The Practical Guide to High-Leverage Practices in Special Education

The Purposeful "How" to Enhance Classroom Rigor

Series Editor
Dee Berlinghoff, PhD

The Practical Guide to High-Leverage Practices in Special Education

The Purposeful "How" to Enhance Classroom Rigor

Ruby L. Owiny, PhD
Minnesota State University, Mankato
Mankato, Minnesota

Kyena E. Cornelius, EdD
University of Florida
Gainesville, Florida

SLACK Incorporated
6900 Grove Road
Thorofare, NJ 08086 USA
856-848-1000 Fax: 856-848-6091
www.slackbooks.com

ISBN: 978-1-63091-884-2

Senior Vice President: Tony Schiavo
Vice President, Editorial: Jennifer Kilpatrick
Director of Editorial Operations: Jennifer Cahill
Cover: Tinhouse Design
Project Editor: Brianna Benfield

Instructors: *The Practical Guide to High-Leverage Practices in Special Education: The Purposeful "How" to Enhance Classroom Rigor* includes ancillary materials specifically available for facility use. Included is an *Instructor's Manual.* Please visit www.efacultylounge.com to obtain access.

The procedures and practices described in this publication should be implemented in a manner consistent with the professional standards set for the circumstances that apply in each specific situation. Every effort has been made to confirm the accuracy of the information presented and to correctly relate generally accepted practices. The authors, editors, and publisher cannot accept responsibility for errors or exclusions or for the outcome of the material presented herein. There is no expressed or implied warranty of this book or information imparted by it. Care has been taken to ensure that drug selection and dosages are in accordance with currently accepted/recommended practice. Off-label uses of drugs may be discussed. Due to continuing research, changes in government policy and regulations, and various effects of drug reactions and interactions, it is recommended that the reader carefully review all materials and literature provided for each drug, especially those that are new or not frequently used. Some drugs or devices in this publication have clearance for use in a restricted research setting by the Food and Drug and Administration or FDA. Each professional should determine the FDA status of any drug or device prior to use in their practice.

Any review or mention of specific companies or products is not intended as an endorsement by the author or publisher.

SLACK Incorporated uses a review process to evaluate submitted material. Prior to publication, educators or clinicians provide important feedback on the content that we publish. We welcome feedback on this work.

Library of Congress Control Number: 2023949735

Printed in the United States of America.

Last digit is print number: 10 9 8 7 6 5 4 3 2 1

Contents

Instructors: *The Practical Guide to High-Leverage Practices in Special Education: The Purposeful "How" to Enhance Classroom Rigor* includes ancillary materials specifically available for facility use. Included is an *Instructor's Manual.* Please visit www.efacultylounge.com to obtain access.

Acknowledgments

I would be remiss not to thank my family for the countless hours they tolerated my absence (with minimal whining) as I was sequestered in my office writing or off at a secluded cabin to have multiple hours of uninterrupted writing. David, the love of my life, who keeps all the plates spinning in my absence, thank you for supporting me and encouraging me to keep doing this work when I get exhausted. Addy, Emma, and Matthias, you continually inspire me. It is a joy to watch you grow and come into yourselves with your goofy jokes and shenanigans that keep me giggling. My mom does not understand what in the world I do sometimes, but encourages me anyway and is proud when I show her a published copy of my writing.

To my co-author, colleague, and "conference spouse," but more than that, a dear friend who does life with me even from afar. I am grateful to you, Kyena, for taking on this challenge with me and jumping into the deep end of the book writing pool when we had no idea what we were getting ourselves into!

Finally, to my students who inspire me to learn and grow so I can continue doing this work to the benefit of the children who deserve our best, I say thank you.

—Ruby L. Owiny, PhD

This book would not have been possible without the love and support of my family. To my husband, Rob, thank you for your daily encouragement and support. You always believe in me! Thank you for following me where this dream leads. To my children, birthed and bonused, Curtis, Caity, and Julia, thank you for listening, brainstorming, and sounding impressed! I love you to the moon and back, twice around the sun, and to infinity and beyond (ok, that was for my grandkids, I love you too Colin and Caroline). At the beginning of this journey, my biggest cheerleader was diagnosed with pancreatic cancer. And even though she is not here to see the final product, I still feel her love and encouragement every day. I love you, Mama!

Of course, a huge thank you goes to the magnificent Ruby Owiny! I have to share how this journey began. My partner in crime, my conference (and I mean EVERY conference) roommate, my friend, and now my co-author, says to me one day, "I want to write a book!" So what do two overcommitted, overvolunteered professors do—we brainstorm ideas, and decide, "WE ARE GOING TO WRITE A BOOK!" We did it! We wrote a book! We have laughed, cried, and laughed some more, and although we are finally finished with this endeavor, I know our journey together will never end. I love you girl!

A final thank you to all of my friends and special educator colleagues who didn't run away when I asked them to write a chapter with me. You all are amazing!

—Kyena E. Cornelius, EdD

About the Authors

Dr. Ruby L. Owiny is an Assistant Professor of Special Education at Minnesota State University, Mankato, where she primarily teaches courses in single subject research methods and methods of teaching students with emotional and behavioral disorders, along with classroom and behavior management, with a focus on applied behavior analysis. Prior to her work at Minnesota State, Dr. Owiny was an Associate Professor at Trinity International University and the Director of the Division of Education. While at Trinity, she also designed and directed the Access Program, which supported students with autism as they completed their bachelor's degree. Dr. Owiny believes everyone deserves to be an accepted, contributing member of their community, starting at school. This drives her professional research of inclusive education. She examines how teacher preparation programs prepare teacher candidates to implement Universal Design for Learning, High-Leverage Practices, and evidence-based practices. She has 13 years of public school teaching in Title I elementary schools in both general and special education, providing instruction in multiple teaching roles and service delivery models. She has experience consulting around the United States and in four other countries, training teachers in co-teaching and inclusive practices, such as embedding specially designed instruction into instruction in the general education classroom, Universal Design for Learning, instructional strategies, and behavioral interventions. She enjoys meeting teachers to learn about the impact they have on their students, particularly the ways they seek to meaningfully include students with disabilities and effectively provide instruction to improve post-secondary outcomes.

She is a Past President of the Teacher Education Division, and has served on multiple committees and workgroups for the Council for Exceptional Children. Dr. Owiny has been active in the Teacher Education Division caucus, Small Special Education Programs Caucus (SSEPC), for several years and, in 2022, was honored with the Nasim Dil Service Award for Outstanding Service to Teacher Education in Small Special Education Programs. She is currently chairing the workgroup that prepares resources to support student teachers who participate in the Student Teacher Support Network. She is a frequent manuscript reviewer for the *Journal of Special Education Preparation, Educator Perspectives Journal*, and *Teachers Connecting to Advance Retention and Empowerment* (TCARE). Dr. Owiny also frequently reviews books for SLACK Incorporated and Rowman & Littlefield Publishing.

In her limited free time, Dr. Owiny enjoys scrapbooking to chronicle the life of her family. She loves traveling, especially visiting her in-laws in Tanzania. Her favorite activities are being a basketball, lacrosse, baseball, and band mom for her three children. She cannot get enough of the outdoors. She takes every chance she can to camp, hike, bike, snowshoe, and enjoy a good book on the beach.

Dr. Kyena E. Cornelius is a Clinical Associate Professor of Special Education at the University of Florida. She primarily teaches and advises students in the online EdD program. This program aligns with Dr. Cornelius's passion of developing expert practitioners who are truly scholarly professionals. Prior to moving to Florida, Dr. Cornelius was an Associate Professor of Special Education at Minnesota State University, Mankato, where she taught courses for initial licensure programs and served as the College of Education's Accreditation Coordinator. It was through this work that she developed her interest in teaching standards and the need for common language in our field, driving her research and professional goals to elevate the teaching profession.

Dr. Cornelius travels the country providing professional development for in-service teachers on the High-Leverage Practices, co-teaching, and formative assessment. She is the President Elect of the Teacher Education Division of Council for Exceptional Children (CEC) and currently co-leads a national workgroup commissioned by CEC for special education teacher recruitment. She is on the editorial boards and frequently reviews manuscripts for two journals: the *Journal of Special Education Preparation* and *Rural Special Education Quarterly*. She is also the co-editor for *TEACHING Exceptional Children*.

When Dr. Cornelius is not traveling the country for work, she is traveling to visit her children and grandchildren who live in Virginia. If she is not traveling, you can find her in the kitchen pursuing her other passion—baking. She not only bakes, she bakes with spirits, and often contemplates starting a new career/business of Kyena's Boozy Bakery.

Contributing Authors

Kelly Acosta, PhD (Chapter 4)
Rhode Island College
Providence, Rhode Island

Amber Benedict, PhD (Chapter 4)
Arizona State University
Tempe, Arizona

Kathleen A. Boothe, PhD (Chapter 3)
Southeastern Oklahoma State University
Durant, Oklahoma

Shantel M. Farnan, EdD (Chapter 8)
Northwest Missouri State University
Maryville, Missouri

Amy I. Gaines, MA/MS (Chapter 1)
William S. Hart Union High School District
Santa Clarita, California

Kiersten K. Hensley, PhD (Chapter 15)
Minnesota State University, Mankato
Mankato, Minnesota

Kimberly M. Johnson, PhD (Chapter 7)
Minnesota State University, Mankato
Mankato, Minnesota

Michael J. Kennedy, PhD (Foreword)
University of Virginia
Charlottesville, Virginia

Marla J. Lohmann, PhD (Chapter 3)
Colorado Christian University
Lakewood, Colorado

Lawrence J. Maheady, PhD (Chapter 17)
SUNY Buffalo State
Buffalo, New York

Wendy W. Murawski, PhD (Chapter 1)
California State University Northridge
Northridge, California

Jodie Ray, MA (Chapter 4)
Arizona State University
Tempe, Arizona

Alice L. Rhodes, PhD (Chapters 13 and 19)
Asbury University
Wilmore, Kentucky

Sarah M. Salinas, PhD (Chapter 11)
Minnesota State University, Mankato
Mankato, Minnesota

Jennifer A. Sears, PhD (Chapter 21)
University of North Georgia
Gainesville, Georgia

Victoria Slocum, PhD (Chapter 13)
Asbury University
Wilmore, Kentucky

Dana L. Wagner, PhD (Chapter 14)
Minnesota State University, Mankato
Mankato, Minnesota

Jennifer D. Walker, PhD (Chapters 9 and 10)
University of Mary Washington
Fredericksburg, Virginia

Foreword

I recall a cold, blustery day at the Council for Exceptional Children's (CEC) old headquarters in Virginia when the High-Leverage Practices (HLPs) for students with disabilities were finalized. A few months earlier when Drs. James McLeskey and Mary Brownell from the CEEDAR Center and University of Florida asked me to serve on the workgroup, I wasn't even aware of the term HLP—how quickly things change (now I can't go 5 minutes without saying or talking about HLPs)! Speaking purely for myself, as we wrapped that initial phase of production, I had no idea the work would permeate the field in such a thorough and substantive manner. I must admit it is pretty cool to see how an idea as deceptively simple as HLPs grew to inform and transform an entire field—there is a lesson there for anyone wondering how you might also leave your mark through a combination of knowledge, persistence, teamwork, creativity, timing, and vision. Here's a hint: If a visionary leader like James or Mary asks you to be part of an authoring team, even if you don't know what they're talking about, say yes.

Being part of a group of professionals representing numerous agencies and stakeholders from across the country was an honor, but also a fun and challenging opportunity to think through the question: What are the essential practices all special educators should have in their repertoires? Now, almost 10 years later, I often wonder if we got things right and what other choices the team could have made. For example, I worry while there are obviously at least 22 key practices special educators need to know and be able to implement, is it possible during a preparation program or professional development session (or series) to learn and master that many complex and intertwined practices (not to mention also leaving room to learn about evidence-based practices)? If pinned down, I would say the answer to that question is probably no. Instead, I argue focusing on a smaller set of key practices that are essential to serving the unique population of students and families in each setting is wiser. To elaborate, selecting key practices like HLP 16—"*Use explicit instruction*" is needed to implement a huge number of other practices (HLPs and evidence-based practices). Thus, ensuring all educators know and use key practices with automaticity is a strategic move when planning where to invest limited time and energy for learning. Once a practice such as "*Use explicit instruction*" is mastered, professionals can more easily add related practices given their understanding of foundational instructional principles.

This is why I (and the field) am so lucky and appreciative of colleagues in the field like Drs. Ruby L. Owiny and Kyena E. Cornelius who are smart, creative, and dedicated to dissemination of high-quality practices all around. They skillfully and effortlessly weave what many cannot: They break the complex into manageable bites and craft a message that is digestible by professionals at any level of skill and experience. In this new text, *The Practical Guide to High-Leverage Practices in Special Education: The Purposeful "How" to Enhance Classroom Rigor*, Ruby and Kyena deliver to readers a way to make something big (the full list of 22 HLPs) into a consumable menu of critical practices to be mixed and matched depending on students' needs. They conceptualize the HLPs as I do: that while learning and mastering all is a terrific goal, professional learning happens in increments, and professionals need time to breathe and implement one or a small number of new practices at any given time (while receiving feedback) in order to be successful.

As I read the various chapters, Ruby, Kyena, and their collaborators present a logical and manageable roadmap for building knowledge about the HLPs. In addition, the chapters have a consistent thread: how to make huge practices like the HLPs and bring them back to the ground level where professionals of all levels can make sense of them. As you plan your professional learning and development journey with HLPs, this text will be a significant guidepost to think through which practices to focus on first, and which combinations of practices make the most sense given your setting. Each chapter provides practical examples from real classrooms, figures, and other exhibits to illustrate key points and materials that can be adapted for immediate use. In sum, this book is essential reading for anyone working in the field of education who shares my concern that we're always trying to do too much with too little time.

In conclusion, the HLPs are here to stay in our field. Therefore, policymakers, researchers, teacher educators, state and local administrators, teachers, staff, family members, and students need to come together to make important choices about where to invest our limited resources devoted to professional learning. The 22 HLPs are vast in their implications for how professionals should construct their identity and repertoire for supporting students with disabilities and others who struggle. I recommend doing all you can, at least at first, to make what can seem like an overwhelming challenge of learning all of the HLPs (and don't forget evidence-based practices) into smaller segments to manage your cognitive load. Ruby and Kyena's book will be your companion and guide as you make these decisions and will then help you expand readiness to add more and more complexity and sophistication to your daily practice.

—Michael J. Kennedy, PhD

Introduction

The High-Leverage Practices (HLPs) for special education emerged from the idea that teacher preparation programs needed to be more organized in how they prepared teacher candidates. A research team from the Council for Exceptional Children (CEC) and the Collaboration for Effective Educator Development, Accountability and Reform (CEEDAR) Center partnered for this very purpose: to identify a set of core practices that were known to improve student outcomes—practices that are fundamental to effective special education teaching. Naturally, as teacher educators, we wanted to know what do pre- and in-service teachers need to know in order to fully implement the HLPs with high levels of fidelity? As we pondered this question and did some searching, we remembered McCray et al. (2017) wrote about HLPs and evidence-based practices (EBPs) being a "promising pair." That was the answer! We decided to provide a tool for both pre- and in-service teachers to learn how to use EBP as the *how to* in order to enhance classroom rigor. That led us to the title, *The Practical Guide to High-Leverage Practices in Special Education: The Purposeful "How" to Enhance Classroom Rigor.* To be effective special educators, implementation of the HLPs with EBPs will lead to highly effective instructional practices.

The Intertwined Functionality of the HLPs

You will find in every chapter a description, with a corresponding table, of how other HLPs work in tandem with the HLP highlighted in that chapter. The table also includes some EBPs described in the chapter that would require using the HLP to implement, along with some resources for further exploration of the EBPs. This section in each chapter is meant to highlight that HLPs are not stand-alone actions. Rather, they work together to provide a robust professional practice for teachers to teach and students to learn at high levels. As John Donne is quoted to have said, "No man is an island." The same is true of the HLPs. In other words, no HLP functions effectively in isolation. Taking a cursory glance at a list of HLPs gives the illusion that HLPs are a checklist to mark off as each one is accomplished. That is simply not the case. The HLPs are more like a 22-circle Venn diagram with each one overlapping with several others, if not all of them. Maybe a better illustration is a toddler's drawing with lines all intertwined in what looks to be a big mess, but indeed has structure and order, at least in the eyes of the artist, like in Figure I-1. In this toddler's drawing, without the colors to distinguish the lines, it is difficult to know which line is which, where it begins, and where it ends. This is akin to how the HLPs function. They each have a distinctive function and features, such as the colors used in the toddler's drawing, yet like the lines in the drawing, the HLPs fluidly intertwine with no clear beginning of one or end to another.

To put it another way, it is important that all teachers use practices supported through research, those that have garnered enough evidence to impact student growth (Leko et al., 2019). As teachers become more proficient with using the HLPs, the interconnected links between the HLPs and EBPs (McCray et al., 2017) become more evident, and serve as a reminder that teaching is not a series of independent actions but a symphony of well-orchestrated practices. It is important to note that this book is not an exhaustive list of all EBPs that should be used in classrooms. This is but a sampling to get you started. It is also important to understand the differences between EBPs and HLPs. Figure I-2 points to their similarities and differences through a Venn diagram. Both are identified through research, shown to improve student outcomes, and should be taught to pre-service and in-service teachers. The EBPs address a specific skill, researchers are always encouraged to develop more, and due to the nature of the practice there may be a cost associated with certain EBPs, either in the materials or the training. Meanwhile, the HLPs can be used across contents and skills, there are a finite set of practices, and can be implemented at no cost.

Figure I-1. Toddler's drawing.

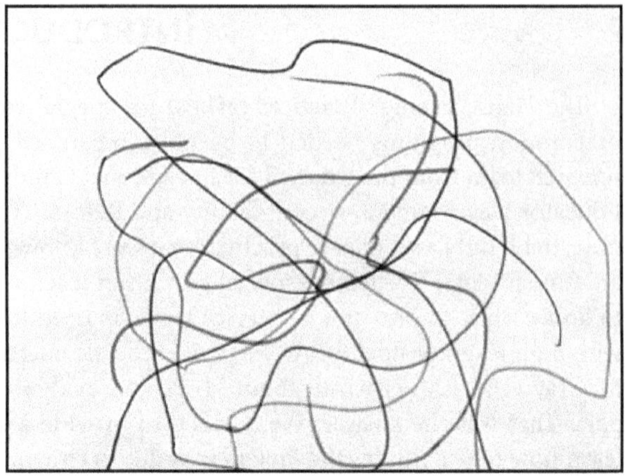

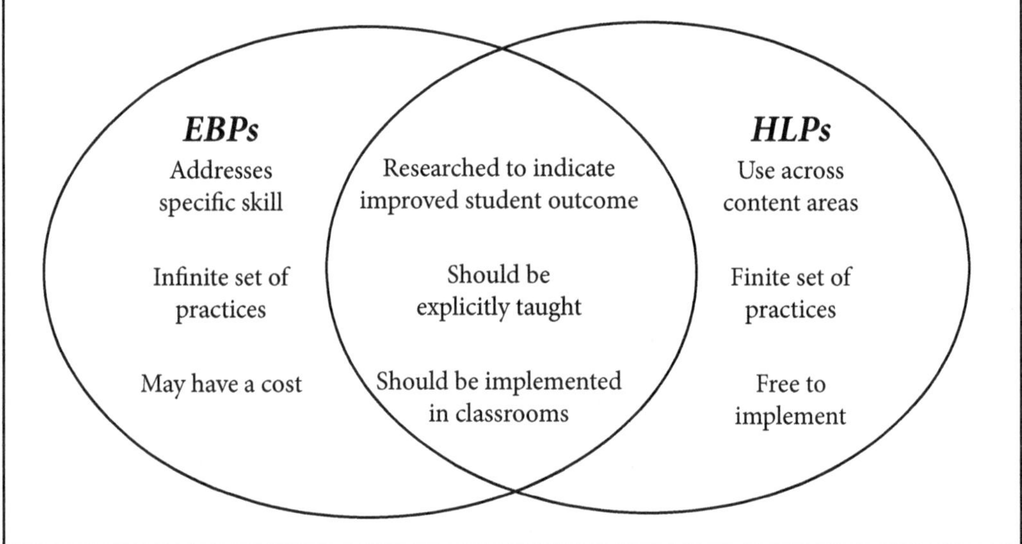

Figure I-2. Comparing EBPs and HLPs.

Readers may notice that chapters generally take on an inclusive tone. This is for at least two reasons, and you, the reader, can probably think of more. First, the premise of the book is to help special education teachers implement the HLPs, which can be accomplished in any setting, resource room, *and* an inclusive classroom. Second, students with disabilities (SWD) are general education students first. Evidenced by the Least Restrictive Environment (LRE) discussion during individualized education program (IEP) meetings, the general education classroom is the first placement discussion in determining the appropriate educational setting for SWD. When special educators implement the HLPs, the general education classroom will become a more suitable place for all students, and as noted, more SWD are included in the general education classroom more frequently, and thankfully, this continues to increase. In fact, from 2009 to 2020, the percentage of SWD who were placed in a general education classroom for 80% or more of the school day rose from 59% to 66% (National Center for Education Statistics, 2022). All educational environments must be high quality to meet the academic, behavioral, social, and emotional needs of SWD and their non-disabled peers. The implementation of HLPs can be an integral part of a holistic approach.

Why Universal Design for Learning?

Universal Design for Learning (UDL) is addressed in several chapters of this book. As a framework, UDL facilitates removing barriers to students' learning while making learning accessible to allow students to meet learning goals (CAST, 2022). The National Center for Education Statistics (2022) highlights the changing demographics of American classrooms with increased numbers of SWD, English-language learners, and overall gaps in student achievement between student groups being reported. Because of this variability in any given classroom, teachers can ill afford the previous model of "one size fits all" (Chardin & Novak, 2021), rather they must consider the range of backgrounds, strengths, and needs in their classroom. Scott et al. (2017) remind us that, as a framework, UDL assists teachers in providing access to the general education curriculum for SWD. Furthermore, the Every Student Succeeds Act (2015) replicates the notion found in the Higher Education Opportunity Act (2008) that UDL is a "scientifically valid framework for guiding educational practice" and states the expectation that UDL be included in state education plans and implemented in classrooms. This means special educators must be prepared to help their general educator counterparts to meet the needs of SWD also. The beauty of UDL, and the HLPs and the EBPs described in this book, is that they benefit students without disabilities as well as students with them. Therefore, UDL can be implemented in any setting, with appropriate decision-making based on the data (HLP 6), to meet the instructional needs of any student. As a special educator, implementing UDL in a resource room or pull-out situation is just as important as implementing UDL in a co-teaching or collaborative relationship in a general education classroom.

One of the features of UDL is its ability to include culturally responsive pedagogy to create learning environments that reflect "themselves, their communities, and their lived realities" (Chardin & Novak, 2021). This notion is extended as educators seek to disrupt the cycles of inequality and oppression by first honoring every student for who they are and what they bring to the classroom and second by recognizing race, ethnicity, and other differences are barriers in instructional design and work toward culturally sustaining practices through UDL (Fritzgerald, 2020). These ideas align with the fact that the HLPs naturally incorporate culturally responsive practices (McLeskey et al., 2017), as well. A key feature in special education is that of inclusive practice to help guarantee SWD are meaningfully educated in the general education classroom, to the maximum extent possible. It is, in part, this aspect of diversity, equity, and inclusion (DEI) that the special education HLPs were written. Pugach et al. (2020) define inclusion "as a *broad, shared equity agenda* designed to assure educational success for every group of marginalized learners." The HLPs serve as a piece of the puzzle to meet the needs of SWD and to consider their cultural and linguistic backgrounds as well as other aspects of their intersectionality. UDL, implemented with the HLPs, provides an additional layer of responsiveness to ensure meaningful access to the general education curriculum that is culturally, linguistically, neurologically, and physically inclusive for SWD while also benefitting all students.

Specially Designed Instruction

As much as we believe in the UDL framework and inclusive practices, we still believe in specially designed instruction. Please do not misinterpret our zest for UDL and the general education environment as a means of escaping our professional responsibility. After all, the federal law defines special education as "specially designed instruction, at no cost to parents, to meet the unique needs of a child with a disability" (IDEA 2004, 20 U.S.C. § 1401(29)). As you read through the chapters of this book you will see a heavy slant toward the general education classroom. Of course, you will! As we stated earlier, more than 65% of SWD receive their education there. We also believe you will see how the UDL framework will allow both special and general education teachers to provide intensive instruction as well as specially designed instruction when needed in the general education classroom. Being included in the general education classroom does not mean a student is missing out on their promised services, just as being in a special education setting does mean the student is getting their specially designed instruction. Remember, special education is a service, not a place! As long as the teachers continue to implement EBPs with fidelity, monitor student progress, and change instructional practices when needed, specially designed instruction can take place anywhere.

Professional Development for Evidence-Based Practices

As you read through the book, and as stated in the first paragraph, and in the title, you will see many EBPs discussed and even have resources about them provided to you. However, as teacher educators and professional developers, we must remind you that some of these practices require you to receive professional development. After all, we know that to be effective, EBP must be implemented with fidelity (Cook et al., 2009). How can you have fidelity if you are unsure what to do? This is especially true for, but not limited to, the University of Kansas SIM Learning Strategies as well as Direct Instruction, a model of instruction that is highly scripted, explicit, and sequenced, developed by Dr. Zig Engelmann and colleagues at the University of Oregon in the 1960s (National Institute for Direct Instruction, 2023).

Contributors

As we started working on this book, we realized that it could be much richer if we invited other experts in the field to contribute on chapters where their expertise could shine. Therefore, you will notice that several chapters include authors besides the two of us. We want to thank these contributors for their willingness to work with us and share their expertise in this book. Like us, they too believe in the power of implementing HLPs with EBPs.

To-Do Items for You, the Reader

Besides read and enjoy this book, if you are new to implementing HLPs or want to go deeper in your understanding, we urge you to do as Desmond Tutu is quoted to have said—how do you eat an elephant? One bite at a time. Therefore, please choose one HLP, one EBP, and become proficient at implementing it and then bite off another chunk and become proficient at that. Do not make the mistake of trying to do it all at once. One small bite at a time will help you to digest the full thing. Pay particular attention to the applications titled "What Does HLP _ Look Like in a K-12 Classroom?" You may want to choose an EBP from the scenario to implement in your classroom. All we ask is that you move forward one step at a time to implement the HLPs. You will be glad you did when you see the growth in yourself, as a professional, and in your students!

Finally, we would be remiss if we did not mention the CEC. This is the premier professional organization providing support to educators, parents, and other stakeholders to ensure high-quality services are provided to SWD. We urge you to check them out at https://exceptionalchildren.org/ and glance through the resources available to you. Throughout this book, you will notice many citations from *TEACHING Exceptional Children*. This is the practitioner journal published by CEC to help special educators become even more proficient in their service to SWD.

Now, get comfy, get your favorite drink (Kyena's is coffee, and Ruby's is Coca-Cola), get ready to learn (at least reflect), and get a pen ready to sketch out a plan to try an HLP!

Cheers,
Ruby and Kyena

References

CAST. (2022). *About the UDL Guidelines*. https://www.cast.org/impact/universal-design-for-learning-udl

Chardin, M., & Novak, K. (2021). *Equity by design: Delivering on the power and promise of UDL*. Corwin.

Cook, B. G., Tankersley, M., & Landrum, T. J. (2009). Determining evidence-based practices in special education. *Exceptional Children, 75*(3), 365-383. https://doi.org/10.1177/0741932514557271

Every Student Succeeds Act, 20 U.S.C. § 6301 (2015). https://www.congress.gov/bill/114th-congress/senate-bill/1177

Fritzgerald, A. (2020). *Antiracism and universal design for learning: Building expressways to success*. CAST.

Higher Education Opportunity Act of 2008, Pub. L. No. 110-315, 122 Stat. 3078 (2008). https://www.govinfo.gov/content/pkg/PLAW-110publ315/pdf/PLAW-110publ315.pdf

Individuals With Disabilities Education Act, 20 U.S.C. §§ 1401 (2004).

Leko, M. M., Roberts, C., Peyton, D., & Pua, D. (2019). Selecting evidence-based practices: What works for me. *Intervention in School and Clinic, 54*(5), 286-294.

McCray, E. D., Kamman, M., Brownell, M. T., & Robinson, S. (2017). *High-leverage practices and evidence-based practices: A promising pair*. CEEDAR Center. https://ceedar.education.ufl.edu/wp-content/uploads/2017/12/HLPs-and-EBPs-A-Promising-Pair.pdf

McLeskey, J., Barringer, M.-D., Billingsley, B., Brownell, M., Jackson, D., Kennedy, M., Lewis, T., Maheady, L., Rodriguez, J., Scheeler, M. C., Winn, J., & Ziegler, D. (2017). *High-leverage practices in special education*. Council for Exceptional Children & CEEDAR Center.

National Center for Education Statistics. (2022). *Students with disabilities*. Condition of Education. U.S. Department of Education, Institute of Education Sciences. https://nces.ed.gov/programs/coe/indicator/cgg

National Institute for Direct Instruction. (2023). *DI vs. di: The term "Direct Instruction."* https://www.nifdi.org/what-is-di/di-vs-di.html

Pugach, M. C., Blanton, L. P., Mickelson, A. M., & Boveda, M. (2020). Curriculum theory: The missing perspective in teacher education for inclusion. *Teacher Education and Special Education, 43*(1), 85-103. http://doi.org/10.1177/0888406419883665

Scott, L. A., Thoma, C. A., Puglia, L., Temple, P., & D'Aguilar, A. (2017). Implementing a UDL framework: A study of current personnel preparation practices. *Intellectual and Developmental Disabilities*, 55(1), 25-36.

Disclaimer

The authors and contributors would like to acknowledge the importance of culturally inclusive practices, both through the language used within the text and the classroom practices discussed. For example, the term *stakeholder* may have emotional connotations for some Indigenous Peoples. As we, ourselves, advocate for a marginalized group of citizens, it is not our intention to hurt or dishonor any group, nor do we wish to lift one group above another. However, as this term is still used within the field of special education and within the law itself, we want readers to know that it is used throughout the book as a term that encompasses key people and decision-makers involved in the education process.

Additionally, we would like to acknowledge the Council for Exceptional Children's introduction to the High-Leverage Practices (HLPs) for special education noted the incorporation of culturally responsive approaches as central to their identification and organization (McLeskey et al., 2017). As such, the HLPs for special education were identified based on the belief that the work of special educators is more nuanced and specialized than that of general educators. The TeachingWorks HLPs for General Education (Ball & Forzani, 2009) are more broadly defined and not detailed for differences in instructional practices. This is not to say that general education practices are not culturally responsive. However, we do suggest that providing researched effective practices for students with disabilities will contribute to more social equitable practices in schools (Artiles et al., 2011). Not to imply these HLPs are the pinnacle of cultural inclusivity, merely a beginning, we encourage other scholars to explore how the HLPs for special education can evidence more cultural responsivity for all students.

References

Artiles, A. J., Kozleski, E. B., & Waitoller, F. R. (2011). *Inclusive education: Examining equity on five continents.* Harvard Education Press.

Ball, D. L., & F. M., Forzani. (2009). The work of teaching and the challenge for teacher education. *Journal of Teacher Education*, *60*(5), 497-511. https://doi.org/10.1177/0022487109348479

McLeskey, J., Barringer, M.-D., Billingsley, B., Brownell, M., Jackson, D., Kennedy, M., Lewis, T., Maheady, L., Rodriguez, J., Scheeler, M. C., Winn, J., & Ziegler, D. (2017). *High-leverage practices in special education.* Council for Exceptional Children & CEEDAR Center.

Collaboration High-Leverage Practices

Special education is built on collaboration. It is appropriate for these High-Leverage Practices (HLPs) to be included first in the 22 HLPs. Special educators work with a range of stakeholders to ensure high-quality programming for students with disabilities. From parents and other caregivers to general education teachers, related service providers, and students themselves, special educators understand the value of building these relationships to better understand their students, their strengths, likes and dislikes, and the areas requiring intervention. The collaboration of these stakeholders allows for a better understanding of the student and helps to create more accurate individualized education programs that effectively meet students' needs by taking into account a wide range of information from various perspectives. HLPs 1 through 3 are explained in Chapters 1 through 3 with a description of the evidence-based practices to help special educators facilitate quality collaborative relationships.

Why Collaborate With Other Professionals?

Amy I. Gaines, MA/MS
and Wendy W. Murawski, PhD

HLP 1

Collaborate with professionals to increase student success.

INTRODUCTION

Collaboration is a cornerstone component to building and maintaining the very foundation upon which effective supports, services, and pedagogical techniques for all students are designed. In this chapter, we define collaboration as it relates to meeting the unique needs of students with disabilities (SWD). We describe what effective, meaningful collaboration between professionals looks like across settings, with particular emphasis on practical and applicable strategies that practitioners can implement in the short and long term to immediately enhance their skills. We provide evidence that doing so will consequently improve educational outcomes for SWD in the areas of academics, behavior, and social-emotional learning. Teacher-friendly suggestions for streamlined implementation are coupled with short vignettes and a description of potential roles and responsibilities when collaborating. Practical resources for further research and professional development are also provided.

Owiny, R. L., & Cornelius, K. E. *The Practical Guide to High-Leverage Practices in Special Education: The Purposeful "How" to Enhance Classroom Rigor* (pp. 3-21).

CHAPTER OBJECTIVES

- Define collaboration as a High-Leverage Practice as it relates to the interaction between professionals on behalf of PreK-12 students.
- Identify the benefits of collaborating with other school-based professionals.
- Describe evidence-based practices with collaboration that lead to improved academic, behavioral, and social outcomes for PreK-12 students.
- Implement the collaboration skills, resources, suggestions, and examples provided in the chapter.

KEY TERMS

- **accommodations:** Change *how* a student learns the same material as their peers.
- **collaboration:** When individuals work together, sharing resources, responsibilities, goals, and decision-making.
- **co-teaching:** When two or more educators co-plan, co-instruct, and co-assess a group of students with diverse needs (Murawski, 2010); though typically shared for an extended period, co-teaching can occur for one lesson, unit, or subject.
- **educational professionals:** Professionals who are employed in the educational sector and who possess a credential, degree, or certificate in a related field (e.g., teachers, psychologists, counselors, administrators, etc.).
- **interprofessional (or interdisciplinary) collaboration:** The use of collaborative skills and behaviors by multiple professionals from different areas of expertise who share their expertise and assume common responsibility to solve a variety of problems.
- **Least Restrictive Environment (LRE):** Refers to the supports and services a student will access to be educated, to the greatest extent possible, alongside their non-disabled peers. It is less a physical location than a concept and cascade of services. LRE is a legal concept required by the Individuals with Disabilities Education Improvement Act (IDEIA).
- **modifications:** Change *what* the student learns, often resulting in a reduction in depth, complexity, and/or grade level content.
- **paraprofessionals:** Teaching assistant within the classroom/school. These include instructional assistants, one-to-ones, educational assistants, etc.

Robust, effective school-wide collaboration is neither a luxury nor a passing fad. Rather, it is the very foundation upon which effective, inclusive, and organizationally adaptable schoolwide communities are cultivated and maintained. Simply put, collaboration is the glue that holds a school together. This may seem like an overstatement, but consider how much collaboration is required for schools to function. Gajda and Koliba write,

> Collaboration is a ubiquitously championed concept and widely recognized across the public and private sectors as the foundation on which the capacity for addressing complex issues is predicated. For those invested in organizational improvement, high-quality collaboration has become no less than an imperative. (2007, p. 26)

In short, without an effective building level collaborative culture, forward momentum is stalled, and student outcomes will not be maximized. One could easily argue that this is a compelling reason for playing nicely with others.

High-Leverage Practice (HLP) 1 relates not only to collaboration in general, but specifically to the collaboration between professionals. In the context of this chapter, we define school professionals as those individuals who are employed in the educational sector and who possess a credential, degree, or certificate in a related field (e.g., teachers, psychologists, counselors, administrators, and so on). Consider the plethora of collaborative meetings that occur on a school site regularly: departmental and grade-level teams, curriculum and instructional meetings, school site council, student success team meetings, individualized education program (IEP) meetings, and more. Many of these collaborative meetings bring classroom teachers and other educational professionals to work together toward the common goal of acting in the best interest of students. When it comes to supporting students who have a disability or are neurodiverse, there are many professionals who work within a school environment who could be included in ongoing collaborative efforts; it is this interaction around mutual goals and shared responsibilities that is termed *interprofessional collaboration*. While classroom teachers may first come to mind, other critical professionals include administrators, special education teachers, a variety of therapists (occupational, physical, speech), mental health providers (school counselors, psychologists, social workers), physical health providers (school nurses, adaptive physical education teachers), and more. Others with whom teachers may need to collaborate include paraprofessionals, staff (office, janitorial, custodial, transportation, food service), and community stakeholders. While families are incredibly valuable collaborators, that interaction is addressed in Chapter 3.

If you are an educational professional, regardless of your particular role in education, HLP 1 relates to you. Though we may joke that collaboration is taught as early as pre-school ("sharing is caring"), it is a difficult skill for many to master. For most of us, effectively collaborating with other professionals does not come easily or naturally. It is a skill we must first explicitly learn and continue to practice and hone as our professional responsibilities evolve. As a professional educator working with students with disabilities (SWD), collaboration is not merely a suggestion; it is a professional imperative (Gajda & Koliba, 2007). Per the Individuals with Disabilities Education Improvement Act (IDEIA; 2004), SWD are to be taught in their Least Restrictive Environment (LRE; Rodriguez & Murawski, 2020); to do so requires a significant amount of strategic and intentional collaboration between professionals. There is no template to this collaboration, just as there is no template to each student. To meet a student's individual needs, a "whole child" approach must be taken. What academic, behavioral, social, physical, and other needs does that student have and how can we as professionals work together to meet those needs? That is the goal of interprofessional collaboration.

What Is HLP 1?

HLP 1 is explicitly stated as, "collaborate with professionals to facilitate student success." According to the Council for Exceptional Children (CEC) and the Collaboration for Effective Educator Development, Accountability and Reform (CEEDAR) Center, this is defined:

> collaboration with general education teachers, paraprofessionals, and support staff is necessary to support students' learning toward measurable outcomes and to facilitate students' social and emotional well-being across all school environments and instructional settings (e.g., co-taught). Collaboration with individuals or teams requires the use of effective collaboration behaviors (e.g., sharing ideas, active listening, questioning, planning, problem-solving, negotiating) to develop and adjust instructional or behavioral plans based on student data and the coordination of expectations, responsibilities, and resources to maximize student learning. (McLeskey et al., 2017, p. 17)

In this chapter, we break this rather long definition into its constituent parts, identify the key elements of each, provide the research and evidence-based practices (EBPs) that connect with each section, and offer anecdotes with examples for practitioners for immediate use.

As mentioned in the introduction, collaboration is the glue that holds special education together. Collaboration is important across the spectrum of school settings—from early childhood programs to high school and beyond. Effective collaboration at a school site translates directly to improved outcomes, in a multitude of ways, for SWD across service domains, content areas, and grade levels.

In fact, all students benefit when effective collaboration occurs at the school site. While the sheer number and variety of professionals in schools can make collaboration daunting, they also serve to emphasize why it is so critically important. Without professionals engaging in effective collaborative skills and sharing responsibilities, resources, and expectations, students will not benefit from the robust capacity and professional expertise available to them and will not glean the same significant academic, behavioral, and social benefits which they require, and are entitled to, per their IEP.

How Are the HLPs Connected?

There is a total of 22 HLPs, none of which exist in a vacuum, nor should any one of them be implemented in isolation (McLeskey et al., 2017). Each HLP was identified to name specific "improved methods for supporting special education teacher candidates as they learn to use effective practices in their classrooms" (McLeskey et al., 2017, pp. 2-3). Each of the four interlocking domains—Collaboration, Assessment, Social/Emotional/Behavioral, and Instruction—lends itself to the others such that each HLP should be broadly understood and applied in the context of other HLPs.

In the context of developing and maintaining a highly effective collaborative culture, HLP 1 is at the forefront because all other HLPs are predicated on the utility of effective collaboration. Clustered around HLP 1 (the focus of this chapter) is HLP 2, which reflects the importance of organizing and facilitating effective meetings with professionals and families, and HLP 3, which addresses collaboration with families to support student learning and to secure needed services. HLP 4 asks professionals to use multiple sources of information to develop a comprehensive understanding of a student's strengths and needs, while HLP 5 requires professionals to interpret and communicate assessment information with stakeholders to collaboratively design and implement educational programs. Gathering these multiple sources of information and communicating information with stakeholders all require collaboration.

Collaboration is also a requisite skill for addressing students' social, emotional, behavioral, and academic needs. For example, the Social/Emotional/Behavioral area (such as HLP 9—"*Teach social behaviors*" and HLP 10—"*Conduct functional behavioral assessments [FBAs] to develop individual student behavior support plans*") will require the collaboration of general education teachers. It may also require the collaboration of other professionals, such as social workers, special education teachers, behavior experts, school psychologists, and so on. The HLPs in the area of Instruction also require collaboration. For example, to address HLP 13—"*Adapt curriculum tasks and materials for specific learning goals*" or HLP 19—"*Use assistive and instructional technologies*," a special education teacher may need to collaborate with the school's instructional technology specialist; communicate with an administrator regarding resources and funding; and coordinate these tasks, materials, and technologies with the student's multiple general education teachers and family members.

How Can Collaboration Among Professionals Increase Academic Outcomes?

While there are many aspects of students' development that should be addressed by schools, none is more obvious than that of their learning or academic outcomes. For SWD as well as those that struggle, collaboration between professionals is crucial for their outcomes to be maximized. Historically, students are taught by one teacher in a closed-door classroom; much more is involved for SWD. However, in recent years, research supports interprofessional collaboration, to include collaboration between classroom teachers, to improve student learning for all students (Weiss et al., 2017), demonstrating that this is not merely a "special education thing." Collaboration among those who work in, for, or with schools is simply a requirement for the benefit of all students.

While it can be difficult to do quantitative research on how people "work together" (a common definition of collaboration; Zigmond et al., 2013), especially as those collaborative efforts or actions can look so different depending on the situation, needs of the students, and personalities of the professionals, there are sufficient data to indicate that the collaboration among professional educators results in higher-quality academic outcomes for students (Borg & Drange, 2019; King-Sears et al., 2021). In fact, McLeskey and colleagues (2017) write, in their description of collaboration, that "collaboration is ethereal in that it is never an end in itself, instead operating as a culture or a means through which any goal can be reached" (p. 2).

Collaboration among professionals can certainly take many different avenues as it relates to impacting student academic achievement. Here, we first consider the impact of collaboration on school climate and the subsequent impact of climate on student achievement. Next, we look at professional collaboration and its impact on SWD in segregated settings. Finally, we share the EBPs related to collaboration between adults in inclusive settings, to include those in which educators are co-teaching. Though collaboration with families is of paramount importance, and is certainly a form of adult collaboration that can impact student achievement, the focus of this chapter, HLP 1, more narrowly focuses on interprofessional collaboration.

Why Are Collaborative Climates Important to Academic Outcomes?

Let's start with the overall need for a collaborative school climate. The Every Student Succeeds Act (ESSA) encourages states to include school climate as an indicator of school quality as part of their accountability and improvement systems (Kostyo et al., 2018; Rodriguez & Murawski, 2020) because of the increasing data demonstrating correlations between school climate and student outcomes. In one research study that included 38 high schools, researchers demonstrated how staff relations contributed positively to school climate, and climate in turn contributed to academic achievement (Back et al., 2016). Ronfeldt and colleagues (2015) collected data on more than 9,000 teachers and determined that students' achievement gains in reading and math were indeed improved in those schools that had higher collaboration quality among their instructional teams. Indeed, they found that "these results support policy efforts to improve student achievement by promoting teacher collaboration" (Ronfeldt et al., 2015, p. 475). Waldron and McLeskey concur, stating that "research has shown that school change that improves teacher practice and student outcomes may be achieved through Comprehensive School Reform. Key aspects of this reform include the development of a collaborative culture" (2010, p. 58). Thus, when there is a positive collaborative culture in a school, professionals are willing to work together to solve problems, improve instruction, and ultimately, increase student academic outcomes.

How does one improve the collaborative school climate? There are a variety of resources available to enhance and even measure the collaborative climate in a school. These will be discussed later in the chapter. Other simple methods include creating a school-wide inclusion committee, engaging in both goal-directed and social activities as a faculty and staff, and taking a survey of students and faculty to determine how they view the culture of the school and what suggestions they might make to improve its collaborative nature.

Can Collaboration Exist in Segregated Settings?

Some educational professionals work with students in segregated settings (e.g., homes, institutions, self-contained classes). Although one may be inclined to think those individuals work independently and without the need for collaboration, nothing could be further from the truth! Students

Table 1-1. Student/School Collaboration Accountability Chart

MEETING DATE:					
TOPIC/GOAL:					
STUDENT/STUDENT GROUP:					
OBJECTIVE/ TASK TO COMPLETE	PERSON RESPONSIBLE	LOCATION	BY (DATE)	FOLLOW-UP	
				Date	*With Whom*

whose LRE is in a segregated setting typically have more extensive support needs (academic, behavioral, social, emotional, or physical), making collaboration among service providers even more imperative. Research has found that interprofessional collaboration is beneficial between educators and social workers (Allen-Meares et al., 2013), school psychologists and school counselors (Stone & Charles, 2018), school nurses (Cappella et al., 2011), and others. This is true, for students' academic outcomes as well as their mental and physical health. Even collaborating with community members can lead to a decrease in students' absenteeism, which in turn increases academic outcomes (Childs & Grooms, 2018). Overall, researchers (e.g., Allen-Meares et al., 2013) have found that the most effective interprofessional programs and interventions are those that target all students, as opposed to pulling out small groups of students, a result that emphasizes collaboration and inclusive practices. Table 1-1 provides a Student/School Collaboration Accountability Chart that can be used to document and organize the collaboration between professionals.

How Does Co-Teaching Improve Student Outcomes?

Increasingly, SWD are being taught in inclusive settings and with their typically developing, grade-level peers. One of the most prevalent collaborative activities to support students in inclusive settings is the service delivery model of co-teaching, whereby two professionals (most often a general and special education teacher) co-plan, co-instruct, and co-assess a diverse group of students in the same classroom (King-Sears et al., 2014; Murawski, 2010). As McCray et al. (2017) explain, HLPs should be used in conjunction with EBPs to ensure student success. While co-teaching itself cannot be considered an EBP without additional empirical research (Cook et al., 2017), the data available on co-teaching continue to grow. Meta-analysis, a systematic process to evaluate and synthesize the body of research literature around a particular topic, assists researchers and practitioners to identify outcomes of research, often with the purpose of identifying EBPs (Lane & Carter, 2013). Murawski and Swanson's (2001) seminal meta-analysis on co-teaching identified only six eligible empirical studies and identified a moderate effect size (0.41); more recently, King-Sears and colleagues' meta-analysis included a comprehensive search of published and gray literature and included 26 eligible studies, finding a similar moderate effect size (g = 0.47) for students in co-taught settings compared to those in special education settings (King-Sears et al., 2021). Specifically related to academic outcomes, numerous researchers (e.g., Bottge et al., 2018; Brusca-Vega et al., 2011; Cole et al., 2020; Fontana, 2005; Hang & Rabren, 2009; Lochner, et al., 2019; Murawski, 2006) have found that co-teaching can increase students' academic outcomes. While more research is always helpful and the literature on co-teaching continues to provide cautions on its implementation without appropriate professional development and administrative support (Lochner & Murawski, 2018), it is clear that two educators working together can employ EBPs to enhance student success for all learners.

What would co-teaching around EBPs to enhance student academic outcomes look like? Using strong collaboration and communication skills, two educators would share their expertise to ensure students have access to grade-level curriculum, high expectations, and rigorous instruction, as well as any scaffolding (HLP 15), supports, accommodations, or differentiation (HLP 13) they may require (Karten & Murawski, 2020). Parity between co-teachers is important as it models respect, trust, and a true understanding that both individuals bring something valuable to the experience that is beneficial both to students and to themselves. As the general educator typically takes the lead on ensuring standards-based curriculum, the special educator typically takes the lead on suggesting pedagogical approaches to instruction that are universally designed and able to be differentiated for individual needs and ensuring that students with IEPs receive their specially designed instruction, often able to be implemented through universal design and/or differentiation.

Table 1-2 provides concrete examples of how two educators can collaborate, using the co-teaching models originally described by Cook and Friend (1995). When professionals can demonstrate key characteristics of collaboration such as parity, respect, trust, conflict-management, and problem-solving skills (Karten & Murawski, 2020), they can maximize the impact they have on their students—and subsequently their students' academic outcomes. Co-teaching requires far more than merely putting two adults in the same classroom, it truly requires those adults cultivating a collaborative relationship as described in HLP 1. A resource to help educators share their goals and expectations around co-teaching, and to start them discussing their potential roles and responsibilities, is the SHARE worksheet provided by Murawski and Dieker (2004) and available at www.2TeachLLC.com. Additional articles, resources, and templates for co-planning (to include more information on the various co-teaching approaches and lesson plan examples of their use) are also accessible at the 2Teach website.

What Professional Collaboration Can Facilitate Students' Social and Emotional Well-Being?

School success is clearly not only defined as academic success. Educators, policy makers, and the public concur that students should not only learn core curriculum while spending 13 or more years in the public school system, but should also graduate proficient in soft skills, such as being able to collaborate, being responsible citizens, demonstrating respectful behavior, and building their own positive social and emotional health (ASCD, 2007). Without a doubt, "Teaching and learning in schools have strong social, emotional, and academic components... Students typically do not learn alone but rather in collaboration with their teachers, in the company of their peers, and with the encouragement of their families" (Durlak et al., 2011, p. 405). All of this begs the question: Are we collaborating enough as adults to model and teach the social, emotional, and behavioral skills students need?

Research by Benson (2006) would answer that question with "no." In a national sample of almost 150,000 secondary students, fewer than 45% felt competent in skills such as empathy, conflict-resolution, or decision-making, while under 30% reported having a school that provided a caring, encouraging environment. Under a third! No wonder as many as 40% to 60% of high school students become "chronically disengaged" from school (Klem & Connell, 2004). The critically low engagement

Table 1-2. Co-Teaching With Evidence-Based Practices to Enhance Academic Outcomes

EBP	CO-TEACHING APPROACH	GENERAL EDUCATOR	SPECIAL EDUCATOR	HLPS USED
Begin lessons with short reviews of previous learning	Station Teaching	5-minute station to review a particularly difficult homework problem. Independent Station: Students check their homework against an answer key with model responses for a 5-minute station	5-minute station to review general concepts already taught.	Station 1: HLPs 16, 20 Station 2: HLP 21 Station 3: HLPs 15, 22 All: HLP 17
Ask many questions and observe student responses	One Teach-One Support/ One Teach-One Observe	Provide direct instruction and ask open-ended questions of students.	During instruction, also ask questions and record responses of students to review with co-teaching partner later.	Teacher 1: HLPs 16, 18 Teacher 2: HLPs 4, 6, 18
Provide models such as demonstrations or think-alouds	Team Teaching	As teachers describe a math problem, they question each other regarding their different ways of approaching it, showing students that there are multiple ways to achieve the same answer.		HLPs 14, 18, 21, 22
Provide scaffolds, or temporary supports, for difficult material	Alternative Teaching	Take a small group of students who are struggling with higher order concepts and work with them directly.	Monitor the class and circulate, answering questions, as students work on independent or group work.	Teacher 1: HLPs 8, 15 Teacher 2: HLPs 7, 8 Both: HLP 17
Check that students understand the material	Parallel Teaching	Take half of the class and review for an upcoming test using Kahoot, checking understanding with the smaller group	Take half of the class and review for an upcoming test using Quizlet, checking understanding with the smaller group	Both: HLPs 4, 6, 7, 8, 12, 14, 15, 17, 18, 19

from students, especially at the secondary level, has been exacerbated by the COVID-19 pandemic, issues around equity, and socio-educational differences, resulting in a "wicked problem" that requires collaborative strategies amongst key stakeholders (Seymour et al., 2020, p. 244). Schools clearly need support in addressing the mental health, social-emotional, and behavioral aspects of a student's upbringing; one teacher alone in a room may have difficulty addressing all the academic diversity, not to mention these other needs. Banks and colleagues (2014) recommend that "school-based mental health programming can be integrated with an academic curriculum and designed both to address the emotional and behavioral problems of students and, more importantly, give them the tools necessary to be able to prevent and manage them" (p. 759).

As educators struggle to do everything currently asked of them, it behooves us to first ensure the impact of such additional programming. Is it worth this additional collaboration, time, and effort to also focus on behavioral and social needs? In a meta-analysis of 213 school-based, universal social and emotional learning (SEL) programs involving more than 240,000 K-12 students, Durlak and colleagues (2011) demonstrated that participants in SEL programs not only significantly improved their social, emotional, behavioral, and attitudinal skills, but their academic performance even reflected an 11–percentile point gain in achievement. In fact, surprisingly, it was the programs implemented in the classrooms by teachers that were more effective across the board than those conducted by non-school (e.g., consultants, specialists) personnel. "Student academic performance significantly improved only when school personnel conducted the intervention" (Durlak et al., 2011, p. 413). Clearly then, the outcomes are worth having teachers and other school personnel embed SEL-focused activities and interventions into academic classes. Enter again the need for collaboration between school professionals.

Without a doubt, professionals are needed in school settings to promote the early identification and intervention for the mental health of students. Many SEL programs have been created to work in schools and many teachers, school counselors, and school psychologists find themselves implementing preventative mental health programs with students. These programs aim to help students with an awareness of themselves, their identity, their feelings, their decision-making and problem-solving skills (Trip et al., 2007), and to help them gain skills in self-instruction, self-control, and self-determination (Banks et al., 2014). As more and more children enter school with both internalizing (e.g., depression, anxiety, suicidal ideation) and externalizing (e.g., aggression, impulsivity) behaviors, teachers need to be prepared not only to address those behaviors as they occur but to proactively work with students to help them learn to manage their own behaviors and feelings (Peck et al., 2012). This takes collaboration with those individuals (e.g., school counselors, nurses, psychologists) who have been trained as experts in doing so. Interdisciplinary collaboration is critically important in addressing these mental health and behavioral needs.

So, you may be asking, if school psychologists and counselors have expertise in psychological and therapeutic interventions, why not simply let them continue to provide pull-out services independently? Pugh (2010) reflects on the fact that, while these individuals may be better educated in social-emotional and mental health curricula, they have limitations—such as access to a large classroom of students, the knowledge of the class culture and specific needs, and daily interactions with students. Teachers, on the other hand, are positioned not only to implement universally designed curriculum with a class but also to observe, generalize, modify, assess, and match interventions with students' needs (Miller et al., 2010). Collaborative partnerships between school-based mental health professionals and teachers result in the implementation of higher-quality interventions with treatment integrity, an ability to bridge the gap between research and practice, and the application of supportive programs that positively impact a larger group of students (Pugh, 2010). In addition, collaboration builds the skills of both individuals, supports the reliability of implementation, and models best practices for students. Classroom teachers need not do it alone; they just need to reach out to their school colleagues and begin to identify ways to incorporate social/emotional/behavioral/mental health supports into the school day through co-teaching, a daily or weekly unit, or a planned curriculum. See Table 1-3 for some collaborative resolutions pertaining to social-emotional/behavioral situations.

Table 1-3. Collaborative Resolutions Around Social-Emotional/Behavioral Situations

EXAMPLE SITUATION	NON-COLLABORATIVE RESOLUTION	COLLABORATIVE RESOLUTION
Kindergarten student is hitting peers, won't share toys, doesn't follow directions.	Student would receive 1:1 or small group pull-out from school psychologist or teacher to teach appropriate behavioral skills.	School psychologist is invited into kindergarten classroom three times a week to do mini-lessons to whole class on sharing & conflict-resolution. Paraprofessional and teachers work on supporting student with proximity control and simple one-step directions.
Student in third-grade class has difficulties with his "R" and "S" sounds.	Student would receive 1:1 or small group pull-out instruction from SLP, missing some of his class activities.	SLP teaches the third-grade teacher how to work with the "R" & "S" sounds. During peer reading for fluency practice, the teacher pairs with the student and helps him practice "R" and "S" in the context of his reading. He isn't pulled from class.
Middle school student is becoming isolated and has begun cutting herself.	Student would receive counseling from school counselor or psychologist. Most teachers would not know about situation unless the family knows and decides to share the information.	Meeting is held with teachers, counselor, psychologist, paraprofessionals, nurse, and family. Student might be invited toward the end of the meeting. Team collaboratively identifies ways to assist student, address mental health and physical needs, and help her develop friendships/supports by finding and acknowledging any cultural/ racial/ gender identity groups that may provide her with more specific advocates.
High school student is starting to miss class more often and is suspected of drinking and smoking pot.	Student might be suspended or expelled, which may result in him dropping out of school.	Collaborative meeting of teachers, counselor, administrators, family, and student is held to proactively identify ways to address substance abuse and truancy. Co-teachers meet with student to help identify areas of interest and for increased class engagement. School counselor helps student identify future goals and shares these with teachers. Administrators help make connections with teen substance abuse programs.

What Are Effective Collaboration Behaviors When Interacting With Other Professionals?

The term *collaboration* implies some type of partnership or a positive form of working together toward a mutual goal. Collaboration typically involves mutual accountability, responsibility, sharing of resources, open communication, and a feeling of equality in pursuit of the shared goals (Connolly & James, 2006). Coming together is just the beginning, however. For that partnership or interprofessional collaboration to have a positive outcome, individuals need to utilize strong communication skills and collaborative behaviors. These behaviors include communicating of ideas, using active listening skills, asking open-ended questions, and sharing in the planning and problem-solving. An excellent resource for learning more of these skills as applied to the interprofessional educational context is Lynne Cook and Marilyn Friend's book, *Interactions: Collaboration Skills for School Professionals*, now in its ninth iteration.

Prater and Sileo (2015) remind us that

> you can't collaborate if you can't communicate. In fact, genuine communication is harder to achieve than you might think! For example, non-verbal actions like where you stand, facial expressions, and whether you touch someone or not, all communicate something regardless of what you say. You might say all the right things, but unknowingly roll your eyes communicating "I don't have time for this." (p. 324)

Clearly then, it is important for professionals not only to be aware of the words they are using, but also the way in which they match their words to their actions. For example, a co-teacher may tell her partner that she wants to be an equal in the process and that she respects the partnership, but if she is constantly late to class or fails to follow through with promised planning, her actions communicate the opposite.

These collaborative and communicative behaviors also require us to consider unconscious bias, cultural norms and expectations, and communication styles. "A better understanding of the cultural and linguistic differences expressed in differing communicative styles could prevent many miscommunications and misunderstandings..." (Fallah & Murawski, 2018, p. 69). While it is not possible to know the nuances of every culture, programs and trainings in cultural competence, cultural awareness, and cultural sensitivity now abound in schools in an effort to help educators recognize how much our different frames of reference and backgrounds can both enhance collaboration and cause barriers to that collaboration when they are not actively addressed. In addition, language differences can create challenges to already difficult communication between individuals from different cultures (Turney & Kao, 2009).

When is all this collaboration and communication supposed to occur? Time is the primary resource requested by those who want to be able to meet, plan, and find additional ways to collaborate (Strauss, 2013), yet also continues to be one of the most noted barriers to collaboration in the research. Strauss cites educational guru Dr. Linda Darling-Hammond as saying,

> Old style factory-model thinking could undercut richer student learning if we follow traditional patterns of education reform implementation. Like a contractor who is paid a bonus to finish a project on a tight timeline, school systems that cut corners by trying to "automate" teaching decisions through pacing guides, scripted curriculum, or frequent, narrow testing are likely to produce rickety, undeveloped student learning skills...educators are committed to common-sense changes to improve teaching and learning practices: they most value time to co-plan with colleagues to create new lessons or instructional strategies and to analyze how their students are developing and what they can do together to advance progress. (p. 2)

Yet, that valued collaborative time is rarely given sufficiently. Research from the National Center for Literacy Education found that only 32% of educators have a chance to frequently co-create or reflect with colleagues about how a lesson worked, only 21% are given time to frequently examine student work with colleagues, only 14% frequently receive feedback from colleagues, and only 10% frequently have the opportunity to observe the teaching practice of a colleague (Strauss, 2013). Time to collaborate is one of the best resources that can be given to educational professionals to improve outcomes for students. Here are some suggestions for finding and using collaborative time, while implementing strong and appropriate communicative behaviors.

- Identify one professional learning community meeting a month for collaborative planning time that cannot be usurped by meetings, professional development, or other more formal or informational sessions.
- Hang a sign on the classroom door, indicating that co-planning is occurring and deterring students and others from interrupting the meeting.
- Invite guest speakers to classes once a month to enable co-teachers or small groups of teachers to share and collaborate.
- Use Google Docs and other online resources for collaborating between classroom teachers and other school-based professionals (e.g., psychologist, counselor) and paraprofessionals regarding upcoming in-class activities and instruction.
- Self-advocate for planning time with administrators by demonstrating how the time will be used and how the interprofessional collaboration will ultimately benefit students.
- Add your collaborative partner as a co-teacher on online learning platforms (e.g., Google Classroom, Quizizz, GoFormative, Edulastic, BrainPop) so each of you can remotely develop learning materials when it is more convenient for you.

What Collaborative Strategies Support Professionals in the Development and Adjustment of Instructional or Behavioral Plans?

"I was a wonderful parent before I had children" (Faber & Mazlish, 2002, p. 1). In that wonderful first line of *How to Talk So Kids Will Listen and Listen So Kids Will Talk*, the authors acknowledge how easy it is to make judgments and give opinions from the outside. Once you have your own children, or in this case, a classroom of children, you realize that things do not always go according to plan or textbook. Data-based decision-making is about using objective information to drive a continuous improvement cycle (Lochner & Murawski, 2018). Simply teaching "to the middle" and hoping all students will somehow learn the content has been debunked time and again as a losing battle. A beautiful illustration of this losing battle is the video of Todd Rose in his TedX talk when he describes "the myth of average." (A link to the video is provided in the resources.) Simply put, average does not really exist. Everyone is different; learning, behavior, and social skills all exist along a continuum. Strong educators recognize diversity in students and themselves and can collect formative and summative assessment data on a variety of factors to help them make informed decisions (HLPs 4 and 6). In addition, strong educators recognize that they are not alone in being able to collect said data.

With the sheer amount of information that needs to be shared between professionals—from grades to behaviors to parent requests to language skills to team meeting information—strong communication skills are critical. Educators need to be able to relay and respond to information through both oral and written means, in both formal and informal manners. The sharing of data to create or adjust instructional and behavioral plans occurs daily, far more than merely at an IEP meeting or when the results of standardized tests or quarterly grades come out. Teachers might share information about a student's writing abilities while passing in the hall; a school counselor might email a group of teachers about a student's recent familial loss; a speech pathologist might write up a report regarding a student's receptive and expressive language skills from a recent session; a teacher and paraprofessional might meet to discuss the results of a formative assessment; and co-teachers might sit together to co-plan an upcoming lesson, discussing students' needs and strengths as they do so. Each of these are examples of collaboration and communication that occur regularly in schools and are key to student success.

Too often, teachers feel they are solely responsible for what happens in their classes and that is simply untrue, especially when it comes to SWD. Right from the start, a collaborative group of teachers, family members, and other stakeholders are required to form the IEP team to help determine a student's eligibility, goals, strengths, and needs. This collaboration is actually legally mandated because the law recognizes the importance each individual, with their differing expertise and frame of reference, brings to the interaction (Rodriguez & Murawski, 2020). Teams with a variety of names (e.g., IEP, 504, Student Study) meet for a variety of purposes (e.g., designing behavior plans, reviewing data, determining necessary accommodations). In all of these situations, it is the collaboration and communication that enables educators and families to learn from one another, gather valuable information, and make necessary adjustments to better meet students' academic and behavioral needs.

What Does HLP 1 Look Like in a K-12 Classroom?

Knowing they had limited time to co-plan, Ms. Gutierrez and Mr. Webb came to their meeting prepared. As the general education teacher, Ms. Gutierrez identified the pacing plan, content standards, and lesson objectives that were required for the unit. She shared with Mr. Webb the materials and lessons she had used in the past, making it clear that she was eager for feedback and more ideas. As the special educator, Mr. Webb helped identify areas in which students might struggle so that the co-teachers could proactively create strategies to address those areas, using EBPs like modeling, as with explicit instruction (HLP 16), using visuals, breaking down information step-by-step (HLP 15), and progress monitoring (HLP 6). Because both co-teachers believed in the principles of Universal Design for Learning (UDL), they were comfortable offering their students choices in how they would learn, engage in the material, and demonstrate their mastery of the competencies. When they had a disagreement about anything related to grade-level standards or the curriculum, Mr. Webb deferred to Ms. Gutierrez; she deferred to him when they could not come to consensus on topics related to accommodations or differentiation practices for students. Together, they were able to maintain high academic standards for students and proactively address needs so that there was less of a need for academic modifications.

Elementary Example

"I've tried everything!" Dr. Kiernan smiled to herself as a new teacher complained about his inability to make headway with Maddie, a particularly challenging student in his fifth-grade classroom. This wasn't an atypical situation; so many teachers tried to "do it all" themselves. After encouraging the teacher to take a breath—and a piece of candy from the jar on her desk—Dr. Kiernan began to share all of the options still available. When she mentioned the behavior intervention specialist who could come and do an observation and collect data (HLP 6), the student's special education teacher who was eager to co-teach in that class, the paraprofessionals who might offer additional in-class support, and the family members (HLP 3) who had yet to be approached to ask their suggestions for additional strategies, the teacher's eyes grew wide. Dr. Kiernan continued, "There is so much more we can do together to figure out what works for Maddie. You're not in this alone and you are not expected to come up with all of the ideas. And, you know what? We'll probably have to keep coming up with ideas and tweak them as we go! Kids are complex, but luckily, we have a lot of really bright and experienced adults around we can reach out to."

Secondary Example

Elijah is a seventh-grade student on the autism spectrum. He is enrolled in a self-contained class where he is learning the order of operations for solving complex math problems. Although his classmates have mastered the skill and are ready to move on, Elijah continues to struggle. His teacher has noticed that he is having trouble organizing his paper and remembering the order of the steps to use. He is also acting out by crying and crumpling up his paper when he becomes frustrated or overwhelmed. Rather than problem-solving independently, his teacher reaches out to the school counselor and the occupational therapist to develop a targeted lesson that will benefit the entire group (HLP 12). Together, they plan a "push in" lesson in which the occupational therapist teaches the entire class several actionable strategies for organizing their math work and the therapist conducts a separate lesson with the group on strategies to self-regulate (HLP 14) after experiencing setbacks in the classroom. Although Elijah's teacher initially believed that she could independently target these skills with her students, enlisting the help of her colleagues elevated the experience for all students in the classroom and capitalized on the strengths and expertise of other professionals.

Summary

All of the collaboration and communication required daily to meet students' needs cannot simply occur randomly. If that were the case, significant and important information might be lost. In addition, teachers can feel they suffer from what Murawski and Dieker (2013, p. 73) call the "Chicken with Its Head Cut Off Syndrome." Instead, strategic collaboration, to include the coordination of expectations, responsibilities, and resources among professionals, is required. It is this strategic collaboration that can enhance student learning and outcomes academically, behaviorally, and socially. Table 1-4 provides example strategies of what this coordination and collaboration between professionals might include.

In the ever-changing world of education, some things remain constant—students learn best when they are engaged, supported, and nurtured in the care of adults who are mutually invested in their progress. This holds true for children with and without disabilities across all settings. In this chapter, we offered a research-based rationale for engaging in interprofessional collaborative practices, demonstrating why educators and school-based service providers need to have the time, resources, and motivation to work together. The strategies and actionable, useful resources (Table 1-5) provided in this chapter for implementing collaborative practices in school settings can support students' academic, behavioral, and social outcomes. What better rationale is there for adults to let go of their egos, open their doors, and reach out to one another for support?

Chapter Review

1. How does HLP 1 connect to some of the other HLPs? Give an example by using one of the co-teaching approaches.
2. Describe collaboration and why it is important to student success.
3. Why is collaboration also important to meet students' social/emotional/behavioral/mental needs?
4. Choose a strategy identified in this chapter and consider how to apply it in your current or future classroom.

Table 1-4. Coordination of Expectations, Responsibilities, and Resources

COORDINATION OF...	STRATEGIES
Expectations	• Co-teachers can complete the SHARE worksheet (Murawski & Dieker, 2004) to proactively discuss their expectations for the class. • Gifted education coordinators, or experts in twice-exceptional learners, can provide mini-lessons to general education teachers regarding what appropriate expectations are for these students. • Special education teachers can create "IEP at a Glance" sheets for their colleagues that summarize the overall strengths, goals, objectives, accommodations, and needs of a particular student. • Counselors, psychologists, consultants, and coaches can be invited into classrooms to observe and collect data on justice-oriented praxis, helping teachers identify areas of unconscious bias or microaggressions. Teachers need to be open to feedback for improvement. • Behavior specialists can provide information to teachers and family members regarding the expectations for responses to specific student behaviors to help with treatment fidelity and continuity.
Responsibilities	• Co-teachers can identify regular activities (e.g., take roll, update website, photocopy, call parents, do warmup) and divide and conquer so there is consistency in their schedules. • Special educators can teach paraprofessionals specific skills that can be done with small groups, to include collecting frequency, duration, and other basic data. • Special service providers (e.g., school psychologists, SLP, OT, PT) can be encouraged to provide services in the inclusive classroom, especially around social-emotional and behavioral areas. Using regrouping approaches like Station or Parallel teaching, these professionals can support the formal needs of students with IEPs as well as some yet unidentified needs of other students. • Teachers can work collaboratively with sign language interpreters or paraprofessionals in class, demonstrating respect for their positions and support while also communicating that these individuals are not expected to be "the teacher" of students. • At Back-To-School Night, co-teachers can introduce themselves to families as equal partners ready to support all children in the class equally. They can identify their own areas of strength and how they will use those strengths to support their diverse learners.

(continued)

Table 1-4 (continued). Coordination of Expectations, Responsibilities, and Resources

COORDINATION OF...	STRATEGIES
Resources	• Teachers can work collaboratively to identify resource needs as a department or collective to share with their administrators. Self-advocating for resources can be difficult but is an important communicative skill (Hensley & Huddle, 2021). • Special educators can bring together multiple general educators to agree on specific ways to do things, which will reduce the variability between teachers and the load on special educators to make specific changes for each general educator with whom they work. • Teachers can embrace UDL principles, allowing for multiple means of representation, engagement, action, and expression, in their lessons. These UDL lesson plans can be digitally stored in a school database, accessible to other grade-level colleagues to use and adapt, thereby reducing workloads for all and increasing accessibility for students. Two excellent resources for educators are *What Really Works with Universal Design for Learning* (Murawski & Scott, 2019) and *Anti-Racism and Universal Design for Learning: Building Expressways to Success* (Fritzgerald, 2020). School professionals from varying cultures can help classroom teachers identify books and other classroom materials and instructional lessons that are more culturally relevant and responsive. • Co-Teachers can use a Google Drive to store their shared co-planned lessons, materials, differentiated assessments, and more. • School counselors, social workers, and psychologists can help schools identify strong Social-Emotional Learning (SEL) programs and initiatives, while the whole school can embrace Positive Behavioral Interventions and Supports (PBIS).

References

Allen-Meares, P., Montgomery, K. L., & Kim, J. S. (2013). School-based social work interventions: A crossnational systematic review. *Social Work, 58*, 253-262.

Association for Supervision and Curriculum Development (ASCD). (2007). The learning compact redefined: A call to action—A report of the Commission on the Whole Child. ASCD. http://www.ascd.org/learningcompact

Back, L. T., Polk, E., Keys, C. B., & McMahon, S. D. (2016). Classroom management, school staff relations, school climate, and academic achievement: Testing a model with urban high schools. *Learning Environmental Research, 19*, 397-410. https://doi.org/10.1007/s10984-016-9213-x

Banks, T., Squires, G., & Anhalt, K. (2014). Interdisciplinary collaboration: Cognitive behavioral interventions in special education and school psychology. *Creative Education, 5*, 758-768. http://dx.doi.org/10.4236/ce.2014.510089

Benson, P. L. (2006). *All kids are our kids: What communities must do to raise caring and responsible children and adolescents* (2nd ed.). Jossey-Bass.

Borg, E., & Drange, I. (2019). Interprofessional collaboration in school: Effects on teaching and learning. *Improving Schools, 22*(3), 251-266. https://doi.org/10.1177/1365480219864812

Bottge, B. A., Cohen, A. S., & Choi, H. J. (2018). Comparisons of mathematics intervention effects in resource and inclusive classrooms. *Exceptional Children, 84*(2), 197-212. https://doi.org/10.1177/0014402917736854

TABLE 1-5. USEFUL RESOURCES TO SUPPORT IMPLEMENTING COLLABORATIVE PRACTICES IN SCHOOL SETTINGS

TOPIC	RESOURCE
Co-Teaching	https://2teachllc.com/
Share Worksheet	https://img1.wsimg.com/blobby/go/7ad6ae6c-f442-4fd3-8002-7c319a765a1c/downloads/1c56n8uai_436648.pdf?ver=1664312865002
Collaborative Culture Resources	http://bit.ly/HLP1-Collaboration
Editable School/Student Collaboration Accountability Chart	https://docs.google.com/document/u/0/d/1GWUh5SP_ZaDcXqEMvse3oea65dJzMUMenj7ZJ8CivfA/mobilebasic
"The Myth of Average"	https://www.youtube.com/watch?v=4eBmyttcfU4

Brusca-Vega, R., Brown, K., & Yasutake, D. (2011). Science achievement of students in cotaught, inquiry-based classrooms. *Learning Disabilities: A Multidisciplinary Journal, 17*(1), 23-31.

Cappella, E., Jackson, D. R., Bilal, C., Hamre, B. K., & Soule, C. (2011). Bridging mental health and education in urban elementary schools: Participatory research to inform intervention development. *School Psychology Review, 40*, 486-508.

Childs, J., & Grooms, A. A. (2018). Improving school attendance through collaboration: A catalyst for community involvement and change. *Journal of Education for Students Placed at Risk (JESPAR), 23*(1-2), 122-138. https://doi.org/10.1080/10824669.2018.1439751

Cole, S. M., Murphy, H. R., Frisby, M. B., Grossi, T. A., & Bolte, H. R. (2020). The relationship of special education placement and student academic outcomes. *The Journal of Special Education, 54*(4), 217-227. https://doi.org/10.1177/0022466920925033

Connolly, M., & James, C. (2006). Collaboration for school improvement: A resource dependency and institutional framework of analysis. *Educational Management Administration and Leadership, 34*(1), 69-87. https://doi.org/10.1177/1741143206059540

Cook, L., & Friend, M. (1995). Co-teaching: Guidelines for creating effective practices. *Focus on Exceptional Children, 28*(3), 1-16.

Cook, S. C., McDuffie-Landrum, K. A., Oshita, L., & Cook, B. G. (2017). Co-teaching for students with disabilities: A critical and updated analysis of the empirical literature. In J. M. Kauffman, D. P. Hallahan, & P. C. Pullen (Eds.), *Handbook of special education* (pp. 233-248). Routledge.

Durlak, J. A., Weissberg, R. P., Dymnicki, A. B., Taylor, R. D., & Schellinger, K. B. (2011). The impact of enhancing students' social and emotional learning: A meta-analysis of school-based universal interventions. *Child Development, 82*(1), 405-432.

Faber, A., & Mazlish, E. (2002). *How to talk so kids will listen & listen so kids will talk*. Wade Publishers.

Fallah, S., & Murawski, W. W. (2018). Special education and CLD families: Challenges and strategies for establishing strong partnerships. In K. E. L. Norris & S. Collier-Stewart (Eds.), *Social justice and parent partnerships in multicultural education contexts* (pp. 65-83). IGI Global.

Fontana, K. C. (2005). The effects of co-teaching on the achievement of eighth grade students with learning disabilities. *Journal of At-Risk Issues, 11*(2), 17-23.

Fritzgerald, A. (2020). *Anti-racism and Universal Design for Learning: Building expressways to learning success*. CAST.

Gajda, R., & Koliba, C. (2007). Evaluating the imperative of intraorganizational collaboration: A school improvement perspective. *American Journal of Evaluation, 28*(1), 26-44. https://doi.org/10.1177/1098214006296198

Hang, Q., & Rabren, K. (2009). An examination of co-teaching: Perspectives and efficacy indicators. *Remedial & Special Education, 30*(5), 259-268. https://doi.org/10.1177/0741932508321018

Hensley, K. K., & Huddle, S. M. (2021). Know what you need: A special educator's guide to locating and asking for classroom curricular resources. *TEACHING Exceptional Children, 53*(3), 226-233.

Individuals With Disabilities Education Improvement Act, 20 U.S.C. § 1400 (2004).

Karten, T., & Murawski, W. W. (2020). *Co-teaching do's, don'ts, and do betters*. ASCD.

King-Sears, M. E., Brawand, A. E., Jenkins, M. C., & Preston-Smith, S. (2014). Co-teaching perspectives from secondary science co-teachers and their students with disabilities. *Journal of Science Teacher Education, 25*(6), 651-680.

King-Sears, M. E., Stefanidis, A., Berkeley, S., & Strogilos, V. (2021). Does co-teaching improve academic achievement for students with disabilities? A meta-analysis. *Educational Research Review, 34*. https://doi.org/10.1016/j.edurev.2021.100405

Klem, A. M., & Connell, J. P. (2004). Relationships matter: Linking teacher support to student engagement and achievement. *Journal of School Health, 74*, 262-273.

Kostyo, S., Cardichon, J., & Darling-Hammond, L. (2018). *Making ESSA's equity promise real: State strategies to close the opportunity gap*. Learning Policy Institute.

Lane, K. L., & Carter, E. W. (2013). Reflections on the special issue: Issues and advances in the meta-analysis of single-case research. *Remedial and Special Education, 34*(1), 59-61. https://doi.org/10.1177/0741932512454582

Lochner, W. W., & Murawski, W. W. (2018). *Beyond co-teaching basics: A data driven, no-fail model for continuous improvement*. ASCD.

Lochner, W. W., Murawski, W. W., & True-Daley, J. (2019). The effect of co-teaching on student cognitive engagement. *Theory and Practice in Rural Education, 9*(2), 6-19.

McCray, E., Kamman, M., Brownell, M. T., & Robinson, S. (2017). *High-leverage practices and evidence-based practices: A promising pair*. CEEDAR.

McLeskey, J., Barringer, M.-D., Billingsley, B., Brownell, M., Jackson, D., Kennedy, M., Lewis, T., Maheady, L., Rodriguez, J., Scheeler, M. C., Winn, J., & Ziegler, D. (2017). *High-leverage practices in special education*. Council for Exceptional Children & CEEDAR Center.

Miller, L. D., Short, C., Garland, J., & Clark, S. (2010). The ABCs of CBT: Evidence-based approaches to child anxiety in public school settings. *Journal of Counseling and Development, 88*, 432-439. http://dx.doi.org/10.1002/j.1556-6678.2010.tb00043.x

Murawski, W. W. (2006). Student outcomes in co-taught secondary English classes: How can we improve? *Reading & Writing Quarterly, 22*(3), 227-247. doi.org/10.1080/10573560500455703

Murawski, W. W. (2010). *Collaborative teaching in elementary schools*. Corwin.

Murawski, W. W., & Dieker, L. A. (2004). Tips and strategies for co-teaching at the secondary level. *TEACHING Exceptional Children, 36*(5), 52-58.

Murawski, W. W., & Dieker, L. (2013). *Leading the co-teaching dance: Leadership strategies to enhance team outcomes*. Council for Exceptional Children.

Murawski, W. W., & Scott, K. L. (Eds.). (2019). *What really works with Universal Design for Learning*. Corwin.

Murawski, W. W., & Swanson, H. L. (2001). A meta-analysis of co-teaching research: Where are the data? *Remedial and Special Education, 22*(5), 258-267. https://doi.org/10.1177/074193250102200501

Peck, A., Albrecht, S., George, C., Mathur, S., Paget, M., Ryan, J. B., White, R., & Baker, D. (2012). Reflections on the future of Council for Children with Behavioral Disorders: A response to Colvin, Forness, & Nelson. *Behavioral Disorders, 37*, 123-125.

Prater, M. A., & Sileo, N. (2015). Fantastic family collaboration. In W. W. Murawski & K. L. Scott (Eds.), *What really works with secondary education* (pp. 322-334). Corwin.

Pugh, J. (2010). Cognitive behaviour therapy in schools: The role of educational psychology in the dissemination of empirically supported interventions. *Educational Psychology in Practice, 26*, 391-399. http://dx.doi.org/10.1080/02667363.2010.521312

Rodriguez, J., & Murawski, W. W. (2020). *Special education law and policy: From foundation to application*. Plural Publishing.

Ronfeldt, M., Farmer, S. O., McQueen, K., & Grissom, J. A. (2015). Teacher collaboration in instructional teams and student achievement. *American Educational Research Journal, 52*, 475-514. https://doi.org/10.3102/0002831215585562

Seymour, K., Skattebol, J., & Pook, B. (2020). Compounding education disengagement: COVID-19 lockdown, the digital divide and wrap-around services. *Journal of Children's Services, 15*(4), 243-251. https://doi.org/10.1108/JCS-08-2020-0049

Stone, S. I., & Charles, J. (2018). Conceptualizing the problems and possibilities of interprofessional collaboration in schools. *Children & Schools, 40*(3), 185-192. https://doi.org/10.1093/cs/cdy011

Strauss, V. (2013). What teachers need and reformers ignore: Time to collaborate. *Washington Post*.

Trip, S., Vernon, A., & McMahon, J. (2007). Effectiveness of rational-emotive education: A quantitative meta-analytical study. *Journal of Cognitive & Behavioral Psychotherapies, 7*, 81-93.

Turney, K., & Kao, G. (2009). Barriers to school involvement: Are immigrant parents disadvantaged? *The Journal of Educational Research, 102*(4), 257-271. https://doi.org/10.3200/JOER.102.4.257-271

Waldron, N. L., & McLeskey, J. (2010). Establishing a collaborative school culture through Comprehensive School Reform. *Journal of Educational and Psychological Consultation, 20*(1), 58-74. https://doi.org/10.1080/10474410903535364

Weiss, M. P., Pellegrino, A., & Brigham, F. J. (2017). Practicing collaboration in teacher preparation: Effects of learning by doing together. *Teacher Education and Special Education, 40*(1), 65-76. https://doi.org/10.1177/0888406416655457

Zigmond, N., Magiera, K., Simmons, R., & Volonino, V. (2013). Strategies for improving student outcomes in co-taught general education classrooms. In B. G. Cook & M. Tandersley (Eds.), *Research-based practices in special education* (pp. 116-124). Pearson.

I'm Supposed to Lead Meetings? How Do I Do That Well?

Ruby L. Owiny, PhD

HLP 2

Organize and facilitate effective meetings with professionals and families.

INTRODUCTION

Special education placement requires many meetings. These meetings can include a variety of stakeholders from school personnel, parent liaisons, parents, or community partners. Special educators frequently are called upon to lead these meetings. No one wants to spend time in a meeting that wastes time and does not accomplish the goals or even have goals. Instead, the best use of stakeholders' time is to conduct meaningful, effective, and efficient meetings with the purpose of addressing the need of students with disabilities and planning supports to guide them toward success. This chapter addresses how to lead effective meetings with careful planning, providing opportunities for each voice to be heard, respecting a variety of perspectives, active listening, and eliciting feedback from all stakeholders in order to arrive at consensus.

Owiny, R. L., & Cornelius, K. E. *The Practical Guide to High-Leverage Practices in Special Education: The Purposeful "How" to Enhance Classroom Rigor* (pp. 23-38).

CHAPTER OBJECTIVES

- Describe effective meetings.
- Explain how to organize effective meetings.
- Articulate the components of effective meetings.

KEY TERMS

- **active listening:** Part of effective leadership and communication; evidenced by a conscious effort to hear what is being said, eye contact, body language, head nods, and nonverbal communication; paraphrasing what you hear, asking clarifying questions.
- **agenda:** A list of priorities to address in a meeting; a type of schedule.
- **consensus:** Everyone agreeing to the decision, knowing their voice and ideas were heard.
- **facilitator:** Typically, a special educator or district employee; leads special education meetings, takes care of paperwork, and ensures timelines are observed and met.
- **home visits:** School personnel meeting with students and their families in their home.
- **individualized education program (IEP) meeting:** A meeting for a student with a disability who receives specially designed instruction through an IEP; by law to have the meeting, must include, at a minimum, a general educator, special educator, parents, and a school/district representative.
- **pre-planning:** Preparing for a meeting ahead of time, including the agenda, communication with stakeholders, and gathering relevant documents, communication, and data.

Meetings in special education are as common as waking up in the morning. They can be an effective means of communicating and collaborating with stakeholders. It may seem simple; you have a need to meet with a parent, colleague, or individualized education program (IEP) team, so you send out an email, text, or make phone calls and schedule the meeting. When the meeting convenes, you discuss the issue at hand and come to agreement on a solution. While it seems simple, we have all been in meetings that have not been effective nor efficient and may not have ended with a solution. This outcome is frustrating and time consuming in an already busy schedule for stakeholders. No one wants to attend a meeting in which no solution is determined. This chapter addresses the need for effective meetings and gives practical suggestions for how to effectively lead a meeting. Heeding the tips in this chapter will help you to be a stronger leader when in charge of meetings with colleagues and families.

What Is HLP 2?

High-Leverage Practice (HLP) 2—"*Organize and facilitate effective meetings with professionals and families*" is defined by McLeskey et al. (2017) as:

> Teachers lead and participate in a range of meetings (e.g., meetings with families, individualized education program [IEP] teams, individualized family services plan [IFSP] teams, instructional planning) with the purpose of identifying clear, measurable student outcomes and developing instructional and behavioral plans that support these outcomes. They develop a meeting agenda, allocate time to meet the goals of the agenda, and lead in ways that encourage consensus building through positive verbal and nonverbal communication, encouraging the sharing of multiple perspectives, demonstrating active listening, and soliciting feedback. (p. 18)

When broken down into its components, this HLP makes perfect sense for meeting the needs of our students with disabilities (SWD) through collaboration with relevant stakeholders and is quite practical. Special educators will lead an abundance of meetings over the course of their careers, meetings of many types such as parent–teacher conferences or IEP team meetings and, for a variety of reasons, quick check-ins to inquire about how a student is performing in a different setting or identifying ways the student needs further supports, problem-solving a need, answering questions, and the list can go on and on.

What goes into preparing for an effective meeting and then leading it? This HLP tells us. We will break it down here and go into further detail in later sections. First, one must identify the purpose of the meeting. In most cases, this purpose revolves around student outcomes and determining the best instructional and behavioral approaches to meeting those identified outcomes. Second, to help stay on track and focused on the meeting goal, an agenda is helpful. An agenda ensures that all stakeholders understand what will happen in the meeting. Consider it like an advanced organizer that we give our students at the beginning of a class session. Additionally, including an estimated time for each agenda item helps to keep the meeting on track and participants focused. Finally, a third component of HLP 2 is to lead the meeting in a collaborative manner and to come to consensus, which promotes all participant voices being heard. Encouraging sharing of individual perspectives while demonstrating active listening is important while leading a meeting. Providing positive feedback, both verbally and non-verbally, and asking for feedback on ideas help to put members at ease and demonstrate that everyone's voice is heard and valued.

We know what HLP 2 is, but it is not always so easy to do. As mentioned earlier, we have all sat in meetings of various types that have been ineffective, leaving us feeling voiceless with a lack of accomplishment. The following sections will help you to avoid this pitfall of ineffective, non-collaborative meetings. This chapter will give you some concrete suggestions to implement, which will build your confidence and capacity to lead effective meetings and will lead to a strong sense of accomplishment for you and those attending.

How Is HLP 2 Connected to Other HLPs?

As discussed in the Introduction, the HLPs have this feature of intertwined functionality, thus it will come as no surprise that HLP 2 functions in tandem with other HLPs. Certainly, all three collaborative HLPs work together for the most effective collaboration. We must collaborate with colleagues (HLP 1), which can include co-teaching and sharing strategies to implement with students, among other things, as discussed in Chapter 1. It goes without saying that we must collaborate with parents (HLP 3) as they are certainly the most important partners in educating students. Additionally, the Assessment HLPs must be considered when planning meetings. It is expected that teachers will share assessment data from multiple sources with stakeholders (HLP 4) while also determining the best way to communicate those results in a meaningful, understandable way without using the educational jargon educators are prone to using and that parents frequently do not understand (HLP 5). With all this, educators must also collaborate to make the best instructional decisions possible, based on the available data (HLP 6), as all stakeholders have different perspectives of the student, helping to create a broader picture of who the student is and how best to meet their needs in light of their strengths.

As though the Collaboration and Assessment HLPs are not enough, HLP 10 also directly applies to collaboration. A single person cannot effectively or accurately complete a functional behavioral assessment (FBA) and develop a behavior support plan (BSP). Careful planning with school personnel is vital in completing the FBA and certainly involving caregivers in providing information and determining what to include in a BSP is important to providing the student with the care and mindful decision-making necessary to best meet their needs. You can read more about this unique and specific form of collaboration in Chapter 10.

Table 2-1. Alignment of HLPs and Resources for Evidence-Based Practices

EBP SUPPORT WITH HLP 2	RELATED HLPS	RESOURCES
Home visits	3, 4, 5, 6, 10	https://www.edutopia.org/article/home-visits-101-cristina-santamaria-graff https://ies.ed.gov/ncee/rel/regions/midatlantic/pdf/REL_MA_home_visits.pdf
Regular communication	3, 4, 5, 6, 10, 11	https://affect.coe.hawaii.edu/lessons/establishing-channels/ http://www.edutribe.com.au/educator-resources/12-tips-for-effective-communication-with-parents-for-educators/
Progress reports	3, 4, 5, 6, 11	https://iris.peabody.vanderbilt.edu/module/iep01/cresource/q3/p09/ https://www.readingrockets.org/article/student-progress-monitoring-what-means-your-child
Positive phone call home	3	https://www.edutopia.org/blog/power-positive-phone-call-home-elena-aguilar https://www.pbisrewards.com/blog/positive-phone-call-home/
Pre-meeting planning	1, 3, 10	https://www.specialedlawinsights.com/2019/02/this-one-mistake-can-turn-pre-iep-meeting-planning-into-prohibited-predetermination/ https://www.theintentionaliep.com/what-to-do-before-during-and-after-an-iep-meeting/
Meeting agenda	1, 3, 6, 10, 11, 19, 21	https://modernteacher.net/iep-meeting-agenda/#Types_of_IEP_Meetings_with_Sample_Agendas https://www.smcoe.org/assets/files/About_FIL/San%20Mateo%20County%20SELPA_FIL/Staff%20Resources_FIL/IEP%20Process_FIL/iep-meeting-outline-agenda.pdf
IEP guide	3, 10, 19, 21	https://creatingbutterflies.com/the-iep-process-for-parents-simplified/ https://www.theedadvocate.org/a-visual-guide-to-the-special-education-process/
Encourage multiple perspectives	1, 3, 4, 6, 10	https://researchautism.org/iep-meetings-from-multiple-perspectives/ https://www.ascd.org/el/articles/iep-meetings-building-compassion-and-conversation

(continued)

Table 2-1 (continued). Alignment of HLPs and Resources for Evidence-Based Practices

Active listening	1, 3, 4, 10	https://www.forbes.com/sites/womensmedia/2012/11/09/10-steps-to-effective-listening/?sh=24f3f9c93891 https://www.mindtools.com/CommSkll/ActiveListening.htm
Solicit feedback	1, 3, 5, 6, 10	https://iris.peabody.vanderbilt.edu/module/iep02/cresource/q2/p04/#content https://citeseerx.ist.psu.edu/viewdoc/download?doi=10.1.1.601.6318&rep=rep1&type=pdf

Finally, some of the instructional HLPs apply to collaboration and may require separate meetings, or be agenda items with other points for discussion, with school personnel and parents. Identifying and prioritizing long- and short-term learning goals (HLP 11) is a large part of IEP development in IEP team meetings. Both school personnel and parents should be involved in determining those goals. As teachers make decisions about instruction, it is important to keep parents informed, but especially helpful is to include parents and school personnel in determining instructional and assistive technologies (HLP 19) that can support a student throughout the school day, during extracurricular activities, at home, and in the community to meaningfully participate in the environment. Teaching generalization across settings (HLP 21) is another instructional HLP requiring communication. School personnel and parents can help a student generalize skills across settings with appropriate communication on how to perform the skill, what to expect from the student, and how to support the student in performing that skill across a variety of settings, at school, home, and in the community. For a list of HLPs related to HLP 2, and some of the evidence-based practices discussed in this chapter, see Table 2-1.

How Do I Lead and Participate in Meaningful Meetings to Support Positive Student Outcomes?

As HLP 2 states, we need to clearly identify measurable student outcomes and develop instructional and behavioral plans to support the outcomes. This is typically accomplished in an IEP team meeting but can be part of on-going communication throughout the school year. Identifying measurable student outcomes and developing an instructional plan is one of the main goals of developing an IEP. Student outcomes drive specially designed instruction including the instructional strategies implemented, determining the appropriate provider to work on the stated outcomes with the student, and the amount of time required daily, weekly, or monthly to accomplish those outcomes within the year. To accomplish this, a special educator must develop competency in leading effective meetings to write the IEP and obtain approval by stakeholders.

A foundation of effective relationships and effective meetings is relationship building and clear, open communication (Beck & DeSutter, 2020; Diliberto & Brewer, 2014). Taking steps to build relationships, with colleagues, of course, but especially with caregivers, and to clearly and openly communicate with them, will help reduce the feeling that many families experience—that of not feeling heard, feeling left out of the decision-making process, and sensing the need that they must "fight" to get their child what they feel their child needs (Rossetti et al., 2017). Rather than fostering this adversarial relationship, with limited or no communication, or even unduly promoting a subdued or submissive role on the part of the parent, the ideal relationship is that of mutual respect and mutual sharing of ideas which comes with communication and building trust.

Home visits before the school year begins or shortly thereafter can help put families at ease in communicating a message of care, concern, and mutual respect. Families frequently feel honored that a teacher would take time from their day to visit their home. This positive first experience can set the stage for a strong school-family relationship throughout the year. In fact, Meyer et al. (2011) noted that after conducting home visits before the school year began, teachers reported improved communication with families as compared to working with families who did not receive a home visit, and teachers recognized stronger relationships with families developed as a result of the home visits. A caution, however, in conducting home visits is to never go alone. Teachers should always go in pairs for safety. One may also wish to consider alerting the family to the visit either by email, phone call, or even mailing a card or postcard to their home. This gives families an opportunity to communicate their desire not to have a home visit by the teacher.

There is a myriad of ways to develop relationships and establish clear communication with families. Diliberto and Brewer (2014) recommend regular communication (e.g., daily, weekly, monthly) with families to discuss student progress, successes, and needs. Additionally, regular progress reports (Diliberto & Brewer, 2014), such as mid-way through a quarter, can assist parents in understanding how their child is progressing toward meeting their IEP goals and developing proficiency in general education standards. An oft-used strategy is a phone call or note home to inform a caregiver of a positive experience the child had, or a success experienced, which helps set a tone that the teacher is committed to the student's success. Thus, the first step in leading and participating in meaningful meetings to support the student is open lines of communication with all stakeholders, with an emphasis on building relationships with caregivers.

To set the stage for an effective IEP meeting, it is recommended to do some pre-meeting planning. This assists an educator to be adequately prepared (Beck & DeSutter, 2020) when the meeting occurs and provides an opportunity for connection with a student's caregivers and help them to feel a stronger connection to the team. Prior to the meeting, especially an IEP meeting, Diliberto and Brewer (2014) suggest reaching out to team members to share student strengths, areas of concern, ideas for goals, and any other relevant information they would like to share. This can be written into the Present Levels of Academic Achievement and Functional Performance (PLAAFP) section of the IEP in advance and gone over for revisions during the meeting. Any brainstormed IEP goals can be drafted and ready for final discussion at the IEP team meeting.

Another thing to remember is the special educator should carefully consider how to maintain the dignity of the student and the family during meetings (Rosser, 2021). Special education meetings can be difficult for parents as they listen to education professionals discuss the weaknesses and needs of their child, which often stems from a deficit model of thinking. One must guard against that mindset and demonstrate honor for the individual while also promoting necessary interventions for the student's growth. Rosser (2021) recommends carefully selecting and preparing which data to highlight during the meeting, to not get bogged down in a deficit mindset or overwhelming families with all that is "wrong" with their child (Chapter 5 provides more detail on this skill). Instead, consider providing the overall picture of evaluation results rather than getting bogged down in the minutiae. Providing families with an overview of the IEP process through an infographic or slide will also help them to better understand the process, help keep the momentum going, and allow them to follow along more seamlessly (Rosser, 2021). Additionally, creating a handout of key terms and commonly used acronyms, with a brief definition, can be helpful to allow parents to feel comfortable in the meeting with a basic understanding of the terminology (Rosser, 2021).

In your pre-planning, it is important to remember your culturally and linguistically diverse families. Plan to have materials available in the families' native languages (Rossetti et al., 2017), along with securing an interpreter during the meeting. If possible, consider having a conversation with the interpreter prior to the meeting to provide a glimpse into the material that will need to be translated. This will help the interpreter to identify terms in the parents' language that will most closely translate to English for a more accurate translation. Do not assume that because a parent appears to be fluent in English, they do not need an interpreter during the meeting or materials translated. Conversational English is quite different from academic language, thus having materials and conversation translated into the families' native languages can help ensure understanding and demonstrates respect for the families' native language.

It should be noted that parents, by law (Individuals with Disabilities Education Act [IDEA], 2006) are required to be members of the IEP team and decision-making. Therefore, any pre-meeting communication related to an IEP should include the whole team and not just school personnel. Not only is this law, but it certainly assists in relationship development and trust with parents. In fact, Rossetti et al. (2017) cite several authors who note that family engagement directly affects student outcomes for those who have IEPs.

As relationships are built and pre-meeting planning is conducted, special educators have laid a strong foundation for the meeting. Yell et al. (2022) note schools should and must go beyond mere invitations for parents to participate in educational decision-making for their child to encourage full, meaningful participation. This should include allowing parents to share their ideas about what could work best for their child, and the team should give careful consideration into how to incorporate their ideas into the IEP (Yell et al., 2022) or into the school day, in general. The efforts spent on the front end of the process stand a better chance of families feeling more comfortable with school personnel, reducing the potential for conflict to escalate, and eliminating the need for due process hearings. Rather, families will be more apt to feel comfortable addressing their concerns and questions to school personnel.

Leading a meeting when families know they have full rights and responsibilities as the rest of the team will help special educators to lead meetings that are more amiable than antagonistic. With an amiable team, the meeting can run more smoothly with shared respect being the key component for decision-making. Leading an effective meeting involves a focus on what the child needs and how to best meet those needs. When relationships have been built, a team can be led through the lens of open communication, sharing of ideas, and coming to consensus in decision-making with each team member knowing their ideas were heard and considered (Weaver & Ouye, 2015). As such, every meeting should include more than just information sharing, but should include an exchange of ideas, open communication, and shared decision-making.

What Are the Components of Effective Planning to Accomplish Meeting Goals?

A meeting agenda should be prepared several days in advance of any meeting, whether it is an annual IEP review, a parent-teacher conference, a meeting requested by the parents or school personnel to discuss an issue, or any other reason. Once the agenda is drafted, it should be shared with parents and other participants, asking for input on additional items they would like discussed (Weaver & Ouye, 2015). Kurth et al. (2019) noted that not only are parents outnumbered on an IEP team, which can leave them feeling intimidated, but it often inhibits their ability to speak up because school personnel have not actively sought their input nor affirmed it.

IEP Team Meeting Agenda

Student:
Day: Time: Location:
Type of Meeting: Initial **Annual Review** Triennial Review
Meeting Facilitator:
Team Members:

1. Welcome (2 min)
2. Introductions (10 min)
3. State purpose of meeting (2 min)
4. Establish meeting norms (2 min)
5. Review agenda - any additions? (2 min)
6. Review of parental rights (5 min)
7. Review of current IEP data related to goals (10 min)
8. Parent input on current goals and other information they wish to share (10 min)
9. Discuss continued eligibility (5 min)
10. Develop updated PLAAFP (include strengths and needs; 15 min)
11. Determine appropriate goals (15 min)
12. Determine how goals will be measured and progress communicated to parents (5 min)
13. Determine services and placement (ensure appropriate LRE; 5 min)
14. Transition plan (if applicable; 20 min)
15. Ask for any questions, concerns, or additional input (5 min)
16. Secure signatures (if parents are ready and IEP is finalized; 2 min)
17. Adjourn

Notes: Include action items and necessary communication with stakeholders not present in the meeting

Figure 2-1. Sample IEP meeting agenda: annual review.

When creating the agenda, include time estimates for each item to help all team members to stay on track (see Figure 2-1 for an example of an agenda for an IEP meeting and Figure 2-2 for an example of a parent-teacher meeting). However, the agenda should be viewed as flexible in case additional items come up for discussion. In addition, after welcoming attendees and doing introductions, the next item should be stating the purpose of the meeting to ensure everyone is on the same track. Plan to go over the posted agenda in the meeting, too, and allow a brief time for additions to it (Diliberto & Brewer, 2014; Weaver & Ouye, 2015).

Furthermore, it is important to plan which documents will need to be shared and how that information will be shared in a way that makes sense to all participants, free of educational jargon and stated in terms understandable to those outside of the field (Rosser, 2021). Carefully consider what data members of the team should provide to help answer questions participants might have or to justify a suggestion (Beck & DeSutter, 2020). Additionally, when sending the agenda out, confirm with team members their availability to attend the meeting and to remain in the meeting for its duration. This sends a message that this meeting, this student, and this family are important to school personnel (Beck & DeSutter, 2020). This careful planning will allow for meetings to run more smoothly and decisions to be more collaborative.

Parent-Teacher Meeting Agenda

Student:
Day: Time: Location:
Attendees:

1. Welcome
2. Introductions, if needed
3. State purpose of meeting
4. Information Sharing
    a. Student's overall well-being, attitude toward school
    b. Strengths (academic, social, dispositions, etc.)
    c. Current achievement
    d. Other
5. Questions/Concerns
6. Decisions Made
7. Adjourn

Notes: Include action items and necessary communication with stakeholders not present in the meeting

Reminder: Share meeting notes with parents and other relevant stakeholders within 3 school days to ensure accountability on action steps

Figure 2-2. Sample parent-teacher meeting agenda.

How Can Special Educators Facilitate to Build Consensus and Include All Members of the Team in Meaningful Decision-Making?

Teachers must develop skills to lead meeting participants to arrive at consensus in decisions made on behalf of SWD. Each team member must know they have a voice at the table with parents being assured of their equality with other team members (Rossetti et al., 2017). A key word in the question for this section is *facilitate*. Leading an IEP meeting or most any meeting where decisions are made for SWD requires a team decision, making facilitation a must. The IEP team consists of experts in various areas of education and knowledge of the student; their voices are important. As Williams (2007) states, the facilitator's role is one of guiding the group to a decision rather than unilaterally stating what will be done. To guide the team in making decisions based on consensus, "school-based decision-making between parents and professionals should be framed within a conversation that is equally balanced among all participants" (Connor & Cavendish, 2018). This only happens when school personnel position themselves as allies for the student and the parents, rather than the experts who have the best answers. This posturing as one member of the larger team, who understands that the collective expertise creates the opportunity for better decision-making, sets the stage for "authentic communication and decreasing power differentials" (Connor & Cavendish, 2018). There are three ways within HLP 2 that facilitators of meetings can guide a team to consensus: allowing and even soliciting multiple perspectives, engaging in active listening, and soliciting feedback from all team members. Each of these principles will be discussed in more detail.

Encourage Multiple Perspectives

When a team is meeting to discuss how to adequately meet the needs of an SWD, each team member's perspective of the student is important. The facilitator should set some ground rules, such as reminding meeting participants that everyone remains quiet when someone is talking so they can listen to what is being said (Yell et al., 2022). Each perspective, when shared and put together, helps to create a fuller profile of the student's strengths, needs, likes, and dislikes. This profile allows the team to make wise decisions. The IDEA (2004) requires a collaborative effort for IEP development, specifically. Decisions should be made as a team and include goals, accommodations, placement location, etc., to meet the individual needs of the student. In fact, IDEA explicitly requires parents to be meaningfully involved in these decisions (Cheatham et al., 2012). When parents are meaningfully involved, their perspective is heard and considered. As experts on their child, this perspective could be argued to be the most important. It should be noted that soliciting parent input to their insights of their child is vital to a fuller understanding of the student, yet Kurth et al. (2019) identified that parent input was not always reflected in IEPs. This possible unintentional undermining of parent insights sends a message to parents that their perspective is not valued. Therefore, teachers should be cautious and alert to ensure the parent's perspective is heard and valued, evidenced by those insights becoming a part of the IEP, as appropriate. Asking for clarification (Yell et al., 2022) or further details is a key to ensuring the team understands each other and key ideas are included in the IEP or other decisions being made about the student.

It is important to also mention the unique situation families from culturally and linguistic backgrounds find themselves in when navigating the special education process in schools. They may appear passive in their participation in their child's education and in the IEP process. Special educators should investigate why this may be the case. Chang et al. (2022) note that the language barrier can be a big deterrent, along with poor translations of documents or poor interpretation of spoken language. To overcome these barriers, special educators should be aware of the challenges families from culturally and linguistically diverse backgrounds experience and identify ways to overcome these barriers.

Active Listening

Yell et al. (2022) note that all school personnel must be cognizant to "create and maintain a professional and courteous environment" during meetings. The responsibility falls heavily on the facilitator to ensure this happens. One way to ensure courtesy is to remind participants to allow one person to finish their idea before interjecting. Additionally, engaging in active listening, often considered to be an important aspect of collaboration (Thistle & McNaughton, 2015), is important as the facilitator of the meeting. As each team member provides input about the student, the facilitator should be actively engaged in listening to take accurate notes and to synthesize the information into the IEP or other decisions being made. Active listening serves a dual purpose: It is both a tool for gathering information about the child, and also portraying an attitude of interest and care to the parents (McNaughton & Vostal, 2010). The meeting facilitator should be intentional in seeking parental insights into their child and ensure their ideas, along with those of other team members, are adequately addressed when coming to consensus on the development of the IEP or for problem-solving a challenge the student is facing.

Solicit Feedback

To solicit feedback, one must listen carefully to what is being said and ask for feedback on what was shared. It is important for each team member to feel comfortable in providing feedback on ideas in order to reach consensus and hear each person's point of view. To solicit feedback, the facilitator could ask questions such as, "Mrs. Juarez, what do you think of Mr. Simba's idea?" or "The speech pathologist would like to see the student three times a week to work on communication skills. How does the team feel about that recommendation? Is it an appropriate amount of time to meet goals while balancing other service needs?" Given that the IEP is intended to help the student develop missing skills and grow in areas of weakness, while shoring up strengths, it is vital for all team members' voices to be heard (Beck & DeSutter, 2020), asking team members to respond to other team members' ideas helps to ensure everyone has a say and to develop a more robust IEP; develop a broader, more accurate view of the student; and ensure sound decisions are determined.

What Does HLP 2 Look Like in a K-12 Classroom?

Elementary Example

Mr. and Mrs. Sutton reached out to Mrs. Hunter, a second-grade teacher, via email to request a meeting due to some concerns they have about their son, Johnathan. They are concerned that, while they agreed to pull-out services for him in English Language Arts (ELA), that his needs may not be getting met and that he is missing out on full access to the general education curriculum and peer models. Mrs. Hunter quickly responds with days and times in the next week that she is available and asks if any of those times might work. If not, she asks if Mr. and Mrs. Sutton will provide her with their availability, and she will work to arrange her schedule accordingly. Additionally, she asks if they would be amenable to her inviting the special educator, Mrs. Messner, to get her input into Johnathan's progress also.

Mr. and Mrs. Sutton respond with a date and time that works for Mrs. Sutton, and they are willing for Mrs. Messner to participate in the meeting as well. Mrs. Hunter calls Mrs. Messner to inform her of this request and inquire if that date and time will work for her. It does and Mrs. Messner is happy to meet with them and had even been recently considering discussing a placement change with Mrs. Hunter and Johnathan's parents. With the meeting set up, Mrs. Hunter emails the agenda to Johnathan's parents and Mrs. Messner (Figure 2-3) and asks for their input on the agenda. Everyone approves the agenda and accepts the calendar invitation for the meeting.

On the morning of the meeting, Mrs. Hunter makes a phone call to Mr. and Mrs. Sutton to confirm they are still able to attend the meeting and confirmed with Mrs. Messner when they had hallway duty earlier that morning. When Johnathan's parents arrive in the school office, Mrs. Messner is waiting for them to walk with them to Mrs. Hunter's classroom. On the walk there, she asks about their family, jobs, etc. When they arrive in Mrs. Hunter's room, she warmly greets them and directs the group to a table in a corner of the room while she closes her classroom door for privacy. Once seated herself, she begins the meeting by thanking Johnathan's parents for their involvement in Johnathan's education and their request for the meeting. She asks them to share how Johnathan is doing overall and what activities he is currently involved in as he has mentioned basketball coming up and a ski trip that has been booked for winter break. Mrs. Messner interjects that Johnathan chose to write his how-to paper on skiing, based on his excitement for the upcoming trip. After getting an overview of their perspective of how he is doing (HLP 3), Mrs. Hunter asks them to share their ideas for Johnathan related to his ELA placement. While Mr. and Mrs. Sutton share, Mrs. Hunter and Mrs. Messner take notes and ask questions for clarification, such as "Can you tell us more about Johnathan's perspective about being in the special education resource room for ELA?" and "That's an interesting thought. Can you tell us more?" When Mr. and Mrs. Sutton finish explaining why they have made this placement change request, Mrs. Messner shares some data that support their idea. Johnathan has improved in both reading and writing as evidenced by his performance on I-Ready progress monitoring (HLP 6), his in-class work, and performance on check-outs from the *Reading Mastery* curriculum (HLP 4) Mrs. Messner uses for reading intervention. Mrs. Hunter affirms Johnathan's parents' concern that he is missing out on peer models during ELA while explaining that, based on the data, Johnathan is benefitting from *Reading Mastery* and is concerned his progress might stall if that intervention was removed. Mrs. Messner recommends that Johnathan's time in the special education resource room

Parent-Teacher Meeting Agenda

Student: Johnathan Sutton
Day: November 15, 2023 Time: 1 pm - 1:45 pm Location: Mrs. Hunter's room #18
Attendees: Mr. and Mrs. Sutton, Mrs. Hunter, Mrs. Messner

1. Welcome
2. State purpose of meeting: Johnathan's current ELA placement
1. Information Sharing
   a. Student's overall well-being, attitude toward school
   b. Strengths (academic, social, dispositions, etc.)
   c. Current achievement in ELA
   d. Other
2. Questions/Concerns: Could Johnathan benefit from ELA placement in the general education setting rather than the special education resource room?
3. Decisions Made
4. Adjourn

Notes: Include action items and necessary communication with stakeholders not present in the meeting

Reminder: Share meeting notes with parents and other relevant stakeholders within 3 school days to ensure accountability on action steps

Figure 2-3. Meeting agenda for Johnathan Sutton.

be reduced to 30 minutes daily from 60 minutes daily so he can receive instruction in the *Reading Mastery* curriculum and continue to make progress toward achieving grade level reading skills. Mrs. Hunter recommends that Johnathan receive his specially designed instruction for writing goals in the general education classroom with her implementing the IEP goals for written expression with consultation from Mrs. Messner on a weekly basis to ensure proper monitoring of goals is occurring and sharing ideas for strategies Johnathan could be taught. Mr. and Mrs. Sutton are pleased with the progress Johnathan has made and appreciate the data his teachers have provided to show them how much he has improved, including a graph with a trend line showing that if he continues making progress in *Reading Mastery* lessons, he is projected to be reading on grade-level by the end of the school year. They are pleased that Mrs. Hunter is willing to provide the specially designed instruction necessary for Johnathan to be included in the general education classroom for writing instruction.

Mrs. Messner makes note of these changes on Johnathan's IEP and documents the decisions made while adding to the bottom of the agenda that she needs to inform the full IEP team of this change to Johnathan's IEP. Once decisions are finalized, Mrs. Messner and Mrs. Hunter both thank Mr. and Mrs. Sutton for their time and their participation in making wise decisions for Johnathan's academic progress and adjourn the meeting. Mrs. Hunter walks Mr. and Mrs. Sutton back to the office in much the same fashion as Mrs. Messner who met them in the office. She shows interest in them as individuals and asks about their jobs, their family who lives on the East Coast where a hurricane is expected to make landfall within the next few hours, and inquires about their other children. Once in the office, Mrs. Hunter thanks them and reminds them to never hesitate to contact her with any questions they may have and thanks them again, wishing them a great afternoon.

Secondary Example

Mr. Daniels is prepping for Angel's IEP meeting. First he wants to make sure everyone who needs to be there (i.e., parents, general educator, administrator, and the student) is included in the invitation. He has already cleared and saved the date for 2 weeks from now. He sends the electronic invitation to members, but also allows the invitation to be shared just in case the parents want to bring someone from outside the school. Angel has been participating in a community program to obtain her cosmetology license, and her mother mentioned she might want to invite Ms. Herch, the director of the program. Mr. Daniels offered to invite her, but Mrs. Grace, Angel's mom, wanted to check with Angel first, and she was not sure if Ms. Herch would want to attend.

Mr. Daniels then looks over the progress monitoring data and graphs, he cannot wait to share the progress Angel has made over the past year. He checks all the notes from meetings with general educators and aligns their information to help formulate a clear, concise, and complete PLAAFP for Angel. He then reviews the interview notes and data from her post-secondary transition assessment. Mr. Daniels starts to draft preliminary statements to share with the team. He wants to be sure to share draft statements with the family ahead of the meeting for their input.

The day of the meeting arrives and after double checking the invitation, Mr. Daniels sees everyone, including Ms. Herch from the cosmetology program, will be attending. He prints off personalized agendas (see Figure 2-1) so that everyone will have their own for easy reference. He gathers Angel's data portfolio with progress monitoring graphs, work samples, and the drafted PLAAFP statements. He goes to get Angel from class, and together they meet Mrs. Grace and Ms. Herch in the front office. He helps them sign into the school and escorts them to the conference room where Ms. Wilson, Angel's general education English teacher, and Mr. Scott, the building administrator, are waiting. Mr. Daniels is so glad the school invested in a round conference table; now IEP teams can sit together and not have school staff appear domineering by having parents sit alone across from school personnel.

Mr. Daniels starts with introductions, and as he introduces himself, he passes out the printed agendas. He then invites others to introduce themselves as well. He reminds everyone the purpose of the meeting and then explains the norms; they are committed to honoring everyone's time and commit to follow the agenda, everyone will have a chance to share, when someone is talking no one will interrupt or cut them off. If anyone feels the meeting is getting too emotional, they are free to ask for a break and that request will be honored. We honor different opinions and multiple ways of looking at an issue. We use person-first language (i.e., the student's name or "student with a disability" vs. "the disabled child"). We recognize when more information is needed and will not rush to decisions if we need to collect more information. We ask clarifying questions and do not assume everyone understands what we mean. To model this norm, Mr. Daniels provides examples and checks for understanding and agreement.

Mr. Daniels then goes over the agenda and asks for questions on what they will be covering in this meeting. Then he reviews the parental rights documents and offers Mrs. Grace another copy. She smiles and says, "That's okay, I have plenty of these at home." Once he is sure everyone is ready to start, Mr. Daniels begins with sharing the goals from Angel's IEP from last year. He shares the writing goal, explains how the progress was monitored, and shares the graph of steady progress. He briefly talks about the specialized instruction Angel received and asks Ms. Wilson to share information about the general education curriculum. Together they express how pleased they are with Angel's progress. Mr. Daniels then hands Angel a copy of an essay she wrote last week, and she shares with the group how she developed her opinion, found evidence to support her opinion, and wrote more. When she said that last bit, she turned to Mr. Daniels and smiled. She said, "He is always telling me, 'You have more to say, so say it. Write more.' That is Mr. Daniels's favorite thing to say!" This routine continues with all the goals.

Mr. Daniels asks Mrs. Grace after each goal presentation if she has anything to add or share. She stays quiet through the first couple of goals and then shares how proud she is of Angel and thankful to Mr. Daniels, Ms. Wilson, and the entire school. They have all worked so hard to make Angel feel accepted, and she finally sees Angel is starting to enjoy school and talks about her assignments at home. Mr. Daniels takes notes and adds them to the IEP documents. He then reminds the team that this is Angel's annual review; she was found eligible to continue services last year in 10th grade and so they will now discuss the goals for this coming year.

Ms. Wilson begins by discussing the general education curriculum; she describes the demands of the class and the expectation for meeting the state standards. She highlights the strengths that Angel has related to the curriculum. Mr. Daniels shares current baseline data collected from district benchmarks, progress monitoring data, and makes a connection to how Angel's current ability level is still impacting her ability to progress in the general education curriculum. He suggests a goal that would be meaningful to Angel's progress and related to the general education standard, and then shares how and when progress toward that goal will be monitored.

Mr. Scott asks to speak. He commends both teachers for working together to meet Angel's needs and thanks Mrs. Grace for all her support, reminding them they are a team and Angel's success is due to all of their hard work, but states no one has worked harder than Angel. He asks Mrs. Grace how she feels about the goals, and asks Angel if she feels these are goals she can achieve. Angel says she will continue to work hard but wants to know if she can be moved to the class with Ms. Wilson. "I don't mean no disrespect, Mr. Daniels; it's just I think I'm ready to do it alone. Ms. Wilson knows me, and we work real good together." Mr. Daniels jokes that he is no longer her favorite teacher and then Mrs. Grace pops in and corrects Angel's grammar. Angel rolls her eyes and repeats the statement using her mother's words. Mr. Scott says, "Well, Angel, you brought us right to our next agenda item."

The team discusses reducing Angel's direct service minutes and moving her out of the team-taught class and having her finish the year in Ms. Wilson's non–co-taught English 11 classroom. They discuss the accommodations that would be needed, and how Mr. Daniels will still consult with Ms. Wilson and Angel as he monitors her reading comprehension goals. However, he suggests she remain in the resource class where she can continue to receive instruction for writing strategies. Angel is happy with the choice, and Mrs. Grace states she is thrilled to see Angel take more ownership of her learning.

Mr. Daniels then turns to Ms. Herch and tells her that so much of Angel's success is due to her program. Angel added, she loves her classes and is so excited to continue in the program. Mr. Daniels then explains the process of the secondary transition plan. As they review Angel's plan, Ms. Herch becomes more active in the conversation. Explaining more details about cosmetology and potential income. She shares the talent and natural ability Angel is showing and then encourages Angel to consider some business classes at the local community college. Angel frowns and says she is tired of school; she just wants to get out and start living on her own and begin her career. Ms. Herch tells her she knows exactly how she feels, she had those exact feelings when she was graduating from high school. Then she explains that with some business classes she could also manage her own salon one day. Mrs. Grace was so excited to hear Ms. Herch say these things and said Angel should further her education. After further discussion on the topic, Mr. Daniels then added a post-secondary goal of attending the local community college for business classes. The meeting was winding down. Mr. Scott then asked everyone if there were any more questions. Mr. Daniels asked if everyone was in agreement on the IEP that they developed, and then secured signatures. Ms. Herch thanked Mrs. Grace for the invitation and admitted she had never been invited to a school meeting before; she was thrilled to be included.

Summary

Given the quantity of meetings related to special education, it is imperative that special educators have the skills to "organize and facilitate effective meetings with professionals and families" as HLP 2 states. This chapter has provided you with tools to lead meetings well by first getting to know families and establishing a trusting relationship with them. Please refer to Figure 2-2 to guide you as you prepare for, and lead, special education meetings. Additionally, preparing ahead of time for meetings, with all documentation, data, and information gathered and an agenda prepared, leads to a well-organized meeting. Demonstrating respect for others' perspectives, actively listening, and eliciting feedback from stakeholders will help to make wise, informed decisions to best support the student.

HLP 2 easily integrates multiple other HLPs. The concepts explained in this chapter apply to co-planning with a co-teacher or collaborating to implement a new strategy for a student as HLP 1 articulates. It will be obvious that HLP 3, collaborating with families to support student learning and secure needed services, is an integral part of those with whom meetings will be held. In those meetings with stakeholders, it is inevitable that data will be shared (HLPs 4, 5, and 6) and must be communicated effectively so all participants understand. When conducting an FBA and developing a BSP, a team is best suited to gathering all the necessary data for the FBA and subsequently analyzing the data, determining a function of the behavior, and developing an appropriate BSP (HLP 10).

When meeting for IEP development, a main piece of the IEP is identifying learning goals (HLP 11), determining what, if any, assistive or instructional technology (HLP 19) is needed to support the student, and determining how to best teach maintenance and generalization of skills across time and settings (HLP 21). These three HLPs are frequently part of the IEP team meeting, along with being discussion points in other meetings, as well. It is vital to the decision-making process for the meeting to be efficient and effective to ensure that a plan can be in place promptly to meet the needs of students and to clearly communicate that plan to stakeholders.

Chapter Review

1. Restate HLP 2 in your own words.
2. What is the most important part of effective meetings?
3. What should be included in pre-planning for a meeting?
4. How can one establish consensus in decision-making?
5. What documents or other materials might be necessary to have available during an IEP meeting or a parent-teacher conference?

References

Beck, S. J., & DeSutter, K. (2020). An examination of group facilitator challenges and problem-solving techniques during IEP team meetings. *Teacher Education and Special Education, 43*(2), 127-143.

Chang, Y. C., Avila, M., & Rodgriquez, H. (2022). Beyond the dotted line: Empowering parents from culturally and linguistically diverse families to participate. *TEACHING Exceptional Children, 55*(2), 132-140. https://doi.org/10.1177/00400599221099868

Cheatham, G. A., Hart, J. E., Malian, I., & McDonald, J. (2012). Six things to never say or hear during an IEP meeting: Educators as advocates for families. *TEACHING Exceptional Children, 44*(3), 50-57.

Connor, D. J., & Cavendish, W. (2018). Sharing power with parents: Improving educational decision making for students with learning disabilities. *Learning Disability Quarterly, 41*(2), 79-84. https://doi.org/10.1177/0731948717698828

Diliberto, J. A., & Brewer, D. (2014). Six tips for successful IEP meetings. *TEACHING Exceptional Children, 44*(4), 30-37. https://doi.org/10.1177/004005991204400404

Individuals With Disabilities Education Act, 20 U.S.C. §§ 1400 et seq. (2004, 2006 & Supp. V. 2011).

Kurth, J. A., McQueston, J. A., Ruppar, A. L., Toews, S. G., Johnston, R., & McCabe, K. M. (2019). A description of parent input in IEP development through analysis IEP documents. *Intellectual & Developmental Disabilities, 57*(6), 485-496.

McLeskey, J., Barringer, M.-D., Billingsley, B., Brownell, M., Jackson, D., Kennedy, M., Lewis, T., Maheady, L., Rodriquez, J., Scheeler, M. C., Winn, J., & Ziegler, D. (2017). *High-leverage practices in special education*. Council for Exceptional Children & CEEDAR Center.

McNaughton, D., & Vostal, B. R. (2010). Using active listening to improve collaboration with parents: The LAFF don't CRY strategy. *Intervention in School & Clinic, 45*(4), 251-256.

Meyer, J. A., Mann, M. B., & Becker, J. (2011). A five-year follow-up: Teachers' perceptions of the benefits of home visits for early elementary children. *Early Childhood Education, 39,* 191-196. https://doi.org/10.1007/s10643-011-0461-1

Rosser, C. (2021). *Preserving the dignity of young clients and their families*. Leader Live. https://leader.pubs.asha.org/do/10.1044/leader.MIW.26032021.26/full/

Rossetti, Z., Sauer, J. S., Bui, O., & Ou, S. (2017). Developing collaborative partnerships with culturally and linguistically diverse families during the IEP process. *TEACHING Exceptional Children, 50*(4), 172-182. https://doi.org/10.1177/0040059918758163

Thistle, J. J., & McNaughton, D. (2015). Teaching active listening skills to pre-service speech-language pathologists: A first step in supporting collaboration with parents of young children who require AAC. *Language, Speech, and Hearing Services in Schools, 46*, 44-55.

Weaver, A. D., & Ouye, J. C. (2015). A practical and research-based guide for improving IEP team meetings. *NASP Communiqué, 44*(3), 1-8.

Williams, B. R. (2007). *More than 50 ways to build team consensus*. Corwin Press.

Yell, M. L., Bateman, D. F., & Shriner, J. G. (2022). *Developing educationally meaningful and legally sound IEPs*. The Rowman & Littlefield Publishing Group, Inc.

How Can Collaborating With Families Ensure Successful Outcomes for Students?

Kathleen A. Boothe, PhD
and Marla J. Lohmann, PhD

HLP 3

Collaborate with families to support student learning and secure needed services.

INTRODUCTION

Family–school collaboration is key to providing appropriate and effective services to students with disabilities (SWD). High-Leverage Practice (HLP) 3 focuses on the importance of collaboration with families to ensure SWD are receiving appropriate services and to ensure student learning is occurring. Teachers need to remember that families know their child best. Therefore, it is vital to the student's success that teachers make an effort to partner with families. This chapter provides background information on HLP 3 and how it intersects with other HLPs to improve student outcomes. Strategies and examples of implementation of HLP 3 with related evidence-based practices will also be provided in the chapter.

Owiny, R. L., & Cornelius, K. E. *The Practical Guide to High-Leverage Practices in Special Education: The Purposeful "How" to Enhance Classroom Rigor* (pp. 39-54).

CHAPTER OBJECTIVES

- → Explain the rationale for building collaborative relationships with the families of SWD.
- → Articulate the ways in which schools and families can partner to support SWD.
- → Create a plan for building family–school relationships in your classrooms.

KEY TERMS

- **advocacy:** Advocacy is communicating with one another the strengths, weaknesses, and desires of oneself, a person, or a group of people.
- **collaboration:** Collaboration occurs when two or more people or groups of people work together to achieve a common goal.
- **parent involvement:** Parent involvement occurs when schools actively reach out to families and ask for their input. This occurs when there is two-way communication between the school and the home.
- **person-centered planning:** Person-centered planning occurs when schools work together with students and families on identifying gifts/talents, achievements, needed resources, etc. to assist in planning for the child's future.

This chapter offers practical implementation tips for High-Leverage Practice (HLP) 3—"*Collaborate with families to support student learning and secure needed services.*" Partnering with families is a critical aspect of serving students with disabilities (SWD) and is supported by research and mandated under IDEA. This chapter will present an overview of the rationale for teaming with families, a synopsis of the research regarding family–school relationships, and practical strategies that special educators can use to implement HLP 3 in their own classrooms and schools. The Council for Exceptional Children (CEC) and the Collaboration for Effective Educator Development, Accountability, and Reform (CEEDAR) Center have described HLP 3 as,

> Teachers collaborate with families about individual children's needs, goals, programs, and progress over time and ensure families are informed about their rights as well as about special education processes (e.g., IEPs, IFSPs). Teachers should respectfully and effectively communicate considering the background, socioeconomic status, language, culture, and priorities of the family. Teachers advocate for resources to help students meet instructional, behavioral, social, and transition goals. In building positive relationships with students, teachers encourage students to self-advocate, with the goal of fostering self-determination over time. Teachers also work with families to self-advocate and support their children's learning. (McLeskey et al., 2017, p. 18)

This HLP can be broken down into four main components:

1. Communication
2. Advocating
3. Building relationships
4. Supporting families in building their own skills

This chapter will address the importance of each component and provide practical suggestions for supporting each component.

When we talk about teaming with parents, it is critical to consider the different types of family–school relations. Not all families want, or need, the same kind of relationship with school personnel. Epstein (1992) describes six types of parent involvement and recommends that all schools and teachers are prepared for families who may need some, or all, of these involvement strategies. Family–school relationships may include (a) ensuring positive home conditions, (b) two-way communication, (c) volunteering, (d) learning at home, (e) shared decision-making, and (f) community collaboration. Table 3-1 offers an overview of these types of relationships, as well as the roles of the school and the family. To implement HLP 3, teachers and schools will need to be aware of, and be prepared to fulfill, their role in each relationship type.

Decades of research have shown benefits of family–school relationships for individual students as well as the school community. Students, schools, families, and communities all benefit when families and schools work as a team. Benefits include (a) long-term planning for the student's education and future endeavors (Epstein, 2008), (b) increased student engagement and motivation for learning (Gonzalez-DeHass et al., 2005), (c) increased student school attendance (Sheldon & Epstein, 2004), (d) increased academic achievement (Cooper et al., 2010; Hampden-Thompson & Galindo, 2017), and (e) improved school climate (Lohmann et al., 2018). Despite the benefits of family involvement in the school setting, family participation in schools and collaboration between families and schools remains minimal (Huscroft-D'Angelo et al., 2018).

How Is HLP 3 Connected to Other HLPs?

As you have and will read throughout this book, the special education HLPs do not work in isolation, but instead the HLPs combine to ensure a comprehensive program of support for SWD. While effectively implementing any one HLP requires a special educator to also be implementing other HLPs, teaming with families is explicitly stated in HLPs 2, 4, 5, and 6, as well. As they facilitate individualized education program (IEP) meetings (HLP 2), special educators work with families and other stakeholders. HLP 4 explicitly states that special educators should include information from families in comprehensive assessments. When implementing HLP 5, special educators help families understand assessment data and team with families to use the data to make educational decisions. Finally, HLP 6 asks special educators to talk to stakeholders, including families, about student learning and make adjustments to meet student needs. There are several more HLPs that work alongside HLP 3 but are not explicitly stated. These include HLPs 10 (data collection for functional behavioral assessments [FBAs] and behavior support plans [BSPs]), 11 (prioritizing learning goals), 17 (flexible grouping), and 18 (student engagement). As you read through the remainder of the chapter, you will see how HLP 3 works together with all of these HLPs.

What Are the Best Ways to Communicate With Families?

The first part of HLP 3 involves communicating with families. Communication may take a variety of forms including (a) talking to families in-person at school drop-off and pick-up, (b) scheduled face-to-face or technology-based meetings, (c) telephone calls, (d) emails, (e) written paper-based communication, and (f) communications via apps, such as GroupMe or Remind. In addition, some communication is written for all families served by the special educator, while other communication needs to be one-on-one. The special educator may write a weekly email with information about the curriculum or may host information sessions for families to learn about the special education process; these types of communications would be sent to all families. Additionally, the special educator will need to maintain confidentiality and communicate one-on-one with the family of each student to discuss student strengths, needs, and progress.

When special educators speak to families, it is important that they focus on the child's strengths and the positives instead of focusing the conversation on the child's needs (Carlson et al., 2020; Fish, 2008) in order to reflect the special educator's respect for the child both as a student and as a person (Fontil & Petrakos, 2015). One way that special educators can communicate they care about

Table 3-1. Types of Family–School Relations

TYPE OF RELATIONSHIP	ROLE OF SCHOOL	ROLE OF FAMILY	HLP ALIGNMENT WITH RELATIONSHIP TYPE
Ensuring Positive Home Conditions	Supporting families by offering training and parent education as appropriate.	Ensuring children have a positive home environment, including health and safety.	Supporting families in building their own skills
Two-Way Communication	Using a variety of methods to communicate with families about school events and individual student progress.	Communicating with schools and responding to communication from the school.	Communication Building relationships
Volunteering	Offering opportunities for families to volunteer for the school in a variety of ways and at various times. Providing training/support for volunteers.	Volunteering in the school and for school events and/or attending school events.	Building relationships
Learning at Home	Provide families with guidance regarding supporting learning at home.	Assist children in completing homework and other learning activities at home.	Supporting families in building their own skills
Shared Decision-Making	Treating families as equal decision-makers and inviting families to participate in PTA/PTO, advisory councils, committees, and other school-based organizations.	Participating in PTA/PTO, advisory councils, committees, and other school-based organizations.	Advocating Building relationships
Community Collaboration	Collaborate with community organizations to organize programs that families need, such as after school care and health services. Communicate information about community-based resources to families.	Take advantage of community-based resources to ensure children's needs are met.	Advocating

Adapted from Epstein, J. L. (1992). *School and family partnerships report no. 6.* Johns Hopkins University Center on Families, Communities, Schools & Children's Learning.

the student is through high expectations and an enthusiastic attitude about supporting the child (Carlson et al., 2020). Contacting parents early and often at the beginning of a school year to praise the student, show that enthusiastic attitude, and explain their high expectations for the student is helpful for building a relationship before any challenges may arise. One way to accomplish this is by sending home a family questionnaire at the beginning of the school year (Hogan et al., 2013). This

Dear Mrs. Smith,

I want to thank you for the support you have given us here at school. Ever since we discussed Mario's late work a few weeks ago, he has turned in all the missing assignments and has stayed caught up. He is now passing math!

Recently I have noticed that Mario has been sleepy, close to falling asleep, once he gets to homeroom class. He comes into class and goes directly to his desk and puts his head down. I was wondering if you have noticed this or if there have been any changes on your end that I should be aware of. I want Mario to be successful, and I know he will be, we just have to figure out this next hurdle and get him back on track. Please contact me and let me know when you would be available for either a phone call, a Zoom meeting, or a face-to-face meeting.

Thank you and I look forward to hearing from you soon so we can continue to help Mario be successful in 3rd grade!

-Mrs. Suarez-

Go Hawks!!!!

Figure 3-1. Sample email to family.

questionnaire can include questions about (a) the best time to contact the family, (b) their expectations of their child and the teacher, (c) their beliefs regarding their child's strengths and weaknesses, and (d) their hopes and dreams for their child. This is one example of HLP 3 working in tandem with other HLPs, specifically HLP 4 and HLP 6. Please see Chapter 4 for more detail on parent questionnaires. In addition, families appreciate when special educators bring concerns to them as early as possible instead of waiting until the problem becomes larger and more challenging to manage (Carlson et al., 2020).

Figure 3-1 offers a sample email that a teacher may send home. Note that the email starts and ends with positives, the special educator's concerns about the student are sandwiched between the positives and the concerns are written in a way that does not project blame, but instead shows the teacher is seeking a solution to support the student by simply stating the facts without any interpretation of what the teacher thinks could be going on.

Hogan et al. (2013) recommend that special educators use communication logs to keep track of when they talk to families and list a general overview of the topics discussed, as well as any follow-up responsibilities for either the family or the teacher. Table 3-2 shows a sample communication log that can be used for documenting the discussion when communicating with parents.

Communication with families must be intentional, and it can be beneficial for special educators and families to establish structured communication systems and clear guidelines for how all communication will occur (Fishman & Nickerson, 2014). For example, a student may have a physical communication notebook that they take to and from school each day. Each day, the teacher writes about the student's day and any important information that must be shared with parents. Parents are asked to use the notebook to share information and ideas or ask questions of the teacher. This form of communication system is especially common for students with significant disabilities and for younger children. Similarly, some teachers choose to create daily or weekly communication forms that they send home to parents. Figure 3-2 shows an example of one of these forms. Other structured communication systems included regularly scheduled phone calls or meetings, as well as options for communications when challenges arise. When teachers use these types of communication forms with parents, they are not only beginning to build relationships and open the line of communication with families to collaborate for the success of the student, but they are also facilitating and organizing themselves for future meetings with families and other professionals (HLP 2). These communication forms can also be used to meet the Assessment HLP 4, by providing data from the families that can be used to develop an effective educational program for the student.

Table 3-2. Sample Family Communication Log

DATE AND TIME	PARENT OR GUARDIAN NAME—INCLUDE STUDENT NAME	FORM OF CONTACT—EMAIL, PHONE, OTHER (SPECIFY)	WHAT WAS DISCUSSED?
08/25	Jeannette Lawson (mom)—Miles Davey (son)	Phone call	Welcomed them to class Thanked them for returning the questionnaire Discussed their concern regarding Miles's poor organizational skills Teacher will work on color-coded folders with Miles and a daily communication log for Mrs. Lawson to sign each evening

When teachers communicate with parents, there are a few critical considerations. First, communication with families should be done in their home language (Burke et al., 2021). Teachers should ensure materials are written in the languages represented in their classroom to offer to their families. Some families may feel uncomfortable disclosing that they do not understand fully and may nod along with the conversation but have many questions. Providing communication in a family's native language demonstrates respect and honor for families' backgrounds and recognition that some terms may be unfamiliar in English. Thus, providing documents in both languages provides an opportunity for families to have access to materials in their home language, if desired, and facilitates

A Note from Mr. Alvarez

Today's Date:

Dear (Families Name),

Today, (Student Name) worked on the following academic skills:

Today, (Student Name) worked on the following life skills activities:

Today, (Student Name) worked on the following behavior skills:

Behavior Notes:

Homework:

Parent Comments/Questions:

Figure 3-2. Sample communication form.

a productive meeting in which families can more fully participate and potentially understand the information more deeply. When this occurs, educators are addressing HLP 2. Effective communication with culturally diverse families is often hindered due to language barriers (Burke et al., 2021). If the teacher does not speak a family's home language, the school needs to identify an interpreter to ensure clear communication. It is critical that schools do not rely on the special education students or their siblings to fulfill this interpreting role, which is a practice known as "language brokering" and that is currently utilized by many schools (Lee, 2021). Additionally, schools must be cognizant of not relying on faculty and staff who speak a native language or even using foreign language teachers in the school to be interpreters as this takes those professionals away from their primary duties in the school (Cormier & Scott, 2021). The best way to ensure we do not over-rely on the faculty and staff in our schools is by budgeting financial resources for hiring outside professionals to serve as interpreters.

A second consideration is that schools must strive for two-way communication, which means that both families and schools are sharing information with one another. However, Meier and Lemmer (2015) indicate that schools tend to focus more on one-way communication from the school to the families, with less focus on soliciting communications from families. Similarly, Conus and Fahrni (2019) found that families also expect that most communication will be one-way. Because this is often the expectation of both groups, it is especially critical for special educators to be intentional about seeking frequent and meaningful communication from families. The focus of HLP 2 is on organizing and facilitating effective meetings with professionals and families and by partaking in two-way communication you are working toward meeting this HLP as well as HLP 3.

Third, all communication must show respect for adult family members; one way to do this is to ensure that both correspondence and conversations address others by their names. Show the same respect for family members as you would for colleagues; instead of referring to a student's parent as "Mom" or "Dad," use their names and refer to them as "Mrs. Jones" or "Mr. Phiri" just as you would refer to a colleague as "Miss Smith" and not "teacher" (Graham-Clay, 2005). In addition, special educators can show their respect for families by always approaching communication from the knowledge that families and schools each want what is best for the student, even if they disagree on what is best.

Is Advocacy a Component of Teaming With Families?

In addition to communication, effectively implementing HLP 3 requires being an advocate for children and families. To best advocate for the needs of the child, we recommend a person-centered planning approach (Lohmann et al., 2018). Person-centered planning involves listening to the concerns of the family and seeking their input on the child's needs and progress, so that you can help them address those concerns and seek out the appropriate support when needed (Coots, 2007; Kirmani, 2007). Families desire educational planning for their children that is individualized to their child's unique needs (Carlson et al., 2020), and children should be involved in their own educational decision-making to the extent possible (Pounds & Cuevas, 2019). Because each student has unique skills, needs, and interests, the person-centered planning process ensures that individualized decision-making occurs. It also means that the special education services that each student receives will be unique and that two students in the same classroom and school are unlikely to receive the exact same supports. Person-centered planning is also associated with the HLPs of Assessment because it is another form of data collection that is used to create educational programs for SWD.

The person-centered planning process is a research-based practice that allows for schools to identify the specific needs of students and then use this information to advocate for the individual student (Tournier et al., 2021). In addition to advocating for individual students, special educators should engage in advocacy efforts that support all learners with disabilities and their families. When making recommendations regarding services or supports for a student, Whitby et al. (2013) suggest explicitly stating that your recommendations are designed for the individual needs of the student and that you share the student data and the peer-reviewed research that support your recommendations. It is also important to remember that when you advocate for a student, the family and/or your colleagues may disagree about what the student needs and may also have data and research to support their beliefs (Sears et al., 2021). This means that you must approach advocacy with a willingness to consider the ideas of others and solutions for supporting the student and must seek to collaborate to achieve the common goal of supporting the student (Friend & Cook, 2017).

Sears et al. (2021) talk about three ways that teachers can advocate and involve families: (a) with families, (b) for families, and (c) to families. Advocating with families involves supporting caregivers in communicating their desires and needs, as well as explicitly asking for family input before IEP meetings and helping families to understand the role of special education in supporting their children. To ensure quality family input for IEP meetings, we recommend two strategies: sending a family input form home for parents to complete and return at least 2 weeks before each meeting (Figure 3-3) and scheduling a parent–teacher meeting in preparation for the IEP meeting to talk about family needs, desires, and goals for the student. These two suggestions demonstrate the connection between HLP 2 and HLP 3 working together for successful outcomes for students. Furthermore, this is another great way to incorporate data from multiple sources on a student's strengths and needs (HLP 4), as well as to help you with prioritizing your short and long-term goals (HLP 11). In Chapter 11 you will read about specific strategies to engage parents from diverse cultures.

What are your child's strengths related to academic skills?
What are your child's strengths in the home and community settings?
What are your child's interests in school?
What are your child's interests outside of school (free time activities, sports/clubs, friends, etc.)?
What are your child's academic needs?
What are your child's social-emotional needs?
What supports does your child require in order to be successful in the academic setting?
What supports does your child require in order to be successful in the home and community settings?
What supports do you need in order to help your child be successful?
What are your short-term dreams for your child?
What are your long-term dreams for your child?
Describe how you envision your child's life as an adult.
What else do you want the IEP team to know about your child?

Figure 3-3. Sample family input form.

When special educators advocate for families, they use their expertise about instruction and interventions to ensure the children's learning needs are met and support families in locating credible resources for academic and behavioral supports (Sears et al., 2021). Parent training is an important part of advocating for families and will be discussed later in this chapter. Finally, special educators can advocate for families by providing professional development and support to colleagues regarding supporting SWD in the classroom (Kramer & Murawski, 2017; Sears et al., 2021).

The third form of advocacy noted by Sears et al. (2021) is advocating to families, which involves setting clear boundaries that encourage families to support some of their own needs and taking care of oneself as a teacher. Research indicates that special educators frequently experience vicarious trauma due to the amount of support they provide to students and families (Borntrager et al., 2012) and the impacts of that trauma can be addressed through intentional self-care (Lesh, 2020). Self-care can be done in many ways and can cost as little or as much as you can afford and can take 20 minutes or a full weekend. Find out what works best for you. Examples of self-care can include the following: (a) exercising, (b) taking a vacation, (c) finding a hobby such as sewing or volunteering at a local animal shelter, (d) attending a sporting event or the theater, or (e) having a spa day. You may even choose to create yourself a self-care planning form. Figure 3-4 provides a few examples.

In addition to advocating with, for, and to families, special educators can support students and their families through intentional legislative advocacy. Special educators can contact local, state, and national legislators to share information about the needs of SWD and their families, as well as joining advocacy efforts led by local teacher groups and professional organizations (Fisher & Miller, 2021).

I am WORTH it!
I MUST take care of myself in order to make a positive difference in my students' lives!

At the end of the week (specify time frame), I will reward myself with spending the day with my family OUTSIDE! (specify specific activity)

At the end of the grading period (specify time frame), I will reward myself by coming "unplugged" from my work emails (specify specific activity).

This school year, I will get to have a spa day (specify specific activity) at the end of each grading period (specify time frame).

Figure 3-4. Self-care planning examples.

One good way to advocate for students alongside other special educators is to participate in the Council for Exceptional Children Special Education Legislative Summit, which is held every summer (CEC, n.d.). By using many of the suggestions discussed, we have shown how HLP 3 works in tandem with HLPs 2, 4, 5, and 6.

How Can Teachers Build Relationships With Families?

A third aspect of HLP 3 is building relationships with students' families. Families of SWD often feel as though they are not considered an equal member of their child's IEP team and that they are not given an opportunity to contribute their opinions in educational decision-making (Mueller & Vick, 2019). Some parents of SWD have even reported being mistreated and disrespected during IEP meetings and other interactions with school personnel (Fish, 2006; Lo, 2008).

There are a variety of strategies that special educators can use to build relationships with families. The first strategy is the use of home visits (Kirmani, 2007; Rosenberg et al., 2002). A home visit occurs when a teacher visits a student and their family in their own home. Home visits help teachers better understand the family and the unique needs and circumstances of the student (Korfmacher et al., 2008). Staples and Diliberto (2010) recommend working with families to arrange a mutually convenient time for the home visit and ensuring that you are following all policies from your school and district. If families are not comfortable with a home visit, offer to meet them at a public place, such as a coffee shop, a park, or a restaurant. Who doesn't love an ice-cold fountain drink from McDonald's and good company? Just us?

A second strategy is to invite families into the classroom (Kirmani, 2007). Families may be invited to help with regularly scheduled or one-time tasks in the classroom (Yermanock Strieb, 2010). This might include directly working with students by listening to students read, leading activities, hosting parties and other special events, or helping with tasks such as creating bulletin boards, making copies, or preparing art projects. In addition, we recommend inviting families into the classroom to observe their child's learning. This can be especially beneficial for aiding families in learning to implement interventions at home as they can observe the special educator implementing the intervention in the classroom. In addition, parent observations in the classroom can lead to parental insight for academic or behavioral challenges the student may be exhibiting.

You may want to consider ways families could get to know one another. Having an SWD can be an isolating journey for many families (Breitkreuz et al., 2014). Consider hosting a meet-up at the school playground for preschool- and elementary-aged students and their families. For older students, depending on their abilities, a meet-up in the school cafeteria, local mall food court, or a bowling alley could help families come together and build some support networks. When students meet outside of school you can see who the child interacts with and what their interests are.

Building relationships with families also involves learning about, and showing respect for, their cultural beliefs and values. Recent research (Burke et al., 2021) indicates that non-White families report frequent discrimination and social stigma when interacting with school personnel. Francis et al. (2017) recommend making connections with community members who share the same cultural background as students and their families to better understand the culture and cultural perceptions of disabilities. In addition, special educators should spend time in the community where students live to better understand the culture (Buchanan & Buchanan, 2017). By following these suggestions, you are not only meeting HLP 3, but you are also addressing HLP 18. Identifying ways in which the student is engaged outside of school can help you in creating more engaging activities to include in your classes.

What Are the Best Ways to Support Parents?

The final component of HLP 3 is supporting families in improving their own skills to support their children. Previous research indicates that the families of children with disabilities often have limited knowledge of special education (Burke et al., 2020) and may feel confused about the special education process (Stoner et al., 2005), which can lead to challenges with accessing and utilizing services available to their children (Trainor, 2010). When special educators support families in better understanding the special education process, families can become more actively involved and advocate for the needs of their children. Additionally, increased parental knowledge and understanding of the IEP process also improves relationships between schools and families (Fish, 2008). Parent training regarding special education services may be conducted through formal training sessions led by school personnel or other agencies (Citil, 2020). Special educators should be aware of training sessions that are occurring so they can recommend them to families. Additionally, when families better understand the IEP process you are ensuring that you have the knowledge to meet HLP 2 when preparing for, and facilitating, your IEP meetings. Meetings will run much smoother because parents will know what to expect.

In addition to helping parents learn more about the special education process, special educators may also need to offer support to help families learn parenting skills. These parent trainings may occur through structured group sessions, may be individualized training for each parent, or may include a combination of group sessions and one-on-one family instruction (Ingersoll & Dvortcsak, 2006). In the previous section, we presented the idea of home visits; while these can be a great way for building relationships with families, they can also be used as an avenue for providing families with instruction and support to meet their children's needs at home (Rosenberg et al., 2002). For students with emotional and behavioral disabilities, special educators can use these home visits to explicitly teach family members evidence-based interventions for addressing behavior challenges (Lukowiak, 2010).

In addition to these structured methods of parent education, special educators can offer informal parent education in a variety of ways. We have seen teachers include a "Tip of the Week" in their classroom newsletters or share specific evidence-based strategies that work for a student during conversations with parents or in notes sent home. Figure 3-5 provides a list of "tips of the week" that a special educator may consider including in a classroom newsletter. As special educators consider engaging in parent education, though, they must be sure to demonstrate respect for all families and approach this education with an attitude that demonstrates their knowledge that families are the experts on their own children.

- Have a dedicated time and space for homework each evening.
- Read to your child at least a few times per week.
- Movement increases brain functioning, so encourage your child to play before beginning homework.
- Be consistent. Set expectations for behavior in the home and follow through with consequences when behavioral expectations are not met.
- Let your children see you reading - this will encourage them to read.
- The car ride home from school is a great time to practice math facts!

Figure 3-5. Sample tips of the week.

What Does HLP 3 Look Like in a K-12 Classroom?

Elementary Example

Mr. Phiri is a special education teacher in an elementary school, and he provides inclusion support and case management for the students in the first- and second-grade classrooms who receive special education services. Mr. Phiri knows that it is crucial for him to collaborate with his students' families to ensure success. To team with families, Mr. Phiri uses several strategies. First, he knows that almost half of his students' families are Spanish speakers, so he asks the school administrative assistant, who is also a Spanish speaker, to translate all written communications that he sends home; each communication has English on one side and Spanish on the other so that every family has access to the information in both languages and may choose which language to use to access the information. Each of his newsletters includes information about upcoming parent training sessions offered by the school or community organizations, as well as a "study tip of the week." In addition, he alerts his school district in advance that he will need an interpreter for all parent–teacher conferences and IEP meetings, as well as for other communications with families. Before the school year begins, Mr. Phiri visits each family in their home or a location of the family's choosing in the community; several families prefer to meet at the park instead of in their own homes. Before each IEP meeting, Mr. Phiri conducts another home (or community) visit with the family to gain parental input about the student's needs, as well as to answer any questions the family may have regarding the IEP process and their child's rights.

Secondary Example

Mrs. Chavos has been teaching ninth-grade resource math for the past 15 years but recently attended training where the importance of family collaboration was discussed. She knows how important this is to the success of her students, but many times other duties get in the way, and she fails to communicate with her students' families. She left the training reinvigorated and has made a vow to develop a plan to better communicate with families. In her plan she will advocate for her students both at school and in the community, and to teach advocacy skills to her students and their parents. She will first send out a parent information letter and a student information letter at the beginning of every semester. This will allow her to find more information about the families and the student which will include: (a) preferred language, (b) names/pronouns, (c) preferred communication style, (d) best times to contact them, and (e) their goals and aspirations. Mrs. Chavos also plans to create a newsletter, remembering what she learned at the training about the importance of communicating often with families. In the newsletter she will highlight parent trainings in the community and other

Table 3-3. Alignment of HLPs and Resources for Evidence-Based Practices

EBP SUPPORT WITH HLP 3	RELATED HLPS	RESOURCES
Parent training	4, 5	Center for Parent Information and Resources: https://www.parentcenterhub.org/
Communication	2, 4	Apps & Websites for Improving Parent-Teacher Communication: https://www.commonsense.org/education/top-picks/apps-and-websites-for-improving-parent-teacher-communication Parent-Teacher Communication Templates: https://www.educationworld.com/tools_and_templates/parent-teacher-communication-templates
Advocacy	2, 4, 5, 6, 11	Partnerships for Action, Voices, and Empowerment: https://wapave.org/ The Pacer Center: https://www.pacer.org/ The ARC: https://thearc.org/ Center for Parent Information & Resources: https://www.parentcenterhub.org/ Wrightslaw: https://www.wrightslaw.com/
Building relationships	18	CONNECT Module: Family/Professional Collaboration: https://connectmodules.dec-sped.org/connect-modules/learners/module-4/

community resources that may assist the families. She will also include any information on events the school will be hosting for families. The final part of Mrs. Chavos's plan is to ensure she is better at collaborating for IEP meetings. She will plan to send home a list of recommended IEP goals at least 5 days prior to the IEP meeting so that parents have time to review and offer their suggestions. She will also call them a few days before the IEP meeting to ask them if there is anything they want addressed in the IEP meeting.

Summary

Teaming with families is a critical component of being an effective special educator. HLP 3 outlines the need for teachers to (a) communicate, (b) advocate, (c) build relationships, and (d) support families in building their own skills. Table 3-3 offers a list of resources that special educators can use and share with families as they work to fully implement HLP 3 in their own classrooms. By utilizing the strategies outlined in this chapter and continuing to grow their own skills regarding collaboration with families, special educators will aid SWD in being more successful in their classrooms and communities.

Chapter Review

1. Why is it important for *you* to collaborate with families to ensure successful outcomes for your students?
2. Choose at least one of the other HLPs discussed in this chapter that can be used in conjunction with HLP 3 and develop a plan on how you could integrate the two HLPs.
3. Thinking back to the strategies provided in this chapter, what is one strategy that you have not implemented that you would like to implement? Describe how you will begin implementation.
4. Discuss how you involve person-centered planning into your everyday routine. If you do not already include this, develop a plan on how you can begin implementing this in your classroom. Create a plan for building family–school relationships in your classroom.

References

Borntrager, C., Caringi, J. C., van den Pol, R., Crosby, L., O'Connell, K., Trautman, A., & McDonald, M. (2012). Secondary traumatic stress in school personnel. *Advances in School Mental Health Promotion*, *5*(1), 38-50. https://doi.org/10.1080/17547 30X.2012.664862

Breitkreuz, R., Wunderli, L., Savage, A., & McConnell, D. (2014). Rethinking resilience in families of children with disabilities: A socioecological approach. *Community, Work, & Family*, *17*(3), 346-365. https://doi.org/10.1080/1366880 3.2014.893228

Buchanan, K., & Buchanan, T. (2017). Six steps to partner with diverse families. *Principal, January/February*, 46-47.

Burke, M. M., Rios, K., Garcia, M., & Magana, S. (2020). Examining differences in empowerment, special education knowledge, and family-school partnerships among Latino and white families of children with autism spectrum disorder. *International Journal of Developmental Disabilities*, *66*(1), 75-81.

Burke, M. M., Rossetti, Z., Aleman-Tover, J., Rios, K., Schraml-Block, K., & Rivera, J. (2021). Comparing special education experiences among Spanish- and English-speaking parents of children with disabilities. *Journal of Developmental & Physical Disabilities*, *33*(1), 117-135.

Carlson, R. G., Hock, R., George, M., Kumpiene, G., Yell, M., McCartney, E. D., Riddle, D., & Weist, M. D. (2020). Relational factors influencing parents' engagement in special education for high school youth with emotional/behavioral problems. *Behavioral Disorders*, *45*(2), 103-116.

Citil, M. (2020). Informative parent training on parental advocacy and legal rights for families with children with special educational needs. *International Journal of Psychology and Educational Studies*, *7*(3), 178-193.

Conus, X., & Fahrni, L. (2019). Routine communication between teachers and parents from minority groups: An endless misunderstanding? *Educational Review*, *71*(2), 234-256.

Cooper, C., Crosnoe, R., Suizzo, M., & Pituch, K. (2010). Poverty, race, and parental involvement during the transition to elementary school. *Journal of Family Issues*, *31*, 859-883.

Coots, J. J. (2007). Building bridges with families: Honoring the mandates of IDEA. *Issues in Teacher Education*, *16*(2), 33-40.

Cormier, C. J., & Scott, L. A. (2021). Castaways on Gilligan's Island: Minoritized special education teachers of color advocating for equity. *TEACHING Exceptional Children*, *53*(3), 234-242. https://doi.org/10.1177%2F0040059920974701

Council for Exceptional Children. (n.d.). *Special education legislative Summit*. https://specialeducationlegislativesummit.org/

Epstein, J. L. (1992). *School and family partnerships report no. 6*. Johns Hopkins University Center on Families, Communities, Schools & Children's Learning.

Epstein, J. L. (2008). Improving family and community involvement in secondary schools. *The Education Digest*, *73*(6), 9-12.

Fish, W. W. (2006). Perceptions of parents of students with autism towards the IEP meeting: A case study of one family support group chapter. *Education*, *127*(1), 56-68.

Fish, W. W. (2008). The IEP meeting: Perceptions of parents of students who receive special education services. *Preventing School Failure*, *53*(1), 8-14.

Fisher, K., & Miller, K. M. (2021). Legislative advocacy for special educators. *TEACHING Exceptional Children*, *53*(3), 244-252. https://doi.org/10.1177/0040059920970988

Fishman, C. E., & Nickerson, A. B. (2014). Motivations for involvement: A preliminary investigation of parents of students with disabilities. *Journal of Child & Family Studies*, *24*(2), 523-535.

Fontil, L., & Petrakos, H. H. (2015). Transition to school: The experiences of Canadian and immigrant families of children with autism spectrum disorders. *Psychology in the Schools, 52*(8), 773-788.

Francis, G. L., Haines, S. J., & Nagro, S. A. (2017). Developing relationships with immigrant families: Learning by asking the right questions. *TEACHING Exceptional Children, 50*(2), 95-105. https://doi.org/10.1177/004005991772077

Friend, M., & Cook, L. (2017). *Interactions: Collaboration skills for school professionals* (7th ed.). Pearson.

Gonzalez-DeHass, A. R., Willems, P. P., & Doan Holbein, M. F. (2005). Examining the relationship between parental involvement and student motivation. *Educational Psychology Review, 17*, 99-123. https://doi.org/10.1007/s10648-005-3949-7

Graham-Clay, S. (2005). Communicating with parents: Strategies for teachers. *School Community Journal, 15*(1), 117-129.

Hampden-Thompson, G., & Galindo, C. (2017). School-family relationships, school satisfaction and the academic achievement of young people. *Educational Review, 69*(2), 248-265. https://doi.org/10.1080/00131911.2016.1207613

Hogan, K. A., Lohmann, M. J., & Champion, R. (2013). Effective inclusion strategies for professionals working with students with disabilities. *Journal of the American Academy of Special Education Professionals, Spring/Summer*, 27-41.

Huscroft-D'Angelo, J., January, S. A., & Duppong Hurley, K. L. (2018). Supporting parents and students with emotional and behavioral disorders in rural settings: Administrator perspectives. *Rural Special Education Quarterly, 37*, 103-112. https://doi.org/10.1177/87568705177508

Ingersoll, B., & Dvortcsak, A. (2006). Including parent training in the early childhood special education curriculum for children with autism spectrum disorders. *Topics in Early Childhood Special Education, 26*(3), 179-187.

Kirmani, M. H. (2007). Empowering culturally and linguistically diverse children and families. *Young Children, 62*, 94-98.

Korfmacher, J., Green, B., Staerkel, F., Peterson, C., Cook, G., Roogman, L. A., Faldowski, R., & Schiffman, R. (2008). Parent involvement in early childhood home visiting. *Child Youth Care Forum, 37*, 171-196.

Kramer, A., & Murawski, W. W. (2017). Beyond just "playing nicely": Collaboration and co-teaching. In W. W. Murawski & K. L. Scott (Eds.), *What really works with exceptional learners* (pp. 152-168). Corwin.

Lee, J. (2021). A survey of Korean elementary schoolteachers on their communication with students and parents from migrant backgrounds and the need for quality language services. *The International Journal for Translation & Interpreting Research, 13*(1), 118-135.

Lesh, J. J. (2020). Don't forget about yourself: Words of wisdom on special education teacher self care. *TEACHING Exceptional Children, 52*(6), 367-369. https://doi.org/10.1177/0040059920936158

Lo, L. (2008). Chinese families' level of participation and experiences in IEP meetings. *Preventing School Failure, 53*(1), 21-27.

Lohmann, M. J., Boothe, K. A., & Hathcote, A. R. (2018). Addressing the barriers to family-school collaboration: A brief review of the literature and recommendations for practices. *International Journal of Early Childhood Special Education, 10*(1), 25-31. http://doi.org/10.20489/intjecse.454424

Lukowiak, T. (2010). Training and support for parents of children with emotional and behavioral disorders. *Journal of the American Academy of Special Education Professionals*, 25-35.

McLeskey, J., Barringer, M.-D., Billingsley, B., Brownell, M., Jackson, D., Kennedy, M., Lewis, T., Maheady, L., Rodriguez, J., Scheeler, M. C., Winn, J., & Ziegler, D. (2017). *High-leverage practices in special education*. Council for Exceptional Children & CEEDAR Center.

Meier, C., & Lemmer, E. (2015). What do parents really want? Parents' perceptions of their children's schooling. *South African Journal of Education, 35*(2), 1-11.

Mueller, T. G., & Vick, A. M. (2019). Rebuilding the family-professional partnership through facilitated individualized education program meetings: A conflict prevention and resolution practice. *Journal of Educational & Psychological Consultation, 29*(2), 99-127.

Pounds, L., & Cuevas, J. (2019). Student involvement in IEPs. *Georgia Educational Researcher, 16*(1), Article 4.

Rosenberg, S. A., Robinson, C., & Fryer, G. E. (2002). Evaluation of paraprofessional home visiting services for children with special needs and their families. *Topics in Early Childhood Special Education, 22*(3), 158-169.

Sears, J. A., Peters, B. L., Beidler, A. M. S., & Murawski, W. W. (2021). Using relationships to advocate with, for, and to families. *TEACHING Exceptional Children, 53*(3), 194-204. https://doi.org/10.1177/00400599209823

Sheldon, S. B., & Epstein, J. L. (2004). Getting students to school: Using family and involvement to reduce chronic absenteeism. *School Community Journal, 14*(2), 39-56.

Staples, K. E., & Diliberto, J. A. (2010). Guidelines for successful parent involvement: Working with parents of students with disabilities. *TEACHING Exceptional Children, 42*(6), 58-63.

Stoner, J. B., Bock, S. J., Thompson, J. R., Angell, M. E., Heyl, B. S., & Crowley, E. P. (2005). Welcome to our world: Parent perceptions of interactions between parents of young children with ASD and education professionals. *Focus on Autism and Other Developmental Disabilities, 20*(1), 39-51.

Tournier, T., Wolkorte, R., Hendriks, A. H. C., Jahoda, A., & Embregts, P. J. C. M. (2021). Family involvement in person-centered approaches for people with intellectual disabilities and challenging behaviors: A scoping review. *Journal of Mental Health Research in Intellectual Disabilities, 14*(4), 349-374. https://doi.org/10.1080/19315864.2021.1959689

Trainor, A. A. (2010). Diverse approaches to parent advocacy during special education home-school interactions: Identification and use of cultural and social capital. *Remedial and Special Education*, *31*, 34-47.

Whitby, T. J. S., Marx, T., McIntire, J., & Wienke, W. (2013). Advocating for students with disabilities at the school level. *TEACHING Exceptional Children*, *45*(5), 32-39. https:/doi.org/10.1177/004005991304500504

Yermanock Strieb, L. (2010). *Inviting families into the classroom: Learning from a life in teaching.* Teachers College Press.

Assessment High-Leverage Practices

Assessment creates the structure of specialized instruction. From initial eligibility to designing meaningful instruction it all starts with assessment. Assessment is a process, it is always **ongoing**! It is not an event, a "do this one thing" once and consider the job complete. Effective special educators must know how to collect assessment data from multiple sources, because no one assessment tool can provide enough information to guide our work with students with disabilities. Special educators need to explain the results to everyone involved. They understand the assessment, its implications, and can translate that information into understandable information for all stakeholders. Communication and common understanding of student strengths and needs are barriers that can impede effective specialized instruction. Special educators should navigate these conversations to remove obstacles for student learning. It is also critical that special educators intentionally make assessment a process. They should then reflect on and use assessment data to inform and guide instruction changes for both curricular change and intensification of instruction. The chapters that follow explain High-Leverage Practices 4 through 6 while providing information and helpful strategies to complete and use assessment well.

How Can I Use Multiple Sources of Information to Paint a Comprehensive Portrait of My Students' Strengths and Needs?

Kelly Acosta, PhD; Jodie Ray, MA; Amber Benedict, PhD; and Kyena E. Cornelius, EdD

HLP 4

Use multiple sources of information to develop a comprehensive understanding of a student's strengths and needs.

INTRODUCTION

Have you ever heard the adage, "A picture is worth a thousand words"? Then consider this, if one picture can convey such complex meaning what can multiple snapshots tell you about a student? Just as an artist uses texture, lines, color, shapes, and space to create a picture, a special education teacher uses multiple sources of information to create meaningful educational decisions for students with disabilities. Those decisions impact that student's academic and social development and often set the course for their successes or potential failures. To help you fully implement and benefit from High-Leverage Practice (HLP) 4, this chapter explains the elements and rationale for this practice, as well as provides examples of several evidence-based practices and measures that align with HLP 4. We will illustrate how effective teachers interpret and use data from a variety of sources to develop a comprehensive learner profile that enables their ability to differentiate and provide individualized instruction for a diverse population of learners.

Owiny, R. L., & Cornelius, K. E. *The Practical Guide to High-Leverage Practices in Special Education: The Purposeful "How" to Enhance Classroom Rigor* (pp. 57-71).

CHAPTER OBJECTIVES

- → Define a comprehensive learner profile.
- → Develop a learner profile that is sensitive to the linguistic and cultural needs of students with disabilities.
- → Identify evidence-based strategies to draw on students' strengths to support their academic and social-emotional needs when providing individualized instruction.
- → Identify formal and informal assessments to gather information to learn about potential barriers to students' academic, behavioral, and social-emotional learning goals.

KEY TERMS

- **curriculum-based measurement (CBM):** CBMs are assessments based on grade level curriculum material that teachers can use quickly and easily to measure student progress toward a learning objective.
- **formal assessment:** Assessments with specific guidelines for administering, scoring, and interpreting results. The purpose of a formal assessment is to gather overall achievement data.
- **informal assessment:** Assessments that are often teacher developed to be closely aligned with instruction. The purpose of an informal assessment is to help teachers monitor student progress on a specific targeted skill.
- **Multi-Tiered System of Supports (MTSS):** A multi-tiered framework that incorporates the use of data with instructional interventions to support students' academic, behavioral, and social-emotional needs.

When making important decisions for students with disabilities (SWD), we want as much information as possible. A "one moment in time" snapshot has too many loose ends. What if the child is feeling bad, or they had a disagreement with a friend or family member that morning? Maybe it is just the opposite. What if it is a really good day? Is this what we want to use to make important decisions? Probably not. For our most vulnerable students, we need several pieces of information that are the most accurate and up to date. We need multiple sources of information so that we can truly understand students' needs, and also their strengths.

This chapter is dedicated to helping you identify what those sources may be and how to use them to develop a comprehensive learner profile. That profile will help guide programing decisions, develop learning goals, and create learning opportunities to advance student learning. When you fully understand the student, their background, their prior learning experiences, and their academic and behavioral strengths, you will be able to focus on their needs in more powerful ways. You can design and deliver instruction that is tailored to that particular student, the specially designed instruction they need to learn and thrive.

What Is HLP 4?

High-Leverage Practice (HLP) 4 states that special educators need to "use multiple sources of information to develop a comprehensive understanding of a student's strengths and needs" (McLeskey et al., 2017, p. 19). This is an imperative step that will allow you to provide specialized instruction to SWD. Educators compile multiple sources of information to paint a comprehensive portrait of their learner. Information should be gathered from formal assessment data as well as informal assessments such as observations, interviews, and work samples. Compiling these data helps identify students' learning and behavioral needs and enables teachers to provide scaffolding and support to overcome anticipated barriers to learners' progress. Leveraging students' interests and cultural backgrounds enables you to tailor your instruction to meet students' needs.

What Is the Purpose of HLP 4?

HLP 4 was developed to support special educators in providing specialized instruction. By compiling data from a variety of sources, teachers gain an understanding of students' individual learning and behavioral needs and strengths. Not only is this a best practice, but one of the five core propositions of the National Board's Professional Teaching Standards (NBPTS; 2010b). Knowing your learners is even a federal requirement of the Individuals with Disabilities Education Act (IDEA; 2004). The IDEA mandates that all educators must gather data from a variety of sources to support students' learning needs and use this information to determine students' Present Levels of Academic Achievement and Functional Performance (PLAAFP), identify accommodations (HLP 13), and document students' progress toward specific learning and/or behavioral goals (HLPs 8, 11, and 12; Hosp et al., 2016). Information gathered from a comprehensive learner profile is a critical component of designing and implementing instruction within a Multi-Tiered System of Supports (MTSS) framework (Bailey et al., 2020) and key to using Universal Design for Learning (UDL) in your classroom (Meyer et al., 2014). Additionally, leveraging information about students' cultures, interests, personalities, and preferences will enable you to optimize the learning environment and tailor instruction to all students (HLPs 6 and 11 through 13). It should be noted that we, the authors, are by no means advocating for teaching to learning styles. Learning styles are a myth, proven multiple times over to not serve any purpose in educating children and certainly not evidence-based practice (Newton & Miah, 2017; Westby, 2019). What we are advocating is that all students have preferences in how they like to do things. Taking those preferences into account is not bad practice, in fact it is the opposite—it honors the student for the way they are "wired" and helps increase motivation when they are able to engage in learning activities that are in line with the way they most enjoy learning. See Table 4-1 to see how HLP 4 is aligned with other HLPs and resources for the evidence-based practices (EBPs) discussed throughout this chapter.

What Is a Comprehensive Learner Profile?

Building a relationship with your students is essential. A comprehensive learner profile allows teachers to know each student's academic, socio-emotional, and personal learning needs and goals. It allows you to provide accommodations and adapt curriculum (HLP 13) that enable students to be successful. A comprehensive learner profile is a way to collect and document information regarding your students' strengths and weaknesses, helping you to implement HLP 12, which is to "systematically design instruction toward a specific learning goal" (McLeskey et al., 2017, p. 22). It is important to understand that a learner profile is not a one-time snapshot of your student, but an ever-changing portrait of your student that evolves throughout the year as your teacher–student relationship develops and your students progress. Comprehensive learner profiles are flexible and can include information from a variety of sources. In addition to formal standardized assessment data, you should use information about students' preferences, gender, and culture to begin thinking about how to best reach students as you plan instruction (Bray & McClaskey, 2017; Tomlinson, 2001, 2014).

Knowing your student is not just best practice but is an integral part of special education law. The IDEA regulations (2006) require special educators to gather information from a variety of sources to determine students' needs. Compiling multiple data sources including both quantitative and qualitative information gathered in formal and informal ways helps to provide a deeper understanding of students. On the student's individualized education program (IEP), teachers note the student's

Table 4-1. Alignment of HLPs and Resources for Evidence-Based Practices

EBP SUPPORT WITH HLP 4	RELATED HLPS	RESOURCES
Collaborative teaching (Aceves & Orosco, 2014)	1, 3	Module on Communication and Collaboration offered through the CEC Division for Early Childhood: https://connectmodules.dec-sped.org/connect-modules/learners/module-3/ Black, K., & Hill, P. (2020). The quick collaborative meeting promoting success in an inclusive setting. *TEACHING Exceptional Children*, *53*(2), 114-120. https://doi.org/10.1177%2F0040059920919128
Responsive feedback (Aceves & Orosco, 2014)	6, 11, 12, 13, 15, 16	Iris Center module on Classroom Diversity: An Introduction to Student Differences: https://iris.peabody.vanderbilt.edu/module/div/ https://www.ascd.org/el/articles/personalization-and-udl-a-perfect-match
Modeling (Aceves & Orosco, 2014)	12, 16	HLP 12 video example: https://highleveragepractices.org/hlp-12-systematically-design-instruction-toward-specific-learning-goal HLP 16 video example: https://highleveragepractices.org/hlp-16-use-explicit-instruction Archer & Hughes Explicit Instruction (2011): https://explicitinstruction.org
Instructional scaffolding (Aceves & Orosco, 2014)	6, 11, 12, 15	Iris Center module on Differentiated Instruction: Maximizing the Learning for All Students: https://iris.peabody.vanderbilt.edu/module/di/#content Article on Differentiation for Learning Profile: https://pdo.ascd.org/LMSCourses/PD11OC138M/media/DI-Instruction_M3_Reading_LP.pdf
Implement culturally responsive instruction (Aceves & Orosco, 2014)	6, 11, 12, 13, 15, 16	Module on Cultural and Linguistic Differences: What Teachers Should Know: https://iris.peabody.vanderbilt.edu/module/clde/#content Iris Center module on Teaching English Language Learners: Effective Instructional Practices: https://iris.peabody.vanderbilt.edu/module/ell/#content CEEDAR Center Innovation Configuration on Culturally Responsive Teaching: https://ceedar.education.ufl.edu/wp-content/uploads/2014/08/culturally-responsive.pdf CEEDAR Center Innovation Configuration on Evidence-based practices for English Learners (Document No. IC-18): https://ceedar.education.ufl.edu/wp-content/uploads/2016/11/EBP-for-english-learners.pdf

(continued)

Table 4-1 (continued). Alignment of HLPs and Resources for Evidence-Based Practices

Teaching self-advocacy	14, 18, 21	The Self-Determined Learning Model of Learning Instruction (SDLMI): https://selfdetermination.ku.edu/homepage/intervention/ PACER Center videos and resources on self-advocacy: https://www.pacer.org/students/transition-to-life/advocating-for-myself.asp
Using formal assessments to screen for areas of concern	5, 6, 11, 12	Iris Center module on collecting and analyzing data for data-based individualization: https://iris.peabody.vanderbilt.edu/module/dbi2/
Utilize curriculum-based measurement to determine risk and monitor progress across tiers with English learners as part of a school site or district's comprehensive MTSS model (Richards-Tutor, 2016)	1, 2, 3, 5, 6, 11, 12	Intervention Central: https://www.interventioncentral.org easyCBM: A website where teachers can administer CBMs in reading and math, track and monitor progress, and develop individual student reports, profiles, and instructional learning needs: https://app.easycbm.com
Tertiary behavior interventions: conducting functional behavioral assessments	1, 2, 3, 5, 6, 8, 10	Lewis, T. J., Hatton, H. L., Jorgenson, C., & Maynard, D. (2017). What beginning special educators need to know about conducting functional behavioral assessments. *TEACHING Exceptional Children*, 49(4), 231-238: https://doi.org/10.1177%2F0040059917690885 Shippen, M. E., Simpson, R. G., & Crites, S. A. (2003). A practical guide to functional behavioral assessment. *TEACHING Exceptional Children*, 35(5), 36-44: https://doi.org/10.1177%2F004005990303500505 Iris Center Module on FBA: https://iris.peabody.vanderbilt.edu/module/fba/ Center for Positive Behavioral Interventions & Supports (PBIS). Efficient Functional Behavior Assessment: The Functional Assessment Checklist for Teachers and Staff (FACTS): https://www.pbis.org/resource/efficient-functional-behavior-assessment-the-functional-assessment-checklist-for-teachers-and-staff-facts
Error analysis	6, 12, 13, 16	Iris Center module on collecting and analyzing data for data-based individualization: https://iris.peabody.vanderbilt.edu/module/dbi2/ *Specifically: page 6 (Error Analysis for Reading) and page 7 (Error Analysis for Mathematics)
Anecdotal seating chart (Cornelius, 2013)	6, 7, 10	Cornelius, K. E. (2013). Formative assessment made easy: Templates for collecting daily data in inclusive classrooms. *TEACHING Exceptional Children*, 45(5), 14-21: https://doi.org/10.1177%2F004005991304500502

strengths and weaknesses. During this stage of the IEP process, input is collected from the student's special education teachers, general education teachers, family members, the student themselves, and any additional related services, such as speech and language pathologists, occupational therapists, physical therapists, behavioral management teachers, guidance counselors, or nursing staff. If the student is of transition age (IDEA requires a transition plan at age 16; however, it varies based on state), a vocational rehabilitation counselor may also be a part of the multidisciplinary IEP team. Documenting a student's current performance ensures that every teacher is knowledgeable about all academic, social and emotional needs.

Using information gathered from a comprehensive learner profile, teachers can differentiate instruction and "adjust the curriculum and presentation of information to learners rather than expecting students to modify themselves for the curriculum" (Hall et al., 2004, p. 2). Differentiating and adjusting instruction aligns with HLP 13, which states educators should "adapt curriculum tasks and materials for specific learning goals" (McLeskey et al., 2017, p. 22). Additionally, information gathered from a comprehensive learner profile will allow you to employ UDL practices (Hall et al., 2012). By fostering flexible teaching practices emphasized by UDL, you actively work to tear down barriers to students' academic progress and optimize learning for all (Meyer et al., 2014). Moreover, it is also an essential component of the NBPTS Exceptional Needs Standards (2010a). The NBPTS underscores the importance of recognizing students' individual differences and adjusting their instructional practice based on "observation and understanding of their students' interests, abilities, skills, knowledge, language, family circumstances and peer relationship" (NBPTS, 2010a p. 8). Thus, effective teachers know how to draw on knowledge of their learners and provide multiple modes of teaching and learning to provide meaningful individualized instruction and appropriate support to meet their learners' diverse needs.

What Is the Benefit of Compiling a Comprehensive Learner Profile?

A comprehensive learner profile is an important step in getting to know your learners' unique cultures, interests, personalities, preferred modalities, strengths, and needs, a key component to providing culturally responsive instruction (Gay, 2010). The information gained from compiling a comprehensive learner profile is beneficial, as it can be used to guide instruction (HLPs 11, 12, and 13), create an equitable and inclusive learning environment, and foster strong relationships between you and your students (Lynch, 2018). Using strategies and supports that have enabled students to be successful in the past will allow teachers to ensure students' continued successes. Success builds success. Using the knowledge about the student's preferred approaches to learning and demonstrating knowledge gathered by the teacher when compiling the learner profile, teachers can effectively implement UDL (CAST, 2018) and differentiate instruction to optimize the learning environment (HLP 13), thus, enabling more students in diverse classroom settings to experience success. Differentiating instruction, while implementing UDL, based on the distinct learning profiles of your students supports all learners and is aligned with the individualized nature of specially designed instruction, "that one student's road map to learning is not identical to anyone else's" (Tomlinson, 2014, p. 4).

As you work to develop a comprehensive learner profile, it is important to also utilize HLP 3 and work collaboratively to leverage the knowledge and expertise from parents, families, and the students themselves. Learner profiles are collaborative and dynamic because the learner is constantly growing and changing. A strong learner profile weaves together information from multiple sources like a richly woven tapestry to depict the many facets of the student as a learner and as an individual. It is imperative that educators adopt a strengths-based approach when engaging in the task of creating a learner profile. Identifying the student's strengths supports the student by allowing the teacher to teach through the student's strengths and celebrate each student's unique contribution to the learning environment. This practice fosters a supportive learning community by promoting students to encourage each other, thereby empowering students to become leaders at different times depending on the task at hand.

Once a comprehensive learner profile has been created, the special educator can use the information to teach through students' strengths to further support their areas of need (HLP 13; Tomlinson, 2001). Drawing on students' comprehensive learner profiles enables teachers to make informed decisions about their practice and adapt their classroom environment, instructional approach, and methods of assessment to respond to the various levels of background knowledge, preferred methods of learning, and interests (Hall et al., 2004). Armed with this knowledge teachers can employ other HLPs, such as use assistive and instructional technology (HLP 19), make accommodations and adaptations to instruction (HLP 13), and personalize the learning environment in order to make learning accessible for every student (HLP 6).

How Do I Develop a Learner Profile That is Sensitive to the Linguistic and Cultural Needs of My Learners?

When developing a comprehensive learner profile, it is imperative that educators pay close attention to the linguistic and cultural needs of every learner. Gathering knowledge of the students' background, values, communication styles, and preferences for learning is crucial to meet the students' needs and nurture their academic, linguistic, and cultural growth. To develop a learner profile that is sensitive to the linguistic and cultural needs of the learners in your classroom, you first need to know each student's level of English language proficiency, their level of linguistic proficiency in their home language, as well as their cultural identity. Compiling this information, you can design evidence-based culturally and linguistically responsive lessons. Although research is still emerging on EBPs for culturally and linguistically diverse learners, there are four emerging EBPs that have been identified that promote academic and social-emotional growth in students with diverse backgrounds: collaborative teaching, responsive feedback, modeling, and instructional scaffolding (Aceves & Orosco, 2014).

With collaborative teaching, teachers not only engage in collaboration with their colleagues, but also with students' families. Students' families play a fundamental role in providing information about their child's linguistic and cultural needs, cultural background and history, family values, and communication preferences, which is why using HLP 3 (collaborate with families to support student learning), in conjunction with HLP 4 is essential. Engaging in responsive feedback includes utilizing information from language proficiency assessments to garner knowledge about students' levels of language proficiency and identify areas of strength and areas for improvement. Using this data to identify students' linguistic needs can support teachers with implementing other emerging culturally responsive EBPs and HLPs, such as adjusting their instructional practices (HLP 6), identifying and prioritizing long- and short-term goals (HLP 11), systematically designing instruction (HLP 12), adapting the curriculum (HLP 13), providing scaffolded supports (HLP 15), and using explicit instruction (which includes modeling; HLP 16).

Developing a comprehensive learner profile with students can also increase their awareness of how they learn best, further promoting students' agency. Students' development of metacognitive skills is important to help them develop self-advocacy. Supporting the development of student agency and self-advocacy is important as it is a research-based practice identified as a strong predictor of post-secondary school success (Mazzotti et al., 2021). Teachers of elementary school students often model metacognitive processes through think-alouds; however, these students rarely achieve independent discovery of their metacognition. Middle school students need to be taught to recognize their unique learning idiosyncrasies and learn how to advocate for themselves to request adaptations, specifically accommodations, to the learning environment so that they can be successful. For instance, Lazaro, a Deaf middle school student, recalls words through his visual memory file. If he does not have a visual reference of a concept in his mind's eye, then he is not able to comprehend that word or concept. In this situation, it is critical for Lazaro to communicate with his teacher that he does not understand; this should prompt the teacher that there is a breakdown in Lazaro's comprehension. Using this information, the teacher should stop and provide a visual that explicitly builds his knowledge of the concepts rather than merely using the word in sign, written, or spoken English. Until this concept is built and can be connected to his existing schema or background knowledge, he is unable to make meaningful connections to the words or concepts. Often it requires tangential side trips to build students' background knowledge and ensure that all students, regardless of their linguistic and cultural needs, can access the curriculum and comprehend the subject matter. Knowing your students' linguistic and cultural needs is a key step to being able to meet your learners' individual learning needs and provide meaningful instruction. Developing interactive lessons that regularly allow active student participation enables the teacher to see if the students are comprehending the information (HLP 18).

How Can I Draw on Students' Strengths to Support Their Academic and Social-Emotional Needs When Individualizing My Instruction?

Effective educators utilize information gained from a comprehensive learner profile to implement HLPs 5, 6, 11, 12, and 13, to guide their instructional practice and individualize teaching strategies to meet their learners' needs. Moreover, educators simultaneously draw on culturally responsive teaching practices and strongly believe that all students can learn and have unique strengths to contribute to the learning community. Just as every person has a unique fingerprint, they also have a unique learning profile, and there are countless ways to differentiate your instruction to engage students (Tomlinson, 2001).

When planning instruction that is culturally responsive, teachers should use recommended teaching practices backed by research (Aceves & Orosco, 2014) to optimize student success. Creating child-centered instruction is one recommended practice that incorporates learners' interests to entice them to grow and stretch their skill level. For instance, imagine a student who loves art and despises math. Incorporating art into math lessons will encourage them to get through difficult problems, if, for example, at the end they are able to use their answers to discover a hidden picture by coloring their answers. This small adjustment in the instructional practice considers that the teacher knows their student's strengths, weaknesses, and interests. Encouraging students to strengthen their skill level by using their interests or skillset is a positive way to support learner growth and an effective way to implement HLP 18 to promote active student engagement. As teachers get to know their students, they can find an appropriate learning fit for students and plan accordingly. It is important that teachers continually employ observations and knowledge of their students' interests, abilities, skills, knowledge, family circumstances, and peer relationships to support students and provide instructional scaffolding.

How Can I Assess the School-Based Learning Environment to Determine Potential Support Students Need to Be Successful or Anticipate Potential Barriers That May Impede Students' Academic and/or Social-Emotional Progress?

Assessing a student's learning environment is a critical step in developing a comprehensive learner profile. Collecting information using multiple sources of data across a variety of settings is a requirement of the IDEA (2006) and part of an MTSS framework (Bailey et al., 2020). Thus, a special educator must be knowledgeable about the various data sources available and how to use data to develop a comprehensive learner profile so they can meet the needs of each individual learner. The data special educators collect should come from both formal and informal sources within a variety of settings. Understanding how your student performs using multiple data sources in various learning environments can help you, as the teacher, identify ways to implement UDL, differentiate instruction, and develop a more robust IEP that meets the needs of the individual learner (Stecker et al., 2005; Tomlinson, 2001). It is important to take into consideration that assessment results may be skewed because of cultural and linguistic bias (Klingner et al., 2005). More about the types of formal and informal assessment data special educators should gather to help develop a comprehensive profile is described below.

Formal Assessments

Formal assessments are those with specific guidelines for administering, scoring, and interpreting results (Kritikos et al., 2018). These types of assessments are often summative in nature and used to determine mastery within a specific content area when compared to other students within the same age and/or grade (Cornelius, 2013). Often these assessments are used to determine student competency towards completion for a standard high school diploma or for meeting basic college entry requirements. Some examples of formal assessments are mandated state tests such as the Florida Standards Assessment (FSA) or the Scholastic Aptitude Test (SAT) students take as part of the college application process. Other formal assessments such as the *Woodcock-Johnson IV Tests of Achievement* (Schrank et al., 2014) and the *Wechsler Intelligence Scale for Children, Fifth Edition* (Wechsler, 2014) are used as part of, but cannot be the sole diagnostic criteria in, determining special education eligibility (IDEA, 2006).

Within an MTSS framework, using formal assessments as a screener to identify students who may require additional supports is an EBP (Bailey et al., 2020). Researchers recommend that to effectively identify students who may require additional supports and services, that schools should administer universal screeners at least twice a year (Bailey et al., 2020). Examples of formal assessments school districts might use as screening tools are the iReady (Curriculum Associates) or STAR (Renaissance) assessments.

The information from formal assessments serves as a compass to guide the special educator towards identifying more specific areas of need (HLP 6). For instance, you may find that your student struggled to pass the math portion of the state assessment and also scored within the low range on the mathematics portion of their last formal diagnostic achievement test. Based on this information you can anticipate this student will need additional support to make progress in math. However, these formal assessments paint only a broad picture of your student's overall academic abilities. These assessments do not tell you, the teacher, which specific math concepts the student may struggle to comprehend. These tests are also often administered only once at the end of the school year, or at best three times per year at the beginning, middle, and end of the year, and do not provide teachers with enough information on student progress toward learning goals in the interim. Thus, gathering additional information more often using informal assessments is necessary (Bailey et al., 2020; Cornelius, 2013).

Informal Assessments

Informal assessments are assessments more closely aligned to instruction and are often teacher developed (Kritikos et al., 2018). Using informal assessments throughout the school year to help support teams with making educational decisions is an established EBP (Hamilton et al., 2009). Special educators can use information from informal assessments to help determine students' PLAAFP, identify accommodations, and document students' progress toward specific learning and/or behavioral goals (HLPs 6 and 11; Hosp et al., 2016). They are administered to students more frequently and provide teachers with valuable insights as to how their students are progressing on an ongoing basis. Different types of evidence-based informal assessments are curriculum-based measurements (CBMs), observations, or approaches used to gather information from parents, families, and the students themselves (Kritikos et al., 2018). Where formal assessments are the compass that guides the teacher to identify a student's areas of need, informal assessments provide teachers with specific directions on how to best support a student in their identified areas of need.

Curriculum-Based Measurements

CBMs are assessments based on grade-level curriculum material that teachers can use quickly and easily to measure student progress toward a learning objective (Stecker et al., 2005). Special educators should use information gathered from formal assessments in combination with informal assessments such as CBMs to help develop a comprehensive learner profile. For example, for the student whose formal assessments demonstrate math as an area of weakness, a CBM on more targeted math skills should be administered. CBMs that assess a student's ability to compute basic math facts or, for an older student, basic algebraic concepts can help the special educator identify and target specific instructional needs or accommodations (HLP 13). For instance, if the student struggles to complete a math fluency CBM on two-digit addition, they may require additional time to complete math work and more intensive and targeted instruction on numeracy.

To gain a more complete picture and create a comprehensive student learning profile, teachers should dig even deeper and use the information from the CBM to conduct an error analysis (Lemons et al., 2014; Powell & Stecker, 2014). Analyzing information from an error analysis is an EBP (Lemons et al., 2014) that can help the teacher identify specific targeted skill areas in which the students will require more intensive instruction (HLPs 6 and 20). Let's go back to the example of the math fluency probe. If we closely examine the errors, we may notice that although the student struggled to complete enough math problems in a timely manner, they only incorrectly answered problems that required regrouping. This information tells her teacher that this student will require more intensive and individualized instruction on place value in addition to the mathematical concepts of numeracy.

Observations

A comprehensive learner profile should also include information from observations conducted in a variety of settings. Observations conducted in a variety of settings help the special educator learn how factors in various learning environments could also potentially be impacting a student's social-emotional, behavioral, and academic progress (Kritikos et al., 2018). For instance, perhaps during the student's math class the heater is particularly loud, making it challenging for the student to concentrate and stay on task. Knowing this information can help the teacher identify a more appropriate seat for this student.

If your student has more challenging behaviors, they may have had a functional behavioral assessment (FBA) completed (see Chapter 10). The purpose of an FBA is to help identify the function, or purpose, of challenging student behaviors (Lewis et al., 2017; Shippen et al., 2003). While FBAs are the most widely used assessments to identify and support students with challenging behaviors within Tiers 2 and 3, research determining it as an EBP is still developing (Gage, 2015). The information gathered from an FBA helps educators develop a plan to target these behaviors through a behavior intervention plan (BIP) or also called a behavior support plan (BSP). Not all of your students may have or need an FBA or a BIP/BSP, however, information gathered from these sources will help you, as the special educator, develop a more comprehensive learner profile so you can understand how you might address your learners' needs.

Teachers can gather information from observations on not only a student's social and emotional behaviors, but academic behaviors or skills as well (Cornelius, 2013). One of the most simplistic ways special educators can gather data on a variety of behaviors is through the use of an anecdotal seating chart (Cornelius, 2013). Teachers can use the EBP of anecdotal seating charts to make notations of off-task behaviors, time to complete tasks, or student responses during instruction. For instance, during independent math work, the teacher may walk around the room with a copy of an anecdotal seating chart on a clipboard and make a notation every time they notice students off-task. Alternatively, the teacher could make a note each time a student correctly or incorrectly responds orally to a math problem when prompted by the teacher. Using anecdotal seating charts provides teachers with a quick and easy way to gain valuable insights about your students' learning progress and needs.

How Can I Leverage the Student Learner Profile to Identify Opportunities to Provide/Coordinate Support?

It is impossible for a special educator to put together a comprehensive profile without collaborating with others. Collaboration is such an essential component of a special educator's role that there are two HLPs, HLP 1 and HLP 3, related to collaboration and it is included as one of the Council for Exceptional Children's (CEC) professional standards (Berlinghoff & McLaughlin, 2022). In addition, it is a hallmark of working within an MTSS framework (Bailey et al., 2020). So, for the special educator to put together a comprehensive learner profile, it is essential that they collaborate with the student's general educators, school counselors, and any additional support staff the student may see, such as a speech-language pathologist (see HLP 1). Collaborating with families and the student (see HLP 3) is also essential, especially when supporting a student's post-secondary transition planning (Mazzotti et al., 2021). Community-based partners may also be involved in collaboration to help the special educator develop a comprehensive student profile.

What Does HLP 4 Look Like in a K-12 Classroom?

Elementary Example

It is the end of the first grading period and Richard just moved to the Paradise Valley Unified School district from Everett, Washington. He joined Ms. Markle's fifth-grade English Language Arts class. When Ms. Markle, a first-year teacher, calls on Richard, she notices that he is struggling to read aloud. She dismisses her concerns at first, assuming that it may be because he is shy. However, after several weeks, Ms. Markle determines that there is more to Richard's slow and laborious reading. After mentioning her concerns to the special educator during passing, Ms. Markle is advised to administer a series of CBMs for reading to diagnose Richard's specific area of need and learn more about how to support Richard in reading. From these assessments and subsequent error analysis, Ms. Markle pinpoints that Richard's listening comprehension is strong, but he is lacking fundamental decoding skills, indicating a breakdown in phonics. Ms. Markle identified that Richard could benefit from more explicit and systematic instruction in phonics with a specific focus on letter patterns

(HLPs 6, 12, and 16). Ms. Markle has begun to coordinate instruction through Tier 2 under the guidance and support of her mentor teacher, Mrs. Sanchez (HLPs 1 and 5).

One afternoon, on an early release day, Mrs. Sanchez drops by Ms. Markle's classroom to inquire more about Richard's background. Other than the fact that he is new, and his father is in the Army, Ms. Markle is not able to answer any of the questions Mrs. Sanchez asks. During the conversation Ms. Markle has with her mentor, it becomes clear that in order to provide more appropriate support and tailor her instruction to her learner, she needs to gather more information about Richard. Mrs. Sanchez explains that it is important to gain an in-depth understanding of the students' strengths and areas of improvement to align her instruction to meet the needs of diverse populations of students. She invites Ms. Markle to her classroom to show her how she compiles data from multiple sources to create a comprehensive learner profile on each of her learners. Mrs. Sanchez explains that knowing the cultural and linguistic background, values, family circumstances, communication styles, and preferences for learning are important clues to understanding the portrait of the learner. She goes on to add that by gathering information from the student's family and the student themself, she can figure out ways to leverage student's strengths, interests, abilities, and skills to optimize learning.

Energized with this new knowledge Ms. Markle sets out to develop a comprehensive profile based on Richard's history. She reaches out to Richard's mother, Mrs. Jackson, and sets up a time to discuss Richard's strengths and her goals for her son (HLP 3). Ms. Markle learns that Richard has struggled with reading since third grade, and even had to repeat that grade. Mrs. Jackson admits that she was hoping that the move would help Richard gain confidence in his reading abilities and forge new connections with his peers. She acknowledges the impact staying back had on his self-esteem and motivation. Mrs. Jackson described her son as a creative kid with a lively spirit. When asked what he enjoys doing, his mother shared that Richard likes to engage in drama and was active in his town's improv theater.

Equipped with this insight, Ms. Markle brainstormed ideas to integrate Richard's love of acting and theater into her instruction (HLP 18). Ms. Markle decided to do a reader's theater with her class to celebrate Veteran's Day. As Ms. Markle shared the news with the class, Richard's face beamed. Richard was thrilled to be able to engage in reading with the class and felt comforted by the familiarity of acting and proud to be the son of a military dad. Ms. Markle had already gone over the vocabulary and previewed the script with Richard during their morning small group time (HLPs 15 and 21). Ms. Markle modeled and provided explicit instruction in the phonics skill (HLP 16). This enabled Richard to feel comfortable reading in front of his peers.

Secondary Example

It is the beginning of the school year and Ms. Sharpe, a high school special education teacher, is spending time collaborating with others (HLPs 1 and 3) to gather information from a variety of sources to develop comprehensive learner profiles on her students. One of her students, Eduardo, is a 10th grader in her co-taught math and resource room classes. To develop a learner profile on Eduardo, she first coordinates with the school's guidance counselor (HLP 1) by pulling information from Eduardo's cumulative file to learn his overall academic history. From this file, she obtains his most recent scores on the state-mandated tests, score reports from diagnostic achievement testing, and grades from previous report cards. She notes on her profile that Eduardo just missed the cut-off score to pass the state-mandated math assessment required for him to receive his high school diploma. She also notes that Eduardo scored below average on math on his last diagnostic achievement testing, and previous report cards show a history of struggling to pass math courses. Other important information she gathers from the cumulative file is that his family speaks Spanish at home. Even though Eduardo speaks Spanish at home, his last state-mandated English language proficiency exam indicates he is proficient in English and does not require additional English language support.

To learn more about how to support Eduardo in math, Ms. Sharpe administers a series of math CBMs and then conducts an error analysis. From these assessments, she learns that Eduardo is able to compute basic math facts but struggles to complete these in a timely manner. Because Eduardo is in high school and needs to learn more complex math skills, she notes he should use a calculator for all math assignments and tests (HLP 13). From her error analysis on basic algebraic functions, she learns that Eduardo consistently makes mistakes on balancing equations to correctly solve problems. She uses this information to make a note that she should provide more direct and explicit instruction during Eduardo's resource class on understanding how to solve basic algebraic problems (HLPs 6, 16, and 20). She knows he will need to learn this information to help him pass his math courses and the state-mandated math assessment required for graduation.

Next, she collaborates with her math co-teacher, Ms. Johnson, to conduct a series of short observations on Eduardo's current academic and behavioral progress during his classes. She uses an anecdotal seating chart and notes Eduardo is consistently off task. When she asks Eduardo about this later, he tells her that he struggles to follow along with the teacher's instruction and that he is distracted by others in the classroom. After learning this information, Ms. Sharpe moves Eduardo's seat closer to the teacher and away from some of his friends and notes his on-task behaviors improve.

Lastly, she conducts a series of interviews with Eduardo and his family to learn more about Eduardo, his interests, and future career aspirations to support his post-secondary transition planning. From the interviews, she learns that Eduardo is responsible for babysitting his two younger siblings after school, making it challenging for him to complete homework. She also learns Eduardo enjoys playing videogames and would love to become a videogame designer. Based upon this information, Ms. Sharpe makes a plan to support Eduardo with completing some of his homework before school starts and during his resource room class. She also collaborates with his guidance counselor to enroll him in a graphics design course next semester to support his future career aspirations of becoming a videogame designer (HLP 1).

Summary

Educators draw on multiple sources of data to gather information in order to paint a rich portrait of their learners' academic and behavioral strengths and needs. It is important to remember that learner profiles are dynamic, continuously morphing as students accomplish each milestone and embark on the next. As you have seen throughout this chapter, the HLPs are interconnected. Effective teachers weave together multiple HLPs to create a strong tapestry of diverse teaching practices. Developing a comprehensive learner profile is beneficial, as it can be used to guide instruction, create an equitable and inclusive learning environment, and foster strong relationships between you and your students (Lynch, 2018). To develop a learner profile that is sensitive to the linguistic and cultural needs of the learners in your classroom, it is imperative to know each student's level of English language proficiency, their level of linguistic proficiency in their home language, as well as their cultural identity. Incorporating learners' interests can enable them to develop their skillset. Formal and informal sources within a variety of settings can provide the special educator nuggets of information that are pivotal in compiling a comprehensive learner profile. In addition, information from observations and collaboration with general educators, special educators, support staff, and families can lead to a deeper understanding of students' strengths, interests, and needs. This collaboration is a fundamental part of the MTSS framework and supports all students.

Chapter Review

1. Describe the key components of HLP 4 in your own words.
2. What is the purpose of a comprehensive learner profile?
3. Name two informal assessments discussed in this chapter that you would use in creating a learner profile. Explain why these assessments were chosen.
4. Name two formal assessments discussed in this chapter that you would use in creating a learner profile. Explain why these assessments were chosen.
5. How does family background and cultural expectations inform the learner profile?

References

Aceves, T. C., & Orosco, M. J. (2014). *Culturally responsive teaching* (Document No. IC-2). University of Florida, Collaboration for Effective Educator, Development, Accountability, and Reform Center. http://ceedar.education.ufl.edu/tools/innovation-configurations/

Bailey, T. R., Colpo, A., & Foley, A. (2020). *Assessment practices within a multi-tiered system of supports* (Document No. IC-18). University of Florida, Collaboration for Effective Educator, Development, Accountability, and Reform Center. http://ceedar.education.ufl.edu/tools/innovation-configurations/

Berlinghoff, D., & McLaughlin, V. L. (Eds.). (2022). *Practice-based standards for the preparation of special educators.* Council for Exceptional Children.

Bray, B., & McClaskey, K. (2017). *How to personalize learning.* Corwin.

CAST. (2018). *Universal Design for Learning guidelines, Version 2.2.* http://udlguidelines.cast.org

Cornelius, K. E. (2013). Formative assessment made easy: Templates for collecting daily data in inclusive classrooms. *TEACHING Exceptional Children, 45*(5), 14-21. https://doi.org/10.1177%2F004005991304500502

Gage, N.A. (2015). *Evidence-based practices for classroom and behavior management: Tier 2 and Tier 3 strategies* (Document No. IC-15). University of Florida, Collaboration for Effective Educator, Development, Accountability, and Reform Center (CEEDAR) Center. https://ceedar.education.ufl.edu/wp-content/uploads/2015/11/Behavior-Management-tier-two-and-three-strategies.pdf

Gay, G. (2010). *Culturally responsive teaching: Theory, research, and practice* (2nd ed.). Teachers College Press.

Hall, T., Vue, G., Strangman, N., & Meyer, A. (2004). *Differentiated instruction and implications for UDL Implementation.* National Center on Accessing the General Curriculum. https://sde.ok.gov/sites/ok.gov.sde/files/DI_UDL.pdf

Hall, T. E., Meyer, A., & Rose, D. H. (2012). *Universal design for learning in the classroom: Practical application.* Guilford Press.

Hamilton, L., Halverson, R., Jackson, S., Mandinach, E., Supovitz, J., & Wayman, J. (2009). *Using student achievement data to support instructional decision making* (NCEE 2009-4067). National Center for Education Evaluation and Regional Assistance, Institute of Education Sciences, U.S. Department of Education. http://ies.ed.gov/ncee/wwc/publications/practiceguides/

Hosp, M. K., Hosp, J. L., & Howell, K. W. (2016). *The ABCs of CBM: A practical guide to curriculum-based measurement.* Guilford Publications.

Individuals with Disabilities Education Act, 20 U.S.C. § 1400 (2004).

Individuals with Disabilities Education Act, 34 C. F. R.§ 300.304 (2006).

Klingner, J. K., Artiles, A. J., Kozleski, E., Harry, B., Zion, S., Tate, W., Zamora Durán, G., & Riley, D. (2005). Addressing the disproportionate representation of culturally and linguistically diverse students in special education through culturally responsive educational systems. *Education Policy Analysis Archives, 13*(38). https://doi.org/10.14507/epaa.v13n38.2005

Kritikos, E. P., McLoughlin, J. A., & Lewis, R. B. (2018). *Assessing students with special needs* (8th ed.). Pearson.

Lemons, C. J., Kearns, D. M., & Davidson, K. A. (2014). Data-based individualization in reading: Intensifying interventions for students with significant reading disabilities. *TEACHING Exceptional Children, 46*(4), 20-29. https://doi.org/10.1177%2F0040059914522978

Lewis, T. J., Hatton, H. L., Jorgenson, C., & Maynard, D. (2017). What beginning special educators need to know about conducting functional behavioral assessments. *TEACHING Exceptional Children, 49*(4), 231-238. https://doi.org/10.1177%2F0040059917690885

Lynch, M. (2018). *Here's everything you need to know about learner profiles.* The Edvocate. https://www.theedadvocate.org/heres-everything-need-know-learner-profiles/

Mazzotti, V. L., Rowe, D. A., Kwiatek, S., Voggt, A., Chang, W., Fowler, C. H., Poppen, M., Sinclair, J., & Test, D. W. (2021). Secondary transition predictors of postschool success: An update to the research base. *Career Development and Transition for Exceptional Individuals, 44*(1), 47-64. https://doi.org/10.1177/2165143420959793

McLeskey, J., Barringer, M.-D., Billingsley, B., Brownell, M., Jackson, D., Kennedy, M., Lewis, T., Maheady, L., Rodriguez, J., Scheeler, M. C., Winn, J., & Ziegler, D. (2017). *High-leverage practices in special education.* Council for Exceptional Children & CEEDAR Center.

Meyer, A., Rose, D. H., & Gordon, D. (2014). *Universal Design for Learning: Theory and practice.* CAST.

National Board for Professional Teaching Standards. (2010a). *Exceptional needs standards* (2nd ed.). http://www.nbpts.org/wp-content/uploads/ECYA-ENS.pdf

National Board for Professional Teaching Standards. (2010b). *Five core propositions.* http://www.nbpts.org/five-core-propositions

Newton, P. M., & Miah, M. (2017). Evidence-based higher education—Is the learning styles "myth" important? *Frontiers in Psychology, 8*, 444. https://doi.org/10.3389/fpsyg.2017.00444

Powell, S. R., & Stecker, P. M. (2014). Using data-based individualization to intensify mathematics intervention for students with disabilities. *TEACHING Exceptional Children, 46*(4), 31-37. https://doi.org/10.1177%2F0040059914523735

Richards-Tutor, C., Aceves, T., & Reese, L. (2016). *Evidence-based practices for English learners* (Document No. IC-18). University of Florida, Collaboration for Effective Educator, Development, Accountability, and Reform Center. http://ceedar.education.ufl.edu/tools/innovation-configurations/

Schrank, F. A., McGrew, K. S., & Mather, N. (2014). *Woodcock-Johnson IV Tests of Achievement* (4th ed.). Riverside.

Shippen, M. E., Simpson, R. G., & Crites, S. A. (2003). A practical guide to functional behavioral assessment. *TEACHING Exceptional Children, 35*(5), 36-44. https://doi.org/10.1177%2F004005990303500505

Stecker, P. M., Fuchs, L. S., & Fuchs, D. (2005). Using curriculum-based measurement to improve student achievement: Review of research. *Psychology in the Schools, 42*(8), 795-819. https://doi.org/10.1002/pits.20113

Tomlinson, C. A. (2001). *How to differentiate instruction in mixed-ability classrooms* (2nd ed.). ASCD.

Tomlinson, C. A. (2014). *Differentiated classroom: Responding to the needs of all learners.* ASCD.

Wechsler, D. (2014). *Wechsler Intelligence Scale for Children* (5th ed.). Pearson.

Westby, C. (2019). The myth of learning styles. *Word of Mouth, 31*(2), 4-7. https://doi.org/10.1177/1048395019879966a

How Do You Become a "Steward" of Assessment Information to Engage All Stakeholders?

Kyena E. Cornelius, EdD

HLP 5

Interpret and communicate assessment information with stakeholders to collaboratively design and implement educational programs.

INTRODUCTION

Special education is a jargon-filled profession. We love our acronyms, our standard divisions, and significant findings. We discuss students with disabilities with words like mild/moderate, high incidence, and affect. That does not always mean something to general educators and even more rarely with parents. As special educators you need to welcome all stakeholders, other professionals, and parents onto the ship they were just forced to board together and make this journey as meaningful as possible. Everyone wants to get the most out of the cruise, but if they are not speaking the language, they are going to miss the excitement. In this nautical world metaphor, special educators are the stewards that make the journey pleasant and often help translate the unknown for the passengers.

Owiny, R. L., & Cornelius, K. E. *The Practical Guide to High-Leverage Practices in Special Education: The Purposeful "How" to Enhance Classroom Rigor* (pp. 73-85).

CHAPTER OBJECTIVES

- Describe the purpose of common assessments in a way every stakeholder understands.
- Know how HLP 5 is connected to other HLPs and can be used to involve stakeholders in designing and implementing educational programs.
- Explain how assessments are connected to all special education decisions.

KEY TERMS

- **age and grade equivalent:** A predetermined score set by the designer and publisher of an assessment that represents the average score of a student of a particular age or grade level. These
- **composite score:** Also known as cluster score, is the average score of all the subtests related to the domain on a standardized test. For example, a Reading Composite Score could be the average of the Word Recognition, Reading Fluency, and Read Comprehension subtests.
- **confidence intervals:** A percentage that represents the range of how "good" the estimate of the test score is. In other words, the range of scores that you could expect the student's score to fall between if you retest them again with the same instrument in the same conditions.
- **criterion-referenced tests:** Assessments that compare a student's progress against a preset criterion, usually curriculum skills, without comparing to the progress of others.
- **curriculum-based measurement (CBM):** A practice used both as a universal screening and ongoing monitoring to determine how students are progressing with basic academic skills.
- **high-stakes testing:** A test used to make important decisions about students, educators, and schools. It goes beyond teacher and district designed exams. This term most commonly refers to the end of the year testing administered by the state.
- **norm-referenced tests:** Assessments that are designed to compare students to other students in the same age and grade.

Assessments are the foundation of all things special education (Yell et al., 2020). They drive every decision moving forward, and you, the special educator, are the "steward" of the information from those assessments (Kamman & McCray, 2022). This description of your job, *assessment steward*, is the most accurate. After all, you are responsible for gathering all the assessment data and are charged with sharing it in meaningful, understandable ways with all stakeholders. You manage the data in a responsible way and safeguard those it impacts.

Consider the process; when a student is *struggling*, it is based on some assessment, either compared to their peers, the curriculum-based assessment used to mark progress throughout the year, or the teacher's observation of the student in class. The assessment leads to the student receiving more intensive support based on a multi-tiered system. Sometimes the parents see their child struggle at home. Regardless of who sees the struggle, they are basing this on some assessment data. This leads to a referral to special education, and where you become integral in explaining the information (e.g., assessment results, the process) to all stakeholders. Remember, parents must provide informed consent for a comprehensive evaluation; how can they be informed if they do not understand what is happening, what is driving the decision, and what the end result may look like?

Whether the student received intensive instruction through Response to Intervention (RTI) with limited progress, or goes through a comprehensive evaluation, a team evaluates the assessment data collected to determine the student's eligibility for special education. There are many sources of information you will want to use for these decisions; be sure to read Chapter 4 for more ways to collect data and use them to understand students. Once again, you will need to be able to explain each of the assessments, the purpose of the assessment, and the proposed actions in a way that all stakeholders, especially the parents, feel like equal partners. You must use language they understand; our cute acronyms may mean something to us, but generally outside of special education, they mean nothing and are just confusing.

Once the student qualifies for special education, that same assessment information still sets the foundation of the individualized education program (IEP), and you still need to be able to explain it all. The assessment results help you write the Present Levels of Academic Achievement and Functional Performance (PLAAFP); again, remember to write the PLAAFP in a language all stakeholders understand. Through academic testing and talking with parents and general education teachers, you identify the students' strengths and weaknesses, and discuss them in relation to the assessment that gave you that information. The eligibility assessments also establish the baseline scores you will use to establish goals and monitor progress, which is also documented in the PLAAFP. However, use that data so that everyone on the team understands what it means; raw assessment scores seldom mean anything!

Once the PLAAFP is established, you use the information from assessments to determine the goals, the type and amount of special education services the student will receive and where services will be delivered, the accommodations and modifications the students will need to be successful in an academic setting, and anything else the student will need to be provided a Free Appropriate Public Education (FAPE). You also determine in the IEP how you are going to monitor progress. For more exact ways to use data in daily instruction and to monitor progress, be sure to read Chapter 6. As you can see, assessments really are the foundation of special education, and your job is to manage the information gathered and share it in meaningful ways to all stakeholders. You might say assessments are the ship that drives special education, and you are the steward to share the assessments in a way to make sure every stakeholder gets what they need to understand and be active in the journey.

What Is HLP 5?

When the team of researchers got together to identify a set of High-Leverage Practices (HLPs), they began with the work from a team of general educators (Ball & Forzani, 2011). They then went deeper into the practices of special educators to see how they overlap and if they all apply to special education or if others were needed. There was definite overlap; see Chapter 17 for a prime example. However there were nuances to special education that were not to be found in general education; you can see similarities in HLP 6 to diagnosing student thinking as well as coordinating and adjusting instruction (https://www.teachingworks.org/high-leverage-practices/). However, HLP 5 is unique to special education. McLeskey and his colleagues (2017) on the HLP research team note the importance of the IEP team in not only the evaluation but the ongoing education of students with disabilities (SWD). For 80% of general education students, schooling is so natural that they may not need many different assessment tools to guide their education. They progress through school without ever sitting through hours of testing to diagnose their learning patterns or thinking; teachers merely need to look at their classroom performance to adjust for some reteaching or perhaps enrichment activities to guide instruction. On the other hand, to keep the ship metaphor going, so much data are collected on SWD, it is as if they were applying for a security clearance to cruise on a naval ship, and someone needs to protect that data and explain them to others so together they can plan the ship's route and destination.

Effective special education teachers must explain and clarify all assessment information for stakeholders, no matter if that is another education profession, a family member, or the student. They involve the stakeholders in the assessment process, developing goals, and, of course, implementing the goals. Special educators themselves must understand the purpose of each assessment and how culture and language influence the information and interpretation of the data. They then engage collaboratively with all stakeholders to use data to develop and implement individualized education and transition plans. To ensure the IEP provides an appropriate education and leads the student to independence, the IEP team ensures the goals developed are standards-based, appropriate accommodations and modifications are identified, fair grading practices are decided upon, and transition goals that are aligned with student needs are included. That is a lot to take in, so the purpose of this chapter is to dive into each of these tasks and give you some practical tips on becoming the best steward you can be.

How Is HLP 5 Connected to Other HLPs?

This book continually points out how the HLPs are a collective group; they are not isolated "one-off" acts of teaching, they have an intertwined functionality. So how is this one connected or intertwined? It seems to be easier to see how some of the instructional HLPs are interlaced like one big nautical knot. There are similarities; actually there is more overlap here than with some of the other Collaboration and Assessment HLPs. Obviously, this calls for collaboration with other professionals (HLP 1) and with family members (HLP 3). You will use multiple sources of data (HLP 4) to help with the decisions you make, and sometimes you need to explain the data that change instructional plans and why instruction was adjusted (HLP 6). Also, think about this: you are essentially teaching the stakeholders about the assessment information. As you explain and clarify data, you will want to provide parents with positive and constructive feedback to guide their understanding (HLPs 8 and 22) of assessment information. You may have to adapt the materials you use to explain information (HLP 13). You will have to scaffold the information (HLP 15) as you build their understanding. Finally, you want stakeholders to think about the information and how it relates to other areas of the student's education, and of course you want them to retain the information so you can focus the discussion in succeeding meetings on other topics (HLP 21).

It may be more difficult to see how to use evidence-based practices (EBPs); however, there are some researched frameworks and strategies. We will show you a graphic organizer to use in helping to clarify information, but other than that we will discuss frameworks and best practices, such as the Review, Interpret, Streamline, and Communicate (RISC; Blackwell & Stockall, 2019) process to communicate data. Creating communication strategies (i.e., logs, notebooks) can build collaboration and understanding with families (Davern, 2004). See Table 5-1 for a list of EBPs and other HLPs aligned to implementing HLP 5. So, let's answer some of those questions you might have about truly understanding this HLP.

What Are Practical Ways to Involve Stakeholders in the Special Education Process?

It is important to understand everyone's role in the special education process and then it might be easier to involve them. When considering three of the primary stakeholders, think of the general educator as the expert on the curriculum and standards of the grade and content area. Special educators are the experts on specialized instruction and understand how disability impacts student performance in the curriculum and classroom. You have the knowledge related to specialized services and instruction. You know a range of EBPs to implement to improve student outcomes. To do your job, you need to understand how to bridge the divide of the curriculum and the student. The parent is instrumental in developing a successful plan. The parent is the expert on the child. They have known the child longer and have experienced every milestone as they watched their child develop. They also understand cultural norms and expectations of their family. Families are the most invested in the student's success. You need to collaborate, all of you, to develop a plan for the student's success.

Table 5-1. Alignment of HLPs and Resources for Evidence-Based Practices

EBP SUPPORT WITH HLP 5	RELATED HLPS	RESOURCES
Curriculum-based measurements	4, 6	https://www.interventioncentral.org/ https://dibels.uoregon.edu/ https://iris.peabody.vanderbilt.edu/module/pmm/#content
Graphic organizer	15, 21	https://www.canva.com/graphic-organizers/templates/
RISC	2, 3, 8, 22	Blackwell, W. H., & Stockall, N. (2019). RISC: Four Steps for Interpreting and Communicating High-Stakes Assessment Results. *TEACHING Exceptional Children, 51*(4), 265-275

The first thing you need to do is build authentic relationships where everyone feels valued. Often general educators feel special education teachers do not value their time, which makes them feel less valued. One way you can involve professional stakeholders is to use technology (HLP 19) to collaborate (Charles & Dickens, 2012). With online tools you can collaborate with general education teachers to plan not only for co-teaching but for planning for parent meetings. Create a document on a web-based platform that allows for "live" editing. You can ask questions of the general educator, then they can provide answers and evidence of the student's performance. It will take time to establish, and you will need to build that relationship upfront. Once established, the relationship will be strengthened by both of you appreciating this time-saving tool.

The same principle can be extended to parents. First, you must establish a relationship and make it clear to parents they are equal partners in the process. Listen to them, let them tell you their concerns, as well as their hopes and dreams for their students. Really listen, take notes, and refer to these during conversations. Let them know you value their opinion and want to include them. This can be done at the time of the initial referral. Start building that relationship early. Then along the way of the process keep them informed. No one likes to feel they are being kept in the dark. Talk early and talk often!

We have often used homework logs (Hall et al., 2003) to keep parents up on homework and school events. Why not create a similar home-to-school notebook to communicate progress and upcoming assessment information. Be mindful if parents have access to computers and technology at home. If they do, create a similar document with parents that you do with co-teachers to communicate. If they do not, get a small notebook. We prefer a composition book, because they are more durable and pages will stay intact. After a few weeks of back and forth to school, spiral notebooks seem to fray and loose pages. This notebook or online journal creates powerful data when you are discussing transition assessments and post-secondary plans. It gives you "in time" information when that transition planning becomes more real, an actual event as opposed to some future event.

Keep all stakeholders engaged by staying organized and keeping meetings as brief as possible. We all know special education meetings tend to drag on (refer to Chapter 2 for more information on leading efficient meetings). Use an agenda; share the agenda at the beginning of the meeting and stick to it. When you see the conversation is starting to drift, bring it back to the topic at hand. It is fine to tell a general education teacher you will be glad to schedule time later to discuss their issue, or to tell a parent that you value their input, but you also value their time and ask to move the "fun fact" or story to another time. **Unless** what they are saying is pertinent to the meeting at hand, ask for them to remember that thought and show them where on the agenda it will fit. Then be sure to ask them to share that thought at the appropriate time. To make everyone feel the meeting is not an endless black hole, refer to the agenda often (e.g., "We have done this, now we will be discussing this"). Everyone's time is important; by demonstrating you value the stakeholders' time, they will continue to engage and stay involved.

Blackwell and Stockall (2019) developed a framework to help special education teachers review, interpret, streamline, and communicate (RISC) assessment results. We love using mnemonics so much with students, we even use them ourselves! We will be using this framework along with another practical tool to help you explain and clarify assessment information, communicate the purpose of the assessment, and collaboratively make decisions. The next three sections will be closely tied as we show you a strategy to streamline your duties as the steward of assessment information.

How Do You Explain and Clarify Assessment Information in a Way Everyone Understands?

Think about how you take unknown information and connect it to student learning. You find something they can relate it to, you build on their background knowledge, and you link new learning to that. Sometimes you must build or create that "prior" knowledge so it can relate to what you need to teach. We often use graphic organizers (Dexter & Hughes, 2011) to build and connect knowledge with students. We can do the same thing to explain and clarify assessment information. Figure 5-1 provides a template you can use. Each element of the template, or graphic organizer, is tied to the RISC framework. First, "R" stands for "review." Review the assessment information; are there terms that would not be easy for non–special education teachers or school psychologists to understand? How can you make it clearer? Maybe the assessment report uses terms like *criterion-referenced* or *grade equivalence*. How would you explain that to a parent?

The "S" for "streamline" would also fit into this idea of clarifying assessment information. Think about how you can summarize the information to create a story. This is not represented on the template, but it would be easy for you to create this with other stakeholders together. How do the data collected create a picture of the student; can you visualize them in their classroom engaging with others and with the curriculum? What does the assessment information tell you that helps to create a clearer, more accurate picture?

What Is the Purpose of the Assessment Tools Used?

Every assessment tool has a purpose. It could be to determine student ability or achievement; there are assessment tools for just about everything. If you do not know the purpose of the tool selected, or do not believe the assessment tool is a reliable and valid measure for that purpose, then it is up to you as the special education professional to ask the question of "Why this tool?" On the template provided, make sure you list that purpose in language everyone will understand. For example, high-stakes testing is any test that has important consequences. College entrance exams, like SATs and ACTs, have consequences regarding college admission; even the results of a driver's license test lead to the consequence of getting a license or not. Depending on the person's perspective, it has negative or positive consequences. Yearly state testing is referred to as high stakes, and usually is tied to school accountability measures. These assessments can be used to indicate if a student passes a grade level or even when they can earn a high school diploma. They can also determine if the school

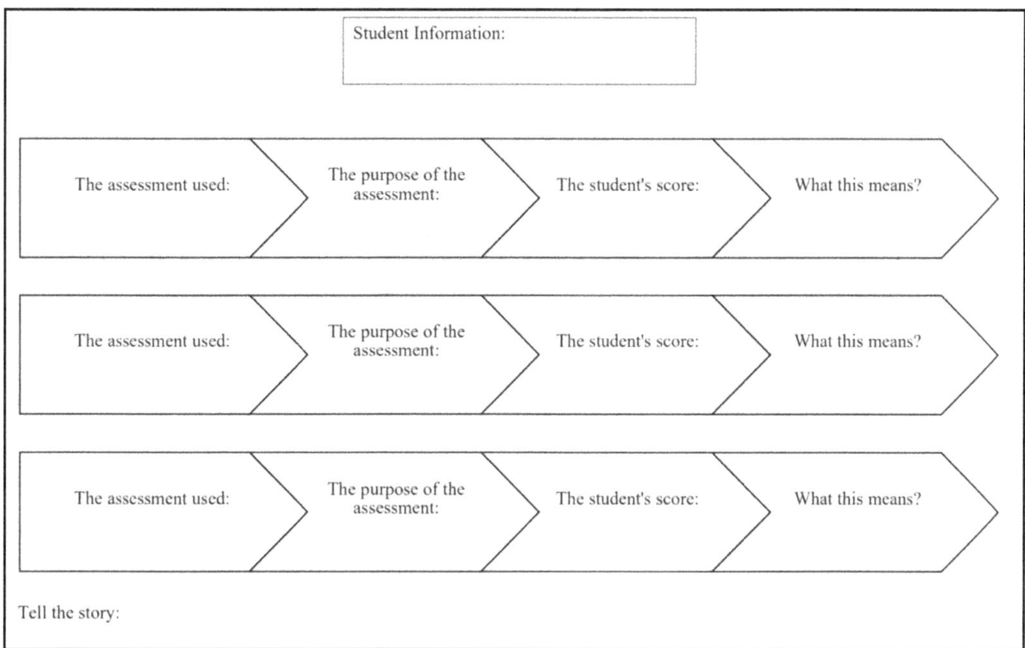

Figure 5-1. Template to guide assessment discussions.

is doing well (enough students are passing) or if they need attention from the state (disproportional results based on race, socioeconomic status, or disability status). These test results are not always aligned with the purpose of the test, so it is important they are only one piece of the decision-making process. It is by knowing the purpose of the assessment and how it is designed (norm-referenced or criterion-referenced) that allows you to interpret the scores. Remember the "I" in RISC is "interpret"; how will you interpret the scores for parents? By understanding and explaining both the purpose and what the score means, you will help parents better understand assessments and what they mean for their student.

Other assessments such as curriculum-based measurements (CBM) can be used for both eligibility and ongoing progress monitoring. The purpose of CBMs is to assess student growth in basic skills easily and quickly (i.e., reading, writing, math; Deno, 2003). CBMs have been identified as an EBP as a valid and reliable assessment of student ability in the grade-level curriculum expectations. The beauty of CBMs is they can be administered quickly, between 1 to 5 minutes, depending on the probe and content, and they are easily scored by counting the number of correct and incorrect student responses given in a set amount of time. There are several probes for each grade level allowing for multiple administrations. CBMs are often used for universal screening at three times during the year for every student K-8, and then used more often for interventions, both through RTI and special education progress monitoring. In the latter two instances the probes are administered weekly to monitor growth and adjust instruction (see Chapter 6 for more details). When schools implement RTI appropriately and collect the ongoing data and the student continues to struggle, making little to no progress, the special education eligibility team is permitted by Individuals with Disabilities Education Act (IDEA; 2004) to use these scores to find a student eligible as a student with a specific learning disability (LD; Hurwitz et al., 2022).

Another common assessment you need to explain to parents is the *Wechsler Intelligence Scale for Children, Fifth Edition* (WISC-V; Wechsler, 2014). The WISC-V measures the intellectual ability of students. This is a common IQ test with 15 different subtests, used in comprehensive evaluations (Gomez et al., 2016). To fully understand each subtest and how they are related, we advise you to meet with your school psychologist. Also, during eligibility testing many school districts use the

Woodcock-Johnson IV Tests of Achievement (WJ IV ACH; Schrank & Wendling, 2018). This battery of 11 to 22 tests, depending on if you administer the standard or the extended battery, measures basic skills, fluency, and the student's ability to apply these skills in the areas of reading, writing, and math. Both the WISC-V and the WJ IV ACH are norm-referenced and designed to compare the student to other students the same age and grade level, based on a national average score.

How Do You Make Sure Every Decision Is Tied Back to the Assessment Information We Gathered?

The "C" in the RISC framework is "communicate." You need to control the story that is communicated to stakeholders. Make sure you know the information that was gathered, what it means in relation to the assessment that was given, as well as the student's progress. Just as you would think about designing a lesson using backward design, start looking at assessment with the end result in mind too (see Chapter 12 for more on backward design). Look at the questions of an eligibility or IEP checklist in your district. When you answer that question, make a direct connection back to the assessment information. For example, when you are writing the PLAAFP, the question the IDEA (2004) asks is: "How the child's disability affects the child's involvement and progress in the general education curriculum (i.e., the same curriculum as for nondisabled children) **or** for preschool children, as appropriate, how the disability affects the child's participation in appropriate activities?" [34 CFR §300.320(a)(1)]. When answering this question, look at the assessment data for achievement tests, the curriculum standard, the teacher information, and parent information to answer the question. To help you better answer questions during eligibility and IEP meetings, we have created a list (Table 5-2) of questions and provide you possibilities of the assessment information that could be used.

What Does HLP 5 Look Like in a K-12 Classroom?

Elementary Example

Ms. Pemrose is preparing for the annual IEP meeting for her student, Crystal Macha, which falls at the beginning of the school year. She is aware that, in the Macha family, high academic achievement is a family value and understanding how disability impacts academic achievement is a struggle for them. Ms. Pemrose remembers how difficult giving permission for special education placement was for them as it felt that, somehow, they had failed as parents and their daughter would not be able to achieve at high levels. Ms. Pemrose decides to ask the school psychologist, Ms. Lynn, to work with her to create an information sheet about Crystal's disability and how it impacts her ability to learn and retain information. She also works with Ms. Lynn to use the graphic in Figure 5-1 to lay out the assessment data from the WISC-V and WJ IV in a visual manner to help them to see Crystal's high level of intelligence and to understand exactly how her LD impacts her academics as revealed in her WJ IV results, along with her classroom performance. Ms. Pemrose hopes that this information sheet will help Mr. and Mrs. Macha better understand that Crystal's LD does not mean she is incapable of high achievement, but rather it means she learns in ways different from her typically developing peers and the plan laid out in her IEP will help her to achieve.

Ms. Pemrose wants Mr. and Mrs. Macha to know how well Crystal is performing in her academics to elevate the notion that Crystal is quite talented in art and capable academically, as well. She asks Crystal's general education teacher, Mr. Maxwell, to help her write the PLAAFP to ensure an accurate picture of Crystal's performance both in the general education curriculum and on her IEP goals. Ms. Pemrose also asks Mr. Maxwell to share during the IEP meeting about Crystal's engagement in the general education classroom, the ways her creativity shine, her friendships, and her academic

Table 5-2. Questions for Eligibility and Individualized Education Program Development Aligned With Assessments

ELIGIBILITY QUESTIONS		
Question	*Assessment*	*Information Gathered*
Is there documentation of inadequate achievement?	• Work samples • CBM • WJ IV ACH	• Evidence of student work • Student's ability compared to the curriculum • Student's ability compared to other students of same age/grade
Is there a documented disorder in one or more of the basic psychological processes?	• WJ IV COG	• Visual processing = difficulty with spatial relation, difficulty with form and direction, not a vision deficit • Auditory processing = difficulty with hearing subtle differences in the sounds of words, not a hearing deficit • Organization/planning sequencing difficulties
Is there a severe discrepancy between ability and achievement?	• WISC-V • WJ IV ACH	• When you compare two scores, usually the composite IQ score from the WISC and the content area cluster scores from the WJ IV, most school districts will want approximately a 20-point difference
Was there an inadequate rate of progress in Response to Intervention?	• CBM	• Student results will be graphed to show the expected goal, and the student's actual progress data taken weekly during a set amount of time, usually 7 to 10 weeks • Evidence of an scientific research-based intervention was used

(continued)

progress in the state standards. By giving her parents a holistic view of how Crystal portrays herself at school, her academic performance, her interactions with peers, her interactions with adults, and her performance in non-academic subjects such as art and music and how those subjects interact with her academics, Ms. Pemrose hopes they will better understand the amazing gifts and talents Crystal has and convince them that an LD does not mean Crystal is destined to fail or that their parenting is at fault.

Through this process, Ms. Pemrose implemented all the Collaboration HLPs while also implementing HLP 4 to ensure that HLP 5 is implemented to ensure appropriate collaboration in developing Crystal's updated IEP. By ensuring that Mr. and Mrs. Macha better understand Crystal's LD and how it manifests itself in her learning, along with how smart she is and how talented she is artistically, they can be more involved in helping to make educational decisions for their daughter. Having the assessment data review from her initial placement the year before, along with current classroom performance data, will allow the IEP team to make informed decisions for Crystal's updated IEP.

Table 5-2 (continued). Questions for Eligibility and Individualized Education Program Development Aligned With Assessments

IEP QUESTIONS		
Question	*Assessment*	*Information Gathered*
What are the areas of need?	• Teacher observation • CBM • Comparison of ability and achievement	• Behavior checklist, anecdotal records • Academic skill deficits—more reliable for baseline data and to write goals • Did the testing indicate a "severe" discrepancy—approximately 20-point difference
What are the student's strengths? What are the student's skills and abilities related to the area of need? Strengths should be stated positively in the PLAAFP.	• All assessment data • Teacher observations	• Explain what the student can do within the area of need—the child may struggle with reading, but they can identify all the letters and most common sound associated with that letter; they can read single syllable words with short vowel sounds • This is where you say the student is eager to please and usually initiates tasks, but disengages when he perceives the task is too difficult • Remember to always note the strength in relation to the area of need; it lets the parents know you know their child has promise
What is the present level of performance? This is where the child is right now.	• Behavior observation checklist • CBM	• After XX consecutive days of observing the student in class, he raised his hand 2 times out of 15 opportunities and blurted out 13 times • Given a XX grade level oral reading fluency passage, XX read 24 words correctly with 65% accuracy

Secondary Example

Mrs. Poppins is the ninth-grade case manager at Cherry Tree Lane High School, and the end of the year test results are in. It is also time for Michael Banks's IEP review, and she has just administered his most recent progress monitoring probes using the Dynamic Indicators of Basic Early Literacy Skill (DIBELS), even though these measures are designed for kindergarten through eighth grade, she still uses DIBELS due to the understanding that most "real world" text is written at the eighth-grade level (Kutner et al., 2006); in addition, Mrs. Poppins's district uses the state's eighth-grade reading test as a requirement for graduation. It should also be noted that DIBELS 8th Edition Administration and Scoring Guide (University of Oregon, 2020) provides direction for "off-grade" progress monitoring. Mrs. Poppins knows this is not ideal tool for typically developing students, and she understands

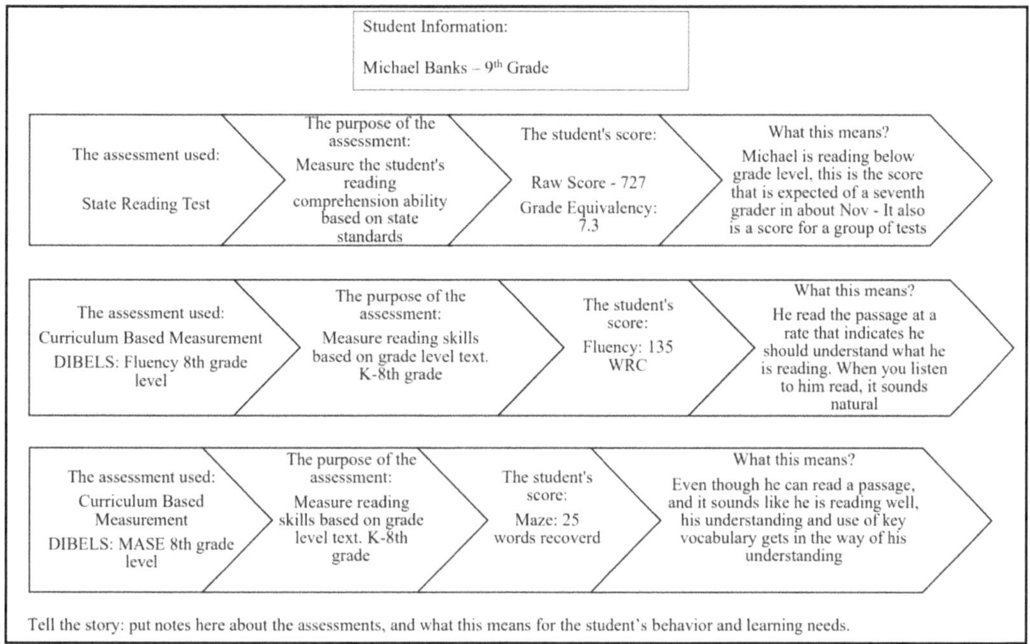

Figure 5-2. Secondary example of completed template to guide assessment discussions.

these results do not allow her to compare to Michael's progress to grade-level peers. However, it does provide a means to measure progress on his reading goals.

When she gets to her desk, Mrs. Poppins pulls out the test results along with Michael's CBM scores and starts to fill out the template she uses to help guide her discussions with stakeholders (Figure 5-2). Using both assessments (HLP 4), she starts crafting the story she needs to communicate with others. Michael's composite score on the exam was 727 (800 is needed for graduation). She is wondering if the parents understand what a composite score is, so she makes a note to add an explanation. Michael has made such gains this year. At the beginning of the year, his oral reading fluency score on the DIBELS was 115, which placed him in the 40th percentile for eighth graders. He was reading independently at a seventh-grade level. Now he is reading 135 words correctly per minute, which places him at a typical eighth-grade level. That is great progress. She places the graph of his results in the meeting folder. This visual will really help her shape the story. She thinks, "I should explain the reading program again to them, so they can see the value of the extra resource class where he had reading interventions. I should also talk to the fact that he is now earning a B in our co-taught English class."

Looking back at the results, she sees the concern—comprehension. She looks at the sub-test scores on the state test. The same pattern is there—some scores are in the 800 but comprehension is 645. Mrs. Poppins also administered a comprehension CBM called a MAZE. In this assessment, the student is presented with a passage that begins with a complete sentence. In the rest of the passage, every seventh word is replaced with a blank space and three word choices. Michael's MAZE score is 25 words recovered; it has improved since the beginning of the year, but not as much as the fluency. She makes a note to take a blank MAZE probe to show Mrs. Banks at their meeting. How can you describe this assessment and its link to reading comprehension without actually seeing it? Reading comprehension is going to be the focus of Michael's IEP goals. This is definitely an area of need in which she can describe both strengths and weaknesses. Mrs. Poppins is ready for the meeting with Mrs. Banks; she has reviewed the assessment results, interpreting the results complete with CBM graph to illustrate Michael's growth. She has all the notes, condensed or streamlined, and the results for everyone to understand. Now she practices telling the story to make sure she catches any jargon she needs to change or define; she is ready to communicate with all stakeholders.

Summary

Effective special educators know how to communicate with all stakeholders. They must translate the technical terminology of assessments as well as the results of the student so that everyone understands. Face it, we use a lot of jargon in special education; it becomes second nature, as if we have taken on a "foreign language." Remember our general education colleagues and parents are not living on our ship and speaking this terminology daily. As we said earlier, you are the steward; it is your job to make the journey more enjoyable. One way you can do that is to translate everything in a way everyone is sure to understand. Be prepared; it will take practice to float back and forth from professional jargon to layperson's terms.

An easy tool for you to use has been provided in Figure 5-1. Fill this out before meetings and use it as your cheat sheet in talking with stakeholders. Be sure to use the RISC process. *Review* the assessment reports before sharing with parents. Look to see where you will need to focus and translate. *Interpret* the results. Break down the type of assessment and scores that are presented; explain what they mean for this student at this time. Do you have graphs that can help illustrate the story you want to tell? *Streamline.* No one wants to read *War and Peace* in one night, nor do they want to read every page of these reports. Determine what is redundant; what can be summarized to tell a clear and coherent story? Finally, *communicate* the story in a way that parents and students feel comfortable and can be more involved in the process. It is only informed consent when the person consenting fully understands the information being presented and all the possible consequences of their decision.

Chapter Review

1. Describe HLP 5 in your own words.
2. Select one high-stakes assessment and describe its purpose related to informing decisions regarding student educational programming.
3. Describe how special educators can ensure all stakeholders understand assessment information.
4. Why is it important for special educators to control the "story" of a student's performance?
5. Which HLPs would you combine to implement HLP 5?

References

Ball, D. L., & Forzani, F. M. (2011). Building a common core for learning to teach: And connecting professional learning to practice. *American Educator*, *35*(2), 17-21.

Blackwell, W. H., & Stockall, N. (2019). RISC: Four steps for interpreting and communicating high-stakes assessment results. *TEACHING Exceptional Children*, *51*(4), 265-275. https://doi.org/10.1177/0040059919826027

Charles, K. J., & Dickens, V. (2012). Closing the communication gap. *TEACHING Exceptional Children*, *45*(2), 24-32. https://doi.org/10.1177/004005991204500203

Davern, L. (2004). School-to-home notebooks: What parents have to say. *TEACHING Exceptional Children*, *36*(5), 22-27.

Deno, S. L. (2003). Developments in curriculum-based measurement. *The Journal of Special Education* *37*, 184-192. https://doi.org/10.1177/00224669030370030801

Dexter, D. D., & Hughes, C. A. (2011). Graphic organizers and students with learning disabilities: A meta-analysis. *Learning Disability Quarterly*, *34*(1), 51-72. https://doi.org/10.1177/073194871103400104

Gomez, R., Vance, A., & Watson, S. D. (2016). Structure of the Wechsler Intelligence Scale for Children–Fourth Edition in a group of children with ADHD. *Frontiers in Psychology*, *7*, 737. https://doi.org/10.3389/fpsyg.2016.00737

Hall, T., Strangman, N., & Meyer, A. (2003). *Differentiated instruction and implications for UDL implementation*. www.cast.org/ncac

Hurwitz, S., Rodriquez, N., & Dixon, A. (2022). Who are students with disabilities? Identification, nondiscriminatory evaluation, and eligibility. In J. A. Rodriguez, & W. W. Murawski (Eds.), *Special education law and policy from foundation to application* (pp. 195-224). Plural.

Individuals With Disabilities Education Act, 20 U.S.C. §§ 1400 et seq. (2004 & Supp. V 2011).

Kamman, M., & McCray, E. D. (2022). Interpreting and communicating assessment information with stakeholders to collaboratively design and implement educational programs. In J. McLeskey, L. Maheady, B. Billingsley, M. T. Brownell, & T. J. Lewis (Eds.), *High leverage practices for inclusive classrooms* (2nd ed.; pp. 71-84). Routledge. https://doi.org/10.4324/9781003148609

Kutner, M., Greenberg, E., & Baer, J. (2006). A first look at the literacy of America's adults in the 21st century. NCES 2006-470. *National Center for Education Statistics.* https://files.eric.ed.gov/fulltext/ED489066.pdf

McLeskey, J., Barringer, M.-D., Billingsley, B., Brownell, M., Jackson, D., Kennedy, M., Lewis, T., Maheady, L., Rodriguez, J., Scheeler, M. C., Winn, J., & Ziegler, D. (2017). *High-leverage practices in special education.* Council for Exceptional Children & CEEDAR Center.

Schrank, F. A., & Wendling, B. J. (2018). The Woodcock–Johnson IV tests of cognitive abilities, tests of oral language, tests of achievement. In D. P. Flanagan & E. M. McDonough (Eds.), *Contemporary intellectual assessment: Theories, tests, and issues* (pp. 383-451). Guilford Press.

TeachingWorks Resource Library. (2022). *Curriculum resources.* https://library.teachingworks.org/curriculum-resources/high-leverage-practices/

University of Oregon. (2020). *8th Edition of Dynamic Indicators of Basic Early Literacy Skills (DIBELS®): Administration and Scoring Guide.* University of Oregon.

Wechsler, D. (2014). *Wechsler Intelligence Scale for Children* (5th ed.). Pearson.

Yell, M. L., Collins, J., Kumpiene, G., & Bateman, D. (2020). The Individualized Education Program: Procedural and substantive requirements. *TEACHING Exceptional Children*, 52(5), 304-318. https://doi.org/10.1177/0040059920906592

Does Assessment Really Drive Instruction?

Kyena E. Cornelius, EdD

HLP 6

Use student assessment data, analyze instructional practices, and make necessary adjustments that improve student outcomes.

INTRODUCTION

Teachers are constantly hearing about data-based decision-making; being asked to let the data "drive" their instruction. How is that possible? What does that even mean? What if we rephrase it and say data informs instruction? Can data really inform instruction? Yes, it can! But only when you know what to do with the data. This chapter provides current and future practitioners with hands-on strategies to collect, reflect, and use data to analyze instructional practice, both teacher practices and students' progress. We then discuss using data to make necessary adjustments to instruction to improve student outcomes.

Owiny, R. L., & Cornelius, K. E. *The Practical Guide to High-Leverage Practices in Special Education: The Purposeful "How" to Enhance Classroom Rigor* (pp. 87-100).

CHAPTER OBJECTIVES

- → Describe multiple ways to collect and systematically use data to make instructional decisions.
- → Know how this HLP 6, is connected to other HLPs and used alongside evidence-based practices to improve student outcomes.
- → Explain the benefits of instructional adjustments that are made after reflecting on data collected.

KEY TERMS

- **curriculum-based measurement (CBM):** A practice used both as a universal screening and ongoing monitoring to determine how students are progressing with basic academic skills.
- **data-based individualization (DBI):** A practice used to individualize and intensify instruction through the systematic use of assessment data.
- **formative assessment:** A practice to monitor student understanding and adjust instruction to increase student learning.
- **opportunities to respond (OTRs):** A practice of teachers asking students academic questions. OTRs are crucial in increasing student outcomes and are often used to measure student engagement.
- **self-reflection:** A practice for teachers to engage in recognizing strengths and weaknesses in their teaching.
- **student self-monitoring:** A practice used by students to engage in monitoring their own progress with interventions.

Special education teachers are charged with creating specialized instruction that is targeted to meet individual student's needs and spur their progress forward. However, to ensure the instruction remains appropriate for students with disabilities (SWD), special education teachers not only monitor student progress toward a goal but also track student response to instruction. They use the data gathered to evaluate instructional practices and then make needed changes to keep student growth as the focus of their work. Data are used for more than just tracking student performance. To increase instructional effectiveness, special education teachers also use different data to evaluate their own teaching practices to make adjustments in their actions that will improve student outcomes. Therefore, it is important that special education teachers collect data on themselves as well as students.

In this chapter we demonstrate how using High-Leverage Practice (HLP) 6—"*Use student assessment data, analyze instructional practices, and make necessary adjustments that improve student outcomes*" is naturally performed with other HLPs, many evidence-based practices (EBP), and practices offering promising outcomes as defined by peer-reviewed research. When teachers routinely (e.g., daily, weekly) consider data collected in their classrooms, they can make any necessary adjustments that truly improve student outcomes by adjusting their instruction to meet student needs.

What Is HLP 6?

Effective special education teachers understand the importance of using data to make instructional decisions. This HLP focuses on how to efficiently and effectively use data to reflect on student data and teacher practice. McLeskey and colleagues (2017) offer a process for implementing this HLP. By providing the steps to meaningfully use data, they demonstrate how you, the teacher, can improve student outcomes. First, plan for instruction with four practices in mind: (a) develop instructional goals, (b) select appropriate EBPs to target an area of need, (c) design specialized instruction, and (d) implement the planned instruction. Second, plan for assessment; during instructional delivery, effective special education teachers collect data (e.g., curriculum-based measurements [CBMs], informal classroom assessments, observations, self-assess their instructions) to analyze the instruction. Finally, plan for analysis; following instruction and data collection, teachers reflect on and evaluate the data collected to determine which practices need to be continued, refined, or extended. When the data indicate a practice is ineffective, quality teachers know to discard this practice, because it did not improve student outcomes, regardless of what others tell them. Quality special education teachers use data to make important decisions, rather than the hearsay or feelings of other teachers.

How Is HLP 6 Connected to Other HLPs?

There are many types of data available to help teachers make instructional decisions. As discussed in HLP 4, multiple sources of data are used to develop a full understanding of both a student's needs and strengths. Effective special education teachers use many assessment tools to develop a comprehensive student profile of strengths, needs, and interests (Benedict et al., 2022) to design programming and instructional opportunities for an SWD. Likewise, HLP 5 focuses on interpreting and sharing the results of all assessment data to others. Kamman and McCray (2022) provide special educators with strategies in sharing results with a variety of stakeholders and working with general educators to provide educational opportunities in general education classrooms (HLP 1). It should not be surprising, then, that this HLP also involves collecting multiple forms of data and discussing results with key stakeholders; after all special education is not a job done well in isolation—it is best done as a team. Effective special educators must productively work with a variety of professionals (HLP 1) as well as families (HLP 3) and students to impact student growth.

Watching a seasoned professional teacher in action, you may miss the fact that they collect and quickly interpret data during instruction. Using "in time" data provides evidence for providing positive and constructive feedback to guide students' learning and behavior (HLPs 8 and 22). The data collected and evaluated in HLP 6 can be the foundation for most of the HLPs of instruction. Special education instructional practices are (a) strategic, based on students' present level of academic and behavioral performance; (b) flexible, able to change at a moment's notice when a student is not progressing; and (c) recursive, to provide students with multiple opportunities to engage with the content (McLeskey et al., 2017). All three of these factors, seen throughout the instructional HLPs 11 through 22, require a special education teacher to collect data, reflect, and adjust instruction to maximize learning opportunities for SWD. See Table 6-1 for a list of HLPs that align with HLP 6 and many useful resources for the EBPs discussed in this chapter.

What Data Should Be Collected During and After Instruction? What Analysis Can Be Done? What Adjustments Should Be Made?

A key component of becoming proficient with this, and many of the HLPs, requires you to be more intentional in your practice. Effective special education teachers reimagine standard practice to tailor their instruction to the individual needs of their students. For HLP 6, this means focusing on assessment as an ongoing process using multiple data sources and carefully including students in the process to help develop the student's ability to self-manage (Lee et al., 2007) or recognize their own progress and take ownership of their learning and behavior. Self-management is the emphasis of

Table 6-1. Alignment of HLPs and Resources for Evidence-Based Practices

EBP SUPPORT WITH HLP 6	RELATED HLPS	RESOURCES
Curriculum-based measurements	5, 11	https://dibels.uoregon.edu/ www.easycbm.com www.pbisapps.org
Formative assessment	4, 5, 13	https://ccsso.org/resource-library/attributes-effective-formative-assessment https://ccsso.org/resource-library/formative-assessment-examples-practice
Data-based instruction	11, 12, 13, 20	https://iris.peabody.vanderbilt.edu/module/dbi2/#content www.interventioncentral.org
Opportunities to respond	12, 16, 18, 20	https://ccsso.org/resource-library/using-crosscutting-concepts-prompt-student-reponses
Student self-management	4, 7, 9, 14, 21, 22	https://afirm.fpg.unc.edu/sites/afirm.fpg.unc.edu/files/imce/resources/SM%20Step-by-Step.pdf https://journals.sagepub.com/doi/abs/10.1177/004005991004300205
Explicit instruction	11, 12, 15, 16, 20, 22	https://explicitinstruction.org/ https://highleveragepractices.org/hlp-16-use-explicit-instruction

HLP 14—"*Teach cognitive and metacognitive strategies to support learning and independence.*" The following sections will help you determine which data to collect, when to collect them, how to analyze the collected data, and finally provide guidance on how to use the data. Throughout these sections we share various EBP, research-based practices (RBP), and best practices.

How Are Data Collected?

Effective special education teachers understand that data come in many forms. A common practice in special education is the EBP of CBM. CBMs are quick assessments used to measure student progress toward specific content knowledge (Stecker et al., 2008) and basic skills (Deno, 2003). These assessments are generally administered weekly and take less than 5 minutes. Results are graphed and teachers can monitor student progress in one visual display. For example, a teacher could use the Dynamic Indicators of Basic Early Literacy Skills (DIBELS; Cummings et al., 2011) CBM to measure student progress on literacy skills. Additionally, validated CBM tools also exist to assess math skills. There are several websites that can assist in collecting CBM data in a variety of content areas:

- https://dibels.uoregon.edu/
- www.easycbm.com
- www.interventionalcentral.org
- www.pbisapps.org

The data collected from CBM assessments allow teachers to reflect upon the intervention and change the course of instruction from week to week. Although these data are the foundation of data-based instruction and IEP progress monitoring (McMaster et al., 2020), in order to make major changes in instruction, you need 6 to 10 weekly CBM data points to create a visual display for analysis of level, variability, and trend of student performance (Lembke et al., 2022). These data cannot provide the data necessary for the teacher to change the course of instruction mid-lesson, nor do they provide information that allows the teacher to reflect upon one day's instructional practice to adjust the lesson that will be taught tomorrow (Cornelius & Johnson-Harris, 2017).

Formative assessment has been defined as "activities undertaken by teachers...that provide information to be used as feedback to modify teaching and learning activities" (Black & Wiliam, 2010, p. 82). Formative assessment can be both planned and spontaneous (Dixson & Worrell, 2016). A planned formative assessment may take the form of a pre-test before a unit begins, an exit ticket at the end of a lesson, as well as homework or quizzes. Spontaneous formative assessment is more difficult to capture; it can be as easy as the teacher "reading" body language to gauge student understanding or being cognizant of the examples and responses students provide during the lesson. These data may be difficult to capture but can be done by intentionally designing a way of recording data on each opportunity to respond (OTR; Haydon et al., 2012) during the lesson, or even students' affect (i.e., attitude, interest, reaction; Cornelius, 2013). This type of assessment provides real-time data that can truly promote reflection and allow teachers to make necessary adjustments during instruction to improve student outcomes (Dixson & Worrell, 2016).

Informal classroom assessments are another form of formative assessment that you can use to gauge student academic performance, behavioral skill improvements, as well as motivation and affect during a single day or class period (Cornelius, 2013). Collecting data on student responses during a beginning warm-up can help determine maintenance of a skill taught yesterday. Collecting data during the guided-practice portion of a lesson informs the teacher if other practice opportunities are needed before moving on to unguided practice. All of these data can be used for daily reflection and instructional adjustments. A simple checklist embedded in a lesson plan template can be a great way to collect data. Figure 6-1 provides an example of a lesson plan template that can be used to plan lessons using the explicit instruction (HLP 16) framework that provides space for anecdotal data while the bottom portion allows you to note specific examples.

The Council of Chief State School Officers (CCSSO) definition of formative assessment includes students' participation in the process. "Formative assessment is a process used by teachers and students during instruction that provides feedback to adjust ongoing teaching and learning to improve students' achievement of intended instructional outcomes" (McManus, 2008, p. 3). One way to involve students is to use the EBP of self-management (Lee et al., 2007), a series of evidence-based strategies that help students become more independent. Self-management skills are important for all students. However, SWD often have negative self-concepts and believe they have no control over their learning, also known as *learned helplessness* (Sutherland & Singh, 2004). Self-monitoring is one strategy in the process of self-management that teaches students to self-assess a targeted skill or behavior and record the results. This does not teach new skills or knowledge. However, self-monitoring does increase (or decrease) the frequency, intensity, or duration of existing behavior. When students collect and monitor data it can serve as a motivator. Studies have shown student outcomes improve when students are involved in the process (Lembke et al., 2022). It also saves some time when students are doing the data collection. Although it does relieve the teacher from collecting all data, student-directed learning does not remove the teacher from the monitoring process. The teacher guides the student through the process to greater independence and control of their learning and

Lesson Plan: Subject ______________ Date __________ Standard Addressed: IEP Goals/Objectives Addressed:		
Opening: • Share today's objectives • Connect to yesterday's lesson	Review/Preview: 1. 2. 3. 4.	Student Response Notes
Model: • Think aloud • Demonstration	Extra Example Based on Student Affect (if needed): 1. 2.	
Guided Practice: What will I do/what will students be asked to do? Specific Tasks: 1. 2. 3.	Extra Example Based on Student Response (if needed): 1. 2. 3.	
Faded Support/Activity (if needed):		
Unguided Practice: What will students be asked to do? Specific Tasks: 1. 2. 3.		

Student	**Warm Up: Review/Preview**					**Guided Practice: OTR**						**Activity: OTR**					**Unguided Practice**			
	1	2	3	4	5	1	2	3	4	5	6	1	2	3	4	5	1	2	3	4

Figure 6-1. Lesson plan template for collecting informal assessment data.

behaviors. It is for this reason that this chapter includes self-management as an EBP to use with HLP 6. The teacher must help the student select the goal, develop a monitoring system, and analyze the data to monitor and evaluate progress. The process is continued with a gradual release of responsibility to the student. This scaffolded support (HLP 15) helps students learn and master the steps of the strategy with confidence as they assume more control and responsibility.

Students should be involved with developing the data collection tools. Depending on the age and independence level of the student, templates for collecting data can be placed on their desk or inside a daily planner for more discrete data collection. A simple frequency chart can be laminated and placed on the student's desk. Looking at the behaviors on the chart, students use an erasable marker to count the occurrence, or collect the data. At a planned time, you and the student conference and the data are logged; the template can be wiped clean and ready for use another day.

Another way to analyze instructional practice is to collect data on your own practice. Nagro and colleagues (2020) provide special education teachers a system to self-analyze instructional practices. The four-step process includes (a) recording instructional segments, (b) reviewing the video, (c) reflecting on what is observed, and (d) revising instructional practice. The video recording serves as another piece of concrete data that promotes reflection, allowing the analysis to shift from perceptions and memories of the experience to actual data-driven decision-making (Nagro et al., 2020).

What Questions Do I Use When Analyzing Data?

An effective special education teacher uses data to analyze instructional practices. Following (and sometimes during) instruction ask questions about student performance. The answers to those questions will help determine later instruction. The questions asked depend on the type of data collected. For example, when analyzing CBM data, ask: Are my students showing improvement? Which skill or element of the skill is still causing concern? The EBP of data-based instruction or data-based individualization (DBI; Fuchs et al., 2010) provides a six-step process for these big instructional questions.

Data-Based Individualization Process

The first step is to use CBM screening measures to confirm the student's current level of performance. Second, using the published norms for the CBM, the teacher sets an ambitious long-term goal (HLP 11) for the student. In Step 3 of the process, the teacher generates a hypothesis to select the appropriate intervention. This is truly the first time analysis takes on professional judgment. Looking at the results from the CBM, you conduct an error analysis to determine common errors. Using reading fluency as an example, you may set an ambitious goal of improving the words read correctly in 1 minute. Now you need to determine the intervention to teach the skill. Here is where you dig more deeply into the student errors to find patterns and areas of need to develop the hypothesis and select the appropriate intervention. Remember when selecting the intervention, you need to be confident in the evidence base of that practice, and that you have the appropriate training to implement it with fidelity.

Once you select the appropriate intervention, and implement that intervention with fidelity, start to collect the data. Within this step of the process, you can make adjustments or adaptations to the intervention (Leko et al., 2019). Some adaptations are necessary for student growth, and some are needed for teacher or setting context. The key is to find the balance by collecting data and making an informed decision.

In Step 4, and within Step 3, when adaptations are being considered, student progress is monitored once or twice a week and plotted to create a visual display of the student's progress. After 6 to 10 weeks, the second analysis happens. During Step 5, teachers start to ask questions based on the graph. These questions pertain to the level, variability, and trend of the data points collected. When considering level, look at the data points in relation to the goal line established in Step 2. Are the points clustered close to the line? Are there more above or below the line? If the points are all close to the goal line, the student is making the intended progress. If more data points are below the line, the student is not making sufficient progress and the instruction will need to change. Another factor to consider is the variability of the data points. If there are one or two points that are surprisingly low or high, the teacher needs to ask why. Consult with the general educator or parent to see if something unexpected happened to cause the student's performance: Did Charles have trouble sleeping the night before? Did something out of the ordinary happen in class or at home? You may also want to consider the timing and date of the lower score: Was the student absent? Was there an extended school break? Did something interrupt instruction? Once these questions are answered, one lower data point may be an "outlier" and not used in the decision-making process. If there is an unusually high data point, the teacher can ask questions about the content. Perhaps there was a reading passage that aligned with the student's interest or background knowledge, and they may have more extensive knowledge of the content vocabulary. However, when there is more variability over time, consider the student's ability to maintain the newly learned skills and to use the skill in other settings (HLP 21), or even their motivation for learning. When fluctuating data does happen, use it for self-reflection and ask, Did I provide the instruction as I planned to? Did I keep to the fidelity of the intervention? The answers to these questions will guide Steps 5 and 6.

In Step 5, the teacher generates a new hypothesis and decides how to continue instruction. Are you going to keep the same intervention, do you need to make any changes? How can I intensify this intervention? Do I need to add more OTRs, provide more time, or change the setting? These questions are considered after fully exploring the questions from Step 4. If you decide a change is needed, note that on the graph with a vertical line and new start date. If the student is making progress, and no instructional changes are needed, keep graphing as normal. During Step 6, the cycle of data collection and analysis continues. Table 6-2 provides examples of questions you can ask during the six-step process.

Formative Assessment Questions

As discussed in the section above, CBM data are not collected every day and will not help you make all instructional changes. For instance, during explicit instruction, which is both an EBP and an HLP (HLP 16), teachers design instruction with a precise series of supports that guide students through the learning process (Archer & Hughes, 2011). It is necessary to collect data on those supports and the students' responses to determine if they are ready to move on to the next phase of the lesson.

During the body of the lesson, explicit instruction has three phases: modeling, guided practice, and independent practice. The teacher begins the lesson with the model, or "I Do" phase, demonstrating and describing what the students will be doing later. During this phase the teacher is doing all the talking, sometimes describing their thinking to the students. The teacher should be watching the students for cues to their understanding. This type of data collection may not look as traditional as CBM graphs, but it very much informs a teacher's instructional decisions (refer to Figure 6-1 for a lesson plan template). By catching that "deer in headlights look," a teacher can choose to provide another example or use different vocabulary to reteach.

During guided practice, sometimes referred to as the "We Do" phase, the teacher provides practice for the students with supports that are faded throughout this phase. Guided practice is the phase of the lesson where many OTRs are important. These OTRs help to provide the data necessary to make instructional decisions. By collecting data on student behaviors and student responses, teachers may determine to re-model, provide additional supports, provide additional practice opportunities, or move on more quickly. Some of this data collection is easily captured in your lesson plan.

Table 6-2. Six-Steps of Data-Based Individualization

STEP	ACTION	QUESTIONS TO ASK
1	Establish present level of performance	What skill is student missing or struggling with? Which assessment will provide a measure of student's ability?
2	Set an ambitious long-term goal	What does the publisher of this assessment suggest as growth rates? What has student's trend data in the past told me?
3	Generate a hypothesis, select intervention, implement with fidelity	What errors occurred during the screening assessment? Is there a pattern? Which EBP will help teach this skill by addressing these errors? Am I proficient with this EBP? What training do I need to become proficient?
4	Monitor student progress	What daily data did I collect to ensure student was ready to proceed? How do weekly monitoring scores compare? Am I administering the assessment correctly?
5	Use decision rules to determine effectiveness of the instruction	How does student's progress align with aim lines and goal? Is he on track to meet the goal? IF NOT: Is this a bad day? Or is this a trend? Did Charles have trouble sleeping the night before, did something out of the ordinary happen in class or at home? OR ask: How can I intensify this intervention? Do I need to add more OTRs, provide more time, change the setting?
6	Repeat cycle of data collection and analysis	Did I implement this process (each step) with fidelity? Did I implement the EBP with fidelity? Did I follow the correct procedures to intensify the intervention?

Some in-time questions you will want to ask include the following: Which concept is causing Brenda to struggle? When did Juan start to lose interest? What happened right before Ron's outburst/shutdown? How many times did Sara ask to leave the room? This anecdotal information can be quickly written down during instruction or immediately following. Teachers should establish a way to log the information in a systematic manner. One way to ensure the data are not lost or forgotten by the end of the day is to embed a way to collect data within your lesson plan (Cornelius & Johnson-Harris, 2017). Another helpful tip is to keep templates and note cards handy on a clipboard or within reach during instruction (Cornelius, 2013).

Student Self-Management Process

Teaching students to manage their own behaviors and learning is one of the primary goals of education. After all, higher levels of self-efficacy and independence are a major focus for teaching SWD. So, it is logical to teach students self-management strategies and help them boost these skills (Rafferty, 2010). One of the five strategies in the self-management process that goes perfectly with HLP 6 is self-monitoring.

Self-monitoring requires students to be able to identify the target behavior and then record if it occurred or not. These data can be the ultimate *student data*. It is important to note that self-monitoring should only be used when the student can not only identify but also perform the target behavior (Rafferty, 2010). This strategy does not work to teach a new skill; however, it can increase or decrease the frequency of already-learned and desired skills (Lee et al., 2007). By teaching students to identify the desired behavior, academic or social, and then record what they observe, the student takes on more ownership of the target behavior and eventually does not need the intervention (Rafferty, 2010).

The student's data collection informs teacher practice as well. In the beginning, the student data are compared to your data. While the student is learning to identify and monitor their behaviors, you are also collecting data in the same manner to compare and help reinforce the behavior and self-monitoring. When comparing the data, you may see differences. For example, if the goal is for "on-task" behavior and the student has more occurrences than you do, you may ask the following: Does Jimmy fully understand the operational definition we developed? Did Marcus use the same intervals I did? These data may tell you to reteach the operational definition of "on task" and spend time modeling both examples and non-examples. Or maybe the student did not understand what and when they were to record occurrences. Either way it does tell you the student is not ready for independence, and you need to change your instructional plan to support the student more. However, when the student becomes more proficient, you spend less time monitoring the behavior, and eventually you and the student create new goals for them to achieve.

Self-Reflection Process

Following instruction, teachers need to analyze their own practice. This can be done by looking at student work to determine common errors or patterns. It can also be done by recording a lesson and reflecting on what is observed. Studies have shown that teachers who purposefully reflect on their practice are not only willing to try new techniques, but they also improve their instructional skills (Nagro et al., 2017).

Self-reflection through video analysis offers a more concrete piece of evidence and allows you to make purposeful decisions, not just based on a feeling or biased memory (Nagro et al., 2020). This process involves four steps: (a) record a lesson, (b) purposefully review it with a recording tool to capture specific elements, (c) reflect using a rubric, and (d) revise instruction. Recording your lesson is even easier today with so many tools at your fingertips. You no longer need bulky camera equipment; chances are you have a recording device by your side right now—your phone or tablet. Set it up and record! When you watch it, you want to make sure you are self-evaluating your instruction, not your posture or clothing choices. It is best if you use a tool to capture what you are focusing on. How many OTRs did I provide? Did I call on one student more than I should have? Do I call on individual students or ask open-ended questions to the group? Do I move around the classroom to provide proximity control to all students?

While watching your video use a rubric that allows you to ask questions about your teaching without causing emotional responses. To analyze your practice, start by describing what you see, using concrete statements that are supported by the video evidence. Next, provide a rationale or justification for your teaching decision, followed by assessing or judging that decision by writing down the impact that decision had on the instruction. These data help validate the final step—application. In the final step, you apply what you have learned through the reflective process to either sustain and extend what works or change what did not (Nagro et al., 2017). Always use student data and ask yourself pointed questions: How did the students react to my instructional decisions? Why didn't Mariah answer any questions? How can I change my questioning techniques to reach Tyce?

What Does HLP 6 Look Like in a K-12 Classroom?

Elementary Example

Elora Elementary School has arranged the master schedule to provide kindergarten and first grade with a common English Language Arts block and mathematics block each day to allow for cross-grade grouping. The same is true for second through fifth grade. Mr. Flores, a special educator, has a caseload of students in second and third grade. The students on Mr. Flores's caseload have IEP goals for reading, writing, math, and behavior needs. Therefore, his ability to group students across grade levels allows flexibility for reading and math groups. If a student in second grade is working on similar skills as a third grader, Mr. Flores can provide specialized instruction in the same reading group to students in different grade levels. Mr. Flores collects data for progress monitoring twice per week to evaluate student responsiveness to the intervention. As data indicate growth, he collaborates with classroom teachers to move students among groups to ensure they are receiving instruction at their correct level.

During instructional groups, Mr. Flores embeds data collection into his instruction. He can collect data on correct and incorrect responses to correctly decoding words, reading accuracy, and comprehension questions. As students practice decoding words aloud, he records, on his clipboard, the word attempted and a + for correct decoding or the type of error if a word is read incorrectly and a 0 for the incorrect word. He follows a similar procedure for reading accuracy and comprehension. Mr. Flores can analyze where errors are being made and adjust his instruction to meet those needs in subsequent lessons. Mr. Flores can also collaborate with the general education teacher to identify how the skills can be reinforced in the general education classroom. Not only is Mr. Flores able to adjust instruction, based on the data collected, he can move students into other groups where students are working on similar skills. This flexibility in grouping (HLP 17) and instructional design allows teachers to meet student needs with the key—using data to make those decisions.

Secondary Example

Miss Rose is a special education at Mountaineer High School; she offers specialized instruction in multiple settings. She plans for instruction both with general education colleagues and alone, for more intensive instruction in smaller group settings. She makes the most of her co-planning time by being ready to discuss many learning strategies to introduce with the content as well as different ways of assessing student learning and their practice. She also talks about how they should use the data collected. She brings anecdotal data she collected from the day's classes and shares areas of concern. Her teaching partner, Mr. Withrow, appreciates these efforts and enjoys the analysis and reflection of their instruction.

During their last algebra class, Miss Rose taught students a mnemonic strategy for problem-solving. Both teachers have become accustomed to engaging with individual students during class to check for understanding. They make note of these "exchanges" and bring the data to planning. They analyzed all data collected: individual and group OTR feedback, any behavioral affect notes they jotted down, as well as student self-monitoring sheets. After considering all the data and discussing the next lesson, they adjust their unit plan. Four students need a remediated mini lesson on using the mnemonic and three need some enhancement to add more rigor. Most of the class, 21 students, will begin the day with review practice opportunities while the two teachers deliver specialized instruction to the seven students who need it. Miss Rose and Mr. Withrow also use the data to design flexible groups (HLP 17). They purposefully group various students within the class so they may experience peer-assisted learning opportunities (Haydon et al., 2010).

While co-teaching, Miss Rose and Mr. Withrow often observe each other and provide their partners with performance feedback, which allows the two to grow professionally and allows each to reflect on their individual practice as well as their co-teaching practice. When teaching alone, they occasionally record their instruction and then self-analyze the videos and then discuss findings with each other. This not only improves their practice but student achievement has also increased.

Summary

Effective special education teachers use student assessment data, analyze instructional practices, and make necessary adjustments that improve student outcomes. Throughout the chapter you have seen how HLP 6 is closely tied to other HLPs and cannot be performed as a single action. It is natural to see how all of the Assessment HLPs are related, collecting multiple sources of information to develop an understanding of student strengths and needs (HLP 4) and interpreting those results to communicate with others to design and implement instruction (HLP 5). HLPs 4 and 5 naturally go hand in hand with using data to analyze your practice and make necessary adjustments. Special educators must collaborate, such as in the case examples we highlighted, using assessment data and interpreting with colleagues to increase student success (HLP 1).

It is also important to note that any time you analyze instructional practices you should analyze your practice in implementing Instructional HLPs. Due to the limits of one chapter and knowing there are many other chapters in this book, we did not highlight all Instructional HLPs, but instead chose to focus on HLPs 11, 14, 15, 16, and 17. Special educators deliver specialized instruction; it is what distinguishes special education from general education. In order to do that, you must use data to identify and prioritize long- and short-term learning goals (HLP 11). You collect baseline data, determine what is achievable for this unique student, and make a plan to get to the end goal. Likewise, during daily instruction you determine the learning outcome for the day, the most fundamental short-term goal. During the process you need to collect and analyze data to ensure the goal was achieved and make real-time changes as needed.

Student independence is the ultimate goal of education. Teaching students to self-manage behaviors and learning is key to achieving that goal (Rafferty, 2010) and the crux of HLP 14. To be successful students need to observe and self-monitor their development and progress. You can work collaboratively with the student, a key stakeholder (remember HLP 5), to assess the data and make necessary adjustments to instruction. Those adjustments may be reteaching the skill or the process, but it could also be in setting new goals and determining the next skill to teach. Along the way of any instruction, you must provide scaffolded supports (HLP 15); without data on student current performance, how would you ever know which scaffold to provide and to what degree? Then without analyzing data, how would you know when it was time to fade the support?

Of course, the backbone to solid specialized instruction is explicit instruction (HLP 16). We know this is the instructional design that offers students the most successful outcomes (Archer & Hughes, 2011). However, how do you know it is time to move on within your lesson or onto tomorrow's lesson without collecting and analyzing real-time data of your instruction? Analyzing the data helps plan tomorrow's instruction and allows you to create flexible grouping (HLP 17) for more specialized instruction as well as more engaging groupings for students.

This chapter also highlights various EBPs that are used in conjunction with this HLP. Another reminder, when you want to implement a new EBP make sure you have done the research to know the necessary steps of the practice. A great place to start is with the resources provided in Table 6-1. We specifically discussed CBM, formative assessment, DBI, explicit instruction, OTRs, student self-management, and video analysis. CBM is used weekly to screen and then monitor student progress toward achieving goals with specific skills. It obviously informs instruction, but since the probes are not administered daily it does not impact daily adjustments. DBI or instruction is used to individualize and intensify instruction through the systematic use of assessment data. This practice goes hand in hand with more formal CBM data and can easily be the focus of HLP 6. You collect the data, determine how the student is progressing, and then make adjustments for the intensification of instruction (HLP 20) based on individual student responses. Whereas formative assessment can be used before, during, and after daily instruction to adjust and plan, data collected is used to determine student understanding and adjust instructional practices in the moment or for the next lesson.

Explicit instruction is so important in the special education process it is not only an EBP, it is also HLP 16. Instruction must be structured so that teachers model, show, and tell students what to do or think about while engaging with content and new skills. Teachers must be strategic in choosing examples and non-examples for students (McLeskey et al., 2017). This strategic planning comes from the data collected from students. What is their current understanding, what motivates them, and what happened with previous instruction? To plan effective explicit instruction, you start with student data. One of the data points you collect during classroom instruction is student responses. How did the student engage with the content? How did they answer the checks for understanding questions? All the OTRs you provide in class need to be captured and used. Why ask a question if you did not log the student responses?

Finally, you must actually reflect on the data to analyze and make those adjustments. Sit with students to review their self-monitoring. Help them record accurately so they become more independent and motivated to take on more of their own learning. Self-monitoring can help increase student motivation and frequency of desired behaviors, both academic and social. You need to analyze the data together to adjust and promote student independence. Make sure you schedule part of your day to reflect on your own practice as well. When you routinely use self-reflection, your teaching practice will improve, and you will be able to explain your instructional decisions based on your and your students' performance. Collect the data, review it, analyze and reflect, and ask yourself hard questions about your teaching practice so that you can adjust instructional practices to improve student outcomes.

Chapter Review

1. Describe what is meant by "let data *drive* instruction."
2. Why is it important to collect data and interpret it daily?
3. Describe one strategy discussed in this chapter that can enhance your data collection.
4. Name three different types of data and how they can be used to adjust instruction.
5. Why is it important to reflect on your practice while analyzing data?

References

Archer, A. L., & Hughes, C. A. (2011). *Explicit instruction: Effective and efficient teaching*. Guilford Press.

Benedict, A. E., Cornelius, K. E., Acosta, K., & Ray, J. (2022). Using multiple sources of information to develop a comprehensive understanding of a student's strengths and needs. In J. McLeskey, L. Maheady, B. Billingsley, M. T. Brownell, & T. J. Lewis (Eds.), *High leverage practices for inclusive classrooms* (2nd ed., pp. 57-70). Routledge. https://doi.org/10:4324/9781003148609-8

Black, P., & Wiliam, D. (2010). Inside the black box: Raising standards through classroom assessment. *Phi Delta Kappan*, 92(1), 81-90.

Cornelius, K. E. (2013). Formative assessment made easy: Templates for collecting data in inclusive classrooms. *TEACHING Exceptional Children*, 45(5), 14-21. https://doi.org/10.1177/004005991304500502

Cornelius, K. E., & Johnson-Harris, K. M. (2017). Progress monitoring: Your classroom itinerary. In W. W. Murawski, & K. L. Scott (Eds.), *What really works with exceptional learners* (pp. 169-185). Corwin.

Deno, S. L. (2003). Developments in curriculum-based measurement. *The Journal of Special Education*, 37, 184-192. https://doi.org/10.1177/00224669030370030801

Dixson, D. D., & Worrell, F. C. (2016). Formative and summative assessment in the classroom. *Theory Into Practice, 55*, 153-159. https://doi.org/10.1080/00405841.2016.1148989

Fuchs, D., Fuchs, L. S., & Stecker, P. M. (2010). The "blurring" of special education in a new continuum of general education placements and services. *Exceptional Children, 76*, 301-322. https://doi.org/10.1177/001440291007600304

Haydon, T., Macsuga-Gage, A. S., Simonsen, B., & Hawkins, R. (2012). Opportunities to respond: A key component of effective instruction. *Beyond Behavior, 22*(1), 23-31. https://doi.org/10.1177/107429561202200105

Haydon, T., Maheady, L., & Hunter, W. (2010). Effects of numbered heads together on the daily quiz scores and on-task behavior of students with disabilities. *Journal of Behavioral Education, 19*, 222-238. https://doi.org/10.1007/s10864-010-9108-3

Kamman, M., & McCray, E. D. (2022). Interpreting and communicating assessment information with stakeholders to collaboratively design and implement educational programs. In J. McLeskey, L. Maheady, B. Billingsley, M. T. Brownell, & T. J. Lewis (Eds.), *High leverage practices for inclusive classrooms* (2nd ed., pp. 71-84). Routledge. https://doi.org/10:4324/9781003148609-9

Lee, S. H., Simpson, R. L., & Shogren, K. A. (2007). Effects and implications of self-management for students with autism: A meta-analysis. *Focus on Autism and Other Developmental Disabilities, 22*(1), 2-13. https://doi.org/10.1177/10883576070220010101

Leko, M. M., Robers, C., Peyton, D., & Pua, D. (2019). Selecting evidence-based practices: What works for me. *Intervention in School and Clinic, 54*, 286-294. https://doi.org/10.1177/1053451218819190

Lembke, E. S., Smith, R. A., & Newman-Thomas, C. (2022). Using student assessment data, analyzing instructional practices, and making necessary adjustments that improve student outcomes. In J. McLeskey, L. Maheady, B. Billingsley, M. T. Brownell, & T. J. Lewis (Eds.), *High leverage practices for inclusive classrooms* (2nd ed., pp. 85-101). Routledge. https://doi.org/10:4324/9781003148609-10

McLeskey, J., Barringer, M.-D., Billingsley, B., Brownell, M., Jackson, D., Kennedy, M., Lewis, T., Maheady, L., Rodriguez, J., Scheeler, M. C., Winn, J., & Ziegler, D. (2017). *High-leverage practices in special education*. Council for Exceptional Children & CEEDAR Center.

McManus, S. (2008). A*ttributes of effective formative assessment*. Council for Chief State School Officers. http://www.ccsso.org/publications/details.cfm?PublicationID=362

McMaster, K. L., Lembke, E. S., Shin, J., Poch, A. L., Smith, R. A., Jung, P. G., Allen, A. A., & Wagner, K. (2020). Supporting teachers' use of data-based instruction to improve students' early writing skills. *Journal of Educational Psychology, 112*(1), 1-21. http://dx.doi.org/10.1037/edu0000358

Nagro, S. A., deBettencourt, L. U., Rosenberg, M. S., Carran, D. T., & Weiss, M. P. (2017). The effects of guided video analysis on teacher candidates' reflective ability and instructional skills. *Teacher Education and Special Education, 40*(1), 7-25. http://doi.org/10.1177/0888406416680469

Nagro, S. A., Hirsch, S. E., & Kennedy, M. J. (2020). A self-led approach to improving classroom management practices using video analysis. *TEACHING Exceptional Children, 53*(1), 24-32. https://doi.org/10.1177/0040059920914329

Rafferty, L. A. (2010). Step-by-step: Teaching students to self-monitor. *TEACHING Exceptional Children, 43*(2), 50-58. https://doi.org/10.1177/004005991004300205

Stecker, P. M., Lembke, E. S., & Foegen, A. (2008). Using progress-monitoring data to improve instructional decision making. *Preventing School Failure: Alternative Education for Children and Youth, 52*(2), 48-58. https://doi.org/10.3200/PSFL.52.2.48-58

Sutherland, K. S., & Singh, N. N. (2004). Learned helplessness and students with emotional or behavioral disorders: Deprivation in the classroom. *Behavioral Disorders, 29*, 169-181. https://doi.org/10.1177/019874290402900208

Social/Emotional/Behavioral High-Leverage Practices

To be most effective, special educators must keep in mind key components of classroom organization and management as well as the social and emotional needs of their students. Additionally, all students need support for pro-social behaviors from time to time, regardless of their diagnosed disability. Building strong teacher–student relationships aids in higher-quality learning and student motivation to persist in their efforts. Even with the most well-organized and respectful classroom with pro-social skills reinforced as a priority, students may need further supports with a functional behavioral assessment and subsequent behavior support plan. High-Leverage Practices (HLPs) 7 through 10 are explained in Chapters 7 through 10, and the evidence-based practices to help special educators to implement these HLPs with greater success are detailed for teachers to implement with confidence.

How Do I Design and Maintain a Positive Learning Environment?

Kimberly M. Johnson, PhD

HLP 7

Establish a consistent, organized, and respectful learning environment.

INTRODUCTION

A unique aspect of teaching is the perennial opportunity to reflect on the prior school year and make adjustments for the new one. The new year presents an opportunity to redesign the physical space of the classroom, reconsider classroom routines and procedures, and update learning, behavioral expectations, and rules. It is an opportunity to rethink how to teach and support classroom routines, procedures, expectations, and rules so that barriers are addressed and all students feel confident navigating the learning environment and are motivated to learn. The purpose of this chapter is to provide an understanding of how to establish and maintain a consistent, organized, and respectful learning environment in these areas: classroom design, organization, and arrangement; classroom routines and procedures; and classroom expectations. Teachers will be provided with recommended practices to transform their classroom from unpredictable and stressful to consistent, organized, and respectful.

Owiny, R. L., & Cornelius, K. E. *The Practical Guide to High-Leverage Practices in Special Education: The Purposeful "How" to Enhance Classroom Rigor* (pp. 103-116).

CHAPTER OBJECTIVES

- Explain practical considerations and recommended practices for classroom design, organization, and arrangement.
- Define and differentiate between *routines* and *procedures.*
- Explain recommended practices for selecting, teaching, and maintaining classroom routines and procedures.
- Clarify distinctions between *expectations* and *rules.*
- Explain recommended practices for determining, teaching, and maintaining learning-related and behavior-related expectations and rules.

KEY TERMS

- **age-appropriate:** Suitable for a particular age group.
- **behavior:** An observable and measurable act.
- **cultural responsiveness:** Having an awareness of the cultural and racial issues faced by others and the ability to reflect and respond according to the needs of individuals.
- **expectation:** Broad guideline for behavior that applies to all.
- **pre-correction:** Providing a reminder of appropriate behavior or correct procedure before an error is made.
- **procedure:** A particular method for performing a task.
- **routine:** A course of action that is followed regularly.
- **rule:** An explicit statement of how to behave in a particular location.

Many teachers enjoy the days right before the school year starts when they get to set up their classroom and prepare for another school year. A non-educator may think this is just about unpacking boxes, putting things away, and decorating the walls, but teachers know that planning for a consistent, organized, and respectful learning environment takes careful consideration of multiple factors. When teachers put effort into planning ahead for (a) the classroom design, organization, and arrangement; (b) routines and procedures; and (c) expectations and rules, the result is a structured learning environment where all students feel confident, valued, and motivated to learn throughout the school year.

As they unpack classroom materials, teachers think about how to organize them and where to place them so that students can easily and efficiently access them. Desks are arranged to promote engagement during a variety of learning activities and to encourage positive social interactions among students. Educational posters are hung and interactive bulletin boards and learning centers are constructed with various learning activities in mind. Once the physical classroom is set up, teachers turn their thoughts to the routines, procedures, expectations, and rules that all contribute to a positive learning environment where instruction and learning take center stage.

Just as teachers thoughtfully plan to maximize learning by the physical arrangement of the learning space, they must also plan ahead for the *mechanics*, or the working parts, of the learning environment. Having routines in place for everyday activities like entering and exiting the classroom, gathering materials for learning activities, or engaging with peers during group work will decrease chaos and confusion and increase instructional time and learning. Having procedures in place for specific tasks such as washing the paint out of paintbrushes or reshelving the lab equipment will not only increase learning time but will also decrease time teachers spend maintaining a neat and organized learning space. Having an organized classroom maximizes instruction and learning, but that is not all it takes to have a positive learning environment. The final thing teachers need to consider when preparing for the start of the school year is classroom expectations and rules.

From the moment of their first smile, handshake, high-five, or fist-bump, teachers are communicating to students how to be students in their classroom—in other words, how to behave toward the teacher and how to behave toward their classmates. This is conveyed to students implicitly when they observe how the teacher interacts with them and their classmates, but it is most directly conveyed to students through explicit development and instruction of classroom expectations and rules. Because of this, teachers must carefully consider their broad expectations for student behavior and the rules that will explicitly outline what is and is not acceptable behavior in their classroom. Having and conveying high expectations for learning-related effort and utilizing instructional routines and procedures to support that effort results in positive learner outcomes. Likewise, having high expectations for behavior-related effort and classroom rules that further define and support that effort results in a positive learning environment.

Establishing a consistent, organized, and respectful learning environment is foundational to all other aspects of classroom management and instruction. When a classroom runs smoothly because there are clear and consistent expectations, rules, routines, and procedures in place, instruction can take center stage. The purpose of this chapter is to provide teachers with a practical understanding of how to establish and maintain a consistent, organized, and respectful learning environment. Common points of confusion will be clarified, and teachers will be provided with recommended practices and specific steps to take in order to transform their classroom environment from unpredictable and stressful to consistent, organized, and respectful.

What Is HLP 7?

High-Leverage Practice (HLP) 7—"*Establish a consistent, organized, and respectful learning environment*" is one of the 22 critical practices that every K-12 special education teacher should master (McLeskey et al., 2017). In order to do this, a teacher needs to think about the classroom design, organization, and arrangement as well as the everyday classroom routines and procedures that need to be in place for a classroom to run smoothly. Additionally, the teacher must determine the learning-related and behavior-related expectations and rules that need to be in place so that learners understand what is expected of them and feel confident to meet the expectations, with support as needed. Once the teacher has determined routines, procedures, expectations, and rules, these must be explicitly taught to students and then consistently supported and practiced throughout the school year. This HLP is foundational to all other HLPs because meaningful instruction and learning become possible when learners feel safe, valued, and respected in the learning environment.

How Is HLP 7 Connected to Other HLPs?

To establish and maintain a positive learning environment, we must determine classroom routines, procedures, expectations, and rules and then we must *teach* them while providing ongoing scaffolding and feedback so that students will maintain the skills and generalize them across all settings where they are applicable. Because the ongoing process of *teaching* the routines, procedures, expectations, and rules is just as important as constructing them, HLP 7 is closely connected to the Instruction HLPs. We systematically design the instruction (HLP 12) for teaching routines, procedures, expectations, and rules, and then we deliver the instruction using an explicit instruction model (HLP 16) while providing, and then systematically removing, scaffolds (HLP 15). We also teach and support metacognitive strategies (HLP 14) that will enable students to self-regulate their use of the new skills and build their confidence as learners in a school community. During instruction, we engage learners (HLP 18) in both the development and learning of the expectations and rules. As we do so, we provide feedback (HLPs 8 and 22) as students practice the new skill with teachers and peers in the classroom and when they move beyond the classroom to other school settings and home (HLP 21).

Because we want to provide consistency across school settings and between school and home, HLP 7 is also closely connected to some Collaboration HLPs. We should collaborate with other school professionals (HLP 1) and families (HLP 3) so that all stakeholders are aware of the routines, procedures, expectations, and rules being taught and practiced so they can provide feedback and positive reinforcement for the same or related skills that are used in other settings.

HLP 7 is also, of course, connected to the other social/emotional/behavioral practices because teaching classroom routines, procedures, expectations, and rules *is* teaching social behaviors (HLP 9). Through this instruction, students are learning the interpersonal skills needed to thrive in school. Additionally, HLP 7 is related to HLP 10 because teachers must know when and how to conduct a functional behavioral assessment and develop an individualized behavior intervention plan, sometimes also called a behavior support plan, when a student's behavior is beyond what can be managed by general classroom expectations and rules. See Table 7-1 to see a snapshot of how other HLPs are used in conjunction with HLP 7 as well as useful resources for the evidence-based practices (EBPs) discussed in this chapter.

What Should I Consider When Designing, Organizing, and Arranging My Classroom?

Classroom aesthetics are as varied as the teachers themselves and teachers can, and should, convey their individual teaching personalities through the spaces that they share with their students every day. There are, however, a few evidence-based and recommended practices that all teachers should consider when planning the classroom design, organization, and arrangement (Table 7-2). First, teachers should ensure that the physical space is safe and that all areas of the classroom and needed materials are organized and accessible to all learners (Trussell, 2008). When classroom materials are organized, students will easily be able to follow routines and procedures (discussed later) for gathering materials and putting them away as needed. All learners, including those who use mobility devices, should have access to all areas of the classroom. Second, teachers should consider the self-regulation and behavioral needs of the learners and arrange the physical space so learners who need frequent support are seated near staff members or peers who will provide support (Korinek & DeFur, 2016). When determining seating arrangements, teachers are encouraged to consider the learning task and what arrangement will be most conducive for the activity (Kern & Clemens, 2007) and the individual needs of the learners (Tobia et al., 2020). Seating arrangements can be designed to provide opportunities for learners to interact with all their peers, which promotes social inclusion (Ng et al., 2013). Seating arrangements can also be strategically designed to reduce peer-related behavior problems and certain externalizing behaviors by seating students who exhibit negatively perceived behaviors near classmates who routinely display pro-social behaviors (van den Berg et al., 2012; van den Berg & Stoltz, 2018). Third, teachers should consider how the learning environment can provide learners with options. When the classroom arrangement has seating options, lighting options, and options for materials, learners feel a sense of ownership over their learning, which can promote engagement and motivation (Evans & Boucher, 2015), also critical to implementing the engagement principle of Universal Design for Learning.

Table 7-1. Alignment of HLPs and Resources for Evidence-Based Practices

EBP SUPPORT WITH HLP 7	RELATED HLPS	RESOURCES
Arrange classroom environment to promote safety, accessibility, and inclusion	9	https://eclkc.ohs.acf.hhs.gov/sites/default/files/pdf/no-search/iss/managing-the-classroom/managing-classroom-teacher-tips-dll.pdf https://www.readingrockets.org/helping-all-readers/english-language-learners/creating-welcoming-classroom-environment-ells
Establish routines and procedures to promote efficiency and maximize instructional time Establish clear rules and expectations to promote positive behavior	1, 8, 14, 15, 16, 18, 21, 22	https://www.naeyc.org/resources/pubs/yc/mar2016/building-environments-encourage-positive-behavior-preschool https://iris.peabody.vanderbilt.edu/wp-content/uploads/pdf_case_studies/ics_norms.pdf
Plan for comprehensive behavior management	12	https://highleverage practices.org/hlp-7-establish-consistent-organized-and-respectful-learning-environment www.pbis.org https://iris.peabody.vanderbilt.edu/module/beh2_elem/ https://iris.peabody.vanderbilt.edu/module/beh2_sec/
Align classroom management with School-Wide Positive Behavioral Interventions and Supports	1, 8, 16, 21, 22	https://www.pbis.org/topics/classroom-pbis

What Should I Consider When Determining My Classroom Routines/Procedures?

Rawlings Lester et al. (2017) suggest that classroom management is a "well-planned set of procedures and routines for avoiding problems" (p. 399). Teachers wear many hats throughout a typical school day. Two main roles are *director* and, of course, *teacher*. Someone can be an excellent teacher, but if they are not a good director, they will struggle to have uninterrupted teaching time and engaged learners. When teachers have routines and procedures in place for a well-managed classroom (director) and seamless instruction (teacher), they will spend less time and energy directing students' movement and behavior and more time teaching. The EBP of incorporating classroom routines and procedures provides predictability, which promotes engagement and reduces behavior problems (Kern & Clemens, 2007).

Table 7-2. Checklists for Areas of Consideration

CLASSROOM DESIGN, ORGANIZATION, AND ARRANGEMENT
• Consider safety and accessibility • Consider seating arrangements that promote self-regulation, social inclusion, and pro-social behavior • Consider options for seating and materials
ROUTINES AND PROCEDURES
• List classroom routines and related procedures • List instructional routines and related procedures • List procedures for everyday activities • Explicitly teach routines and procedures the first time they are needed • Review and provide pre-corrections for routines and procedures before they are used • Provide immediate positive and corrective feedback
EXPECTATIONS AND RULES
• List learning-related expectations and determine the specific rules that will lead to meeting the expectations • List behavior-related expectations and determine the specific rules that will lead to meeting the expectations • Explicitly teach expectations and rules during the first few days of the school year • Review and provide pre-corrections for rules at key times • Provide immediate positive and corrective feedback

Let us begin this section by clarifying the difference between routines and procedures. The term *routine* refers to a course of action that is followed regularly. The term *procedure* refers to a particular method for performing a task. Think of a **routine** as being the way something is always done (e.g., you have a routine for getting ready for work in the morning—one of the things you may do as part of that routine is make coffee). Think of a **procedure** as being the proper way a discrete task is carried out (e.g., you may have a specific procedure for making coffee). Teachers have routines for how they manage the flow of classroom activities (e.g., students are taught to follow a routine for going to the library) and for how they deliver instruction (e.g., teacher uses a vocabulary instructional routine). Students are also taught procedures related to everyday activities that happen in a classroom (e.g., procedures for gathering materials for an activity). These procedures help maintain efficient use of time and manage classroom traffic.

Routines and Procedures for a Well-Managed Classroom

Because every grade level, subject area, classroom, and teacher is different, teachers might find it helpful to think about and list specific parts of their "typical day" when planning classroom routines and procedures. After listing parts of the school day, teachers can think through the routines and procedures necessary for each part. Specific parts of the day at the elementary level might include student arrival; transitions between subjects; movement to and from recess, lunch, library, and special classes like art, music, physical education; and leaving for the day. Specific parts of the day at the secondary level where students move from classroom to classroom throughout the day might include students entering the classroom after passing periods, preparing personal materials for class (e.g., notebooks, textbooks), gathering content-specific materials for the lesson activity (e.g., microscope in a biology class), and packing up at the end of the hour to move to the next class. In addition to the typical day components described, special education resource room teachers will find it helpful to consider routines and procedures for students who enter the classroom at various times throughout the day for behavioral or emotional support and for carrying out components of behavior intervention plans (e.g., Check-In/Check-Out; Mitchell et al., 2011). When thinking about routines for various parts of the day, teachers should break down the routine into a series of steps. To illustrate, consider these scenarios for when students arrive at school and/or enter the classroom. At the elementary level, steps for an arrival routine might include hanging up your jacket, moving your lunch clip to *buy* or *brought*, putting homework in the basket, sitting at your table and greeting your friends, and working on the bell-ringer activity/assignment. At the secondary level, steps for entering the classroom after passing period might include unpacking personal materials for class, collecting content-specific materials from shelves/cabinets, and following directions on the board to prepare for the lesson. In a resource room, steps for entering the classroom to receive support might include sign in, complete a self-monitoring activity, and select a space to work on a self-regulation strategy while waiting for the teacher.

Next, teachers should think about which steps of the routine will require specific procedures to be followed and then determine the sequence of each procedure. Not every step of the routine will require a procedure. For example, most students will not require a procedure for unpacking personal materials for class, but a procedure will likely be important for collecting a microscope and related supplies from the shelves in a biology class. When determining steps for procedures, the teacher will break down the task to be completed into its discrete parts and list those parts as steps. For example, choose one lab partner to gather materials, locate the microscope with the same number as your lab table, carry the microscope to your table with two hands (one on the microscope arm and one under the microscope base), take the microscope to your table and then go back for your supplies, choose the supply basket with the same number as your lab table, do not work with materials or equipment until you receive further instructions. These procedures are important for student and equipment safety, and when students have been clearly taught the proper procedure and a poster listing the steps is displayed by the equipment, there is no ambiguity about how the task should be performed. Also consider including a visual representation of each step beside each item on the list to assist struggling readers or English-language learners.

Routines and Procedures for Seamless Instruction

Routines and procedures that maintain instructional momentum include those that guide students in how they should participate in instruction so that they know what to expect and what is expected of them (Rawlings Lester et al., 2017). This knowledge will give students confidence in their ability to participate in learning activities. When planning for routines and procedures that support instructional momentum, teachers will find it helpful to list the instructional routines that they use on a regular basis such as explicit instruction (Archer & Hughes, 2011; I Do, We Do, You Do; see HLP 16), Content Enhancement Routines (CERs; Bulgren, 2006; see HLP 12), routines for transitioning efficiently from one activity to another (Cangelosi, 2014), and routines related to student engagement (see HLP 18). After listing their commonly used instructional and engagement routines, teachers should determine the behaviors that must be in place for each routine to be used effectively. To illustrate, think about a simple skill and strategy instructional routine—I Do, We Do, You Do (model, guided practice, independent practice; Archer & Hughes, 2011). During the model phase of the lesson (I Do), the teacher will provide a clear explanation of the new skill and model the skill while sharing their thinking process in a think-aloud. During this time, students will look and listen. During the guided-practice phase (We Do), the teacher and students will work together through several examples and non-examples. The teacher will ask questions about what to do next when performing the new skill and students will answer the questions. During the independent practice phase (You Do), the teacher will monitor student progress while students practice the new skill independently. When students know what to do during each phase of a lesson or during various activities, they feel confident in their ability to participate during instruction and instructional time becomes more efficient.

What Should I Consider When Determining My Classroom Expectations and Rules?

Establishing clear classroom expectations and rules is an EBP that results in improved behavior across school settings (Kern & Clemens, 2007). There is no shortage of research on the correlation between teachers' high expectations and learners' positive outcomes (Flanagan et al., 2020; Gentrup et al., 2020). Pre-service teachers learn that having and conveying high expectations for learning and behavior results in positive outcomes, but that having low expectations (even implicitly due to biases) can have the opposite effect (Ayers, 2016). Because of this, teachers must establish and communicate high expectations regarding learning and behavior for all students. Consistently conveying high expectations is difficult, but classroom rules can further extrapolate the expectations (Kerr & Nelson, 2010) providing a structure that guides students and helps teachers consistently support all students.

The terms *expectations* and *rules* are often used interchangeably, so it is helpful to distinguish them. The term *expectation* refers to the way all people should act at school (students and adults). The term *rule* refers to the specific ways teachers want students to behave in their classrooms. Think of **expectation** as being more broad—*be respectful*, and **rule** being more specific about what the expectation looks like—*use kind words*. It is also helpful to conceptualize expectations in terms of *learning expectations* and *behavioral expectations* and to acknowledge a hierarchy of expectations. As teachers, we have expectations of our students related to their effort toward learning and we have expectations of our students related to their behavior. Additionally, there are school-wide expectations, classroom expectations, and community and societal expectations. As children and adolescents develop, they are learning the nuances of these expectations and continually adjusting their behaviors according to new understandings (Ahn et al., 2020). Rules are the building blocks that lead to students meeting expectations. When conveyed clearly, taught explicitly, and supported consistently over time, rules help students navigate the classroom, school, and community social norms.

Learning Expectations

Student achievement is impacted by teacher expectations (Flanagan et al., 2020). To avoid contributing to the achievement gap between different ethnic groups, teachers must acknowledge and confront innate biases (Ayers, 2016) so that they maintain high learning expectations for all students in their classroom. To be consistent over time and with all students, teachers should have, and convey to their students, high expectations for learning. To make this practical, it is helpful to think of expectations for learning in two categories: expectations for academic effort and expectations for work products. Consider a classroom expectation such as *do your best* with supporting rules of *pay attention* and *participate during instruction* and *turn in your best work*. With this expectation and supporting rules in place, students will apply the rules when completing and submitting assignments. With teacher support, students can use self-monitoring (see HLP 14) to ask themselves "Did I pay attention and participate so I fully understand the new skill?" and "Is this my best work?" to move toward meeting the expectation. Likewise, teachers will apply the rules when reviewing student work (see HLP 6), by asking themselves "Did the student pay attention and participate during instruction? Does the student's final work product reflect their best effort?" Applying the rules when reviewing each student's work will prompt teachers to have a conversation with a student whom they perceive did not turn in their best work (see HLPs 8 and 22) and provide additional support rather than simply assigning a poor grade. By applying the rules consistently when reviewing students' work, teachers will maintain and convey high expectations for all students.

Behavioral Expectations

Have you noticed or experienced students behaving well in one teacher's class and then *misbehaving* in another teacher's class? This is due to differences in selection of behavioral expectations and consistency in supporting students to meet them (Myers et al., 2017). Classroom expectations should be aligned with School-Wide Positive Behavioral Interventions and Supports (SWPBIS; Horner et al., 2010; Simonsen et al., 2015), an EBP for enhancing students' understanding of behavioral expectations at school. A school may have some version of the following expectations as part of their SWPBIS framework: *Be Respectful, Be Responsible, Be Safe*. These expectations are somewhat ambiguous, so teachers should develop a more specific set of expectations that align with both their teaching style and student needs. Teachers should think about each school-wide expectation and what it means to them, how they will convey that expectation to students, and how students can demonstrate behaviors that align with that expectation in their classroom. The more specific set of expectations will vary by grade level or content area. *Be Respectful, Be Responsible, Be Safe* may be appropriate for middle or high school students who are familiar with these generalities, but *Be Respectful, Be Responsible, Be Safe* may need to be reworded for students in primary and elementary grades or for students with more intense cognitive delays who need explicit direction. *Be Respectful*, in a primary or elementary classroom, might be worded as *be kind to others* or *use manners*. No matter how the expectations are worded, consistency in the classroom (and over the school year), among teachers and classrooms, and throughout the school is key. When the expectations are aligned, there will be similar expectations in every classroom with every teacher and students will be better able to generalize the appropriate behaviors across all school settings.

Rules

Teachers should consider what specific behaviors students need to demonstrate in order to meet broad expectations and plan to design rules around those behaviors. For example, consider the expectation *be respectful to teacher and classmates*. Behaviors to meet that expectation might include listening when others are talking, using kind words, and including everyone. When designing rules, researchers agree that rules should be few in number, specific, stated positively, and created collaboratively with students (Alter & Haydon, 2017; Kern & Clemens, 2007). More important than sticking to a specific number of rules is making sure that the classroom rules sufficiently support students' understanding of how to meet the related expectation. Three rules may be needed to sufficiently support meeting the expectation of *Be Respectful* and four rules may be needed to support the expectation of *Be Safe*. The number of rules needed will vary according to teacher style and preferences, as well as student needs and classroom dynamics. Rules should be worded to be both positively stated and specific. Wording a rule positively means that the desired behavior, rather than the undesired behavior, is described. For example, "*use kind words*" is preferred over "*don't use mean words*." When determining the wording of rules, we also want to be sure that the rule is specific. To ensure specificity, we should make sure the desired behavior we are describing is observable and that the specific wording is appropriate for the students. Consider a second-grade classroom. The rule, *keep your feet on the floor*, is observable and easily understood by second graders, whereas *sit upright in your seat*, or *don't recline in your seat*, may not be understood. Creating rules collaboratively with students will help to ensure that all student voices are heard, and all students are represented in the classroom community.

When and How Should I Teach Classroom Routines and Procedures, Expectations, and Rules?

It is not enough to simply have routines, procedures, expectations, and rules in place; we must also explicitly teach them so that all students will be successful when applying them in our classrooms. Planning for instruction related to routines, procedures, expectations, and rules is similar to planning for other skill or knowledge lessons. Consider when each skill should be taught and how you will support maintenance of the skill throughout the school year and generalization of the skill across school settings. Consider how each skill should be taught so students are involved and engaged during instruction. Write lesson plans so your instruction is effective and efficient, and so you can reflect on the lesson and make adjustments for future instruction.

First, determine when you will teach each routine/procedure or expectation/rule. Typically, expectations and rules are taught the first few days of school and routines and procedures are taught right before they are needed for the first time (Kern & Clemens, 2007). To promote maintenance of the new skills, teachers should review them each time they are needed—more often at the start of the school year and less often as students demonstrate mastery of the skills. To promote generalization of the new skill, plan to review the skill when it will be used in a new environment. For example, if a rule is to look and listen while the teacher is talking, review the skill with students before they go to a class with a new teacher (e.g., art or physical education), or discuss with students how the skills used at school might also apply at home in certain situations.

Next, consider how each skill should be taught so students are involved and engaged during instruction. Some skills will be completely determined by the teacher (e.g., proper procedure for carrying a microscope) and will be taught by incorporating a simple instructional routine (teacher demonstration and student practice), and some skills will be determined through collaboration with students (e.g., classroom rules) and will be taught through classroom discussions and activities.

When writing lesson plans so your instruction is effective and efficient, determine a measurable lesson objective and how you will know whether students have learned the new skill, then plan learning activities. The sequence of the lessons and the learning activities you choose will depend on the specific skills you are teaching. For example, when teaching classroom rules after reviewing your SWPBIS expectations, you might want students to participate in determining the rules and how they are worded (see Elementary Example; Alter & Haydon, 2017).

Students can also participate in creating visual reminders to place at various locations around the classroom to support students' use of certain procedures. A poster might be placed by the cubbies in a kindergarten class showing what goes in the cubby and where to hang your coat. A poster might be placed near the supply shelves in a high school biology class showing how to properly carry or store a microscope. Teachers should also explicitly teach the social behaviors (see HLP 9) related to classroom rules and expectations. For example, if a classroom rule/expectation is for students to *be kind* to each other, a social behavior that you might need to teach is inviting a classmate to play a game or engaging a classmate in a conversation.

How Can I Maintain a Consistent Learning Environment Across Settings and Throughout the School Year?

Teachers should keep all aspects of the learning environment in mind each day to guard against drift from the use of routines and procedures, which will result in lost instructional time, and from adherence to expectations and rules, which will result in a chaotic learning environment. To do this, teachers should attend to consistency in two areas: across learning environments and throughout the school year. To maintain consistency across learning environments (e.g., other classrooms, cafeteria, playground), teachers should collaborate with colleagues to be sure that everyone knows routines, procedures, expectations, and rules for all school settings. If all teachers and staff align specific rules with SWPBIS expectations, the expectations and rules for each learning environment will be similar and therefore more easily enforced by all faculty and staff.

To maintain consistency throughout the school year, teachers and staff members should provide feedback to students regarding expectations and rules. Pre-corrections, reminding students of the expectation before an error is made, can be provided before students engage in a specific routine or procedure or in situations where remembering a specific expectation might be particularly important (e.g., appropriate behavior during a school assembly). Specific praise can be provided when students engage in appropriate behaviors. In a SWPBIS school, this is easily done through a token system (Ackerman et al., 2020) where students are given tickets when they are "caught being good." Students get to exchange tickets for tangible prizes or special privileges. Teachers should reteach routines, procedures, expectations, or rules when they become aware of patterns of drift or non-compliance. When reteaching is required, teachers should conduct the reteaching and then reflect on their frequency of pre-corrections and praise (see HLPs 8 and 22) to be sure they are providing enough of each.

What Does HLP 7 Look Like in a K-12 Classroom?

The school district where Mr. Davila teaches third grade and Ms. Garrett teaches 10th grade uses a District-Wide Positive Behavioral Interventions and Supports framework. The core expectations in the district are *Be Respectful, Be Responsible, Be Safe*. These core expectations look different in elementary school than they do in high school, and also different in each teacher's classroom, but the unified expectations promote consistency from school to school and teacher to teacher. Read the scenarios below to see how Mr. Davila and Ms. Garrett apply the expectations at their grade levels.

Elementary Example

Mr. Davila has been teaching third grade for 3 years. Over that time, he has reflected on his behavioral expectations and rules and made adjustments each year. Last year he planned a lesson where he and his students constructed the classroom rules together, and he noticed that his students were more invested in the classroom rules and even supported each other in following the rules throughout the school year. This year, he plans to do the same lesson. He starts with a general idea of five rules that relate to the district expectations of *Be Respectful, Be Responsible, Be Safe*. He thinks that the rules *use kind words* and *include everyone* sufficiently address *Be Respectful*; *take care of yourself and your things* and *try your best* address *Be Responsible*; and *keep your area neat* addresses *Be Safe*. With his draft rules in hand, he facilitates a discussion with his third graders about what it means to be respectful. He asks questions like "What does respect mean?", "What does it look like when someone is respectful?", "What do they say or do?", and "How do we know they are being respectful?" Students respond with comments such as "The person is nice," "They don't call someone names," "They aren't rude," "They do what the teacher says," and "They use manners". Mr. Davila writes all comments on the board and then asks students to work in table groups to think about how they can put some comments together to come up with two or three classroom rules about being respectful. Once each table group has a list, Mr. Davila asks each group to share their ideas. They see where groups came up with similar rules, they work through the wording to be sure that the rules are worded simply and positively, and then Mr. Davila writes them on the board. He facilitates the development of rules for *Be Responsible* and *Be Safe* the same way. Once they have all the classroom rules listed on the board, he assigns students to new small groups and supplies them with materials to make posters for each rule. The posters are hung on the wall in the front of the room so Mr. Davila and the students will be able to refer to them easily. Collaboratively creating the classroom rules promotes ownership of the expectations and rules and moves students toward becoming a community of learners that support each other.

Secondary Example

Ms. Garrett is beginning her second year as a 10th-grade biology teacher. At the end of her first year, she met with her colleague and mentor to discuss classroom management. She reported that she spent a lot of time "fussing with students" for improperly handling lab equipment. She was constantly worried about the new equipment being damaged. Her mentor suggested that she create and post visual reminders, with both words and graphics, of classroom procedures in key areas around the room and also spend a class session at the beginning of each semester teaching the proper procedures for handling the equipment. Ms. Garrett planned a lesson for the first class session in which she reviewed proper handling of lab equipment. She explained why it is important to handle the equipment in specific ways and how each item should be handled and stored. She showed students the posters that would remind them and had them practice with their lab partners, so the activity was interactive. As the school year got underway, and the equipment was used, she was sure to provide pre-corrections each time students gathered equipment and put it away. She also made sure to specifically praise students as they followed the procedures. In just the first few weeks of school, she was able to report to her mentor that this aspect of classroom management was going much smoother.

Summary

To establish a consistent, organized, and respectful learning environment, teachers need to carefully consider their classroom environment and how they will convey, teach, and support classroom routines, procedures, expectations, and rules so all students feel confident navigating the learning environment and are motivated to learn.

When considering the classroom environment and how to arrange the physical space of the classroom, teachers should think about safety and accessibility. The teacher and support staff should be able to see all parts of the classroom and all students should be able to access materials as needed. When planning seating arrangements, teachers should think strategically about where students should sit to provide adequate support for self-regulation skills and to promote social inclusion and pro-social behaviors. Teachers should also consider ways to provide students options for seating (e.g., standing desks, beanbags, pillows) so they have ownership over their learning preferences. When considering classroom routines and procedures, teachers should plan for routines and procedures that support efficient student movement in the classroom so that instructional time can be maximized. Additionally, teachers should consider explicitly teaching instructional routines, so students know what to do during certain phases of a lesson (e.g., what to do during a Content Enhancement Routine lesson) or learning activities (e.g., group work).

When considering classroom expectations and rules, teachers should first remember to align their classroom expectations and rules with SWPBIS expectations but adjust for grade level and student needs. Then, they should think about two areas: learning expectations and behavioral expectations. When thinking about learning expectations, teachers should consider having expectations and rules related to work effort and work products. These rules will support students' ownership of their own learning and help teachers to apply expectations consistently with all students. When thinking about behavioral expectations, teachers should be sure that the related rules are few, positively stated, and constructed collaboratively with students.

When a classroom runs smoothly because there are clear and consistent expectations, rules, routines, and procedures in place, instruction can take center stage. This chapter provided teachers with a practical understanding of how to establish and maintain a consistent, organized, and respectful learning environment to transform their classroom environment from unpredictable and stressful to consistent, organized, and respectful.

Chapter Review

1. What do I need to consider when planning my classroom design, organization, and arrangement?
2. What does a typical day look like in my class? What routines will make the day run smoothly? What instructional routines will allow for continued instructional momentum? Which routines include specific procedures that should be followed?
3. What are my school's learning and behavioral expectations for students? What classroom expectations align with these? What rules will support students in meeting expectations?
4. How and when will I teach classroom routines and procedures? How and when will I teach school/classroom expectations? How will I collaboratively determine classroom rules?
5. How can I ensure that I maintain high expectations for academic and behavioral success for all students in my classroom?

References

Ackerman, A. K. B., Samudre, M., & Allday, R. A. (2020). Practical components for getting the most from a token economy. *TEACHING Exceptional Children*, *52*(4), 242-249. https://doi.org/10.1177/0040059919892022

Ahn, J. N., Hu, D., & Vega, M. (2020). "Do as I do, not as I say": Using social learning theory to unpack the impact of role models on students' outcomes in education. *Social and Personality Psychology Compass*, *14*(2). https://doi.org/10.1111/spc3.12517

Alter, P., & Haydon, T. (2017). Characteristics of effective classroom rules: A review of the literature. *Teacher Education and Special Education*, *40*(2), 114-127. https://doi.org/10.1177/0888406417700962

Archer, A. L., & Hughes, C. A. (2011). *Explicit instruction: Effective and efficient teaching*. Guilford Press.

Ayers, W. (2016). These children won't learn. *Kappa Delta Pi Record*, *52*(3), 106-111.

Bulgren, J. (2006). Integrated content enhancement routines: Responding to the needs of adolescents with disabilities in rigorous inclusive secondary content classes. *TEACHING Exceptional Children*, *38*(6), 54-58.

Cangelosi, J. S. (2014). *Classroom management strategies: Gaining and maintaining students' cooperation* (7th ed.). Wiley.

Evans, M., & Boucher, A. (2015). Optimizing the power of choice: Supporting student autonomy to foster motivation and engagement in learning. *Mind, Brain, and Education*, *9*(22), 87-91.

Flanagan, A., Cormier, D., & Bulut, O. (2020). Achievement may be rooted in teacher expectations: examining the differential influences of ethnicity, years of teaching, and classroom behaviour. *School Psychology of Education*, *23*, 1429-1448.

Gentrup, S., Lorenz, G., Cornelia, K., & Kogan, I. (2020). Self-fulfilling prophecies in the classroom: Teacher expectations, teacher feedback and student achievement. *Learning and Instruction*, *66*, Article 101296. https://doi.org/10.1016/j.learninstruc.2019.101296

Horner, R. H., Sugai, G., & Anderson, C. M. (2010). Examining the evidence base for school-wide positive behavior support. *Focus on Exceptional Children*, *42*(8), 1-14.

Kern, L., & Clemens, N. H. (2007). Antecedent strategies to promote appropriate classroom behavior. *Psychology in the Schools*, *44*(1), 65-75. https://doi.org/10.1002/pits.20206

Kerr, M., & Nelson, C. M. (2010). *Strategies for addressing behavior problems in the classroom* (6th ed.). Pearson.

Korinek, L., & DeFur S. H. (2016). Supporting student self-regulation to access the general education curriculum. *TEACHING Exceptional Children*, *48*(5), 232-242. https://doi.org/10.1177/0040059915626134

McLeskey, J., Barringer, M.-D., Billingsley, B., Brownell, M., Jackson, D., Kennedy, M., Lewis, T., Maheady, L., Rodriguez, J., Scheeler, M. C., Winn, J., & Ziegler, D. (2017). *High-leverage practices in special education*. Council for Exceptional Children & CEEDAR Center.

Mitchell, B., Stormont, M., & Gage, N. (2011). Tier two interventions implemented within the context of a tiered prevention framework. *Behavioral Disorders*, *36*(4), 241-261.

Myers, D., Freeman, J., Simonsen, B., & Sugai, G. (2017). Classroom management with exceptional learners. *TEACHING Exceptional Children*, *49*(4), 223-230. https://doi.org/10.1177/0040059916685064

Ng, J., Morbach Sweeney, H., & Mitchiner, M. (2013). Let's sit together: Exploring the potential for human relations education at lunch. *Journal of Thought*, *Summer*, 65-77.

Rawlings Lester, R., Bolton Allanson, P., & Notar, C. (2017). Routines are the foundation of classroom management. *Education*, *137*(4), 398-412.

Simonsen, B., Freeman, J., Goodman, S., Mitchell, B., Swain-Bradway, J., Flannery, B., Sugai, G., George, H., & Putnam, B. (2015). *Supporting and responding to behavior: Evidence-based classroom strategies for teachers.* U.S. Office of Special Education Programs.

Tobia, V., Simona, S., Cerina, V., Manca, S., & Fornara, F. (2020). The influence of classroom seating arrangement on children's cognitive processes in primary school: the role of individual variables. *Current Psychology, 41*, 6522-6533. https://doi.org/10.1007/s12144-020-01154-9

Trussell, R. P. (2008). Classroom universals to prevent problem behaviors. *Intervention in School and Clinic, 43*(3), 179-185.

van den Berg, Y. H. M., Segers-Antonius, H. N., & Cillessen, H. N. (2012). Changing peer perceptions and victimization through classroom arrangements: A field experiment. *Journal of Child Psychology, 40*, 403-412. https://doi.org/10.1007/s10802-011-9567-6

van den Berg, Y. H. M., & Stoltz, S. (2018). Enhancing social inclusion of children with externalizing problems through classroom seating arrangements: A randomized controlled trial. *Journal of Emotional and Behavioral Disorders, 25*(1). 31-41. https://doi.org/10.1177/1063426617740561

What Feedback Guides "Improved" Behavior?

Shantel M. Farnan, EdD

HLP 8

Provide positive and constructive feedback to guide students' learning and behavior.

INTRODUCTION

Teachers are often being given and providing feedback to others. Feedback is important and necessary for both academic instruction and social/emotional and behavioral support. High-Leverage Practice (HLP) 8 focuses on providing positive and constructive feedback to guide students' behavior, while HLP 22 focuses on feedback to guide student learning. They are very connected, as you will see. Most teachers, if reflecting upon their own practice, do provide feedback to their students, but is that feedback substantive enough for replication of positive behaviors or specific enough to change undesired behaviors? This chapter will dive deeper into the specifics of effective feedback including the components, types, methods, and characteristics for improving student behavior in both academic and social classroom situations. Throughout this chapter you will see the complementary practices between HLP 8 and evidence-based strategies integrated together to implement this HLP well in a classroom.

Owiny, R. L., & Cornelius, K. E. *The Practical Guide to High-Leverage Practices in Special Education: The Purposeful "How" to Enhance Classroom Rigor* (pp. 117-125).

CHAPTER OBJECTIVES

- → Define positive and constructive feedback as it pertains to learning and behavior.
- → Describe the various types, methods, and characteristics of feedback.
- → State how HLP 8 is connected to other HLPs and evidence-based practices (EBPs) and the rationale for positive and constructive feedback appearing twice in the HLPs.
- → Explain specific EBPs to deliver feedback for students to improve behavioral performance and reach goals.

KEY TERMS

- **constructive feedback:** The act of giving information through the description of performance in an observed situation.
- **contingent:** Dependent on circumstances, events, or conditions.
- **corrective feedback:** A form of performance feedback used to improve student achievement or behavior typically provided by teachers to reinforce expectations and to correct student errors.
- **Positive Behavioral Interventions and Supports (PBIS):** An evidence-based, tiered framework for supporting students' behavioral, academic, social, emotional, and mental health.
- **self-regulation:** The control of one's behavior through the use of self-monitoring (keeping a record of behavior), self-evaluation (assessing the information obtained during self-monitoring), and self-reinforcement (rewarding oneself for appropriate behavior or for attaining a goal).
- **SMART goals:** Stands for Specific, Measurable, Attainable, Results-oriented, and Time-bound and is often how individualized education program goals are written.

Pre-service and novice special education teachers need and should be provided repeated authentic experiences to apply their knowledge and skills (Leko et al., 2015) and to receive feedback to improve their practice. These feedback practices are important to special education teachers to drive their teaching behaviors and instruction of students, as well as support them in meeting their goals as a teacher. Even though teachers have been taught about feedback, have been given, and received both informal and formal feedback themselves, this does not always "translate into the most effective use of this practice within schools" (Kennedy et al., 2018). Teachers need to be prepared to teach all learners through the coupling of High-Leverage Practices (HLPs) and evidence-based practices (EBPs), including those that focus on both social/emotional/behavioral and instruction domains such as HLP 8.

In this chapter, we demonstrate how using HLP 8—"*Provide positive and constructive feedback to guide students' learning and behavior*" has implications for the domain focused on social/emotional/behavioral and is used to guide behavior and increase student motivation, engagement, and independence. This chapter will also explore the various types and characteristics of feedback and specific EBPs to deliver feedback for students to improve behavioral performance and reach goals. For more information and other examples focused on improving student learning, see Chapter 22.

What Is HLP 8 and How Is It Connected to Other HLPs and Evidence-Based Practices?

As the HLP definition states, "The purpose of feedback is to guide student learning and behavior and increase student motivation, engagement, and independence, leading to improved student learning and behavior" (McLeskey et al., 2017). For feedback to be effective, it must be constructive, strategically delivered, and goal-directed (Kennedy et al., 2018). It is imperative for feedback to expand the student's learning and therefore needs to be specific and focused toward a manageable goal the learner has for themselves. Whether feedback is verbal, nonverbal, or written, the purpose must be to confirm progress while also correcting misunderstandings or confusion the student may be having about their learning. Kennedy et al. (2018) notes, "timely, contingent, genuine, and meaningful feedback helps the student know the areas needing improvement, where they are in relation to their goal, and ways to improve their performance."

Due to the nature of HLP 8 having dual implications for both the instruction and social/emotional/behavioral domains, and it being used to guide student learning and behavior, it is no surprise it is one of many HLPs you will see in many chapters of this book; it is a classic example of the intertwined functionality of the HLPs. It is common to see HLP 8 used in an overarching manner in the following ways:

- When providing explicit instruction regarding behavior (see HLP 16)
- When using modeling as part of explicit instruction
- When students are early in learning new appropriate and expected behaviors or practicing a new behavior skill
- When students are becoming proficient and self-regulating those behaviors (HLP 14)
- When becoming proficient with those behavior skills across multiple settings (HLP 21)

For example, components of explicit instruction such as pacing are often used to

> increase on-task behavior for students that may have difficulty with this behavioral aspect of learning. Self-regulating behavior can come in many forms including self-monitoring and self-instruction or self-talk. The benefits of self-regulation have been found in more than 30 years of research and, specific to behavior, is a way for students to "analyze their behavior, identify problems, determine why certain behaviors occur, predict when problems will arise, and learn how to avoid these incidents. (IRIS Center, 2008, p. 2)

Self-regulation has been noted to have substantial benefits and obviously the attention is on the student. HLP 8 focuses on increasing student motivation, engagement, and independence and these are by-products as a student begins to self-regulate and self-advocate. HLP 3—"*Collaborate with families to support student learning and secure needed services*" strengthens HLP 8 with "the goal of fostering self-determination over time. Teachers also work with families to self-advocate and support their children's learning" (McLeskey et al., 2017, p. 18).

Collaborating with parents is instrumental in behavioral intervention and the most success comes when addressing these challenging behaviors is done in partnership between teachers and parents (Fettig et al., 2013; Marshall & Mirenda, 2002). HLP 3, with its emphasis on collaborating with families to support student learning, is another way to provide feedback to guide student behavior as identified in HLP 8. See Table 8-1 for a list of the EBPs discussed in this chapter, their aligned HLPs, and useful resources to help you understand and implement.

Throughout this chapter, you will be provided a breakdown of the four components of HLP 8, which include feedback being (a) goal-directed, (b) constructive, (c) immediate, and (d) positive. The following sections will help you determine the various types of feedback, the characteristics of effective feedback, and when to provide feedback in order for it to effectively guide student behavior.

Table 8-1. Alignment of HLPs and Resources for Evidence-Based Practices

EBP SUPPORT WITH HLP 8	RELATED HLPS	RESOURCES
Explicit instruction	16	https://youtu.be/N0T5zolYri4 https://explicitinstruction.org/
Self-regulation	14	https://iris.peabody.vanderbilt.edu/module/srs/cresource/q1/p02/
PBIS	3, 9	https://www.pbis.org/

Throughout these sections we will provide you with EBPs, strategies, and examples of feedback to assist in increasing student motivation, engagement (see HLP 18), and independence (see HLP 21), leading to improved student learning and behavior (McLeskey et al., 2017).

What Types of Feedback and Associated Evidence-Based Practices Are Utilized in Both Academic and Social Settings?

When learning more about feedback, it is important to focus on the fact that feedback should be positive and constructive, as well as being utilized in varied formats such as verbal, non-verbal, and written. Positive and constructive feedback can be given through instructive or corrective ways depending on the situation in which the feedback is being provided. The goal of positive and respectful feedback is to focus on student success and progress rather than deficits. This includes making sure to focus on actions rather than personal judgments (Kennedy et al., 2018). While the goal of constructive feedback is to support a student as they progress toward mastery of a new behavioral approach, this includes providing steps for the student to take in response to the feedback (Kennedy et al., 2018). An example of constructive feedback in a behavioral situation would be if a student is attempting to interact with others and is not able to use appropriate and effective communication skills. In this case the student resorts to sarcasm or taking jokes too far. To provide feedback, the teacher may say, "I need to let you know you spoke with your new friends in ways they may not be ready for at this time. When you responded to their request to work with you on the project you said, 'You can't hang.' What are your thoughts on this?" This example of constructive feedback states the purpose, describes what was observed, focuses on the observation, does not infer past it with perceived intentions, and gives the student a chance to respond (Radford University, n.d.). Next steps could involve corrective feedback, which includes suggestions, summarizing, and support.

Corrective feedback is particularly important to student behavioral success and is connected to the EBP of explicit instruction as a key instructional element (see HLP 16; Archer & Hughes, 2011). According to Archer and Hughes (2011), it is necessary to provide students with immediate and affirmative corrective feedback. This includes being specific and informative in your feedback. You then follow up regarding the student's response with a focus on the correct versus incorrect behavioral response. It is also noted corrective feedback should be delivered with appropriate tone and ends with the student giving the correct response. This immediate feedback helps ensure high rates of success and increases the target behavior (Archer & Hughes, 2011; Cornelius & Nagro, 2014). This allows the student to make immediate changes and keeps them from practicing inappropriate behavior. This also helps the student know exactly why they are receiving this feedback (Kennedy et al., 2018).

As future teachers, this type of performance feedback is something that should be modeled for you within your own educator preparation programs. This best practice is known to improve target teacher behaviors to better prepare teachers. Performance feedback, as defined by Cornelius and Nagro (2014), is a "critique of observed behavior that is immediate, specific, positive, and corrective when needed, designed to move the recipient toward a desired performance" (p. 135). In the previous example that began with constructive feedback, it could continue with corrective feedback when needed in order to move the student toward desired communication and interactions with new friends. As a teacher, you could provide corrective feedback by reiterating the main strategies the student could do differently, end on a positive note of confidence in the student, and check to make sure the student understands through summarizing (Radford University, n.d.).

What Are the Characteristics of Positive and Constructive Feedback?

We will break this section down to provide you definitions and examples of the characteristics of positive and constructive feedback.

Goal Directed

When utilizing positive and constructive feedback with students in order to guide their behavior (HLP 8), it needs to be goal-directed. Future teachers of special education, through their courses, are beginning to become familiar with SMART goals. The plan would then be for these teacher candidates to learn to transform those Specific, Measurable, Attainable, Results-Oriented , and Time-bound goals (IRIS Center, 2019) into an action with students and use positive and constructive feedback to meet the goal. This focus on SMART goals provides more clear and specific guidance on what the student is working on achieving in the area of behavior and lends itself to more consistent language that is goal-directed as well. An example of the connection between a student's SMART goal on their individualized education program (IEP) and positive and constructive feedback may be as follows if continuing with the example prior.

- SMART IEP goal: During a 20-minute collaborative class time, the student will independently interact with at least two classmates, without the use of sarcasm or joking on 8 out of 10 collaborative work times by the end of the school year.
- Goal-directed feedback: The above SMART goal example is a clear goal set for the student they should be made aware of and then teachers should provide feedback to inform the student on how to improve the behavior and obtain the goal. This may sound something like, "I really like that you responded with a positive statement when your classmate offered a suggestion within your group. That is how you should respond. When we get new group members in math later today, how about we see if you can say a similar comment to a different group member."

Specific

With such a significant emphasis on feedback being positive, there are many teachers who are incredibly good at using positive praise with students, such as saying statements such as "Good job" or "Super." This may be positive, but it is empty praise. In order for feedback to also be constructive and improve the target behavior, it must be behavior-specific. This is the most powerful positive feedback (IRIS Center, 2014). As noted in the goal-directed section, "specific" is the "S" in SMART goals, and this needs to carry over into the implementation of providing positive and constructive feedback as well. IRIS Center (2014) defines behavior-specific praise as "a positive declarative statement directed toward a child or group of children that describes a desirable behavior in specific, observable, and measurable terms." To give behavior-specific praise, you clearly tell the specific student what they have done correctly. For example, in the example where sarcasm and joking are an issue, you could say, "Nice work telling your classmate you wanted to work with them again in a group." This provides the student specific details about a behavior goal they are working on and about the progress they are making. By saying more than merely "Good job," the teacher is reinforcing the positive behavior while providing details about how the student is performing on their behavioral goal.

Timely and Contingent

Just to reiterate the emphasis on feedback in HLP 8 we are reminded that it states, "Feedback may be verbal, nonverbal, or written, and should be timely, contingent, genuine, meaningful, age appropriate, and at rates commensurate with task and phase of learning (i.e., acquisition, fluency, maintenance)" (McLeskey et al., 2017, p. 21). This section will focus on feedback beginning timely and contingent. Since behavior is observed through the student's actions (performance) based on what is being asked of them, it is important that this feedback be given immediately. Cornelius and Nagro (2014) note this type of "performance feedback has the greatest impact when recipients hear specific descriptions and analyses immediately following their performance, including how to correct their performance when necessary" (p. 135). Timeliness could also be viewed in the sense of whether the feedback fits into the phase of learning and the expectations for the student at that time. For example, giving feedback on how a student approached a spontaneous interaction with a peer they were unfamiliar with may not be appropriate if the student has only been currently working on prompted responses with familiar peers. That student in that situation may not be ready for this type of feedback yet as it does not fit with the current instruction, where they are at in their phase of learning, or what is currently expected of them (Kennedy et al., 2018).

Further exploration of the specifics of timely and contingent feedback suggest it should be given on an appropriate schedule. According to Kennedy et al. (2018), feedback should be provided frequently when the focused behavior is new to the student. Often once a skill or behavior has been mastered, the teachers working with the student look for that behavior to be maintained and generalized (McLeskey et al., 2017), and at that point in the learning process the feedback timeliness could be less frequent than when the behavior was first introduced. The level of frequency needs to be determined on an individual basis depending on the student, the behavior being addressed, and the IEP team's input.

WHAT DOES HLP 8 LOOK LIKE IN A K-12 CLASSROOM?

Elementary Example

Littlefield Elementary School teachers are already familiar with feedback as they have implemented School-Wide Positive Behavioral Interventions and Supports (SWPBIS) and have "implemented the core features of evidence-based practices" (Center on PBIS, 2022) including:

- Establishing a continuum of recognition strategies to provide specific feedback and encourage contextually appropriate behavior.
- Establishing a continuum of response strategies to provide specific feedback, reteach contextually appropriate behavior, and discourage contextually inappropriate behavior.

At Littlefield Elementary School there is a sixth-grade student who has a SMART IEP goal written as follows, "During a 20-minute collaborative class time, Shannon will independently interact with at least two peers, without the use of sarcasm or joking on 8 out of 10 collaborative work times by the end of the school year." Mr. Casey, the teacher working with Shannon, is aiming toward increasing his use of positive and behavior-specific feedback, coupled with additional behavioral intervention strategies and documentation tools to help Shannon reach their goal. Since this goal and behavior skill is new for Shannon, Mr. Casey is implementing strategies to increase the amount of positive, behavior-specific praise and reinforcement used with Shannon. Mr. Casey collaborates with his co-worker and fellow sixth-grade teacher (HLP 1), Ms. Sullivan, to come into his classroom and count the number of times he is currently using positive feedback with Shannon. This is a wonderful way for teachers to monitor their own behavior (HLP 6). Documenting the teacher's behavior using an outside evaluator is a great first step, but will need to move more toward self-management strategies to ensure that Mr. Casey is "providing more positive feedback then giving directions or correcting inappropriate behavior" (IRIS Center, 2014, p. 6).

After Mr. Casey determines his own baseline for the number of times he provides positive feedback by using Ms. Sullivan's data, he then moves onto his next step where he consults the remainder of the IEP team (HLP 1) on how frequent this feedback should occur when addressing the new skill for Shannon involving interacting without the use of sarcasm or joking. Once that frequency level has been determined, Mr. Casey will begin one of the following two strategies to monitor the frequency of the positive feedback. One strategy would be to put the number of rubber bands needed to meet the predetermined frequency count on one wrist and move each rubber band to the other wrist whenever he provides a positive descriptive comment to Shannon with the goal of moving all the rubber bands over throughout the day (Wright, n.d.). The other option would be to tally the number of times positive feedback is used during the day on a sticky note or a clipboard. After these two self-management strategies have been implemented, if Mr. Casey finds he is not meeting the frequency schedule it would be suggested he use a timer to cue oneself to provide positive feedback at regular intervals, which could be done discreetly by using a smartwatch. Another benefit of instituting a schedule is by Mr. Casey modeling timeliness (HLP 16); this leading by example empowers students to do so as well (Crisis Prevention Institute, 2021).

The rubber band strategy in this situation was used for the teacher to self-monitor feedback provided to the student. This can also be used as a behavior management strategy (HLP 14) for students to self-monitor their emerging behavior. A chart for progress monitoring is included in Figure 8-1.

The above example is used to provide strategies focused on goal-directed, positive, constructive, timely, and contingent feedback. This could be coupled with the examples of instructive and corrective feedback shared in the What Types of Feedback and Associated Evidence-Based Practices Are Utilized in Both Academic and Social Settings? section of this chapter earlier. In addition, there are additional interventions and strategies and documentation of these strategies that could be used to support the feedback described in HLP 8. Those strategies will be described as it would pertain to a similar student, but in the secondary classroom.

Secondary Example

Marty is an eighth-grade student who is extremely academically talented but does not like to complete homework and will often disrupt class with interruptions such as jokes, poking fun at others, sometimes getting physical in his approach to other students, and getting out of his seat and even outside of the classroom. The IEP team has completed a functional behavioral assessment (FBA; HLP 10) and has determined the behavior is due to avoidance (mostly of the homework). The team has developed a behavior intervention plan (BIP) and the replacement strategies for the behavior include the adults (teachers, paraprofessionals, etc.) using corrective feedback that is instructive as well. In this situation, when Marty begins to joke, poke, or leave his seat you, as the teacher, would start with reiterating the main strategies Marty could do differently such as, "Marty, my expectation would be that at this time you ask me if you can take a break from your homework or I can help you come up with another new strategy to try." The next step would be to provide a note of confidence in Marty and make sure he understands through summarizing, "Marty, I believe in the fact that you will ask for a break, take a short one, and then go back to work until your watch timer goes off as planned."

<table>
<tr><td colspan="6">Date:
Strategy being monitored or student behavior problem being monitored:</td></tr>
<tr><td>Timeframe
Content area</td><td>8:00 am-9:00 am
______</td><td>9:00 am-10:00 am
______</td><td>10:00 am-11:00 am
______</td><td>11:00 am-12:00 am
______</td><td>12:00 am-1:00 am
______</td></tr>
<tr><td>Teacher signature</td><td></td><td></td><td></td><td></td><td></td></tr>
<tr><td>Frequency of strategy or behavior problem</td><td></td><td></td><td></td><td></td><td></td></tr>
<tr><td colspan="6"></td></tr>
<tr><td>Timeframe
Content area</td><td>1:00 pm-2:00 pm
______</td><td>2:00 pm-3:00 pm
______</td><td colspan="3" rowspan="3">Notes</td></tr>
<tr><td>Teacher signature</td><td></td><td></td></tr>
<tr><td>Frequency of strategy or behavior problem</td><td></td><td></td></tr>
</table>

Figure 8-1. Strategy used to monitor the frequency of positive feedback.

This summarizing and checking for understanding correspond with the "check" step in the HLP of explicit instruction (HLP 16). You can also see in this example the feedback was given as outlined earlier: behavior specific and immediate (timely).

This strategy of corrective and instructive feedback connects with HLP 9 as well in which it is stressed to teach social behaviors, which include communication and self-management (McLeskey et al., 2017). In this case, it is clear Marty is struggling with both of those social behaviors and explicit instruction on them would be beneficial coupled with the components of HLP 8, including the component of feedback. These two HLPs are closely related as HLP 9 requires teachers to prompt the student to use the skill and that can be done through feedback as well. This is also important as otherwise the student continues to, in essence, "practice" the non-examples of disrupting class with interruptions such as jokes, poking fun at others, sometimes getting physical in their approach to other students, and getting out of their seat and even outside of the classroom. If the teacher does not intervene Marty can assume his responses are correct. In Marty's situation it is important to highlight what the correct behavioral response would be and to follow up at another time with instructive feedback through explicit instruction if needed.

Summary

Feedback is used when implementing many of the other HLPs in the Instruction and Social/Emotional/Behavioral domains and is connected to so many of them as described throughout this chapter. This practice of providing positive and constructive feedback could be viewed as one of the most important (Kennedy et al., 2018). HLP 8 focuses on providing positive and constructive feedback to guide students' learning and behavior, and throughout this chapter you saw examples of this and a few EBPs that correspond with this HLP.

Effective positive and constructive feedback can be provided verbally, non-verbally, or written and is goal-directed, specific, timely, and contingent. EBPs such as PBIS, explicit instruction, and self-regulation are embedded within the use of HLP 8 and the further breakdown of the use of corrective or instructive feedback. The implementation of delivering positive and constructive feedback is used to guide behavior and increase student motivation, engagement, and independence. It is also noted this HLP and corresponding EBPs are effective at both the elementary and secondary level.

Chapter Review

1. Describe positive and constructive feedback as it pertains to learning and behavior.
2. How is delivering positive and constructive feedback used to guide behavior and increase student motivation, engagement, and independence?
3. In what aspects does HLP 8 connect with other HLPs and EBPs?
4. Provide examples of the types of feedback and associated EBPs that are utilized to promote student behavioral success.
5. Name and explain the four characteristics of positive and constructive feedback.
6. Choose an EBP or strategy you learned in this chapter and identify how you will use it in your next teaching and learning opportunity with students.

References

Archer, A. L., & Hughes, C. A. (2011). *Explicit instruction: Effective and efficient teaching*. Guilford Press.

Center on PBIS. (2022). *Positive behavioral interventions & supports*. www.pbis.org

Cornelius, K. E., & Nagro, S. A. (2014). Evaluating the evidence base of performance feedback in preservice special education teacher training. *Teacher Education and Special Education*, *37*(2), 133-146. https://doi.org/10.1177/0888406414521837

Crisis Prevention Institute. (2021). *A school-wide approach to managing student behavior*. www.crisisprevention.com

Fettig, A., Schultz, T. R., & Ostrosky, M. M. (2013). Collaborating with parents in using effective strategies to reduce children's challenging behaviors. *Young Exceptional Children*, *16*(1), 30-41. https://doi.org/10.1177/1096250612473127

IRIS Center. (2008). *SRSD: Using learning strategies to enhance student learning*. https://iris.peabody.vanderbilt.edu/module/srs/

IRIS Center. (2014). *Early childhood behavior management: Developing and teaching rules*. https://iris.peabody.vanderbilt.edu/module/ecbm/

IRIS Center. (2019). *IEPs: Developing high-quality individualized education programs*. https://iris.peabody.vanderbilt.edu/module/iep01/

Kennedy, M. J., Peeples, K. N., Romig, J. E., Mathews, H. M., & Rodgers, W. J. (2018). *High-leverage practices #8 & #22: Provide positive and constructive feedback to guide students' learning and behavior*. https://highleveragepractices.org/hlps-8-and-22-provide-positive-and-constructive-feedback-guide-students-learning-and-behavior

Leko, M., Brownell, M., Sindelar, P., & Kiely, M. (2015). Envisioning the future of special education personnel preparation in a standards-based era. *Exceptional Children*, *82*, 25-43. https://doi.org/10.1177/0014402915598782

Marshall, J. K., & Mirenda, P. (2002). Parent—professional collaboration for positive behavior support in the home. *Focus on Autism and Other Developmental Disabilities*, *17*(4), 216-228. https://doi.org/10.1177/10883576020170040401

McLeskey, J., Barringer, M.-D., Billingsley, B., Brownell, M., Jackson, D., Kennedy, M., Lewis, T., Maheady, L., Rodriguez, J., Scheeler, M. C., Winn, J., & Ziegler, D. (2017). *High-leverage practices in special education*. Council for Exceptional Children & CEEDAR Center.

Radford University. (n.d.). *Constructive feedback*. https://www.radford.edu/content/dam/colleges/cgps/dnp/docs/Constructive-Feedback.pdf

Wright, J. (n.d.). *Rubber band intervention*. Intervention Central. https://www.interventioncentral.org/

How Do I Teach Social Skills?

Jennifer D. Walker, PhD
and Ruby L. Owiny, PhD

HLP 9
Teach social behaviors.

INTRODUCTION

Students come to school with a myriad of academic and social needs. While much of instruction is focused on academics, many students have social skill needs that require direct instruction to be successful both in the classroom and outside of school. This instruction should be based on students' needs and targeted at relevant circumstances and settings of students' lives. This chapter outlines the importance of social skill instruction. The varying ways social skills can be embedded into instruction will be outlined, including the development of social skill lessons, practice opportunities, and generalization strategies to ensure not only academic success but social success as well.

Owiny, R. L., & Cornelius, K. E. *The Practical Guide to High-Leverage Practices in Special Education: The Purposeful "How" to Enhance Classroom Rigor* (pp. 127-139).

CHAPTER OBJECTIVES

- → Explain the importance of social skill instruction.
- → Describe how to assess needs and create social skill goals.
- → Identify daily opportunities to embed social skill instruction in the classroom and in the school environment.
- → Deliver social skill lessons based on needs assessments and ongoing data collection.

KEY TERMS

- **character education:** Focuses on moral and ethical values and dimensions such as responsibility, trustworthiness, respect, and citizenship. Definitions may vary widely, depending on life experiences and background.
- **social competence:** Refers to how others evaluate an individual's ability to perform specific social skills across situations and contexts.
- **social skills:** A set of skills individuals perform within situations and contexts. These skills help individuals communicate and interact appropriately with others.
- **social skills instruction:** A way to explicitly teach behaviors to students who need social skills development. This includes assessment, planning, direct instruction, practice, and generalization.

Social skills are a much-needed set of skills for success in school and life. In fact, the "ability to successfully interact and to navigate difficult social situations" is the hallmark of social skills (McDaniel et al., 2022). Additionally, the ability to collaborate, cooperate, communicate clearly, and engage appropriately in teamwork are 21st century skills (New South Wales Department of Education, 2017) and key to success in the workforce, post-secondary education, and life in general. Students must be able to employ 21st century skills for success in school and life. According to the Glossary of Education Reform (2016), 21st century skills are defined as,

> a broad set of knowledge, skills, work habits, and character traits that are believed—by educators, school reformers, college professors, employers, and others—to be critically important to success in today's world, particularly in collegiate programs and contemporary careers and workplaces. Generally speaking, 21st century skills can be applied in all academic subject areas, and in all educational, career, and civic settings throughout a student's life.

Nailing down an exact definition of social skills can be difficult; however, a good rule of thumb when thinking about what constitutes a social skill is asking whether a student needs a particular skill to be successful in interacting with others, such as collaboration, taking turns, and following rules and social norms, or within themselves, such as those skills around motivation, self-efficacy, and self-advocacy. The Universal Design for Learning (UDL) principle of engagement plays a role in social skills as motivation, coping skills, and collaboration are a part of one's ability to be a purposeful, motivated learner. In the context of meeting the needs of students with disabilities (SWD), social skills include working toward appropriate interactions with others and what we often think of as work ethic, the ability to strategize how to begin a task, develop the steps to complete a multi-step project, and to persist when learning gets tough. You may be familiar with social-emotional learning (SEL), which encompasses social skills and is important for students' development. The appropriate use of social skills can be difficult for SWD.

Oftentimes, SWD, particularly those with emotional and behavior disorders, autism spectrum disorder, attention-deficit/hyperactivity disorder, and intellectual disabilities, struggle to engage in appropriate social skills and need intensive, direct instruction to fully and appropriately use social skills (McDaniel et al., 2022). To address the social skill needs of SWD, teachers should embed instruction into their daily curriculum planning. This begins with identifying skill needs through assessments, specifically addressing whether the student does not know the skill ("acquisition") or if the student does not understand when or how to use the skill ("performance"). This distinction is important as it guides instruction and improves skill acquisition and generalization outcomes. Much like an academic lesson plan, students should receive direct instruction on the skill, have numerous opportunities to practice the skill (think about the UDL principle of action and expression to provide practice opportunities in varying ways), and receive specific, immediate positive and corrective feedback (Allday, 2012; Sugai & Lewis, 1996), a feature of explicit instruction (High-Leverage Practice [HLP] 16). Finally, teachers should provide opportunities for generalization to support the longevity of the skill acquisition.

In this chapter, we explain why HLP 9—"*Teach social behaviors*" is important for SWD, and how skills can be embedded into daily instruction. Using needs assessments and instruction, teachers can design social skills lessons that support the learning process, which includes the four following phases: acquisition, performance (also referred to as *fluency*), generalization, and maintenance of new skills. Embedding social skills instruction into daily planning enables students to see the real-world application of the desired skills and will help students experience success both academically and socially. This instruction does not need to be intensive or time-consuming, but opportunities do exist for teachers to provide all levels of support at the classroom, small group, and individual levels.

What Is HLP 9?

For HLP 9, McLeskey et al. (2017) give this direction for teaching social skills:

> Teachers should explicitly teach appropriate interpersonal skills, including communication, and self-management, aligning lessons with classroom and schoolwide expectations for student behavior. Prior to teaching, teachers should determine the nature of the social skill challenge. If students do not know how to perform a targeted social skill, direct social skill instruction should be provided until mastery is achieved. If students display performance problems, the appropriate social skill should initially be taught, then emphasis should shift to prompting the student to use the skill and ensuring the "appropriate" behavior accesses the same or a similar outcome (i.e., is reinforcing to the student) as the problem behavior.

Simply stated, SWD are often challenged with navigating social situations, and because of this, social skill instruction should be integrated into the daily curriculum (McLeskey et al., 2017). This instruction should be aligned with classroom and schoolwide expectations while also considering individualized needs of students. To begin instruction, teachers should identify the social skills needed by individuals or groups of students and when the skill should be used. As teachers assess students' needs, they should also consider whether the student needs the skill due to skill deficits (student does not know how to perform the skill) or skill performance challenges (student does not know when or where to perform the skill). Once a needs assessment has been conducted, instruction can begin.

First, teachers should instruct, or tell, students how to perform the social skill and when to use it. This is the acquisition phase of learning in which direct and explicit instruction occurs (HLP 16). This is the presentation phase of direct instruction. Then, teachers should demonstrate, or provide modeling, of the social skill, which is the I Do phase of learning. Once students are shown what the skill looks and sounds like, plus when to use the skill, they should engage in guided practice, through role plays and other means of practice, the We Do phase of learning. Students should be given plenty of opportunities to practice while receiving feedback (HLPs 8 and 22) to develop fluency in using the skill. In other words, the skill becomes automatic. Finally, generalization and maintenance should be ongoing and supported through specific instruction and feedback, reminders, and/or prompts.

Social skills, as well as academic skills, are important for addressing the needs of the whole child and setting students up for lifelong success. Therefore, special educators should focus not only on the academic success of their students but also on their social success. Further, when students know how to engage in their environment and with their teachers and peers, they may be more available for instruction, creating an enriched learning environment.

How Is HLP 9 Connected to Other HLPs?

When making determinations about students' social skill needs, it is important to review several different sources to develop a complete picture of strengths and weaknesses. As discussed in HLP 4, using multiple sources of data helps develop a more comprehensive profile of a student. Given the challenges with generalization, it is especially important to survey parents, general and special educators, and other stakeholders who regularly work with the student. These conversations hinge on collaboration, as outlined in HLP 1. Collaboration among stakeholders includes sharing the responsibility for decision-making, planning, and resources as well as working toward mutual goals in a voluntary and equal manner (Friend & Cook, 2017; HLPs 5 and 6). Through collaboration, teams and stakeholders can identify social skill needs, plan instruction, and support both reinforcement opportunities and generalization in settings outside of the classroom. In particular, working with families to support students outside of school encourages mastery of social goals (HLP 3). Not only is working with families a key tenet of the Individuals with Disabilities Education Improvement Act (IDEIA; 2004), but partnerships increase parents' engagement in educational planning, potentially promoting students' increased usage of newly acquired social skills. Trust and support can be built when families are provided with culturally responsive training to support positive behaviors in the home (Kim et al., 2013).

As instruction on social skills begins, it is important to establish a consistent, organized, and respectful environment for the student to learn and begin to take risks with practicing new skills. As outlined in HLP 7, this positive learning environment is critical for learning to occur and is the foundation upon which all other HLPs are built, including teaching social skills. See Chapter 7 for more information and detailed strategies to create a positive learning environment. Once this respectful, organized, and predictable setting has been established, instruction can begin. Although many educators equate explicit or direct instruction with academics, explicit instruction should also be applied to teaching social skills. Explicit instruction involves making content, like social skills, explicit by modeling skills and explaining steps to understand and apply new social skills. Further, explicit instruction uses the principles of effective instruction to positively impact student learning and includes scaffolded supports (HLP 15) to help students to be successful. Finally, as skills are taught through explicit instruction (HLP 16), and possibly during more intensive instruction (HLP 20) such as that which is provided in Response to Intervention or Multi-Tiered System of Supports, during guided practice, independent practice, maintenance, and generalization (HLP 21), students should receive positive and constructive feedback (HLPs 8 and 22) throughout each phase of learning—during guided and independent practice and during maintenance and generalization, which is HLP 21.

The emphasis in HLP 8 hinges on the importance of providing feedback on an ongoing basis, specifically until students demonstrate mastery. When students perform skills correctly, in the appropriate social setting, their efforts should be acknowledged. Further, students should receive constructive feedback and praise (a form of positive feedback; HLP 8). Praise includes a statement such as "Nice work" followed by an explicit recap and reminder of the skill, expectation, or social situation that was appropriate. For example, following "Nice work," which is general praise, you can go on to say, "I love that you remembered to ask politely for the pencil and used please and thank you in your request (specific feedback). That's the perfect way to ask for something we want or need." In this manner, you are not only praising the student but offering positive feedback in the form of reinforcing the skill through a brief reminder. (See Chapter 8 for specific ways to provide performance feedback to guide behavior.) When students do not perform the skill correctly or use a skill that does not match the social situation, teachers should review and remind the student about the skill that would have been more appropriate in the specific situation (Lewis et al., 2010), as with corrective feedback (e.g., if a student forgets all of the HLPs listed here support the teaching of social skills in some way and are important for student success). See Table 9-1 for a list of the evidence-based practices we will be discussing in this chapter along with the HLPs you will use when implementing HLP 9.

How Do Teachers Determine Which Social Skills to Teach Students?

Given that poor social skills are associated with a number of at-risk factors, including poorer academic achievement, an increased risk for emotional-behavioral problems, and lower social status (Bloom et al., 2007), it is imperative to teach students how to manage and cope with a variety of social situations and foster acceptance among peers. Broadly, social skills are the skills individuals perform in specific settings. These skills help students navigate their educational and social environments. To determine what skills students may need, teachers must evaluate students' social competence. Social competence is how others, in this case, teachers, judge how an individual uses their social skills across situations and settings (Gresham et al., 2010). An individual has good social competence when they consistently and successfully interact with others in a variety of settings (Spence, 2003). While academic achievement is undoubtedly important, social competence is essential for students to be successful in educational and community settings (Gresham et al., 2010, Merrill et al., 2017). However, determining what to teach to achieve social competence is highly individualized, but achievable.

First, teachers must plan social skills instruction so that it is reflective of students' needs (Schoenfeld et al., 2008). These needs must be assessed in relation to a student's environment, vs. an arbitrary checklist of skills. For example, if a student is working on completing on-the-job training through a school-based program, the needs assessment should include basic work-related skills. Further, a kindergartener might only be assessed on social skills that include those that would be developmentally appropriate, vs. a comprehensive list of all skills. To determine which skills should be targeted, teachers have several options. First, formal or informal assessments can be used to gauge students' proficiency with specific skills. Informal assessments might include running records of observational data, interviews with parents or guardians, or simple checklists of developmentally appropriate skills. Another option is to review a student's individualized education program (IEP) or behavior intervention plan (BIP; sometimes also called a behavior support plan or BSP), if one exists. These documents will guide decision-making about targeted skills, especially if they are included as goals or objectives. Other areas in the IEP to examine include the Present Levels of Academic Achievement and Functional Performance (PLAAFP) and the student's accommodations or modifications. Both of these areas of the IEP could help guide the need for specific skills or provide accommodations that might require direct skill instruction. For example, a student who has extended time on tests and quizzes may need direct social skill instruction on how to ask for help or how to negotiate more time. More formal assessments can be purchased, but if resources are scarce, it may be challenging to make these purchases. Nevertheless, a list of these assessments is outlined in Table 9-2.

How Should Social Skills Be Taught?

After identifying the social skills a student needs, teachers should identify both discrete skills and skillsets that would be helpful to the student. If a student does not know how to ask for help, they may also need instruction on knowing how and when to interrupt or gain the teacher's attention (i.e., discrete skill). Skills should never be taught in isolation, but rather linked to other skills that can be sequenced either before or after the target skill (i.e., skillset). Table 9-3 provides an overview of

Table 9-1. Alignment of HLPs and Resources for Evidence-Based Practices

EBP SUPPORT WITH HLP 9	RELATED HLPS	RESOURCES
Collaborative conversations	1	https://www.tmaworld.com/2019/05/07/9-tips-creating-more-collaborative-conversations/ https://www.nea.org/professional-excellence/student-engagement/tools-tips/benefits-collaboration
Communication with parents	3	https://www.gse.harvard.edu/news/uk/18/07/family-engagement-and-sel https://www.naeyc.org/our-work/families/building-social-emotional-skills-at-home
Comprehensive profile: data collection	4	https://vcuautismcenter.org/resources/factsheets/printView.cfm/1210 https://iris.peabody.vanderbilt.edu/module/fba/cresource/q2/p06/
Positive, welcoming classroom climate	7	https://www.cfchildren.org/blog/2012/08/key-factors-in-creating-a-positive-classroom-climate/#:~:text=Classroom%20climate%20refers%20to%20the,and%20supportive%20of%20student%20learning https://iris.peabody.vanderbilt.edu/module/beh1/cresource/q2/p05/
Positive reinforcement	8	https://www.understood.org/en/articles/the-power-of-effective-praise-a-guide-for-teachers https://anchor.fm/behaviorbabe/episodes/Reinforcement-or-Punishment-e2rb3a
Function-based intervention	10	https://iris.peabody.vanderbilt.edu/module/fba/cresource/q3/p09/ https://ceedar.education.ufl.edu/wp-content/uploads/2014/09/Handout-16-Function-Based-Intervention-Strategies.pdf
Cue cards	14	https://do2learn.com/picturecards/printcards/
Video modeling and video self-modeling	15	https://youtu.be/GS9IFwuM_G8 https://autismpdc.fpg.unc.edu/sites/autismpdc.fpg.unc.edu/files/imce/documents/VideoModeling_Complete.pdf
Explicit instruction	16	https://schoolguide.casel.org/focus-area-3/classroom/explicit-sel-instruction/#:~:text=Explicit%20SEL%20instruction%20refers%20to,on%20social%20and%20emotional%20competencies https://learn.teachingchannel.com/video/social-skills-goals

(continued)

TABLE 9-1 (CONTINUED). ALIGNMENT OF HLPS AND RESOURCES FOR EVIDENCE-BASED PRACTICES

Intensive social skills instruction	20	https://k12engagement.unl.edu/strategy-briefs/Social%20Skills%20Instruction%209-22-14_1.pdf https://chadd.org/for-parents/social-skills-interventions/
Teaching maintenance and generalization	21	https://theautismhelper.com/skill-maintenance-teaching-long-lasting/ https://www.socialthinking.com/Articles?name=strategies-encourage-generalizing-social-thinking-skills
Positive and constructive feedback	22	https://youtu.be/N0T5zolYri4 https://ceedar.education.ufl.edu/wp-content/uploads/2021/02/Professional-Learning-Opportunity-for-HLP-8.pdf

TABLE 9-2. SOCIAL SKILLS ASSESSMENTS

NAME	AUTHORS	LINK
Social, Academic, and Emotional Behavior Risk Screener (SAEBRS)	Kilgus & von her Embse	https://www.illuminateed.com/products/fastbridge/social-emotional-behavior-assessment/
Social Functioning Interviews	Bellini	https://www.ocali.org/project/assessment_guide/page/assessment_measures
Indices of Friendship Observation	Attwood	https://tonyattwood.com.au/resources-research/forms-questionnairs/?_gl=1*1pgrvla*_ga*MTkwNTM4NDgzMy4xNjUzMDcwMTUI*_ga_DW32TFK0LN*MTY1MzA3MDE1NC4xLjEuMTY1MzA3MDI1OS4w*_ga_8HTV2WD33V*MTY1MzA3MDE1NC4xLjEuMTY1MzA3MDI1OS4w&_ga=2.102312450.282766794.16553070155-1905384833.1653070155
Social Skills Improvement System Rating Scales	Gresham & Elliot	https://www.pearsonassessments.com/store/uassessments/en/Store/Professional-Assessments/Behavior/Social-Skills-Improvement-System-SSIS-Rating-Scales/p/100000322.html
Assessment of Social and Communication Skills for Individuals with Autism Spectrum Disorders–Revised	Quill & Brushnahan	https://products.brookespublishing.com/DO-WATCH-LISTEN-SAY-P1010.aspx

Table 9-3. Social Skills Continuum

FOUNDATIONAL SOCIAL SKILLS	TARGET SOCIAL SKILLS	LINKED SOCIAL SKILLS
Introducing yourself, beginning a conversation, active listening, making small talk	Having a conversation	Ending a conversation, sharing personal information, saying thank you
Starting a conversation, waiting for a turn, identifying a problem	Asking for help	Having a conversation, saying thank you, making goals
Identifying a problem, starting a conversation, identifying emotions	Problem-solving	Accepting responsibility, dealing with criticism, making friends
Accepting responsibility, dealing with criticism, starting a conversation	Apologizing	Making friends, accepting feedback

target skills as well as those that might be taught right before or after the target skill. This ensures a continuum of success. Regardless of the skill, teachers should always link these skills to schoolwide expectations whenever possible. If a school utilizes a Positive Behavioral Interventions and Supports (PBIS) framework, all skills should align with the school plan to maintain consistency.

Once the skills or skillsets are identified, students require direct and systematic instruction (HLP 12) of social skills in school environments (Hill & Coufal, 2005; Martens & Witt, 2004). Typically, social skill instruction includes skill acquisition, performance (e.g., developing fluency in using the skill), generalization, and maintenance (Cook et al., 2008), while the most effective programs include direct teaching, modeling, coaching, and generalization (Gresham et al., 2001). In this section, we will focus on direct teaching through skill acquisition and performance by modeling and coaching. Both generalization and maintenance will be covered in the next section of this chapter.

Similar to a lesson plan, social skills instruction should include instruction, modeling, guided practice, and independent practice with reinforcement (Fisher & Frey, 2010). Like any lesson, instruction on social skills should be engaging and implement the principles of UDL. When possible, allow students choice in how to practice the skills, with whom, and where to help build efficacy and motivation. Present various materials and methods for the student to learn from a multitude of models, and while we ultimately want the student to perform the skill in real-life situations, which should also be practiced, allow the student to show knowledge of the skill in a variety of ways as well to keep learning fun and engaging. The principles of UDL can be embedded into any lesson plan.

After introducing the skill, teachers should provide a "hook" to explain why students might need a particular skill. For example, if a teacher were teaching high school students about "asking for help," they might suggest that this skill is needed to ask a boss or supervisor about an assigned task. In elementary school, a teacher might use the example of asking a cafeteria monitor to help with opening a package or carton of milk. After providing a few brief examples, teachers can also ask students for their ideas about the usefulness and potential application of the identified skill. Finally, the skill should be verbally and visually explained in a step-by-step manner, and any steps or vocabulary that are unclear should be discussed and clarified. This is particularly helpful when using words that may have difficult meanings for different people, like "respect," "kind," or "appropriate," to name a few. Understanding the steps and language in learning a new skill creates the foundation for executing the skill later. Keep in mind that the instruction phase of the lesson should be fairly short, not more than 15 to 20 minutes. The majority of the lesson should be spent in guided and independent practice.

Skill: Saying Thank You	I say, "Thank you," when someone
	does something kind for me such as holding a door or picking up something I dropped
	gives me a gift
	does or gives me something I've asked for
	compliments me

Figure 9-1. Sample cue card.

Much like a lesson plan, the next step in teaching social skills includes modeling the skill. During this phase of instruction, the teacher should show students how to execute the skill using a step-by-step approach. Although it may feel uncomfortable, demonstrating how to complete the skill allows students to see the skill in action. As educators, if we ask our students to step out of their comfort zone by practicing the skill, we should be willing to do the same. Modeling should be done in such a way that students can follow each of the skill steps. When modeling, teachers should demonstrate exactly how they expect students to perform the skill. It is helpful to plan for these sessions by creating cue cards or posters and generating a few possible scenarios that students can refer to when modeling the skill. Although the outcome of the role play does not necessarily have to end positively (e.g., a friend says no even after a student asks nicely if they will share), the steps should always be modeled correctly. After an educator models the skill, students should be given the opportunity to role play and practice the skill themselves.

Before the role playing of a skill begins, students should generate their own possible scenarios in which they would need to use the targeted skill. These situations could be in or out of the school setting and could be situations that have already occurred or may occur in the future. Students may record potential role play scenarios individually or as a group, to review later as a reminder of how to perform the skill, much like video self-modeling or video modeling, an EBP. Video self-modeling involves recording the student performing the skill correctly allowing for them to watch the video whenever necessary to review the skill. Video modeling is the same, only the students in the video are not the students who will watch the video. Video self-modeling or video modeling can serve as a method for scaffolding (HLP 15) instruction and provide repeated practice as the student could have access to the video on a personal device to review whenever necessary. These practices have been used with great success for students on the autism spectrum (Mason et al., 2016), but can benefit any student. Either way, students should attempt to develop a meaningful connection to the skill.

Each individual student should attempt to role play their scenario with the teacher or another student. Some students may need prompts, cue cards (Figure 9-1), or reminders to execute the skill correctly, without missing any steps. These supports can be scaffolded and removed slowly as the student develops mastery. During and after the role play, teachers should provide specific, positive, and detailed feedback to the student about the skill steps. This includes role playing all the steps in order and doing so correctly. An example of this feedback might include a phrase like "Marlena, great job going through each of the steps exactly as written and pausing to listen to your 'boss' in this role play" or "John, I noticed you missed step two, can you read that step to me and tell me how you might get your friend's attention?"

Depending on student progress, several modifications or supports can be included in or added to skill instruction. First, if students are having difficulty with learning new skills, teachers can assess whether the student is experiencing difficulty with acquisition or performance. A student with acquisition challenges may miss steps in a skill or may still not know how to execute specific skill steps. Consequently, students may need additional supports. This may include carrying cards with steps, often called cue cards, or receiving prompts for steps when supervised by adults. Cue cards are a tool to support EBP, such as opportunities to respond (OTR) or for scaffolding instruction for students with learning disabilities (Conderman & Hedin, 2011), but are also beneficial for all students as part of differentiated instruction (Conderman & Hedin, 2015). They are a cognitive strategy to help support memory (HLP 14). Teachers can also utilize literature to encourage buy-in from students and explain and reinforce skill steps. Social skill instruction with literature can include character analysis, discussion about conflict, and what-if scenarios that include using specific skills or skillsets. This is a method of implementing UDL also. Use of literature, role play, video modeling, etc., are multiple means of representation, in other words, allowing students to experience the concept in a variety of ways to increase the opportunity for practice toward using the skill fluently.

Other students may know the skill steps and understand them but may have difficulty performing these skillsets. One cause of this performance difficulty may be motivation. If motivation is an issue, reinforcements (goes along with HLP 8 for providing frequent feedback) may be introduced. Students should be surveyed for reinforcers of interest to encourage motivation. Positive reinforcement, in which students essentially earn a reward upon successfully exhibiting a particular behavior, is an EBP (Da Fonte et al., 2016; Scott & Landrum, 2020) and works most effectively when students earn things they like. Da Fonte et al. (2016) identified a three-step process for identifying potent reinforcers for students; however, you can do this more informally through interviewing students, parents, and other stakeholders who may know what the student likes and will work to earn. Students may respond to simply knowing they make a wise choice or to verbal praise from their teachers. Others may need more tangible reinforcers such as earned activities, edibles, or tangibles, such as stickers or prizes. These tangible reinforcers can be faded over time as students are more successful in performing the skill being taught.

Students who have difficulty with performance skills may not have situational understanding of how and when to use specific skills. When this occurs, teachers can provide case studies or scenarios to help a student understand the parameters in which a skill should be used; again, multiple methods of representation for implementation of UDL. As students role play and become more proficient with each skill, teachers can begin to fade supports like cue cards, reminders, and reinforcement.

After students demonstrate foundational knowledge of the skill steps and have role played with proficiency, they should identify opportunities in which they can practice this skill in the classroom, school, or community. This plan should be concrete, and students should be prepared to report back on their success in utilizing the skill steps.

How Do Teachers Teach the Generalization of Social Skills? How Can Students Maintain These Skills?

Although students may learn specific skills and be able to role play them correctly in the classroom, they may experience difficulty when asked to generalize these skills to novel situations. To optimize skill generalization, instruction should happen in situations and locations where skills are needed. This emphasizes the importance of starting social skills instruction with a thorough needs assessment. To further explain where and when skills should be used, teachers should emphasize both examples and non-examples during instruction. This helps students understand situations in which the skill would be a match and those in which the skill would not be appropriate or a good fit. For example, if a student was learning to share in the classroom environment, it would be important to use the non-example of the cafeteria where students are not encouraged to share food or drinks. In a secondary setting, a student may be learning to express disagreement with classmates but might need a non-example in which it would not be fitting to disagree with a supervisor or boss in the workplace. Finally, students should be monitored and evaluated on an ongoing basis to ensure the skill is being performed correctly and in appropriate settings. If necessary, reteaching should occur, or supports or reinforcements should be reintroduced briefly. To promote long-term maintenance of these skills, teachers and students will need to engage in a cycle of monitoring, evaluating, and adjusting until the student has demonstrated mastery across settings and people.

What Does HLP 9 Look Like in a K-12 Classroom?

Elementary Example

Campbell is a third-grade student who frequently argues with her peers. After taking data on the antecedents and consequences (see HLP 10) of Campbell's behavior, her teacher, Mrs. Treiber, discovers that Campbell does not seem to understand how to take turns. While she might agree to allow a student to play with an item she is using in the classroom, and does well with sharing, the give and take of sharing seems to be difficult for her. Mrs. Treiber comes up with a plan to support Campbell in the classroom by utilizing special manipulatives during small group math instruction.

Mrs. Treiber decides to bring one set of manipulatives (HLP 15) to the table where Campbell will be working with her and a small group. She also prepares an index card that outlines the steps for taking turns (e.g., a cue card). As the small group begins working on their math assignment, Campbell begins collecting all the manipulatives and holding them in her seat area, away from her classmates. When Mrs. Treiber reminds Campbell that all manipulatives must be shared with the group and that everyone needs a turn, Campbell pushes them slightly across the table, but still out of reach of her peers.

Mrs. Treiber takes this opportunity to stop and ask Campbell if she understands what she means by "taking turns." When Campbell replies that she gets to hold the manipulatives, Mrs. Treiber decides to seize this teachable moment and quickly teaches a social skill lesson before starting math. With the entire small group, Mrs. Treiber explains what is meant by taking turns and shows the group four actionable steps they can use in this or a similar situation (HLP 16). She further explains what to do while students are waiting for their turn and how to find out whose turn is next.

Although the entire turn-taking social skill instruction only lasted about 5 or 6 minutes, the instruction helped the lesson move much more smoothly than previous lessons with Campbell. While Mrs. Treiber knows that Campbell will continue needing reminders in novel situations, she has started the important process of teaching her a new social skill that will help with peer interactions and group work.

Secondary Example

Mr. Lincoln has been working with Tatum in her inclusive English classroom for the past year. Mrs. Leonard, the special education teacher, co-teaches this class with Mr. Lincoln. They have noticed that, socially, Tatum is successful in small group settings, but once she is in a larger group, she does not know how to get her teachers' attention in a way that is not disruptive to the lessons. Usually, when she wants Mr. Lincoln or Mrs. Leonard's attention, she calls out, even if they are working with another student or are engaged in a small group lesson. Mr. Lincoln knows that it would be beneficial for Tatum to explicitly learn how to ask for help, particularly from adults. He decides to ask her if she would be interested in eating lunch with him and Mrs. Leonard next week to talk about her progress in English. She agrees, but only if Mr. Lincoln can help her go to the front of the lunch line to get pizza, which always runs out before she makes her lunch purchase.

Prior to the day Tatum is to meet with Mrs. Leonard and Mr. Lincoln, her teachers compile a list of ways they both agree Tatum can get their attention outside of raising her hand. Once Tatum arrives, Mrs. Leonard and Mr. Lincoln express their concerns and offer to provide Tatum with a step-by-step process to support her with getting their attention. Since she did not realize how much she was disrupting, she is anxious to improve her behavior. Her teachers go over a series of several steps, including one that gives Tatum a choice about how she wants to get her teachers' attention. Ultimately, she decides to raise her hand, like her classmates, because she does not want to stand out. Before the end of lunch, Mr. Lincoln models (HLP 16) how he thinks through and regulates his own need (HLP 14) to ask for help in large meetings or group events. Then, he asks Tatum to role play with him so she can practice the process before coming to class the next day. During the role play, Tatum realizes she may need some support (HLP 15) with waiting her turn, and Mr. Lincoln assures her that he will acknowledge her hand quickly while she learns this new skill. Tatum and her teachers end their lunch ready for the next English class.

Summary

Effective social skills instruction is important for all students, but especially SWD who might not always understand and use appropriate social skills. Social skills are not taught in isolation, however. They can be taught during academic lessons such as during collaborative groups or playing a review game. Students learn to take turns, encourage teammates, and demonstrate positive sportsmanship while also learning or practicing academic content.

Social skills instruction involves the implementation of other HLPs to be effective. As emphasized throughout this book, no HLP is used in isolation, nor should they be. To effectively teach social skills, collaboration and assessment are crucial to identifying where a student needs to develop skills and what those skills should entail. Parents, therapists, school personnel, and other relevant stakeholders can provide insight into a child's ability to perform a skill. Assessment is necessary to determine what a student can actually do right now and identify the next steps in their development. Establishing a positive, welcoming classroom environment serves as the first line of defense to set up circumstances for appropriate social skills to occur. Positive reinforcement encourages the child to continue doing the same thing because it is correct and comes with favorable consequences. Sometimes an FBA is necessary to pinpoint exactly what the student is getting from engaging (or not) in a particular behavior. The FBA can help us determine the function of the behavior, such as not taking turns during a game of hot potato allows the student to continue holding an object (e.g., the "hot" potato) that gives sensory input. Learning that the student needs that sensory input allows caregivers or school personnel to develop an intervention to allow the student to access sensory input in an appropriate manner.

Several Instruction HLPs relate to teaching social skills. Explicit and systematic instruction are important in helping students to move to independence in performing skills. Scaffolding and feedback are necessary to help the student move from not proficiently performing the skills to performing them proficiently in the correct, real-life situations. Intensive instruction can assist the student in developing fluency more quickly, leading to independence in performing the skill. Instruction in generalization and maintenance of the skill, including positive reinforcement, further develops independence in an efficient manner, allowing the student to more quickly engage in social interactions appropriately, strengthening relationships, and increasing opportunities for academic achievement.

Chapter Review

1. Describe HLP 9 in your own words.
2. How are social skills assessed?
3. How are social skills taught?
4. Choose a skill. How might you teach that skill to an SWD?

References

Allday, R. A., Hinkson-Lee, K., Hudson, T., Nielsen-Gatti, S., Kleinke, A., & Russel, C. S. (2012). Training general educators to increase behavior specific praise: Effects on students with EBD. *Behavioral Disorders, 37*(2), 87-98.

Bloom, E. L., Karagiannakis, A., Toste, J. R., Heath, N. L., & Konstantinopolous, E. (2007). Severity of academic achievement and social skill deficits. *Canadian Journal of Education, 30*, 911-930. https://doi.org/10.2307/20466668

Conderman, G., & Hedin, L. (2011). Cue cards: A self-regulatory strategy for students with learning disabilities. *Intervention in School and Clinic, 46*(3).

Conderman, G., & Hedin, L. (2015). Differentiating instruction in co-taught classrooms for students with emotional/behaviour difficulties. *Emotional and Behavioural Difficulties, 20*(4), 349-361.

Cook, C. R., Gresham, F. M., Kern, L., Barreras, R. B., Thornton, S., & Crews, S. D. (2008). Social skills training for secondary students with emotional and/or behavioral disorders. *Journal of Emotional and Behavioral Disorders, 16*, 131-141. https://doi.org/10.1177/1063426608314541

Da Fonte, M. A., Boesch, M. C., Edwards-Bowyer, M. E., Restrepo, M. W., Bennett, B. P., & Diamond, G. P. (2016). A three-step reinforcer identification framework: A step-by-step process. *Education and Treatment of Children, 39*(3), 389-410.

Fisher, D., & Frey, N. (2010). *Better learning through structured teaching: A framework for gradual release of instructional responsibility.* Association for Supervision and Curriculum Development.

Friend, M., & Cook, L. (2017). *Interactions: Collaboration skills for school professionals* (8th ed.). Pearson.

Glossary of Education Reform. (2016). *21st century skills*. https://www.edglossary.org/21st-century-skills/

Gresham, F. M., Elliot, S. N., Cook, C. R., Vance, M. J., & Kettler, R. (2010). Cross-informant agreement for ratings for social skill and problem ratings: An investigation of the social skills improvement system-rating scales. *Psychological Assessment, 22*, 157-166. https://doi.org/10.1037/a0018124

Gresham, F. M., Sugai, G., & Horner, R. H. (2001). Interpreting outcomes of social skills training for students with high-incidence disabilities. *Exceptional Children, 67*, 331-344. https://doi.org/10.1177/001440290106700303

Hill, J. W., & Coufal, K. L. (2005). Emotional/behavioral disorders: A retrospective examination of social skills, linguistics, and student outcomes. *Communication Disorders Quarterly, 27*, 33-46. https:/doi.org/10.1177/15257401050270010401

Individuals With Disabilities Improvement Education Act, 20 U.S.C. §§ 1400 et seq. (2004 & Supp. V. 2011).

Kim, E. M., Sheridan, S. M., Kwon, K., & Koziol, N. (2013). Parent beliefs and children's social-behavioral functioning: The mediating role of parent-teacher relationships. *Journal of School Psychology, 51*, 175-185. https://doi.org/10.1016/j.jsp.2013.01.003

Lewis, T. J., Jones, S. E., L., Horner, R. H., & Sugai, G. (2010). School-wide positive behavior support and students with emotional/behavioral disorders: implications for prevention, identification and intervention. *Exceptionality, 18*(2), 82-93. https://doi.org/10.1080/09362831003673168

Martens, B. K., & Witt, J. C. (2004). Competence, persistence, and success: The positive psychology of behavioral skill instruction. *Psychology in the Schools, 41*, 19-30. https://doi.org/10.1002/pits.10135

Mason, R. A., Davis, H. S., Ayres, K. M., Davis, J. L., & Mason, B. A. (2016). Video self-modeling for individuals with disabilities: A best-evidence, single case meta-analysis. *Journal of Developmental and Physical Disabilities, 28*, 623-642.

McDaniel, S. C., Zaheer, I., & Scott, T. (2022). Teaching social skills. In J. McLeskey, L. Maheady, B. Billingsley, M. T. Brownell, & T. J. Lewis. (Eds.), *High leverage practices for inclusive classrooms* (2nd ed., pp. 132-144). Routledge. https://doi.org/10.4324/9781003148609-14

McLeskey, J., Barringer, M.-D., Billingsley, B., Brownell, M., Jackson, D., Kennedy, M., Lewis, T., Maheady, L., Rodriquez, J., Scheeler, M.C., Winn, J., & Ziegler, D. (2017). *High-leverage practices in special education.* Council for Exceptional Children & CEEDAR Center.

Merrill, K. L., Smith, S. W., Cumming, M. M., & Daunic, A. P. (2017). A review of social problem-solving interventions: Past findings, current status, and future directions. *Review of Educational Research, 87*, 71-102. https://doi.org/10.3102/0034654316652943

New South Wales Department of Education. (2017). *Key skills for the 21st century: An evidence-based review.* https://vuir.vu.edu.au/35865/1/Key-Skills-for-the-21st-Century-Analytical Report.pdf

Schoenfeld, N. A., Rutherford, Jr., R. B., Gable, R. A., & Rock, M. L. (2008). ENGAGE: A blueprint for incorporating social skills training into daily academic instruction. *Preventing School Failure, 52*(3), 17-27. https://doi.org/10.3200/PSFL.52.3.17-28

Scott, T. M., & Landrum, T. J. (2020). An evidence-based logic for the use of positive reinforcement: Responses to typical criticisms. *Beyond Behavior, 29*(2), 69-77.

Spence, S. H. (2003). Social skills training with children and young people: Theory, evidence and practice. *Child and Adolescent Mental Health, 8*, 84-96. https://doi.org/10.1111/1475-3588.00051

Sugai, G., & Lewis, T. (1996). Preferred and promising practices for social skill instruction. *Focus on Exceptional Children, 29*(4), 1-16.

What Creates and Sustains Behavior Change?

Ruby L. Owiny, PhD
and Jennifer D. Walker, PhD

HLP 10

Conduct functional behavioral assessments to develop individual student behavior support plans.

INTRODUCTION

The ultimate goal of High-Leverage Practice 10 is to positively impact student behavior. When students struggle to engage in school appropriate behavior, a functional behavioral assessment (FBA) should be conducted to collect data and identify the reason, or the function, of that behavior. The FBA should then be used to develop a behavior support plan (BSP). This plan is written to intervene and support students with developing pro-social skills and replacement behaviors to be successful in the classroom and in life. This chapter addresses the process of conducting an FBA and subsequently developing a BSP to teach new behaviors and ensure student success.

Owiny, R. L., & Cornelius, K. E. *The Practical Guide to High-Leverage Practices in Special Education: The Purposeful "How" to Enhance Classroom Rigor* (pp. 141-157).

CHAPTER OBJECTIVES

- → Identify when an FBA should be conducted.
- → Explain the process of conducting an FBA.
- → Describe how to collect and analyze data.
- → Develop a BSP.

KEY TERMS

- **antecedent:** What happens before a behavior occurs that could be causing the behavior to occur.
- **attention-seeking behavior:** Behavior that occurs with the purpose to attract positive or negative attention from peers or adults.
- **behavior:** A measurable, observable, and objective action.
- **behavior intervention plan/behavior support plan (BIP/BSP):** A plan to support and teach replacement behaviors and provide support through reinforcement and consequences.
- **consequence:** A result of a particular behavior; what happens after the behavior occurs.
- **escape-maintained behavior:** Behavior that occurs with the purpose to avoid something undesirable.
- **function-based interventions:** An evidence-based method for reducing aberrant or challenging behavior, targeting the reason, or function, for the occurrence of the behavior.
- **functional behavioral assessment (FBA):** A process of data collection on a behavior of concern for the purpose of determining the reason for, or function of, why a behavior occurs.
- **Positive Behavioral Interventions and Supports (PBIS):** A school-wide tiered system to support behavior universally for all students, in small groups, and individually for specific, intense behavioral needs.
- **positive behavior supports:** Strategies utilized in the environment to support pro-social behavior through reinforcement.
- **punishment:** Adding an undesirable consequence or removing a desirable consequence to decrease the occurrence of an undesired behavior.
- **reinforcement/reinforcers:** Adding a desirable consequence or removing an undesirable consequence to increase the occurrence of a desired behavior.
- **replacement behavior:** The alternative, pro-social behavior that substitutes the behavior of concern.
- **setting events:** A factor (e.g., a specific location, noise, subject, disagreement, argument) that causes or increases the occurrence of a behavior.
- **target behavior:** The behavior of concern in which an intervention is needed to reduce the occurrence.

It is important for all educators to support students' behavior for success in school. However, special educators frequently need to intervene with more intensive support for students with disabilities (SWD) when behaviors impede academic progress (Lloyd et al., 2019). Many schools employ school-wide positive behavioral supports to reinforce students' positive behaviors in a tiered approach that benefits all students. Tier 1 supports are intended to set expectations, teach rules, and provide universal reinforcement. However, there are times when a student will not respond in a desirable manner to Tier 1 supports and more intensive interventions must be employed. This aligns with Individuals with Disabilities Education Act (IDEA; 2004), which states that "in the case of a child whose behavior impedes the child's learning or that of others, consider the use of positive behavioral interventions and supports, and other strategies, to address that behavior" (Section 1414 [d][3][B]). Consequently, there are times when a functional behavioral assessment (FBA) is necessary to determine exactly what is happening with the behavior of concern so supports can be identified and later provided to the student ensuring success. An FBA must be conducted if the school has concerns about whether a student may need special education services or a change in placement or when a student with an individualized education program (IEP) exhibits behaviors that lead to removal from school for 10 days or more as a disciplinary action (IDEA, 2004, Section 1415 [k][1][F]).

This chapter provides you, the special educator, with evidence-based practices to conduct an FBA, use the data generated from the FBA to develop a behavior support plan (BSP; also frequently called behavior intervention plan [BIP]), and determine if the BSP is effective. The FBA process requires a team approach; therefore, you will notice frequent overlap with High-Leverage Plan (HLP) 1. In addition, assessment is important, it is the A in FBA, after all. Therefore, you will notice an overlap with the Assessment HLPs. Collaboration and assessment are key components of conducting an FBA with fidelity and reliability.

What Is HLP 10?

HLP 10 includes conducting FBAs to develop individual student BSPs as a means of intervening when a student's behavior impacts their academic achievement. McLeskey et al. (2017) define HLP 10—"*Conduct functional behavioral assessments to develop individual student behavior support plans*" as follows:

> Creating individual behavior plans is a central role of all special educators. Key to successful plans is to conduct a functional behavioral assessment (FBA) any time behavior is chronic, intense, or impedes learning. A comprehensive FBA results in a hypothesis about the function of the student's problem behavior. Once the function is determined, a behavior intervention plan is developed that (a) teaches the student a prosocial replacement behavior that will serve the same or similar function, (b) alters the environment to make the replacement behavior more efficient and effective than the problem behavior, (c) alters the environment to no longer allow the problem behavior to access the previous outcome, and (d) includes ongoing data collection to monitor progress.

FBAs are key to supporting the behavioral needs of students who struggle with disruptive, dangerous, or socially unacceptable behaviors. The key to behavioral assessments is the functional component of an FBA. It is important to identify the function, or the reason, for the occurrence of the target behavior, and to correctly develop a BSP that allows for the student to access the function more appropriately. The function of a behavior occurs for the purpose of making a "desired change in the environment" (Alberto & Troutman, 2013). That change could be for escaping a task or getting attention from a peer. Identifying the function allows the special educator to develop an intervention that allows the student to access the function in an appropriate way. For example, instead of ripping up worksheets in class (escaping), completing part of a task and taking a break (escaping) could be written into the BSP.

How Do I Conduct a Functional Behavioral Assessment?

Interestingly, an FBA is an evidence-based practice (EBP; Sam & AFIRM Team, 2015). Therefore, this section will explain the process of conducting an FBA by relying upon decades of research on behavior and applied behavior analysis (ABA), in which FBA is firmly grounded. ABA is "the science in which tactics derived from the principles of behavior are applied systematically to improve socially significant behavior and experimentation is used to identify the variables responsible for behavior change" (Cooper et al., 2019, p. 19). In other words, an FBA relies on the knowledge that behavior follows patterns, and identifying these patterns in individuals can help us understand a particular target behavior to intervene in an appropriate manner (Gage et al., 2012). On the surface, behavior seems to be quite complex, however, you can consider it as a "series of interactions between a student and his or her surroundings" (Lewis, et al., 2017). The premise for FBA is three-fold: behavior serves a function or purpose, behavior is contextual, and identification of the function leads to interventions (Gable et al., 2014).

An FBA helps teams determine how antecedents and consequences impact and reinforce behavior. We know all behavior serves a function. What function does the act of brushing your teeth have? To *get* a fresh-tasting mouth and *avoid* tooth decay. What function does the act of turning the alarm clock off have? To *escape* the loud buzzing sound. The *behavior* of brushing your teeth happens in the morning, after eating a meal, and at bedtime. It typically occurs in a bathroom, the context. If one did not like to brush their teeth and was *avoiding* the toothpaste and toothbrush in their mouth, and ran away when told to brush their teeth, we would need to identify what was causing the *escape-maintained* behavior. Why is the person running away when told to brush their teeth (context: direction to brush teeth)? Maybe the toothpaste burns their mouth or the bristles on the toothbrush are too stiff. Knowing this can help to develop an intervention. Change the brand or flavor of the toothpaste. Get a new toothbrush with softer bristles.

Conducting an FBA can be summarized in three steps: gather indirect data, develop a hypothesis of the function of the behavior from those data, and gather direct observational data to confirm the hypothesis or change it (Lewis et al., 2017). You are probably wondering what exactly is involved in those three steps. Keep reading, we fully explain each step for you to be able to conduct your own FBA.

Gather Indirect Data

Prior to gathering data, clearly define the target behavior or behavior of concern. Identify what is keeping the student from experiencing success in the classroom. The behavioral definition must be measurable, observable, and objective (or MOO). Everyone who observes the behavior should agree when it is occurring and how long it is occurring (the duration) or how frequently (the rate) simply based on the operational definition. For example, a student is off task. What actions define the off-task behavior? The student does not have the necessary materials out, is looking around the room, is not actively engaging in the classroom activity for 30 or more consecutive seconds, or is not completing assigned tasks for 2 or more consecutive minutes. This operational definition allows any observer to see the student and determine within a few seconds whether they are on- or off-task. Conversely, a non-operationalized definition might include words like "appropriate," "respectful," or "aggressive." These words do not "MOO" and would not be the same for all observers.

Informal data can help determine the function of the behavior and provide context for when, where, and how often the target behavior occurs. The data collected at this stage is considered informal as it typically relies on student self-reports or teacher memory and perception. Informal data can also include a records review to identify patterns in attendance, tardiness, or behavioral referrals, which could assist in identifying setting events. Also included in informal data is a review of a student's records, IEP, or interviews with key stakeholders, possibly including the student, parents, other teachers, or support staff. The Functional Assessment Checklist for Teachers and Staff (FACTS; March et al., 2000) is one option for a directed interview with a classroom teacher in an elementary classroom or a group of teachers in middle or high school. The FACTS helps teachers to consider all aspects of the student's day to determine when the behavior is most likely to occur, what the behavior looks like and sounds like when it does occur, and identify possible setting events and the consequences of the behavior. The data collected in the FACTS assist in narrowing down a hypothesized function of the behavior. In addition, behavior rating scales can be used to help determine the function of the behavior as well as the frequency, duration, and intensity of the behavior. One behavior rating scale, the Behavior Assessment System for Children, Third Edition (BASC-3), contains behavior rating forms for the student, a teacher, and parents/caregivers.

Develop a Hypothesis of the Function of the Behavior

From the informal data, a hypothesized function of the behavior can be developed. A functional assessment matrix (an example can be found in the IRIS Center module on FBA at https://iris.peabody.vanderbilt.edu/module/fba/cresource/q2/p08/#content) can be used to organize the data to determine a hypothesized function. When identifying the hypothesized function of behavior, keep in mind that it should be objective, which includes factual statements, without judgment. For example, we want to state that the student is engaging in **target behavior** during **a particular condition** to **avoid/gain attention/escape X situation**. We do not want to state why we think this is happening, such as the student is engaging in target behavior during a particular condition to avoid/gain attention/escape X situation **because the student is frustrated or unhappy**. We simply state the conditions, the target behavior, and the hypothesized function (Lewis et al., 2017).

Gather Direct Data

Indirect data are important for starting conversations about a student, identifying a hypothesized function of the behavior, and getting to know the student. However, these data are limited in their scope and are subjective in nature (Walker & Barry, 2022). To enhance these indirect data, direct assessment data bring objectivity and accuracy to develop a full scope of data to eventually develop a BIP.

The student should be observed in their everyday environment (e.g., classroom, lunchroom, playground, school bus) when typical routines and activities are occurring (e.g., instruction, taking a test, independent work, station work, transitions from one activity to the next; Wood, 2014) and in circumstances in which the target behavior generally occurs. It may be necessary to observe in multiple settings if a pattern of behavior has not been identified. The FACTS can be a tool to help identify which settings and times of day may need to be observed. The observer could have expertise in ABA and ideally not be the classroom teacher (Lewis et al., 2017). This allows the setting to be as natural as possible and provides the opportunity for objective data collection.

Once the times of day and settings are identified for direct observation, a method for collecting data should be identified. One or both of the following options can be used. An antecedent-behavior-consequence (ABC) analysis is an evidence-based method for identifying antecedents (what occurs before the behavior occurs) and consequences (what occurs after the behavior) that may be contributing to or maintaining the behavior. The observer uses a chart such as the one provided in Table 10-1 to record the antecedents, behavior, and consequences. Observations should continue until a clear pattern of the behavior is evident. Observations can be conducted in 15-minute segments across multiple settings, time frames, subject areas, or days to help identify the behavioral pattern.

A second option is to directly observe the target behavior and collect data only on its occurrence. However, prior to observation, the observer should identify the best way to collect data on the target behavior. The data collection system should be appropriate for both the target behavior and the intended replacement behavior (Alberto & Troutman, 2013). There are several options. *Event recording* or frequency recording identifies the number of times the student engages in the target behavior. This data collection system is appropriate for target behaviors that are discrete in nature, meaning they have a distinct beginning and end. These could be out of seat, shout-outs, tantrums, tasks completed, etc. *Interval recording* records the occurrence or non-occurrence of the target behavior in smaller increments of time, such as 10 or 15 minutes, and breaks the time into smaller intervals ranging from 5 to 30 minutes. Shorter intervals give more accurate data (Alberto & Troutman, 2013). For

Table 10-1. Antecedent-Behavior-Consequence Analysis Chart

ANTECEDENT: WHAT HAPPENS JUST BEFORE THE BEHAVIOR OCCURS?	BEHAVIOR: DESCRIBE THE BEHAVIOR AS IT OCCURS.	CONSEQUENCE: WHAT HAPPENS JUST AFTER THE BEHAVIOR OCCURS?
Teacher gives direction to turn to page 113 in the math textbook, get a pencil, and begin working on the first three math problems on the page.	Student raises hand and asks the teacher to go to the bathroom.	Teacher grants permission to use the bathroom.
Student given permission to go to the bathroom.	Student leaves the classroom.	When student re-enters the classroom, teacher reminds student of math task.
Student is reminded of the math task.	Student takes 3 minutes to get textbook out of desk.	Teacher ignores student while helping other students.
Teacher ignores student while helping other students.	Student looks for pencil in desk.	Teacher ignores student.
Teacher ignores student.	Students sits at desk with book open, but no paper or pencil to begin working.	Teacher tells student to get to work.
Teacher tells student to get to work.	Student says they need a pencil.	Teacher directs student to get one from the teacher's desk.
Teacher directs student to get pencil from their desk.	Student walks around the back of the room to go to the front corner to the teacher's desk for a pencil.	Teacher continues supporting other students.
Teacher continues supporting other students.	Student walks the long way back to their seat.	Teacher continues supporting other students.

each interval of time, the teacher records a + if the behavior occurred in that interval and a 0 if the behavior did not occur. Once the observation is complete, a percentage of intervals in which the target behavior occurred can be calculated by dividing the number of intervals by the number of times the target behavior occurred. *Rate* is an option for identifying the ratio, or percentage, of behavior occurrence. Rate provides data such as the number of shout-outs in a 50-minute class period, the rate of correct responses in 1 minute, or how long repetitive behaviors occurred in a 6-hour school day. *Duration* measures how long a student engages in the target behavior. We might need to know how long a temper tantrum lasts or how long the student was out of the room for a bathroom break. The amount of time from the occurrence of a stimulus, such as a teacher's direction, and when a student begins a task or completes a directive can be measured with *latency*. To understand a behavior more completely, *topography* can be used to describe what the behavior looks and sounds like. This includes a narrative description of the target behavior. We want to know exactly what a tantrum looks like (e.g., falling on the floor, yelling, crying until tears are present) or what completion of a task looks like, such as the markings made on a paper to complete a task (include a snapshot of the paper in your final report). The markings on a paper might be incorrectly formed letters and numbers, not writing top to bottom, left to right, or doodles alongside the margins with few items completed. *Intensity* or *force* provides a quantitative measure for the target behavior. This might be in the form of a Likert scale, such as with a temper tantrum: 0 = not intrusive to other students; 1 = intrusive to students in the immediate vicinity; 2 = intrusive to students in the classroom; 3 = intrusive to students in other classrooms. A final option for a data collection system is *locus*. The locus describes where the behavior occurs and is in narrative form. The tantrum occurs in physical education, off-task behavior occurs by watching the fish swim in the fish tank, or stimming occurs by slapping the thigh.

There may be an occasion to gather data using multiple systems. You may decide to use rate, frequency, or intensity for temper tantrums, depending on how the behavior is manifesting. It may also be helpful to use multiple systems for one behavior. The key is to identify which recording system will give you the most accurate data for developing an intervention to reduce the occurrence of the target behavior and increase the occurrence of the replacement behavior. Table 10-2 summarizes data collection methods and provides pointers in making recording system decisions.

A further method to test the hypothesized function of the behavior is to conduct a functional analysis. A functional analysis involves testing a behavior to verify the hypothesis of the function. While an individual specializing in ABA will have more expertise in this area, a classroom teacher can attempt to "test" behaviors by providing the function of the behavior to the student and then monitoring how, or if, the behavior changes. For example, if the team believes a student is interrupting the teacher for attention, the teacher could use planned ignoring to ignore the student. If the hypothesis is correct, the teacher would expect the student's behavior to increase. If the teacher intentionally and deliberately gave the student attention prior to, or during the lesson, the team would expect the student's behavior to decrease. In this way, behaviors can be tested through functional analysis.

In the full process of conducting an FBA, you may have noticed that multiple sources of data are collected (HLP 4) and, while we have not explicitly addressed this, sharing concerns, processes, and data with stakeholders (e.g., parents/caregivers of the student and relevant school personnel). Parents or caregivers should be notified as soon as a problem arises and provided with information on how the school is working to address the student's needs, as well as get their input on how the behavior of concern manifests at home (HLP 3). You may not want to show all data in their raw form to parents, as this could easily overwhelm them and they may not fully grasp what the information is saying; instead, summarize the data in a brief narrative and with a visual, such as a graph or chart (HLP 5). This sharing of information is part of HLP 2, and it includes organizing and facilitating effective meetings with professionals and families. This step is vital to students' success. Not only do multiple voices and perspectives aid in gathering and analyzing data, but those same individuals can assist in identifying interventions and in BSP implementation. Additionally, collaboration with families to support student learning and secure needed services (HLP 3) is a benefit to supporting the student. Families may identify the need to secure counseling services outside of school or school personnel can offer expertise on interventions or assistance in gathering data or conducting observations. A team approach to the FBA and BSP is the only way to ensure to positive behavioral change. The African proverb "It takes a village to raise a child" is especially relevant when planning for behavioral interventions because multiple voices, expertise, and ideas allow for a more robust process and plan.

These authors recommend using both options, ABC analysis and using a data collection system. The ABC analysis can assist in confirming the hypothesized function of the behavior and determining any antecedents or consequences that may be contributing to the occurrence of the target behavior. Gathering data specific to the occurrence of the target behavior provides more specific information, and when collecting data for three to five sessions, a baseline for the occurrence of the behavior is established. These data will provide necessary information on the improvement of the target behavior once intervention begins. An example of a completed ABC Analysis Chart can be found in Table 10-1.

Table 10-2. Data Recording Systems

METHODS	QUESTIONS TO ASK	ADVANTAGES	DISADVANTAGES	EXAMPLES
Event Recording (Frequency)	Has the behavior been defined in measurable, observable, and objective terms? Does this behavior have a discrete beginning and end? Can I tally this behavior on my own while teaching?	Does not interfere with instruction. Can be done discreetly. Can be recorded in short increments. Easy to implement.	Does not capture behaviors that occur continuously or for long periods of time. May not capture behaviors that do not have a discrete beginning and end.	Shout-outs; hand-raising; out of seat or assigned area; toileting accidents; number of items completed (e.g., sentences written, words spelled, problems solved)
Interval Recording	Has the behavior been defined in measurable, observable, and objective terms? Can I tally and time this behavior on my own while teaching?	Provides an estimate of behaviors. Subtle behaviors may captured within smaller time frames.	Provides an estimate of behaviors. Observer must be fully focused on the behavior. Teaching is difficult, if not impossible, to do at the same time. May not fully capture the entire behavior due to the snapshot nature of the recording.	On/off-task behavior; cooperative play or interactions; self-injurious behaviors
Rate	Has the behavior been defined in measurable, observable, and objective terms? Do I have both duration or frequency and the total time for the calculation of rate?	Provides a clearer picture of the behavior by putting it into context (e.g., class period, entire day).	Not always possible to determine unless two sets of data have been collected.	Out of seat; shout-outs; tantrums; number of items completed (e.g., sentences written, words spelled, problems solved)

(continued)

Table 10-2 (continued). Data Recording Systems

METHODS	QUESTIONS TO ASK	ADVANTAGES	DISADVANTAGES	EXAMPLES
Duration	Has the behavior been defined in measurable, observable, and objective terms? Can I time this behavior on my own while teaching? Does the behavior have a clear beginning and end?	Provides not only duration of behavior but also the frequency of the behavior. Helpful for capturing behaviors that occur frequently.	Timers must be used to capture duration and this may not be possible while teaching. Observer must be fully focused on the behavior.	Refusing to work; out of seat or assigned area; washing hands; tantrums
Latency	Has the behavior been defined in measurable, observable, and objective terms? Can I time this behavior on my own while teaching? Will reminders or prompts be provided and will that data be collected?	Provides a clearer picture of the behavior by putting it into context (e.g., class period, entire day).	Timers must be used to capture duration and this may not be possible while teaching. Observer must be fully focused on the behavior.	Following directions; getting materials out; starting a task
Topography	Has the behavior been defined in measurable, observable, and objective terms?	Provides a descriptive picture of the data.	Observer must be fully focused on the behavior. Does not give any information about the amount of time the behavior occurs.	Tantrums; analysis of work (e.g., formation of letters or numbers); self-injurious behavior; self-stimulation; panic attack

(continued)

Table 10-2 (continued). Data Recording Systems

METHODS	QUESTIONS TO ASK	ADVANTAGES	DISADVANTAGES	EXAMPLES
Intensity (Force)	Has the behavior been defined in measurable, observable, and objective terms?	Provides a descriptive picture of the data.	Observer must be fully focused on the behavior. Does not give any information about the amount of time the behavior occurs.	Impact of handwritten work (e.g., makes indents or rips in the paper); tantrums; screaming; hitting head against wall
Locus	Has the behavior been defined in measurable, observable, and objective terms?	Provides a descriptive picture of the data.	Observer must be fully focused on the behavior. Collaboration may be necessary to determine breadth of behavior across settings. Does not give any information about the amount of time the behavior occurs.	Wandering around the room occurs only in the cafeteria; out of seat (e.g., walks to door and looks into hallway); panic attacks happen in the hallway between class periods

How Do I Develop a Behavior Support Plan?

Once direct observation data have been collected, a baseline has been established, and data analyzed for the behavior of concern, you are ready to develop the BSP (or BIP, depending on what your school district calls it).

Teach Pro-Social Replacement Behavior That Will Serve the Same or Similar Function

The first step in developing the BSP is to clearly define a replacement behavior. Ask, "Instead of the target behavior (e.g., shouting out), what do we want (e.g., hand raising and waiting to be called on)?" Once the replacement behavior is defined, ask if it will generate the same result as the target behavior; in other words, if the target behavior is providing attention to the student, will the replacement behavior allow for the same, but in an appropriate manner (Lloyd et al., 2019)? Once the replacement behavior is determined, an intervention plan can be developed that addresses the behavioral function and explains data collection for the achievement of the replacement behavior (Hirsch et al., 2017).

For the BSP to be successful, the intervention must be based on the hypothesized function of the behavior. If one is hungry, it would not make sense to give them an opportunity to play a game with a friend. The need is one for food, not social interaction. The same principle applies to interventions. If a student is hypothesized to be seeking attention, they would need an intervention that will allow them to access attention in an appropriate manner, for example.

Altering the Environment

Developing the BSP involves identifying when and where, in the environment, teaching the new behavior is necessary. The student will need to practice the new behavior to mastery. It is also important to consider the level of scaffolding (HLP 15) needed for the student's success and how explicit instruction will be provided (HLP 16). For example, if hand raising and waiting to be called on is the replacement behavior, any classroom where hand raising is expected is the target environment for prompting the student to use the behavior. A plan for teaching the student the replacement behavior is vital to the success of the BSP. This is a time to also think about social skills (HLP 9) since teaching social skills since a social skill is often the replacement behavior. It is important to consider (a) how the replacement behavior will be defined, (b) who will teach the replacement behavior to the student, (c) when it will be taught, and (d) where it will be taught. Additionally, the intensity of instruction (HLP 20) must be matched to how challenging learning this new behavior will be for the student. Initially, the plan may need to include a prompt, such as the visual prompt of the teacher looking at the student and raising her hand to remind the student to raise his. However, a plan for slowly fading the prompt is important since there is a danger of the student becoming dependent on the prompt and not moving toward independence. Another piece of the BSP is identifying the rate and type of reinforcement the student will receive. This is a major component of the BSP. Engagement in the replacement behavior must be as desirable, or more desirable than the target behavior (Lloyd et al., 2019). Will the student receive verbal praise when engaging in the target behavior? Will the student receive a sticker, a high-five, a prize, etc.? In the case of hand raising, will the student immediately be called on? (Hint: He should be, if the function is attention. This allows him to access attention in a positive manner.) HLP 8—"*Provide positive and constructive feedback to guide students' learning and behavior*" plays a role in reinforcement. Reinforcement can include positive feedback; however, the teacher should also consider constructive feedback when the student is struggling to perform the replacement behavior. They may need reminders or reteaching of a step so the replacement behavior can be successful. See Chapter 8 for more information about providing feedback to guide student behavior.

Similarly, another key to a successful plan includes one that prevents the student from obtaining reinforcement for the behavior of concern. In other words, the student cannot obtain the function when engaging in the behavior of concern. For example, if the function of the behavior is attention and the student shouts out rather than raising his hand, the teacher should not give any attention to the student. Instead, she should identify a student who has raised their hand and is waiting quietly. Then, the teacher should verbally praise the student for raising their hand and call on them for a response.

Ongoing Data Collection

While the above pieces are important, there is one more critical component of the BSP. That final piece includes planning for data collection. Look back at Chapter 6, using student assessment data, analyzing instructional practices, and making necessary adjustments that improve student outcomes (HLP 6). That chapter provides ideas for how to collect, analyze, and use the data effectively to make informed decisions. Given that a BSP is a living document, data collection and analysis should be ongoing. Important questions to consider include how the behavior of concern and the replacement behavior will be monitored and who will play key roles in collection and analysis? Without data, school personnel, parents, and the student have no way of knowing how the BSP is working. Data collection plus graphing of the data will allow for analyzing the effectiveness of the BSP and making any necessary adjustments.

What Does HLP 10 Look Like in a K-12 Classroom?

Elementary Example

Trevor is a student in Mrs. Shapiro's second-grade classroom who performs very well academically but struggles to maintain self-control and has frequent outbursts. Despite having a strong classroom management plan with frequent opportunities for reinforcement and a well-structured predictable environment, Trevor continues to struggle. When he gets frustrated, he often shouts out and starts calling the teacher or classmates names. As his behavior escalates, he will often begin throwing materials and books, which leads to throwing chairs and desks. This behavior is not only frightening for his classmates and disruptive to instruction, but it also hinders Trevor's growth and social standing within the classroom.

Mrs. Shapiro quickly realizes she needs help to support Trevor's needs. She refers Trevor to the Student Assistance Team (SAT) to request assistance in meeting Trevor's needs. The SAT determines that an FBA would be helpful to determine what might be motivating Trevor's outbursts. Ms. Edwards, the special educator assigned to the second-grade team, agrees to work with Mrs. Shapiro to conduct the FBA and report the results to the SAT to create a BSP.

Mrs. Shapiro is not familiar with FBAs, so Ms. Edwards describes the process and explains the necessity of identifying the reason behind his behavior and the importance of an ABC Analysis to determine if there may be something occurring in the classroom that serves as a trigger for Trevor, which could be a setting event or antecedent. The ABC Analysis will help to identify exactly why he is having such violent outbursts; in other words, it will help to develop a hypothesis for the function of his behavior.

Ms. Edwards works with Mrs. Shapiro to identify the target behavior in measurable, objective, and observable terms. They come up with the target behavior through the FACTS to identify if a pattern occurs around certain times of the day, subject areas, etc. The target behavior is identified as *escalating disruption* defined as increasingly aggressive behavior beginning with shout-outs leading to forcefully shoving or throwing of books, materials (e.g., crayons, pencil boxes), and chairs or desks. After completing the FACTS, attention-seeking behavior is hypothesized to be the function of the behavior.

From that function, a replacement behavior is determined. The replacement behavior is defined as verbally asking the teacher for help, in a non-disruptive manner. Ms. Edwards schedules a time to observe Trevor in the classroom and completes an ABC Analysis to confirm the hypothesized function of the behavior. The ABC Analysis shows that whenever Trevor is ignored, his behavior escalates until he gets the attention he is seeking. Ms. Edwards conducted another observation to further verify the hypothesized function by completing a functional analysis. Mrs. Shapiro is directed to give Trevor attention as soon as he shouts out. The disruptions do not escalate; however, when Mrs. Shapiro is directed to ignore Trevor when he shouts out, the escalating disruptive behavior *does* increase, therefore this verifies the function of the behavior is attention-seeking behavior.

Additionally, Ms. Edwards asks Mrs. Shapiro to record the frequency of the disruptive behavior and the progression from shout-outs, pushing or throwing items off his desk, to pushing or throwing chairs or desks while also shouting such things as "You're so dumb," "I hate this school," etc. Mrs. Shapiro chooses 5 days over 2 weeks to record the occurrence of the target behavior. Data show the occurrence of the target behavior occurs an average of four times per day.

Now that the function of the behavior has been identified, a BSP must be developed. The SAT meets again for Ms. Edwards and Mrs. Shapiro to share the results of the FBA and their ideas for an intervention. The team decides on an intervention to include providing a card in Trevor's favorite color (red) that he can lie on his desk when he needs some attention. When Mrs. Shapiro sees the card, she goes to Trevor's desk to ask him what he needs. After a few days of practice, Mrs. Shapiro gathers data on the replacement behavior as she did in the pre-intervention phase to determine the effectiveness of the intervention. Trevor had one escalated disruption one day for one occurrence across the 5 days of recording data. Mrs. Shapiro noted she had not seen the red card on Trevor's desk and missed providing the attention, which led to the escalated disruptions. Mrs. Shapiro had a conversation with Trevor about this and they collectively decided to add another step. If, after counting to 15, Mrs. Shapiro did not recognize the card on Trevor's desk, he was to raise his hand with the card to help Mrs. Shapiro see the card more easily. This minor tweak to the plan reduced Trevor's escalated disruptions to zero.

Secondary Example

Mrs. Cavich is an eighth-grade science teacher who is struggling to figure out what to do with Stephanie, one of her new students. In Mrs. Cavich's class, students sit at long tables where sinks and science equipment are built into the desk areas. This is great for active learning and science experiments, but so far, the tables have been a mess for Stephanie. Since the first day of class, Stephanie has been playing with the sink, turning on the water, and touching all the science equipment. Despite repeated requests not to touch the equipment, it has not stopped Stephanie. While Mrs. Cavich would like to move Stephanie to a different seat, the room is designed in such a way that cabinets cover every wall, and there are limited choices outside of the tables.

Finally, after water goes all over the table and floor from another instance of Stephanie's choice to turn on the sink during class, Mrs. Cavich reaches out to Ms. Tane, who leads the school's Behavior Support Team (BST). Mrs. Cavich is certain that the behavior is Stephanie's way to get attention from her peers, especially since she has announced on several occasions that she does not like science. Ms. Tane gets as much information as possible about the behaviors Mrs. Cavich is seeing, and they make sure the behavior of concern is defined in such a way that it is measurable, objective, and observable. After they decide on exactly what behaviors Mrs. Cavich is concerned about, Ms. Tane decides to come in and observe Stephanie to better understand the behavior. She plans to visit Mrs. Cavich's room every day for a week to see what might be going on with Stephanie and her behavioral choices.

During the first few days of observation, Ms. Tane uses a frequency chart and records an average of more than 25 instances per 90-minute block where Stephanie is touching, playing, or moving the science equipment. All of these instances occur when Stephanie is supposed to be attending to a lesson. On the third and fourth days of observation, Ms. Tane uses an ABC chart to try and identify the antecedent. After the second day of ABC recording, Ms. Tane thinks she has the answer!

Ms. Tane schedules a time to meet with Mrs. Cavich and share her findings. First, Ms. Tane shares that as the class progresses, the number of instances in which Stephanie is touching the science equipment begins to increase. Ms. Tane also shares that in every occurrence of this behavior, Mrs. Cavich is lecturing or demonstrating an experiment. None of the instances occur during note taking or when Stephanie is engaged in preparing for experiments or cleaning up. Ms. Tane suggests that Stephanie might be trying to satisfy a physiological or sensory need for movement or play and is actually not seeking attention. She suggests that Mrs. Cavich offer Stephanie a bin of fidgets to see if Stephanie's needs can be redirected. Although Mrs. Cavich is not sure about this hypothesis because she believes the behavior is attention based, she agrees to give it a try.

The next day, Ms. Tane brings in a small container of fidgets for Stephanie to use in Mrs. Cavich's class. Ms. Tane makes sure none of the fidgets make sounds or are too large. When Stephanie arrives, Mrs. Cavich offers her the bin and suggests she use a fidget during class that day. Mrs. Cavich follows the offer with the expectation that the fidget stays with Stephanie and is not thrown or shared with peers during class.

To Mrs. Cavich's shock and Ms. Tane's delight, Stephanie keeps the fidget during the entire class and does not touch the science equipment once. Even as the class progresses and Mrs. Cavich begins demonstrating a science experiment, Stephanie uses her fidget and not the equipment. For the next week, Stephanie continues selecting items from the fidget box and Mrs. Cavich does not record a single instance of Stephanie touching the equipment.

Although Mrs. Cavich is thrilled that this challenge is solved, she still has concerns about future classes when they will be engaging in science experiments with chemicals and a burner. She wants to know if Ms. Tane can help her record the observational data and complete an FBA with the team. Mrs. Cavich thinks it might be beneficial for Stephanie's safety to develop a BSP with her team and her parents to address the remainder of the semester.

Given the function of Stephanie's behavior, the team can develop a plan for the remainder of the semester, particularly when chemicals or the burners are involved. The team develops a series of replacement behaviors that include fidgets and other safe materials for each of the experiments moving forward. In addition, the team decides to reinforce Stephanie's choice to use materials as instructed by allowing her to clean and prep stations for the next class since she enjoys the opportunity to get up and move around the room. The small shift to include fidgets for Stephanie's sensory needs keeps Stephanie and her classmates safe throughout a year's worth of science experiments.

Summary

The FBA and BIP process include many HLPs to make the practice successful. As you have read, the HLPs have intertwined functionality and the FBA is another great example of how intertwined they can be. During the FBA and BSP process, it is imperative that teams collaborate with families to support students and their needs (HLP 3) through the organization of meetings with families and other pertinent professionals (HLP 2). As the FBA process gets underway, teams should use multiple sources of assessment information to understand students' needs, strengths, and behaviors (HLP 4). Just as multiple sources should be used to develop a complete understanding of a student, multiple individuals should also be involved when reviewing assessments. During the FBA, a team approach, including all stakeholders and parents, should interpret assessments and communicate the results (HLP 5) to hypothesize and test function and determine if additional assessments are warranted. Using these assessments, teams should begin to develop and plan for instruction (HLP 6) through the BSP. During the implementation of the BSP, it may be necessary to teach students social behaviors that align with classroom or school expectations (HLP 9), as well as satisfy the function of the behavior of concern. These behaviors can be prompted and reinforced until a student demonstrates mastery. This may require scaffolded supports that utilize visual, verbal, or written prompts (HLP 15) or explicit instruction (HLP 16) on the steps necessary to engage in a new replacement behavior. Depending on the intensity of a student's needs, more intensive instruction may be required using frequent monitoring, increased opportunities to respond, and immediate and specific feedback (HLP 20). This feedback should be positive and constructive, so students know where they need improvement to meet their learning goals (HLP 22). While the FBA and BSP process includes a layered approach, the HLPs presented in this chapter and throughout this text will ensure success. Table 10-3 presents an overview of these HLPs as well as some helpful links to other resources.

Chapter Review

1. Describe HLP 10 in your own words.
2. Why is conducting an FBA important when students engage in disruptive behavior?
3. Describe how to conduct an FBA.
4. Describe how to write a BSP.
5. Describe how to collect data, analyze them, and determine the intervention's effectiveness.

Table 10-3. Alignment of HLPs and Resources for Evidence-Based Practices

EBP SUPPORT WITH HLP 10	RELATED HLPS	RESOURCES
Team approach to decision-making	1	Filderman, M. J., & Gesel, S. A. (2022). Data teams: A collaborative approach to intensifying intervention using student data. *TEACHING Exceptional Children*. https://doi.org/10.1177/00400599221096753 https://iris.peabody.vanderbilt.edu/wp-content/uploads/pdf_case_studies/ics_rtidm.pdf
Collaboration with families to support student learning and secure needed services	3	https://iecp-resources.uark.edu/2020/12/01/hlp-3-collaborate-families-support-student-learning-secure-services/ https://highleveragepractices.org/sites/default/files/2020-10/A-Look-at-Collaboration.pdf
Indirect and direct data collection	4	https://iris.peabody.vanderbilt.edu/module/fba/cresource/q2/p06/#content https://sites.google.com/site/jacquelinediazfba/5-steps-in-conducting-an-fba
Share information with stakeholders and families	2, 5	https://www2.ed.gov/programs/readingfirst/support/stakeholderlores.pdf https://iris.peabody.vanderbilt.edu/module/rti-leaders/cresource/q4/p16
Collect, analyze, and use data to make informed decisions	6	https://soeonline.american.edu/blog/data-driven-decision-making-in-education https://iris.peabody.vanderbilt.edu/module/rti-math/cresource/q1/p07/
Replacement behavior	9	https://intensiveintervention.org/intensifying-behavioral-intervention-behavior-course https://iris.peabody.vanderbilt.edu/module/fba/cresource/q2/p05/
Scaffolding instruction	15	https://iris.peabody.vanderbilt.edu/module/sca/cresource/q1/p01/#content https://highleveragepractices.org/hlp-15-use-scaffolded-supports
Explicit instruction	16	https://intensiveintervention.org/training/course-content/explicit-instruction https://highleveragepractices.org/hlp-16-use-explicit-instruction
Match intensity of need to intensity of instruction	20	https://intensiveintervention.org/implementation-intervention/taxonomy-intervention-intensity https://intensiveintervention.org/resource/intensification-strategy-checklist
Reinforcement	22	https://files.eric.ed.gov/fulltext/ED595392.pdf https://www.verywellmind.com/what-is-positive-reinforcement-2795412

References

Alberto, P. A., & Troutman, A. C. (2013). *Applied behavior analysis for teachers.* Pearson Education Inc.

Cooper, J. O., Heron, T. E., & Heward, W. L. (2019). *Applied behavior analysis* (3rd ed.). Pearson Education Inc.

Gable, R. A., Park, K. L., & Scott, T. M. (2014). Functional behavioral assessment and students at risk for or with emotional disabilities: Current issues and considerations. *Education and Treatment of Children, 37*(1), 111-135. https://www.jstor.org/stable/44820720

Gage, N. A., Lewis, T. J., & Stichter, J. P. (2012). Functional behavioral assessment-based interventions for students with or at-risk for emotional and/or behavioral disorders in school: A hierarchical linear modeling meta-analysis. *Behavioral Disorders, 37*, 55-77. http://www.jstor.org.proxy.mul.missouri.edu/stable/23890731

Hirsch, S. E., Bruhn, A. L., Lloyd, J. W., & Katsiyannis, A. (2017). FBAs and BIPs: Avoiding and addressing four common challenges related to fidelity. *TEACHING Exceptional Children, 49*(6), 369-379. https://doi.org/10.1177/0040059917711696

Individuals With Disabilities Education Act, 20 U.S.C. §§ 1400 et seq. (2004 & Supp. V. 2011).

Lewis, T. J., Hatton, H. L., Jorgenson, C., & Maynard, D. (2017). What beginning special educators need to know about conducting functional behavioral assessments. *TEACHING Exceptional Children, 49*(4), 231-238. https://doi.org/10.1177/0040059917690885

Lloyd, B. P., Wills, H. P., & Lewis, T. J. (2019). Conducting functional behavior assessments to develop individualized behavior support plans. In J. McLeskey, L. Maheady, Billingsley, B., M. T. Brownell, & T. J. Lewis (Eds.), *High leverage practices for inclusive classrooms* (pp. 130-144). Routledge.

March, R. E., Horner, R. H., Lewis-Palmer, T., Brown, D., Crone, D., Todd, A. W., & Carr, E. (2000). *Functional assessment checklist for teachers and staff (FACTS).* Educational and Community Supports.

McLeskey, J., Barringer, M.-D., Billingsley, B., Brownell, M., Jackson, D., Kennedy, M., Lewis, T., Maheady, L., Rodriquez, J., Scheeler, M.C., Winn, J., & Ziegler, D. (2017). *High-leverage practices in special education.* Council for Exceptional Children & CEEDAR Center.

Sam, A., & AFIRM Team. (2015). *Functional behavior assessment.* National Professional Development Center on Autism Spectrum Disorder Child Development Center, University of North Carolina. http://afirm.fpg.unc.edu/functional-behavior-assessment

Walker, J. D., & Barry, C. (2022). *Behavior management: Systems, classrooms, and individuals.* Plural Publishing.

Wood, B. K. (2014). An effective approach to developing function-based interventions in early childhood classrooms. *Young Exceptional Children, 17*(1), 3-20.

Instruction High-Leverage Practices

You have probably noticed that half of the High-Leverage Practices (HLPs; 12 of the 22) fall under the domain of Instruction. This is not an accident, but by design. After all, special education teachers are first and foremost teachers—teachers with a need for a markedly wide range of skills and practices. Students with disabilities are one of the smallest populations in schools, but represent the student group with the most diverse needs. Effective special education teachers need to know the curriculum, and their students' needs. They design appropriate learning goals for long and short term. They understand the curriculum and student individualized education program (IEP) goals so they can break it apart, gauge their students' current understanding to design effective instruction that is sequenced in just the right way to help students make the connections to prior and future learning. They use the knowledge of the curriculum and the student to make meaningful accommodations and/or modifications based on the learning goal. Effective special education teachers use specific strategies to help students become more motivated to take ownership of their learning. They understand when to provide scaffolded supports and how to do so appropriately and plan them with the intentionality to remove the supports. They also deliver instruction in a scaffolded manner of providing a clear model to set up the expectations, providing enough practice opportunities they complete with the students to ensure understanding before students are released to practice the new skill or concept alone. Effective special educators also know students learn from their peers and arrange learning opportunities with a variety of groupings (e.g., heterogeneous, homogeneous, large, small); they intentionally group students for a specific goal. They also embed plenty of opportunities to engage in the lesson, because they know that student engagement with the lesson leads to higher outcomes. Special education teachers know how to use educational technology to improve learning and when assistive technology is required, can collaborate to obtain the right technology, and train the student to use technology that will improve academic outcomes. Effective special education teachers do not let learning become stagnant for any student. They know how to use information gathered from all of these practices as well as assessment data to design intensive interventions—when to change pacing, when to add more or change the practice opportunity. They also use data gathered during instruction to know when to change curriculum or select a new evidence-based practice. They also teach skills and strategies to help students achieve the highest level of independence possible. They specifically teach to mastery before moving on to more complex content so students can maintain learning. They also teach in a way to ensure learning is demonstrated across settings, not just across classrooms, but within the community as well. Of course, this is all done while providing students with the right types of feedback in a positive manner that will move student learning forward. Obviously to capture all of this, we need more HLPs than any other domain. Chapters 11 through 22 will highlight how each of the HLPs improve student learning.

How Do I Know What Is Appropriate When Prioritizing Goals?

Sarah M. Salinas, PhD
and Kyena E. Cornelius, EdD

HLP 11

Identify and prioritize long- and short-term learning goals.

INTRODUCTION

Appropriate has to be the most difficult word to define in special education! This may sound oversimplistic, but when designing long- and short-term goals for students with disabilities (SWD), the most important component to write "appropriate goals" is to keep the individual student in mind. With that student in mind, then ask the following questions. What is the grade-level standard being addressed? What are goals identified in the individualized education program (IEP)? What are the content specific skills required? What is the current ability and readiness level of the student? What cultural and linguistic considerations need to be included? Answering these questions will help you ensure the long- and short-term goals are appropriate. This chapter will help you answer these questions to increase student learning and improve academic outcomes.

Owiny, R. L., & Cornelius, K. E. *The Practical Guide to High-Leverage Practices in Special Education: The Purposeful "How" to Enhance Classroom Rigor* (pp. 161-172).

CHAPTER OBJECTIVES

- → Identify and prioritize short- and long-term learning goals based on student data and develop specialized learning goals based on student IEPs and present levels of academic performance.
- → Know how HLP 11 is connected to other HLPs and used to implement evidence-based practices to increase student outcomes.
- → Explain how short- and long-term goals are designed based on student data and curricular standards.

KEY TERMS

- **long-term goal:** A goal that will take several weeks or months to accomplish. This could mean a unit of instruction, a grading period, or even an annual IEP goal. Typically, long-term learning goals are goals more aligned with the expected rate of progress or growth that an IEP team will determine is appropriate for a student with a disability (SWD) to accomplish during an academic year.
- **short-term goal:** A goal that can be accomplished within a time range of several days to several weeks. Short-term goals break up the long-term goals into gradual increments, like benchmarks, or discrete pieces of the skill short-term objectives.

Goals provide the roadmap and direction to move us from point A to point B. It is important when setting these goals for students that they not only meet the individual needs of the student but that they are aligned with grade-level curriculum standards. Even when the student may not be achieving at grade level, it is important to examine and break apart the standard to get at the most foundational skills needed for the student to master these skills so they can progress toward the standard. As students progress, you use data to monitor their progress and prioritize new learning goals.

In this chapter we help break apart High-Leverage Practice (HLP) 11—"*Identify and prioritize long- and short-term learning goals*" to illustrate how you use this along with other HLPs, to implement many evidence-based practices (EBPs) to improve student outcomes. As your ability to implement HLPs increases, you will see the natural way they all are intertwined in your daily practice.

WHAT IS HLP 11?

It is easy to see why the HLP writing team, from the Council for Exceptional Children (CEC) and the Collaboration for Effective Educator Development, Accountability and Reform (CEEDAR) Center, started the instructional practices with goal setting, because how can you start any endeavor without a goal? McLeskey and colleagues (2017) provide teachers with four factors to consider when they identify and prioritize goals. First, they remind teachers to provide meaningful access to the general education curriculum by starting with the grade-level standards. When possible, this access is in the general education classroom, but even when not possible due to individualized needs, instructional planning should always keep the general education curricula at the center of planning. Second, teachers are to use assessment and progress monitoring data to identify the starting point or current baseline of the student. No goal can be achieved without knowing the starting line. Third, take into consideration the student's background knowledge. This does not only pertain to how well students did with previous learning, but also the knowledge and experiences they bring to the classroom from their personal lives. What is important to them and their family, are there cultural experiences that can enrich their learning? Fourth, and finally, refer to the individualized education program (IEP) goals and benchmarks. Remember, the main function of the IEP is to guide the academic and functional advancement of students (Yell & Bateman, 2020). Understanding these four factors will enable teachers to break apart the content they are teaching to improve student learning. Effective teachers should be able to examine the content, determine what prerequisite skills students are missing, create measurable goals, and use associated assessment tools that easily monitor student performance. They do all of this with the understanding that identifying and prioritizing goals is an iterative process. Closely monitoring and revising meaningful goals safeguards a student's Free Appropriate Public Education (FAPE).

How Is HLP 11 Connected to Other HLPs?

The connection between HLP 11 and other HLPs comes in as special education teachers will rarely teach or use one practice in isolation. That is to say, special educators may often find that they use combinations of HLPs together to design and provide effective responsive instruction for students. For example, a teacher may identify a short- and long-term learning goal, and to support students in reaching that goal, they will systematically design instruction toward a specific learning goal (HLP 12) and provide intensified instruction (HLP 20). To be responsive to student needs and deliver systematic and intensive instruction, special education teachers need to use student assessment data, and engage in analysis of their instructional practices to make needed adjustments to increase student achievement (HLP 6). This means that special education teachers use assessment in multiple forms, both formal assessments (summative, end-of-year assessments, and curriculum-based assessments, which is an EBP; Deno, 2003) and informal assessments (such as formative assessment, in reading small group practice).

Effective special education teachers also prioritize learning goals when they use explicit instruction (HLP 16). Special education teachers need to use explicit instruction as part of breaking down tasks or the steps involved in the processes for reading multisyllabic words (for elementary) and use of reading comprehension strategy instruction (adolescent, grades 6 to 12). Explicit instruction is a key tenet of high-quality academic instruction and of systematic instruction; it is also an EBP (Archer & Hughes, 2011).

Special education teachers need to provide intensified instruction (HLP 20) designed to target specific short- and long-term goals to support students with disabilities (SWD) in gaining proficiency and to build the academic skills needed and familiarity with content, or the learning and application of reading comprehension strategies to meet learning goals set at students' current levels of academic performance as well as proficiency attainment to build toward grade-level standards. See Table 11-1 for a list of HLPs related to, and the EBPs implemented with, HLP 11.

How Do I Break Apart the Grade Level Standard?

To break apart the grade-level standard, special education teachers should start by looking up the grade-level learning standard that most aligns to the skill associated with the student's area of need. For this, the special education teacher would first look at the curriculum learning standards for the content area, and locate the grade-level standards for the student's assigned grade. For instance, in English Language Arts/Reading (ELAR), the fourth-grade Reading Foundation Standard 4.3 states that students should "know and apply grade-level phonics and word analysis skills in decoding words" (http://www.corestandards.org). Once you dig deeper, you find what that means for a typical achieving fourth grader, they can "use combined knowledge of all letter-sound correspondences, syllabication patterns, and morphology (e.g., roots and affixes) to read accurately unfamiliar multisyllabic words in context and out of context" (http://www.corestandards.org). From there, you would compare these skills to the student's current levels of reading. Using progress monitoring or

Table 11-1. Alignment of HLPs and Resources for Evidence-Based Practices

EBP SUPPORT WITH HLP 11	RELATED HLPS	RESOURCES
Curriculum-based measurements (CBM)	4, 6, 20	https://www.interventioncentral.org/ https://dibels.uoregon.edu/ https://iris.peabody.vanderbilt.edu/module/pmm/#content
Direct phonics instruction Concrete-Representational-Abstract (CRA)	12, 20, 22	https://education.missouri.edu/ebi/interventions/ https://iris.peabody.vanderbilt.edu/module/rti03/#content https://iris.peabody.vanderbilt.edu/module/math/
Peer-Assisted Learning Strategies (PALS)	15, 17, 21, 22	https://highleveragepractices.org/hlp-18-use-strategies-promote-active-student-engagement https://iris.peabody.vanderbilt.edu/module/pals26/
Explicit Instruction	12, 16, 21, 22	https://highleveragepractices.org/hlp-12-systematically-design-instruction-toward-specific-learning-goal https://highleveragepractices.org/hlp-16-use-explicit-instruction
Collaborative Strategic Reading (CSR)	15, 17, 21, 22	https://highleveragepractices.org/hlp-13-make-adaptations https://iris.peabody.vanderbilt.edu/module/csr/
Family Engagement Framework	3, 4	https://oese.ed.gov/files/2020/10/equitable_family_engag_508.pdf

CBM data, determine what the student can do and how it is aligned with this standard. If the current performance is lower, then look vertically down at the prior grade-level standards to find at what point the student is currently performing. For students with learning disabilities (LD), this means the special education teacher still begins with the learning standard for the grade based on the student's age, and then looks vertically and moves down one grade level at a time until they find the learning standard that is closest aligned to the student's current level. For students with LD, this will most likely be two or more grades below level, although it depends on each individual student. The level at which the student is currently functioning becomes the point for determining what the appropriate short-term and long-term goals should address. Using our fourth-grade standard, you will see that the third-grade standard starts off the same, but the sub-skills are different. Where the fourth-grade standards had one sub-skill, the third-grade standard has four:

RF 3.3: Know and apply grade-level phonics and word analysis skills in decoding words.

A. Identify and know the meaning of the most common prefixes and derivational suffixes.

B. Decode words with common Latin suffixes.

C. Decode multisyllable words.

D. Read grade-appropriate irregularly spelled words. (http://www.corestandards.org)

The second-grade standard has even more, and one of the sub-skills in second grade is to distinguish between long and short vowel sounds. It may be that our hypothetical student is still struggling with all the vowel patterns to be able to consistently distinguish the sounds. With this information from the grade-level standards and the student's current performance, the teacher has a solid starting point to establish goals.

What Do the Students' Assessment Data Tell Me?

Effective special education teachers know how to analyze and interpret students' assessment data to make decisions about instructional design and adjustment, and to inform the crafting of short- and long-term goals. Student assessment data can come in many forms: formal assessments such as statewide standardized assessment scores, CBMs, screening tools like Dynamic Indicators of Basic Early Literacy Skills (DIBELS; Good & Kaminiski, 2002) with the Phoneme Segmentation Fluency (PSF) assessment to evaluate and the Nonsense Word Fluency (NWF) assessments to determine if the student needs, or would benefit from, more intensified instruction (HLP 20) to develop mastery of foundational literacy skills, like phonemic awareness, that are multiple years below grade level. Additionally, a special education teacher may use a more informal assessment based on observation or error analysis to identify the specific letters that a student or group of students are struggling to correctly differentiate, or patterns of frequently misused or mispronounced prefixes and suffixes. Once the teacher has analyzed student data, they can determine the students' present levels of academic performance and skill proficiency level. Analysis of student data, in turn, helps special education teachers to identify those skills that the student needs to build toward mastery. Moreover, analysis of student data supports the special education teacher's ability to identify and set short- and long-term learning goals, and tailor instruction and practice opportunities to support students. Another way that special education teachers can use student data to set short- and long-term learning goals is by looking at the student's reading fluency with multisyllabic words, design short, intensified practice opportunities for the student with timely feedback, like with the word work sheet, https://ies.ed.gov/ncee/rel/regions/southeast/pdf/prefix_base_word_suffix.pdf, and in turn, write specific short-term learning goals, such as "the student will be able to correctly decode multisyllabic words with the prefixes 'un-', 'mis-', and 'dis-' 8 out of 10 times." This is also an EBP known as data-based instruction or individualization (DBI; Fuchs et al., 2010; see Chapter 6 and Chapter 20 for more on DBI). With culturally and linguistically diverse exceptional students, this means special education teachers are also aware of the importance of assessment of students in both languages, with assessment tools that were normed and designed to be accurate with a specific demographic. Regarding the "big" assessments that are most commonly mentioned as it pertains to assessment used for initial placement decisions, effective special education teachers also acknowledge that assessment tools themselves need to be interrogated through an equity lens. For instance, Restrepo and Castilla-Earls (2021) noted that there is still,

> the limited availability of valid and reliable assessment instruments for bilingual children, and assessment policies and procedures that do not take into account students' bilingual development characteristics, results in inaccurate identification or under-identification of these children to early intervention and special education services. (p. 90)

In addition to the day-to-day assessments used such as curriculum-based assessments, quizzes, and tests that are part of pre-packed curricula and district-developed curricula, we point out that special education teachers need to be aware of the ways that certain bias and cultural knowledge, assumptions, and expectations are woven into curricula and other learning materials and assessments. For students who are from culturally and linguistically diverse families, teachers need to take special caution to ensure the assessments are a true measure of the students' ability. One of the six tenets of the Individuals with Disabilities Education Act (IDEA, 2004) is that students have the right to be assessed without racial, cultural, or linguistic bias (20 U.S.C.§1414). The intent for these regulations for assessment is to prevent and protect students from misidentification for special education. So, why is nondiscriminatory assessment important for special education teachers? Well, it is also best practice! Special education teachers can be confident in the use of student data when nondiscriminatory assessments are used.

The same principles need to apply in classroom assessments as well. Teachers cannot make informed decisions unless the information is accurate. Bennett (2011) suggests classroom formative assessments also be free from assumptions, as assumption and inferences lead to unintentional bias. To make the soundest instructional decisions, teachers need to use multiple sources of information (HLP 4) to ensure the data collected are an accurate portrait of the students' understanding.

This does not mean, however, that we are suggesting that special education teachers eliminate assessment altogether. Rather we posit that assessments, be it formal or informal, summative or formative, written or oral, multiple choice or open-ended questions/short answers, are going to measure just as much or as little (or rather narrow a scope) as they are designed to. In other words, teachers need to be aware and attend to the ways in which the assessment they administer aligns with content taught, the targeted learning objectives, and that the assessment provides a way for progress monitoring to help them measure or otherwise observe and document proof of students' engagement in learning. To this end, the careful collection and analysis of student assessment data can inform special education teachers' decisions about how to adjust instruction, practice opportunities, and even learning goals to maintain rigor and high expectations as students further develop their academic skills, in literacy, language, or other content areas.

What Information Can I Learn From the Students' Backgrounds and Families?

Special education teachers should collaborate with families (HLP 3) to learn about the home language and literacy practices; this goes for all students, and especially for students who are from culturally and linguistically diverse backgrounds. Special education teachers can learn a lot about a student's background by collaborating with students' families and/or guardians. What type of information can special education teachers learn about students? Using guidance from the State Support Network, you can build authentic relationships with parents that go beyond the regular practice of parent–teacher conferences and volunteerism in schools to gain knowledge about students and families that can impact their education (Jacques & Villegas, 2018). Understanding the value the family places on storytelling may help you understand the student's language development. Understanding the family structure and roles within collective extended families may inform you which family member supports homework and how that plays out in families. For instance, in some homes, more than one nuclear family, as defined in U.S. White Culture, may live, work, and socialize together, with more value placed on siblings and cousins as the friend group. In this case knowing the shared roles within the family may broaden your definition of *family* and offer the opportunity to build a relationship with an uncle or "distant" relative that can actually inform you of the student's attitude toward, and ability with, school assignments.

Special education teachers can also learn about students' and families' home language and literacy practices and backgrounds across all domains of life from conversations, single and on-going communication. Teachers could use an informal reading inventory to ask the students and their families about home language and literacy practices to learn about what types of text the student and family or household members typically read, and to learn about the family's home literacy practices. For example, perhaps the mother reads to the child in their native language with stories of cultural importance. Or perhaps the grandfather, who serves as the family leader, cannot read, and is intimidated by the printed word. When families feel safe to share this background, you can gain more information to help you make instructional decisions. These conversations are important because when teachers maintain an open, asset-based stance they can get to know students. Through becoming familiar with students' academic background and outside of school communities, they can identify different knowledge and strengths that their students have, and subsequently seek to draw on these strengths in classroom discussions. From these conversations, teachers can get to know students and learn about their interests. By talking with students' families, teachers can learn about their expectations, or hopes for their student's education and life outside of school. Learning about families' expectations, as well as learning about students' expectations and hopes are for future education, even post-secondary education, is important information that can inform the types of short- and long-term goals that special education teachers and IEP teams determine are appropriate for SWD. This is especially true related to transition planning to ensure the student is working toward meaningful goals. Fourth, for students who are multilingual learners, the teacher can learn about the families' preference for first and second language development. This is particularly important for students who are from culturally and linguistically diverse backgrounds as a common misconception about multilingual learners is that all families hold the same beliefs about bilingualism and how the students' first and additional languages are to be used for educational purposes in school (Alvarado et al., 2021).

So, how can teachers learn about students? Teachers can do this using any number of tools, including through conducting informal reading inventories (IRIs) to learn about the student's and family's home language practices. Use of IRIs and cultivation of open communication with parents/guardians of students are both effective and authentic ways to learn about if and how students engage in learning and development of different types of knowledge across domains in and out of school. This may include student home language use and learning about the family's language preferences for their student's education.

Before going further, we also caution readers to not fall into the trap of *essentializing* students' cultural and linguistic practices, particularly for Black, Indigenous, Latinx, and other minoritized students. In other words, do not think that if you learn about the food (comida), traditional clothes (costumbre), and culture (cultura) that you can become an expert on that group or culture. This simplification of culture difference can lead a teacher to make assumptions and biased inferences (Bennett, 2011).

It is important for special education teachers to avoid biased inferences. When special education teachers build authentic relationships with all students and families, and are intentional to not subscribe to stereotypic thinking, they are more likely to avoid the pitfall of seeing non-White, lower socioeconomic status, and linguistically diverse families as barriers and are better able to establish a relationship of trust and respect that treats the parents as equals.

Prefixes/Prefejos
Prefixes are a word part added to the beginning of a word to create a new word.
Examples/Ejemplos
re = again/de nuevo dis = not/no post = after/despues mis = wrong, bad/mal or mala un = not, opposite/no non = not, opposite/no

Figure 11-1. Sample poster for classroom support.

How Do I Specialize Learning Goals If They Are Already in the Individualized Education Program?

Special education teachers can, and should, specialize learning goals. This is equally important when the learning goals are in the IEP because the IEP goals are typically the larger goals that the IEP team has identified and agreed are the big picture goals that the student needs to work on until the next annual meeting. To help the student meet these larger goals, the special education teacher will design and set one or more short-term learning goals and provide intensified, systematic instruction to help the student make adequate progress by mediating student learning in different types of academic, or literacy apprenticeships in reading and reading comprehension, small groups.

Effective special education teachers acknowledge and value students' wealth of experiences, which includes but is not limited to students' cultural and linguistic knowledge and in-and-out-of-school experiences (Pacheco & Gutiérrez, 2009). This means that special education teachers may also seek to draw on these strengths. But what does this look like? Well, it means that the effective special education teacher may look to see how they can draw on or help students leverage their first language knowledge for the development of their second language. One practice that would be in alignment with research on how to support English-language learners with LD is to engage students to draw on their linguistic repertoires (Pacheco & Gutiérrez, 2009), meaning you can look to see if there are cognates, or words, that are similar, in English and Spanish for prefixes. In Spanish, letters added to the front of words that change the meaning are considered affixes rather than prefixes. For example, the use of "no" in Spanish when used before a word makes it opposite, and the use of "in/im" denotes that the meaning of the word is opposite of what the base word would be alone. Using this knowledge, remind emerging language students that they already know many words and how to build words in their first language. In this classroom example, it is Spanish. Showing students examples with bilingual posters can help them bring their first language into their second language knowledge and development by making it bilingual. A sample poster to display in your class can be found in Figure 11-1. Remember, providing reference "posters" around the classroom as students are learning a skill are a wonderful example of scaffolded supports (HLP 15).

After explaining and showing students the connections and commonalities between the prefixes in Spanish and English, you can design intensified instruction with practice opportunities for students to build words with prefixes and base words. The teacher could write on index cards as practice decks for the group of students. You can also have students make individual sets so that each student can sort or mark the cards for prefixes they are becoming more proficient with and those they need to continue to practice in isolation. Additionally, to support the students as they build mastery with reading and understanding the words in context, provide students opportunities to read texts with the prefixes in a small group and to discuss the meaning of the word in context and how the prefixes change the meaning of the word.

What Does HLP 11 Look Like in a K-12 Classroom?

Elementary Example

Mrs. Jones is an LD resource teacher with five fourth-grade students; all have been identified with areas of need in reading. Three students are also from culturally and linguistically diverse backgrounds, to include Latinx students. She is working with a small group of three fourth-grade students for reading small group instruction to target vocabulary and reading comprehension. The student members of the reading small group are a diverse group of learners and include students with high incidence disabilities and dyslexia (LD)—reading in multiple categories, and culturally and linguistically diverse exceptional learners, including Latinx students with LD and Latinx English-language learners/Emergent Bilinguals with LD. The teacher is also aware of the importance of research and the need to use a lens of culturally and linguistically responsive pedagogy, as well as to pay attention to how the learning environment (Gersten & Baker, 2000, 2003), and the social organization of learning (Alvarado et al., 2021), as well as the role of the teacher plays in mediating learning.

Mrs. Jones explains to students what prefixes are and how they change the meaning of the word. The teacher explains, models, and does a guided practice (HLP 16) with the students. During guided practice, she observes that the fourth-grade students are not understanding how the prefix changes the meaning of the base word. Mrs. Jones decides to consult the instructional standards. She works in a state that follows the Common Core State Standards for Language Arts (http://www.corestandards.org), so she goes to those standards for more information. Breaking down the standard for the grade-level expectations for students in fourth grade, she notices that prefixes and suffixes are not explicitly mentioned, but they can be reasonably inferred to be included in morphology. The Standard 4.1.1.1 reads "use combined knowledge of all letter-sound correspondences, syllabication patterns, and morphology to accurately read unfamiliar multisyllabic words in context and out of context." However, in the third grade, the standard does explicitly mention affixes: "identify, know the meaning of, and read words with common *prefixes and suffixes.*" Meaning this is more aligned with explicit instruction of the third-grade curriculum. Remember standards are written as if it is the end of the year so that it is understood what it is to be mastered by the end of the grade level. This standard implies third-grade general education teachers do more explicit instruction of affixes than fourth-grade teachers. For Mrs. Jones to meet the needs of her students and move them toward the grade-level standard, she must strategically plan long-term goals for students to understand the meaning of the common prefixes and suffixes. The short-term goals may break these into steps for when students will learn which prefix or suffix by a date prior to the annual review.

Now, Mrs. Jones consults the students' IEPs, and based on the students' present levels of understanding and academic performance, determines that an appropriate goal and starting point is to design targeted, systematic instruction (HLP 12) to teach the -ar, -er, and -ir sounds. She determines that the students will be able to correctly identify and differentiate between the -ar, -er, and -ir sounds 7 out of 10 times by the time the students participate and complete daily intensified instruction for a 4-week period; 9 out of 10 times correctly in a 9-week period; and maintain (HLP 21) this sound differentiation when applying it to reading multisyllabic words.

In this case, the short-term goal may read, "Given a third-grade text, students will be able to correctly differentiate between the -ar, -er, and -ir sounds in order to understand the function of prefixes and suffixes in changing the meaning of a root word with 70% accuracy within 4 weeks." Relatedly, the long-term goal is to maintain this skill when applying it to reading new and novel words, as well as the reading of multisyllabic words with prefixes and suffixes. To be measurable this goal may read, "When given an instructional level text, students will be able to correctly differentiate between the -ar, -er, and -ir sounds in order to understand the function of prefixes and suffixes in changing the meaning of a root word with 90% accuracy at the end of 9 weeks."

In recognizing that some of the students are also ELs, Mrs. Jones thinks she may need to focus on having the students make and practice the sounds -ar, -er, and -ir, to explain to them, and have them practice the difference between the letter sound correspondence in Spanish and in English. She plans to have them make the sounds while looking at their mouth formation in a mirror. With this strategy she can point to the similarities between her and her students' mouth and lip shapes for the individual sounds.

During her instruction, Mrs. Jones starts with having students practice the sounds in isolation; the teacher can use formative assessment to examine how students decode basic and multisyllabic words when reading and encountering words in context. Such learning and practice opportunities include collaborative work, through direct instruction, modeling, think-alouds, guided practice (Explicit Instruction; Archer & Hughes, 2011) that leads into peer pair work (PALS; Fuchs et al., 1997), and collaborative reading approaches like the use of Collaborative Strategic Reading (CSR; Klingner & Vaughn, 1998). Researchers have documented that peer-paired work is an effective instructional technique to mediate learning for LD students, as well as Emergent Bilinguals with LD (Sáenz et al., 2005).

As instruction continues with other prefixes, Mrs. Jones notices students are at different skill levels with the prefixes, mis-, non-, and un-, and then collects data (HLP 6) to plan more intensive instruction (HLP 20) for some students while continuing the current pace with others. This flexible grouping (HLP 17) allows her to deliver the individualized instruction students need to meet their IEP goals, as well as identify and prioritize her next short- and long-term learning goals.

Secondary Example

Ms. Simons is a high school special education teacher, serving mainly students with LD and Emotional/Behavioral Disabilities (EBD) in the general education classroom. She focuses on math instruction, and co-teaches with a friend and colleague, Mr. Randal. In their Algebra I class, they have a group of 10 SWD, all with needs in math calculation. The group is diverse; there are four Black students, three Latinx students, one of whom is also an English-language learner/Emergent Bilingual with LD, and three White students, which almost mirrors the 18 general education students. This diverse student group has a wide range of backgrounds and experiences, and quite a range of abilities, but all the SWD have an IEP goal related to math calculation, some for solving simple equations, while others have goals related to using integers and combining like terms. Ms. Simons knows these skills can all be easily measured with an Algebra Basic Skills CBM (Foegen & Morrison, 2010).

As the year begins, Ms. Simons and Mr. Randal take time to get to know their students. They have the students create "math biographies" (Seto & Meel, 2006) where students describe their experiences and feelings toward math class. They also administer both the Algebra Basic Skills and Algebra Foundations CBMs to gather instructional baseline data on the students. At first, Mr. Randal is concerned about the time this will take from the assigned curriculum. Ms. Simons explains to him the value this will add to their planning. By understanding students' experiences and anxieties the teachers can explicitly address them and relate successful experiences back when struggles arise. She goes on to explain the benefits of CBMs. Traditional unit quizzes and tests demonstrate mastery of recently taught content; CBMs will help measure growth and mastery over time. A weekly or biweekly administration of the algebra CBMs will let them see what students are learning and have maintained throughout the year, because the weekly probes, which only take 5 minutes to administer, have the same level of difficulty with all algebra skills. Students are also able to assist in setting their goals, graph their own progress, and in turn, become more engaged in their own learning.

> By keeping the timing, content, and difficulty of the measures consistent across each administration, teachers can have greater confidence that learning, rather than differences in test content or conditions, is responsible for changes in the data on a student's performance graph. (Foegen & Morrison, 2010, p. 96)

After collecting student biographies and baseline data, the two teachers sit down to plan the first unit, Quantitative Relationships, Graphs, and Functions. There are several Common Core State Standards addressed in this unit; they focus on two: Reasoning with Equations and Inequalities (REI A.1) Explain each step in solving a simple equation as following from the equality of numbers asserted at the previous step, starting from the assumption that the original equation has a solution. Construct a viable argument to justify a solution method and Creating Equations (CED A.1) Create equations and inequalities in one variable and use them to solve problems. *Include equations arising from linear and quadratic functions, and simple rational and exponential functions.*

They look through the CBM results and determine the students' readiness levels. One area of concern is that 12 of the 28 students, not just those identified with a disability, had difficulty with tasks related to identifying properties (whether using the property correctly or writing an inverse equation). They also note that 6 of the 12 students wrote about being embarrassed during math because they got "things mixed up." Using this knowledge gained from students, as well as wanting to instill the Common Core State Standards Math Practices 5 (use appropriate tools strategically) and 6 (attend to precision), they craft the following goals:

> Long-term goal: Given a linear equation, students will use mathematical properties to manipulate the equation to form multiple equivalent equations to solve.
>
> Short-term goal: Given 10 equations, students will identify the property used and write the corresponding inverse equation with at least 80% accuracy.

They decide to start the unit by having students help create classroom posters describing the properties in both academic language and student-friendly language as well as including example equations (HLP 18). These posters will be placed on the wall and referred to during instruction. Students are reminded to use these supports (HLP 15) during group and independent work.

After the first week of instruction, they review the data from the latest CBM probe, monitor the daily assessment (exit tickets) of the short-term goal (HLP 6), and are satisfied with the group's success. They proceed to make plans for the two students who did not quite get to 80% accuracy (HLPs 17 and 20), while also planning the next short-term goal, aligned to the curriculum. This practice continues throughout the year, strengthening their professional collaborative relationship (HLP 1) and their students' success.

Summary

Effective special education teachers must use multiple resources to determine the short- and long-term goals for their students. Starting with determining where their students are currently performing within the grade-level standard and curriculum, they gather information about the students' experiences by talking to both the student and the family, adjusting their preconceptions of what family means to different cultures. They use all this information and the IEP goals to determine the "road map" of instruction where they are starting to determine where they want to end.

The IEP is the backbone of a student's individualized education. This legal document determines the student will be provided FAPE. Teachers use the IEP to guide students' academic and functional advancement, but never forget SWD are first and foremost a general education student. How does their instruction and educational experience fit into the general education standards of their peers? Gone are the days of special education isolation, where SWD were just "lucky" to attend public school. Thank goodness! Today, we need to ensure all students regardless of ability, socioeconomic experience, and racial and cultural differences have an appropriate education. To do that, we leverage our relationships with professional colleagues and student families, we use the curriculum and data from assessments, and we use our knowledge of instruction to determine the educational journey our students will travel.

Chapter Review

1. Describe what is meant by an appropriate learning goal.
2. Why are learning goals (both short- and long-term) bound by time?
3. Look up a grade-level standard for a grade level you are or want to teach. Determine the "vertical" skills needed to support mastery of that standard.
4. Name two ways you can involve families in determining their students' short- and long-term goals.
5. How often should you re-examine learning goals?

References

Alvarado, S. L., Salinas, S. M., & Artiles, A. J. (2021). Dual language learners with disabilities in inclusive early elementary school classrooms. In D. C. Castro & A. J. Artiles (Eds.), *Language, learning, and disability in the education of young bilingual children* (pp. 64-89). Center for Applied Linguistics.

Archer, A. L., & Hughes, C. A. (2011). *Explicit instruction: Effective and efficient teaching.* Guilford Press.

Bennett, R. E. (2011). Formative assessment: A critical review. *Assessment in Education: Principles, Policy & Practice, 18*(1), 5-25 https://doi.org/10.1080/0969594X.2010.513678

Deno, S. L. (2003). Developments in curriculum-based measurement. *The Journal of Special Education,* 37(3), 184-192. https://doi.org/10.1177/00224669030370030801

Foegen, A., & Morrison, C. (2010). Putting algebra progress monitoring into practice: Insights from the field. *Intervention in School and Clinic, 46*(2), 95-103.

Fuchs, D., Fuchs, L. S., Mathes, P. G., & Simmons, D. C. (1997). Peer-assisted learning strategies: Making classrooms more responsive to diversity. *American Educational Research Journal, 34*(1), 174-206.

Fuchs, D., Fuchs, L. S., & Stecker, P. M. (2010). The "blurring" of special education in a new continuum of general education placements and services. *Exceptional Children, 76,* 301-322. https://doi.org/10.1177/001440291007600304

Gersten, R., & Baker, S. (2000). What we know about effective instructional practices for English-language learners. *Exceptional Children, 66*(4), 454-470. https://doi.org/10.1177/001440290006600402

Gersten, R., & Baker, S. (2003). English-language learners with learning disabilities. In H. L. Swanson, K. R. Harris, & S. Graham (Eds.), *Handbook of learning disabilities* (pp. 94-109). Guilford Press.

Good, R. H., & Kaminski, R. A. (Eds.). (2002). *Dynamic indicators of basic early literacy skills* (6th ed.). Institute for the Development of Educational Achievement. http://dibels.uoregon.edu/

Individuals With Disabilities Education Act, 20 U.S.C. §§ 1400 et seq. (2004).

Jacques, C., & Villegas, A. (2018). Strategies for equitable family engagement. *State Support Network, Partnering for School Improvement.* American Institutes for Research. https://www.air.org/centers/state-support-network

Klingner, J. K., & Vaughn, S. (1998). Using collaborative strategic reading. *TEACHING Exceptional Children, 30*(6), 32-37.

McLeskey, J., Barringer, M.-D., Billingsley, B., Brownell, M., Jackson, D., Kennedy, M., Lewis, T., Maheady, L., Rodriguez, J., Scheeler, M. C., Winn, J., & Ziegler, D. (2017). *High-leverage practices in special education.* Council for Exceptional Children & CEEDAR Center.

Pacheco, M., & Gutiérrez, K. (2009). Cultural-historical approaches to literacy teaching and learning. In C. Compton-Lily (Ed.), *Breaking the silence: Recognizing the social and cultural resources students bring to the classroom* (pp. 60-77). International Reading Association.

Restrepo, M. A., & Castilla-Earls, A. P. (2021). Language learning and language disability: Equity issues in the assessment of young bilingual learners. In D. C. Castro & A. J. Artiles (Eds.), *Language, learning, and disability in the education of young bilingual children* (pp. 90-111). Center for Applied Linguistics.

Sáenz, L. M., Fuchs, L. S., & Fuchs, D. (2005). Peer-assisted learning strategies for English language learners with learning disabilities. *Exceptional Children, 71*(3), 231-247.

Seto, B., & Meel, D. E. (2006). Writing in mathematics: Making it work. *Problems, Resources, and Issues in Mathematics Undergraduate Studies, 16*(3), 204-232.

Yell, M. L., & Bateman, D. (2020). Defining educational benefit: An update on the US Supreme Court's ruling in Endrew F. v. Douglas County School District. (2017). *TEACHING Exceptional Children, 52*(5), 283-290. https://doi.org/10.1177/0040059920914259

How Can I Ensure My Lessons Are Logically Sequenced?

Kyena E. Cornelius, EdD
and Ruby L. Owiny, PhD

HLP 12

Systematically design instruction toward a specific learning goal.

INTRODUCTION

Lesson planning is part of our job as teachers. Making it systematic takes a bit more skill. Instead of just planning a day's lesson, systematic instruction carefully considers a logical sequence of skills and content: starting with students' current understanding, building on prior learning, and following a strategic pathway from simple to more complex. This sequence is well thought out and designed before lessons and learning activities are planned. Systematic instruction requires intentionality on the part of the teacher to carefully sequence concepts and plan instruction. Effective special education teachers create clear goals, carefully crafted instruction, and use data to make in-the-moment adjustments; these are hallmarks of systematic instruction. Teachers also activate prior knowledge and intentionally explain how current learning fits within the learning sequence, past and present, to help students understand its significance.

Owiny, R. L., & Cornelius, K. E. *The Practical Guide to High-Leverage Practices in Special Education: The Purposeful "How" to Enhance Classroom Rigor* (pp. 173-186).

CHAPTER OBJECTIVES

- Define systematic instruction.
- Design a learning segment, or unit, using systematic instruction.
- Identify evidence-based practices that support implementation of systematic instruction.

KEY TERMS

- **Backward design/Understanding by Design (UbD):** A framework for designing instruction with the end goal in mind before developing lessons and teaching them.
- **Content Enhancement Routines:** Created by the University of Kansas Center for Research on Learning to make learning more organized, accessible, and understandable for students by teachers pre-planning key content to be learned.
- **KWL Chart:** A three-column table on which to record what is *K*nown about a topic, *W*hat learning is wanted around that topic, and what has been *L*earned at the end of a lesson or unit about the topic.
- **Universal Design for Learning (UDL):** A framework for removing barriers to learning so all students can achieve at high rates and become independent, lifelong learners.

Planning instruction can be compared to a road map. A lesson plan details where students begin their learning journey; the path you, the teacher/tour guide, will take them on; and the final destination. All of these are instrumental in planning a well-organized lesson and must already be determined before the journey begins. No lesson should be considered an isolated event. It is connected to prior learning and points to future learning. Just as no destination on a map truly sits in the middle of nowhere, a road, or several, connects it to other towns or cities.

Effective special education teachers are deliberate in their lesson planning. They know their individual students so well that they can assess their current understanding of the content, their strengths and needs (not only related to the curriculum but also what motivates the student), and in other words determine the student's starting point of the journey. They then create favorable traveling conditions, meaning they establish a respectful learning environment that is organized and has predictable routines and procedures to ensure every student learns. They understand the content (or the final destination) in a way that they can break it apart to examine student "gaps" and determine the sequence of lessons needed. Next, they present the content in multiple ways to tap into students' background knowledge, understanding that multiple means of representation and expression are necessary for new learning. Teachers also assess student learning regularly and adjust instruction as needed to keep the student on the journey until they have mastered the skills and content. This chapter will focus on designing lessons that sequence the content in a way that today's learning builds on yesterday's and sets the stage for more complex learning to come.

What Is HLP 12?

High-Leverage Practice (HLP) 12 targets planning, specifically, systematically designing instruction toward a specific learning goal. McLeskey and colleagues (2017) provide more detail for teachers to understand how to implement this HLP. Simply stated, the research team provides simple steps for teachers to consider for implementing this HLP. First, effective special education teachers teach foundational skills and concepts to provide a strong foundation for more complex learning. Second, they structure lessons with a logical progression, and make the connections between the lessons explicit, evidenced in both planning and delivery. Third, they start a lesson by activating students' background knowledge and prior learning and show how the current lesson "fits" with previous ones and with future lessons. Fourth, effective teachers understand that planning involves designing meaningful learning goals, what is involved in reaching the goal, and understand they must allocate class time accordingly. Finally, teachers know that instruction must involve ongoing changes (e.g., pacing, examples) based on student performance.

The best way to achieve a systematically designed lesson is to start at the end. Backward design, also known as Understanding by Design (UbD; Wiggins & McTighe, 2005), has been used in education and lesson planning for decades (Childre et al., 2009). This research-based practice challenges the "traditional" method of starting with the text and curriculum guides to determine what to teach and instead looks at the desired end result (McTighe & Wiggins, 2012). Once you determine the specific goal you wish students to master and how you will measure their success, you assess their current level of achievement, determine what unique skills are missing, and then start the planning process (Bulgren et al., 2007). Finally, make sure to communicate a clear goal for students, plan for ongoing assessment, and then monitor progress.

How Is HLP 12 Connected to Other HLPs?

Delivering systematically designed instruction requires using multiple HLPs. As with any high-quality instruction, teachers use multiple practices together to achieve better outcomes. When you start planning, first determine your students' current level of understanding. To do that, use multiple sources of information to better understand not only students' needs, but also their strengths related to those needs (HLP 4). Analyzing these data will help you determine the specific goals you intend to reach, both for the full learning segment or unit (long-term) and individual lessons (short-term; HLP 11), as well as how to measure student success and determine what data to collect along the way to inform other instructional decisions (HLP 6).

As you start to plan instruction, think about the end result and students' current understanding, plan to build on student background knowledge, and connect to what you know they mastered from previous lessons (HLP 21). Next, analyze your resources and the materials available; decide if adapting or modifying those materials (HLP 13) is needed. Ask yourself, what supports will students need, and how will you scaffold those supports (HLP 15)? How can you actively engage (HLP 18) them for meaningful learning? How will technology (HLP 19) benefit student learning? Then, think about guiding them beyond just "earning" a grade and completing the unit; how can you get them to a level of understanding that they demonstrate this skill across time and settings (HLP 21)? All of this is achieved through explicit instruction (HLP 16) and providing positive and constructive feedback throughout the learning experience (HLP 22). Table 12-1 highlights the multiple HLPs needed to implement the planning methods discussed in this chapter.

What Is Systematic Instruction?

Systematic instruction is defined as, "instruction that is carefully and logically sequenced toward a specific goal" (Konrad et al., 2022, p. 172). Systematic instruction is an evidence-based practice (EBP) derived, in part, from applied behavior analysis principles to ensure students are trained in a new concept in a defined, observable, and measurable manner that leads to student mastery of skills (Walker et al., 2020). Systematic instruction can be successfully implemented in both full instructional units, such as how to add fractions or analyze the causes of Napoleon's war strategy in Europe, or in teaching discrete, specific skills, such as sight words or hand washing. Teachers develop systematic instruction through carefully constructed lesson goals, sequencing of skills and concepts, and

Table 12-1. Alignment of HLPs and Resources for Evidence-Based Practices

EBP SUPPORT WITH HLP 12	RELATED HLPS	RESOURCES
Backward design	11, 13, 15, 16, 17, 21, 22	https://www.cultofpedagogy.com/backward-design-basics/ https://youtu.be/4isSHf3SBuQ
Explicit instruction	4, 6, 13, 15, 16, 17, 18, 20, 22	https://www.understood.org/en/articles/what-is-explicit-instruction https://my.vanderbilt.edu/spedteacherresources/what-is-explicit-instruction/
Activate prior knowledge	4, 6, 17, 18, 22	https://www.youtube.com/watch?v=m9TykvvZHWg&t=7s https://strategiesforspecialinterventions.weebly.com/activating-prior-knowledge1.html
Content Enhancement Routines	4, 6, 18, 19, 22	https://kucrl.ku.edu/sim-content-enhancement-routines https://education.wm.edu/centers/ttac/state/sim/contentenhancementroutines/index.php

helping students to organize their learning in a way that makes sense to them (Konrad et al., 2022). In other words, effective special education teachers must choose what to teach, when to teach it, and how to teach based on their students' needs.

Why Is Systematic Instruction Important?

When clear instructional goals are made explicitly known by students, it takes the mystery out of instruction. When students know exactly what they are learning, why they are learning it, and how it is connected to other learning, they are more likely and more quickly able to "buy in" to instruction (Konrad et al., 2022). When teachers understand how each lesson is connected to others, as well as the overarching goal and standard, it is easier to plan and lead students to achieve independence (Wiggins & McTighe, 2005).

How Do I Plan for Systematic Instruction?

We all love a good template! Time and again we create or look for examples of templates to get us started with a specific task. Figure 12-1 provides a graphic to help you in planning high-quality systematic instruction. The graphic is based on Childre and colleagues (2009) four-step approach to designing quality instruction that takes a student from surface knowledge to deeper understanding.

- Step 1: Identify the learners.
- Step 2: Identify curricular priorities.
- Step 3: Design the assessment framework.
- Step 4: Create learning activities.

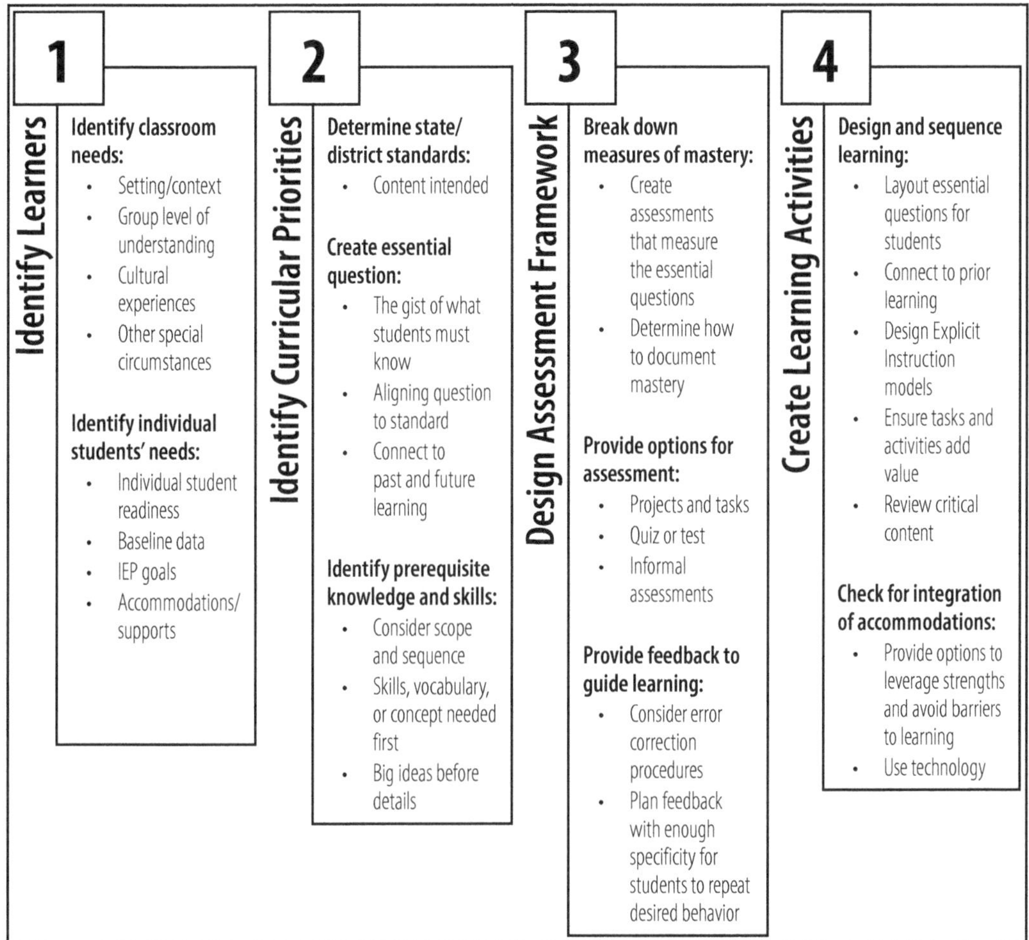

Figure 12-1. Four-step approach to designing systematic instruction. (Adapted from Childre, A., Sands, J. R., & Pope, S. T. [2009]. Backward design: Targeting depth of understanding for all learners. *TEACHING Exceptional Children*, *41*[5], 6-14.)

This chapter builds upon their approach to help you systematically design instruction toward a specific learning goal.

Starting with the first step, you need to understand the needs of your students. Pull from all of those data sources (HLP 4) you have been collecting and think about your setting. Will this instruction take place in an inclusive classroom or maybe a resource room? How is the student or group progressing with universal screening measures? What is the cultural background of the students? What has been their exposure to the topic or skill you will be teaching? What do you know about your students' needs?

During the second step, identify the curricular priorities. What is the state or local standard this lesson is intended to address? As you examine the standard, consider what essential questions this standard was designed to ask. What is the gist of the standard? What are the prerequisite skills needed to access this standard? Make sure you separate those "big ideas" from the details. Think of this as the *need to know* vs. the *nice to know*. Details are fun, but almost trivial points that may not be as important once you dig deeper into the standards. You will also want to consider individualized education program (IEP) goals and objectives and consider the long-term vs. short-term goals (HLP 11) that need to be addressed.

<table>
<tr><td colspan="2">Subject/Topic</td><td colspan="3">Measurable Learning Goal for the Lesson:
(What do students have to demonstrate to say they "learned" this goal?)</td></tr>
<tr><td colspan="2"></td><td colspan="3"></td></tr>
<tr><td colspan="2">CCSS/District Benchmark Standard being addressed</td><td colspan="3">Related IEP Goal/Objective:</td></tr>
<tr><td colspan="2"></td><td colspan="3" rowspan="3"></td></tr>
<tr><td colspan="2">Essential Question</td></tr>
<tr><td colspan="2"></td></tr>
<tr><td colspan="5">Baseline Data (how do you know students are ready for this lesson).</td></tr>
<tr><td colspan="5"></td></tr>
<tr><td colspan="2">Plan for Formative Assessment</td><td colspan="3">Intervention/Evidence-based strategy to be used</td></tr>
<tr><td colspan="2"></td><td colspan="3"></td></tr>
<tr><td>Student</td><td>Planned Support(s): Planned supports can include the learning environment, instructional strategies, learning tasks, materials, prompts, and/or scaffolding</td><td>Targeted Skill/Objective</td><td>Opportunities with targeted skill/objective</td><td>Successful completion/ occurrence</td></tr>
<tr><td></td><td></td><td></td><td></td><td></td></tr>
<tr><td></td><td></td><td></td><td></td><td></td></tr>
</table>

Figure 12-2. Lesson plan template to ensure systematic instruction.

For the third step, design the assessment framework, consider the best method for assessing the learning objectives. What might best allow students to truly demonstrate their understanding in a meaningful way? How can you provide multiple assessments in different ways? What will informal assessment look like? What will formal assessment look like? When will these appear in the lesson sequence? How will you collect data from the assessments? How will you record the data? How will you analyze the data to make informed decisions? All these questions not only apply to systematic instruction but also to HLP 4 (using multiple sources of information to develop a comprehensive understanding of a student's strengths and needs), HLP 5 (interpreting and communicating information with stakeholders to collaboratively design and implement educational programs), and HLP 6 (using student assessment data, analyzing instructional practices, and making necessary adjustments that improve student outcomes).

Many teachers find Step 4, create learning activities, to be the most fun. This is where we can design learning activities to meet the needs of our students and the learning goal while allowing our creative juices to flow. There are some questions to ask to help ensure quality instructional design of the learning activities. First, in line with Universal Design for Learning (UDL), identify any barriers to learning that might need to be addressed. These may likely be addressed in the student's IEP, such as needing a reader for above grade-level material. What activities will best engage students in learning to effectively help them to master the content (HLP 18)? How can those activities be sequenced in the most beneficial way? How will students be grouped during instruction (HLP 17)? How will they actively respond to instruction to stay on task and learn (HLP 18)? What materials are needed to accomplish the activities?

Once these decisions are made, use a full lesson plan template to organize your lessons. We have provided a portion of a lesson plan template to help you ensure the questions from the first and second steps are completely answered (Figure 12-2). The template shared is for one lesson; remember that you are sequencing multiple lessons to create a systematic unit of instruction. Thus, you would want to have an overarching topic and learning goal, then multiple subtopics (logically sequenced) and a meaningful learning objective for each. Once you are ready to plan an individual lesson, start with your topic and subject standard and align the students' IEP goals. For example, your topic may be creating fractions with common denominators, your state standard for fifth-grade math/fractions states; 5.NF.A.1: Add and subtract fractions with uncommon denominators (including mixed numbers) by replacing given fractions with equivalent fractions in such a way as to produce an equivalent sum or difference of fractions with common denominators. The students in this group have related IEP goals, specifically one student's IEP goal states, "Given a set of 10 single-step problems involving addition and subtraction of fractions and mixed numbers with uncommon denominators, the student will solve them with at least 80% accuracy." Consider what students must demonstrate to say they "learned" this goal. Write a measurable learning goal; we are personal fans of the formula: condition, behavior, and criteria for mastery. For instance, "Given 10 sets of 2 fractions, students will identify the common denominator for each set, with 80% accuracy." This goal tells us that for an "aligned assessment" activity you will want students to be successful on 8 out of 10 opportunities to find the common denominator with pairs of fractions. In the previous unit, students were adding and subtracting fractions with common denominators. In that lesson, we taught fractions must have common denominators to add or subtract them. Now, we will reinforce that and teach students to find common denominators before we move on to adding and subtracting uncommon denominators. Following today's learning, we point to the next lesson where students will be learning to convert the set of fractions to have common denominators. Explain that after they find the common denominator they will have to "change" the current fraction, or convert it to an equivalent fraction, another connection to previous learning. You could even make the connection that by the end of the unit or learning segment, the students will be completing multiple steps to add and subtract fractions with uncommon denominators.

Understanding by Design or Backward Design

It is difficult sometimes to think of EBPs involved with planning. However, there are some great ones out there to discuss. Actually, the framework for UbD or Backward design, given that name for starting with the end in mind, comes from research in and out of education. Wiggins and McTighe (2005) highlight the advancements of other fields (e.g., business, sociology) using Backward design, and share this idea as first proposed in education by Ralph Tyler in 1949. The goal of Backward design is the exact goal of systematic instruction at the planning stage, to first consider learning targets (the end goal) before planning the instruction to meet those goals.

Explicit Instruction

Archer and Hughes (2011) have propelled the EBPs of explicit instruction to such an extent that this instructional delivery approach is the recommended instructional delivery method for special education (McLeskey et al., 2017). Highlighting its importance, explicit instruction is also an HLP (HLP 16). When you think about the structured approach of I Do, We Do, You Do, it is easy to see how systematically designing instruction with the explicit instruction principles in mind creates an effective and efficient method for instructional delivery. For more examples of this and more detail on explicit instruction, please read Chapter 16.

Universal Design for Learning

The core components of systematic instruction, "clear instructional goals, logical sequencing of knowledge and skills, and teaching students to organize content" (McLeskey et al., 2017) are relevant in any setting and connect to UDL. Clear instructional goals are key to student engagement. Logical sequencing of knowledge and skills involves decisions on not only the sequence but then the way that knowledge or skill will be taught. Students must be able to actively express their learning and learn

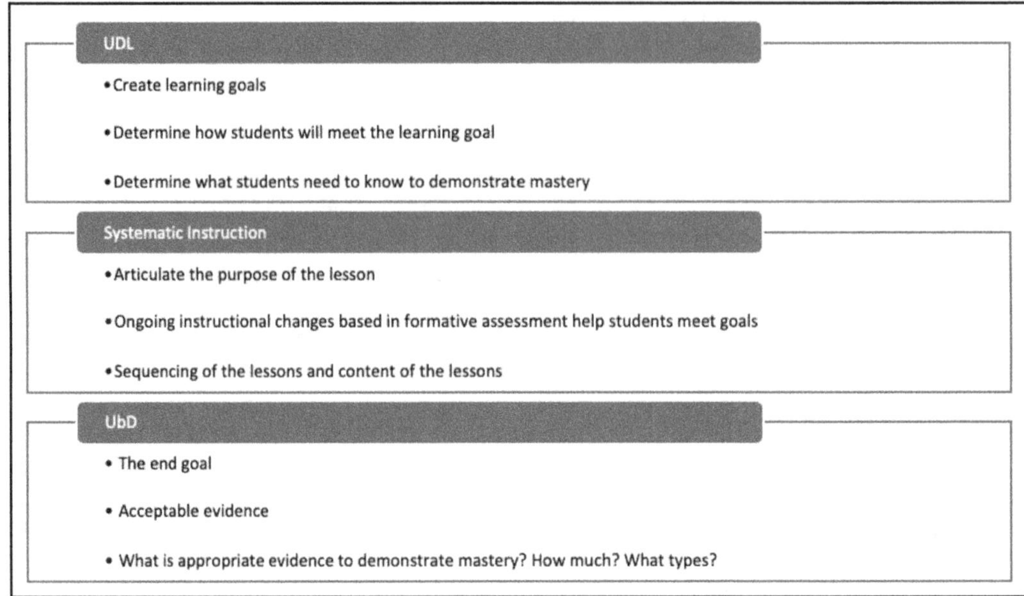

Figure 12-3. Relationship between UDL, systematic instruction, and UbD.

how to organize content, which is embedded in all three principles. Novak (2022) provides a list of prompts for teachers to consider when analyzing their lessons to be UDL-friendly. Several of these items are not only beneficial for ensuring UDL implementation but are essential for implementing systematic instruction and UbD. Figure 12-3 shows this relationship between UDL, systematic instruction, and UbD. Similar questions are asked, and similar decisions are made to ensure quality learning. Systematic instruction is also intertwined with explicit instruction (HLP 16) and multiple other HLPs, but also a myriad of EBPs, specifically UbD and UDL. When implemented in tandem, students learn at higher rates, and when students learn, teachers experience greater job satisfaction.

Content Enhancement Routines

The University of Kansas Center for Research on Learning has developed Content Enhancement Routines. These are "sets of inclusive teaching practices that help teachers organize and present critical information in such a way that students identify, organize, comprehend, and recall it" (University of Kansas Center for Research on Learning, 2022a). Content Enhancement Routines help teachers systematically plan instruction for the diverse needs of the students in their classrooms. These routines are based in research related to student active participation (HLP 18), student self-regulation of their learning (HLP 14), and making abstract concepts more concrete through explicit instruction (HLP 16), along with research on quality instructional design (Schumaker & Fisher, 2021).

Two Content Enhancement Routines, the Unit Organizer Routine and the Lesson Organizer Routine, are designed for teachers to clearly articulate the big picture of the unit and how an individual lesson fits into the unit (University of Kansas Center for Research on Learning, 2022b). Both the Unit Organizer Routine and the Lesson Organizer Routine include principles of systematic instruction. The Unit Organizer Routine includes framing the unit in a way that students know the big picture and can articulate it. This is in line with Konrad et al. (2022) who state that big ideas must be taught, as they are foundational to learning. The big idea allows students to have an anchor by which to hold subsequent information. The Unit Organizer Routine provides a means for students to learn how to organize their learning, which requires the teacher to carefully sequence instruction and teach the organizational method, which in the case of the Unit Organizer Routine is a graphic organizer completed with the teacher. Another key component of systematic instruction and of the

Unit Organizer Routine is making connections by exploring the relationship between background knowledge and new knowledge as well as relationships between and among concepts.

The Lesson Organizer Routine also includes explicitly stating and building a lesson around the lesson's main idea while relating new information to background knowledge. Graphic organizers used in this routine provide students with the opportunity to learn how to organize their learning, a key component of systematic instruction. In addition to these explicit connections to systematic instruction, the Lesson Organizer Routine also provides students with instruction on how their learning has been structured, how to identify the most important content, and to know the expectations for the lesson (University of Kansas Center for Research on Learning, 2022b). When teachers set clear goals in systematic instruction, they are helping students understand the expectations, which in turn will increase efficiency and students will effectively meet learning goals.

How Can I Activate Students' Prior Knowledge and Connect the Content From Previous Learning?

Once sequencing the lesson is completed, strategically planning for students to connect what they learn in a new unit with what they already know helps situate the old concepts around the new ones (Konrad et al., 2022). Many activities that teachers already know are helpful for activating prior knowledge, such as providing a prompt and doing a Think-Pair-Share activity or doing a quick write and directing students to write all they know about a topic for a short period of time (e.g., 1 to 2 minutes; Barrio et al., 2017). These activities create more meaningful learning experiences for students while stimulating their interest in the subject matter and increasing their motivation to master the content (IRIS Center, 2011). The UDL principle of representation includes a checkpoint that is "activate or supply background knowledge" because this idea of situating current learning with prior learning is vital for students to build a bridge from the old to the new to learn effectively and make the new learning accessible (CAST, 2022). The notion that stimulating prior knowledge also increases motivation taps into the engagement principle of UDL, which is the part of the brain that wants to know "why." Making connections helps to answer the "why."

There are multiple methods for tapping into prior knowledge. Only a few have been chosen for this chapter with Table 12-1 providing some further resources for ideas. Tapping into prior knowledge by reviewing vocabulary is one method for ensuring students have the appropriate foundation for new learning. There are many ways to review vocabulary. The activity "I have, who has?" involves the whole class in careful listening for the definition to the word they have on their card. This takes some preparation by preparing cards with a vocabulary word on one side and a definition of a different word on the other. The cards, when laid out in a sequence, become a series of words with definitions.

For the sake of this example, assume a group of three students. When reviewing previously learned government types to learn a new one, you decide to play this game with your students. The procedure is as follows:

1. Prepare index cards. On one card write *democracy* on the front and a definition on the back, "a political and economic doctrine that aims to replace private property and profit-based economy with public ownership and communal control of at least the major means of production (e.g., mines, mills, and factories) and the natural resources of a society" (Britannica, n.d.-a). On the next card write, *communism* on one side and "political system based upon the undivided sovereignty or rule of a single person. The term applies to states in which supreme authority is vested in the monarch, as an individual ruler who functions as the head of state and who achieves his or her position through heredity" (Britannica, n.d.-b) on the back. On the third card write *monarchy* and, on the back, "a form of government based on rule by the people with popular sovereignty as its defining feature (Oxford Reference, n.d.).

2. Pass out one index card to each of the three students.
3. The first student (does not matter who starts) reads the *definition* out loud, starting with, "Who has 'a political and economic doctrine that aims to replace private property and profit-based economy with public ownership and communal control of at least the major means of production (e.g., mines, mills, and factories) and the natural resources of a society'?" The person who has *communism* will say, "I have *communism*" and proceed to read the definition on the other side of the card by saying, "Who has 'political system based upon the undivided sovereignty or rule of a single person. The term applies to states in which supreme authority is vested in the monarch, as an individual ruler who functions as the head of state and who achieves his or her position through heredity'?" The student with *monarchy* will say, "I have *monarchy*. Who has 'a form of government based on rule by the people with popular sovereignty as its defining feature'?" The first student will say, "I have *democracy*." The game is over once the definition is read for the first student's card.

In this example, reviewing *monarchy*, *democracy*, and *communism* lead into the next lesson on *totalitarianism*. Students can connect what they know about the first three governments to this new, fourth, government.

Another way to tap into prior knowledge is to complete a KWL (Know, Want to Know, and Learned). Students can complete a three-column chart of the first two columns (Know and Want to Know) before a new unit begins either as a whole class or individually. As the unit ends, they can complete the Learned column. The K column serves as tapping into prior knowledge while the Want to Know helps the teacher to input information into the unit that interests students and may not already be planned, while the L column serves as both a review for a summative assessment and as a formative assessment for the teacher to have an idea of what students have retained from the unit.

A third, but definitely not final, way to activate prior knowledge is to use questioning through a discussion or using response cards (Owiny et al., 2018). If questions require lengthy responses, discussion could be used to activate prior knowledge. For example, why did the United States of America get involved in the Vietnam War? Yet, if a question requires a discrete response, such as "What is the formula for calculating the area of a rectangle," then response cards could be used in the form of a personal-size whiteboard or laminated construction paper for students to write their response with an erasable marker. Questioning with immediate responses helps the teacher to know what students remember about a prior topic to connect it to the next one.

How Can I Sequence Lessons That Build on Each Other and Make Connections Explicit?

Remember our "learning journey" analogy from the beginning of the chapter? Let's go back to that picture for this answer. We need to see "learning" as a continual motion. We do not start at a random point. We start where we are, or in this case where the student is, and base our destination accordingly. We intentionally break up learning in a way that is logically sequenced and helps students see where they started, where they are, and where they are going. Critically and explicitly sequencing lessons can be achieved with using a template, such as the one provided in Figure 12-2. This helps you to consciously answer questions about your lesson planning and get away from the textbook or curriculum pacing guides. Of course, the scope and sequence of a curriculum can help, but you also want to base these decisions on student information.

Learning Goals

Establish a meaningful goal by asking "What do students have to demonstrate to say they *learned* this goal?" As stated earlier, think about what will be provided to the student (the condition), what you want the student to do (the behavior), and what will be considered an expectation for "learned" (the criteria for mastery). Here is a simple learning goal "formula": When given *this something*, the student *will do this action*, with at least *this percentage* of accuracy.

Teaching Big Ideas Before Details

Just as you would teach a student to give the big idea of a story before they dig into the text to find the supporting details, you want to do the same thing with content and individual standards. When planning your systematic instruction, you need to learn what students already know about the big idea, clear up any misconceptions, and then fill in any "gaps" of learning, before moving on to the details. For example, if you were teaching a unit on the "forms of government," teach the purpose of government first, then dig into the different forms, before starting to compare the forms of government and have students make opinion statements.

Real-Time Changes

This is where you will rely on the use of formative assessment data to make real-time changes. Read student affect; you know that "deer in headlights" look that tells you to stop. Check for understanding. Give more opportunities for practice before moving on. You do not want to keep teaching to complete the lesson plan or meet some district pacing guide. If you move on too quickly, you are not teaching; you are checking the boxes. Real teaching means real learning is happening. Anticipate student errors or misconceptions and plan for them. Plan for ongoing formative assessment. Use an exit ticket, and other in-class formative assessment, to reflect at the end of the day, or class period, to adjust tomorrow's instruction so that learning continues to move forward.

Connect Current Learning With Future Learning

As stated earlier, learning does not happen in isolation. Make sure you connect the stops along the learning journey. At the opening of the lesson, you connect today's learning to yesterday's lesson. You state the purpose and relevance of this lesson and how it connects to the big picture of the content and to real life. Let's face it, every student wants to know why they are learning this thing you want to teach them. Tell them at every opportunity. Make sure you have made clear connections to tomorrow's learning and even the next unit, or the next course in the sequence, and of course share that with students too! End your lesson with how today's learning informs future learning. Not only is making these connections relevant to systematic instruction, it is also a way to implement the engagement principle of UDL—making learning relevant to students helps them to be more fully engaged.

WHAT DOES HLP 12 LOOK LIKE IN A K-12 CLASSROOM?

Elementary Example

Ms. Baker is an elementary school special education teacher who is preparing a math unit related to the Common Core Math Standard 3.2.2.1—"Understand how to interpret number sentences involving multiplication and division of basic facts and unknowns." Create real-world situations to represent number sentences. For example, the number sentence $8 \times m = 24$ could be represented by the question, "How much did each ticket to a play cost, if 8 tickets totaled $24?" (National Governors

Association Center for Best Practices & Council of Chief State School Officers, 2010). She examines the students' current baseline data related to math computation (HLP 6). The students have learned the concept and understand that multiplication is repeated addition of the same number. They are still learning that division is the opposite of multiplication, but they do know the purpose of dividing is to see how many equal groups can be formed. However, they do not have quick recall and fluency of the computation skills. She thinks, "Okay, as they continue to learn, they can use a calculator as an accommodation (HLP 13). I need to make sure they truly understand the concepts of division, that multiplication and division are inverse operations, and what is meant by an unknown. Are they ready for variables right now? Maybe soon. For this unit I will focus on the academic language they will need to understand math and the different operational relationships." The best way to do this is plan the unit so that the lessons are systematically sequenced and logically built upon each other.

She begins the planning process with thinking about the end in mind: What do students need to demonstrate so they know they have learned the topic? She decides for this unit to focus on introducing inverse operations. She will start with vocabulary, and then talk about "inverse operations" with addition and subtraction, move on to multiplication and division, and maybe for a teaser check their readiness for "unknowns" by providing a lesson to demonstrate the relevance of inverse and unknowns. She develops the unit goal: "Given 10 mixed computation problems, students will write an inverse operation problem and solve both problems to check their work with 80% accuracy." Ms. Baker then sequences the lessons and determines each lesson's unique learning objective. She creates multiple practice opportunities (HLP 18) for each lesson, writes down some common errors she anticipates students will make to intentionally plan corrective feedback (HLP 22), designs formative assessments to measure student learning, and prepares to adjust her instruction as needed.

Secondary Example

Ms. Steinman is a high school special education teacher; she and the civics teacher, Ms. Lance, are co-planning a unit on the electoral process. Ms. Lance brings up the social studies standard for civics: "Critique the influence of intermediary institutions on government and policy, such as interest groups, political parties, the mass media, campaigns, caucuses, elections, PACs, and local, state, tribal, and international organizations." They also examine the Common Core Speaking and Listening Standards related to comprehension and collaboration: 11.9.2.2—"Integrate multiple sources of information presented in diverse formats and media (e.g., visually, quantitatively, orally) in order to make informed decisions and solve problems, evaluating the credibility and accuracy of each source and noting any discrepancies among the data" (National Governors Association Center for Best Practices & Council of Chief State School Officers, 2010). Ms. Steinman shares that students in their co-taught civics class have IEP goals of comparing two sources of informational text to identify common themes and differences between sources. They think about how to break up this topic, "the electoral process for president," into separate lessons. Ms. Lance shares the major ideas that must be covered: candidates declare intentions, the primary/caucus process, delegates and conventions, campaigning, electoral college, and transition of power.

Once they agree upon the sequence, they must determine what the students already know (HLP 6). First, they review the text and curriculum materials used in the middle school civics class to see what students were explicitly taught. Next, they design a unit pre-test to assess what students retained from middle school or may already know about the content. They also design an assessment to understand students' ability to compare multiple sources of information and evaluate the source's credibility (HLPs 4 and 6). Based on these results they decide to explicitly teach (HLP 16) a lesson on evaluating the credibility of a source and another lesson on comparing multiple sources. These common core skills are embedded within their unit on the presidential electoral process, using the text students will use for the unit. Using the results of the content pre-assessment, they intentionally plan how much time to dedicate to each subtopic.

After this initial fact gathering, the two teachers now plan the lessons for this unit. They design their overarching goal: "Given two media sources (their textbook and an online article), students will be able to identify the U.S. Presidential electoral process with at least 80% accuracy." They systematically sequence the lessons and determine each lesson's unique learning objective, plan multiple practice opportunities (HLP 18), anticipate common errors to address, so they can plan corrective feedback (HLP 22), and prepare the daily formative assessment to measure student learning and adjust their instruction.

Summary

On a first read, you may be feeling systematic instruction sounds like a lot of work. It is, but so is any effective instructional planning. You must know your content/skills so well you can break them apart and separate big idea from details, assess student learning to gauge where their understanding falls within the scope of the targeted content/skill, and then sequence lessons that build upon each other, while collecting data on student progress and understanding to make in-time changes to strengthen instruction and move student learning forward. An effective teacher starts with the end in mind. Just like any travel plan, you decide your destination, and then look at the current location to find the best route to get you there.

Effective teachers use multiple tools to complete the intricate task of designing instruction. They understand multiple EBPs such as Content Enhancement Routines from the University of Kansas, Unit Organizer Routine and the Lesson Organizer Routine, can help them organize their units and individual lessons. Teachers begin with thinking about the end result; UbD helps them think critically about what student mastery will look like and how ongoing assessment drives instructional choices along the way. Using the UDL framework, teachers remove barriers to learning, and set clear, understandable, and achievable goals while also telling students the purpose for learning the concepts or ideas in the lesson. Effective teachers build on students' prior learning to create meaningful lessons and explicitly link today's learning to tomorrow's. So yes, it is time consuming, and can be a lot of work, but higher student achievement is worth all the time and effort.

Chapter Review

1. Why is systematic instruction important?
2. Describe the four steps discussed in planning systematic instruction.
3. Choose an IEP goal and determine how to break that standard up in a way that promotes student learning.

References

Archer, A. L., & Hughes, C. A. (2011). *Explicit instruction: Effective and efficient teaching.* Guilford Press.

Barrio, B. L., Peak, P. K., & Murawski, W. W. (2017). English language learners with disabilities: Best practices. In W. W. Murawski & K. L. Scott (Eds.), *What really works with exceptional learners* (pp. 262-281). Corwin.

Britannica. (n.d.-a). *Communism.* https://www.britannica.com/topic/communism

Britannica. (n.d.-b). *Monarchy.* https://www.britannica.com/topic/monarchy

Bulgren, J., Deshler, D. D., & Lenz, B. K. (2007). Engaging adolescents with LD in higher order thinking about history concepts using integrated content enhancement routines. *Journal of Learning Disabilities, 40*(2), 121-133.

CAST. (2022). *Activate or supply background knowledge.* https://udlguidelines.cast.org/representation/comprehension/background-knowledge

Childre, A., Sands, J. R., & Pope, S. T. (2009). Backward design: Targeting depth of understanding for all learners. *TEACHING Exceptional Children*, *41*(5), 6-14.

IRIS Center. (2011). *Teaching English language learners: Effective instructional practices.* https://iris.peabody.vanderbilt.edu/module/ell/

Konrad, M., Hessler, T., Alber-Morgan, S. R., Graham-Day, K. J., Davenport, C. A., & Helton, M. (2022). Systematically design instruction toward a specific goal. In J. McLeskey, L. Maheady, B., Billingsley, M. T. Brownell, & T. J. Lewis (Eds.), *High leverage practices for inclusive classrooms* (2nd ed., pp. 172-188). Routledge. https:/doi.org/10.4324/9781003148609

McLeskey, J., Barringer, M. D., Billingsley, B., Brownell, M., Jackson, D., Kennedy, M., Lewis, T., Maheady, L., Rodriquez, J., Scheeler, M. C., Winn, J., & Ziegler, D. (2017). *High-leverage practices in special education.* Council for Exceptional Children & CEEDAR Center.

McTighe, J., & Wiggins, G. (2012). *Understanding by design framework.* Association for Supervision and Curriculum Development.

National Governors Association Center for Best Practices & Council of Chief State School Officers. (2010). *Common core state standards.* www.corestandards.org

Novak, K. (2022). *UDL now! A teacher's guide to applying universal design for learning.* CAST.

Owiny, R. L., Spriggs, A. D., Sartini, E. C., & Mills, J. R. (2018). Evaluating response cards as evidence based. *Preventing School Failure: Alternative Education for Children and Youth*, *62*(2), 59-72. https://doi.org/10.1080/1045988X.2017.1344953

Oxford Reference. (n.d.). *Democracy.* https://www.oxfordreference.com/view/10.1093/acref/9780195148909.001.0001/acref-9780195148909-e-241

Schumaker, J. B., & Fisher, J. B. (2021). 35 years on the road from research to practice: A review of studies on four content enhancement routines for inclusive subject-area classes, Part I. *Learning Disabilities Research and Practice*, *36*(3), 242-257. https://doi.org/10.1111/ldrp.12258

University of Kansas Center for Research on Learning. (2022a). *Components of SIM.* https://sim.ku.edu/components-sim

University of Kansas Center for Research on Learning. (2022b). *The lesson organizer routine.* https://sim.ku.edu/lesson-organizer-routine

Walker, V. L., Douglas, S. N., Douglas, K. H., & D'Agostino, S. N. (2020). Paraprofessional-implemented systematic instruction for students with disabilities: A systematic literature review. *Education and Training in Autism and Developmental Disabilities*, *55*(3), 303-317.

Wiggins, G., & McTighe, J. (2005). *Understanding by design* (2nd ed.). ASCD.

How Do I Adapt Curricula and Materials?

Alice L. Rhodes, PhD
and Victoria Slocum, PhD

HLP 13

Adapt curriculum tasks and materials for specific learning goals.

INTRODUCTION

High-Leverage Practice (HLP) 13 is all about making adaptations for students with disabilities (SWD). This chapter will discuss how to make decisions for choosing the appropriate accommodation or modification under the umbrella of adaptations. When accommodations are accessible to everyone, such as access to an audiobook, it makes it more desirable for SWD who need the accommodation to be successful. Providing accommodations in this manner assists teachers in meeting the needs of all students while ensuring that the specially designed instructions outlined in a student's individualized education program are met. This chapter also explores relevant technology and the selection of materials and tasks for providing appropriate accommodations. The importance of adaptations to the curriculum and materials, specifically regarding accommodations and modifications, will be discussed with examples for provision of the necessary adaptations for student success.

Owiny, R. L., & Cornelius, K. E. *The Practical Guide to High-Leverage Practices in Special Education: The Purposeful "How" to Enhance Classroom Rigor* (pp. 187-202).

CHAPTER OBJECTIVES

- Describe strategies for utilizing relevant technology to meet student needs.
- Explain procedures for selecting materials and tasks based on student needs.
- Describe the process of making modifications through highlighting relevant information, changing task directions, and decreasing amounts of material.
- Define each of these objectives within the Universal Design for Learning framework..

KEY TERMS

- **accessible materials:** Adaptations to make materials accessible to students with disabilities. Adaptations may include strategies for accommodations and modifications as well as adaptations to the materials themselves.
- **accommodations:** Supports or services to compensate for challenges that may be present for individuals with disabilities. Accommodations do not alter the fundamental objectives (or state content standards) of a course, task, or assignment, but provide access to the general curriculum.
- **adaptations:** An umbrella term that includes both modifications and accommodations and can be categorized into general or specific adaptations.
- **assistive technology device:** Any item, piece of equipment, or product utilized for increasing, maintaining, and improving the functional capabilities of students with disabilities.
- **assistive technology services:** Any service that assists a student with a disability select, acquire, and use an assistive technology device. It includes evaluation, purchasing, selecting, coordinating, and training or technical assistance for the students, parents, and professionals.
- **individualized education program (IEP):** A legal document created by teachers, parents, school administrators, related services personnel, and students (when appropriate) in order to provide education for children with disabilities.
- **modifications:** Changes to the instruction, assessments, or curriculum where requirements and expectations are reduced or changed, altering the fundamental objectives of a course (or state content standards), task, or assignment.
- **specially designed instruction:** Adapting, as appropriate, to the needs of a student receiving special education services in areas of content, methodology, or delivery of instruction that (a) meets their unique needs and (b) ensures access to the general curriculum.
- **Universal Design for Learning (UDL):** The design and delivery of curriculum and instruction to meet the needs of all learners by providing them choices for **why** they are learning, **what** they are learning, and **how** they will share what they have learned.

The Individuals with Disabilities Education Improvement Act (IDEIA, 2004) states that special education is "specially designed instruction," which is defined as instruction that "adapts, as appropriate, to the needs of a student receiving special education services in content, methodology, or delivery of instruction that (a) meets their unique needs and (b) ensures access to the general curriculum" (U.S. Department of Education, 2021). Adaptations include modifications and accommodations. Kurth (2013) states, "all adaptations require adjustments in the structure and content of the educational program, as well as the level of curricular mastery expected of students" (p. 35). Once a student qualifies for special education, their individualized education program (IEP) is written based on the assessments and evaluations administered at the time of initial placement. These plans include the student's present level of performance, individualized goals and objectives, individual accommodations or modifications, and specially designed instruction. The IEP teams are required to identify accommodations or modifications necessary for the student to access the general education curriculum.

While both accommodations and modifications are considered adaptations, they differ in how they help students (Disabilities, Opportunities, Internetworking, and Technology, 2021). Accommodations do not alter the fundamental outcomes of a unit, lesson, or assessment. Students with accommodations are responsible for meeting all outcomes, but may have alterations in environment, curriculum format, or equipment to access the curriculum. For example, a student who is Deaf might have an American Sign Language (ASL) interpreter, a student who is blind might use text-to-speech software to read a text, or a student with a learning disability (LD) might have extra time to take a test. On the other hand, modifications change the curriculum for students who cannot comprehend all the concepts the curriculum entails. For example, a student with an intellectual disability (ID) may memorize fewer vocabulary words, write a shorter essay, or even have a lower grade-level standard they are working toward, such as adding whole numbers when the grade-level expectation is calculating fractions. Sometimes the same *device* can be both an accommodation and a modification. For example, in math, a student with a specific LD may fully understand the concepts of numeracy, have a grip on place value, and even understand the principles of addition. However, due to processing deficits, their fluency rate is lower than their peers. In this case a calculator would be an appropriate accommodation. However, for a student with ID, who still does not comprehend these vital concepts, providing them a calculator would be a modification. In this scenario, the student is not demonstrating *their* knowledge, they are merely completing a task.

In reality, however, none of these can be done before collaborating with colleagues to increase student success (HLP 1). It is a lot to consider. After reading this chapter you will understand strategies for utilizing relevant technology to meet student needs, describe procedures for selecting materials and tasks based on student needs, understand the process of making modifications through highlighting relevant information, changing task directions, and decreasing amounts of material, and understand *each* of these objectives within the Universal Design for Learning (UDL) framework.

What Is HLP 13?

High-Leverage Practice (HLP) 13—"*Adapt curriculum tasks and materials for specific learning goals*" is defined as,

> Teachers assess individual student needs and adapt curriculum materials and tasks so that students can meet instructional goals. Teachers select materials and tasks based on student needs, use relevant technology, and make modifications by highlighting relevant information, changing task directions, and decreasing amounts of material. Teachers make strategic decisions on content coverage (i.e., essential curriculum elements), the meaningfulness of tasks to meet stated goals, and criteria for student success. (McLeskey et al., 2017, p. 74)

Adapting curriculum and materials is an umbrella term that includes modifications and accommodations. These are commonly categorized across four groups: (a) presentation, (b) setting, (c) response, and (d) scheduling or timing (Smith et al., 2018). What does this mean? Imagine your student, José, a student with an ID, is in an inclusive 10th-grade science class, and the teacher is beginning a new unit. José's IEP requires him to receive accommodations and modifications to the content. You, the special education teacher, in consultation with the general education science teacher, might think about changing the way you *present* the material by reading aloud directions or highlighting key terms, making changes to the *setting* such as utilizing small groups, changing the way students *respond* such as utilizing assistive technology by using a computer with voice over capability instead of requiring handwritten assignments, or making changes to the *schedule* or *timing* by giving frequent breaks.

Table 13-1. Alignment of HLPs and Resources for Evidence-Based Practices

EBP SUPPORT WITH HLP 13	RELATED HLPS	RESOURCES
Accommodations and modifications	12, 15, 18, 22	https://www.washington.edu/doit/what-difference-between-accommodation-and-modification-student-disability
Universal Design for Learning	12, 22	www.cast.org https://iris.peabody.vanderbilt.edu/module/udl/
Assistive and instructional technology	19	IRIS | Assistive Technology: An Overview www.bookshare.org
Highlighting key concepts and information	15, 19	https://www.adlit.org/in-the-classroom/strategies/selective-highlighting https://iris.peabody.vanderbilt.edu/module/acc/cresource/q2/p05/
Video modeling and video prompting	12, 15, 19	https://autismclassroomresources.com/video-modeling-what-is-it-and-why-use-i/ https://youtu.be/GS9lFwuM_G8
Accessible educational materials	19	https://aem.cast.org/
Guided notes	14, 15	https://www.interventioncentral.org/academic-interventions/study-organization/guided-notes-increasing-student-engagement-during-lecture- http://www.ldonline.org/article/6210/
Mnemonics	14, 15	http://www.ldonline.org/article/5912
Graphic organizers	15	https://www.teachhub.com/classroom-management/2020/09/what-is-a-graphic-organizer-and-how-to-use-it-effectively/ https://www.hmhco.com/blog/free-graphic-organizer-templates

Adaptations can be further broken down into general (used by many students in the classroom and provided across various classroom routines to meet the unique needs of students—including students receiving special education) and specific (addressing specific learning needs and goals of a particular student and activity; Kurth, 2013). For example, let us think about José and his participation in the 10th-grade inclusive science class. Labs, activities, or worksheets may be adapted specifically for José, based on his unique physical, sensory, or cognitive needs (e.g., guided notes, speech-to-text, text-to-speech). However, for activities, labs, and worksheets teachers (both general education and special education) can consider what might meet the needs of many students in the classroom, including José. These general adaptations include scaffolding (HLP 15), technology such as calculators (HLP 19), and peer-mediated instruction. See Table 13-1 for a list of the HLPs and evidence-based practices (EBPs) used alongside HLP 13 with some resources for further exploration.

Table 13-2. Taxonomy of Intervention Intensity

INTENSITY DIMENSIONS	DEFINITION
Strength	How well does the intervention program work for students with intensive needs?
Dosage	Does the intervention program provide multiple opportunities for a student to respond and receive feedback.
Alignment	How well does the intervention program (a) address and target the student's academic needs, (b) not address skills already mastered, and (c) focus on grade-appropriate curricular standards?
Attention to transfer	How well does the intervention program assist the student in (a) transferring skills and (b) making connections between skills?
Comprehensiveness	How well does the intervention program integrate principles of explicit instruction?
Behavior support	What extent does the program integrate the teaching of (a) self-regulation strategies and (b) behavioral principles that minimize non-productive behavior?
Individualization	Does the program use validated data-based processes for individualizing interventions.

How Do Teachers Select Materials and Tasks Based on Student Needs?

Taxonomy of Intervention Intensity

How do you select materials and tasks based on student needs? It is essential to look at HLP 20, providing intensive instruction. HLP 20 states that the intensity of intervention must match the student's needs (both learning and behavior). Sometimes students may be placed in small instructional groups to meet common learning needs and goals (HLP 17). Teachers will use intensive instruction and provide many opportunities to respond while monitoring student progress and adjusting instruction accordingly (McLeskey et al., 2017). For more information and detailed steps to use when intensifying instruction see Chapter 20.

If teachers are to select materials and tasks based on student needs, then the goals must be clearly defined and critical to academic success (McLeskey et al., 2017). To discuss how to select materials and tasks based on student needs, related service providers, special education teachers, and general education teachers must understand the specific needs of students in terms of intensity. Materials and tasks cannot be adapted if the specific needs of the student are not identified. Fuchs et al. (2017) describe a taxonomy of intervention intensity developed to clarify and assist in systematizing intervention intensity (Table 13-2). Further, this taxonomy assists in clarifying intensive intervention programs within the Multi-Tiered System of Supports (MTSS) framework of increasingly intensive interventions.

The taxonomy is divided into seven dimensions: strength, dosage, alignment, attention to transfer, comprehensiveness, behavioral support, and individualization. Teachers must ask themselves questions such as how well a program works for students with intensive intervention needs, how well the program addresses the student's academic needs, and whether there is a process for individualizing to meet changing academic needs?

Once teachers have considered the needs of the student in terms of intensity (HLP 20), prioritized long- and short-term learning goals (HLP 11), and systematically designed instruction toward specific learning goals (HLP 12), they must ask themselves if there are barriers to accessing the materials and tasks: "Do I need to adapt materials to meet the student's needs?" McLeskey et al. (2019) states that "adaptations include any changes teachers make to materials and tasks in order better to meet students' needs" (p. 170). In this chapter, adaptations to materials and tasks will include selecting materials based on student needs, using relevant technology (e.g., computer-based graphic organizers, video modeling, video prompting), and content enhancement (e.g., highlighting important information, graphic organizers).

Universal Design for Learning

UDL is defined as "a framework to improve and optimize teaching and learning for all people based on scientific insights into how humans learn" (CAST, 2021). In other words, UDL influences the design and delivery of curriculum and instruction to meet the needs of all learners by providing them choices for **why** they are learning, **what** they are learning, and **how** they will share what they have learned (Novak, 2019). The Center for Applied Special Technology, now known simply by its acronym CAST, developed the UDL framework and guidelines (https://www.cast.org). The UDL framework guides the development of teaching strategies to make the curriculum accessible to as many different learners as possible. In doing so proactively, teachers can reduce accommodations and modifications for individual students.

The UDL guidelines are used by teachers to implement UDL. The guidelines address three areas: multiple means of engagement, multiple means of representation, and multiple means of action and expression. For more information please be sure to check out the CAST website (https://www.cast.org).

Multiple means of engagement considers all the factors in students' lives that affect how they are engaged or motivated. Some of these factors include neurology (brain function), culture, personal relevance, subjectivity (individual points of view), and background knowledge. Since there is no single means of engagement to address all these variations, the CAST website provides concrete examples teachers can use to enhance engagement among the varied students in a classroom.

Multiple means of representation involve the many ways a teacher, or the students themselves, can present information for the varied students in the classroom. Rather than simply lecturing, a teacher can incorporate visual, auditory, and sensory strategies. Students can make presentations or participate in peer-tutoring or Think-Pair-Share activities to share information in varying ways.

Multiple means of action and expression provides options for students to show what they know. For example, not all students can best demonstrate their knowledge in a written essay or multiple-choice test. Allowing students to demonstrate their grasp of course objectives by other means, such as a video, slide presentation, or model may open up more opportunities for them to demonstrate their mastery of a subject.

UDL allows the teacher to proactively prepare the curriculum for as many different students as possible, reducing the need to retroactively provide accommodations. The CAST website provides many concrete examples of how to meet the needs of the various students in a classroom. Keep UDL in mind when implementing HLP 13.

How Do I Use Relevant Technology?

HLP 19 states that teachers should use assistive technologies (AT) and instructional technologies (IT). In Chapter 19, you will learn about AT and IT technology in depth. In this chapter, relevant technology is addressed in terms of adaptations to meet specific learning goals of the student.

Video Prompting

Evidence-based strategies that have been used in educational settings to help students learn skills and behavior using video prompting (VP). When prompts are included in instruction for students with disabilities (SWD), the opportunity for the student to make a correct response is increased (Collins, 2007). In recent years technology has been used to provide VP on a variety of devices, such as smartphones and tablets, in many settings to increase the effectiveness and efficiency of interventions for SWD (Banda et al., 2011).

VP consists of a student viewing a video of individual steps of a task, stopping the video after each step, performing the step, and going on to view the next step (Collins, 2012). As with video modeling, these videos can be used by one student or a group of students. VP is effective in chained tasks that allow the student to pause between steps, such as following a recipe or brushing their teeth.

Accessibility Software

Accessibility in the classroom can be enhanced with the use of technology such as software and apps. Specifically, accessibility software and apps can be categorized as text-to-speech and speech-to-text.

Text-to-Speech Software

Text-to-speech software and apps are designed to bypass student limitations in reading, due to visual impairment, a specific LD in reading (dyslexia), or ID. Text-to-speech software reads text aloud, either from computer content (e.g., the internet) or a document with optical character recognition scanned into a computer. Students can adjust the speed and volume of the electronic voice and may be able to highlight passages as they are read (Bone & Bouck, 2017).

Hodapp and Rachow (2010) found the students improved in overall comprehension, higher-level thinking, student attitudes, and engagement. Students were able to read twice as much scanned text as print text when using the software. It is, however, important that students be provided with instruction to use text-to-speech software effectively. Bruno et al. (2020) found that students with ID who were provided with direct instruction on using text-to-speech software or apps were less likely to abandon the technology and more likely to continue using it after high school.

Speech-to-Text Software

Speech-to-text software and apps provide students the opportunity to dictate content into a document on a computer. McCollum et al. (2014) found a functional relationship with students identified with an LD, emotional disturbance, and ID through use of speech-to-text software to write a passage in response to a picture prompt. All three participants demonstrated an increase in total words written, multisyllabic words used, and correct writing sequences.

While traditionally used by students with physical disabilities, visual impairments, specific LD in writing (dysgraphia), and ID, speech-to-text software and apps are now utilized by any student to enhance the learning experience (Shadiev et al., 2014).

As with text-to-speech software, it is important to provide instruction and opportunities for students to practice using the software. For example, students create a profile in Dragon Naturally Speaking that "learns" their speech patterns and accents over time, making subsequent dictation more accurate. Students must also "instruct" the software to insert appropriate punctuation while dictating.

Note-Taking Devices and Apps

A subset of speech-to-text software includes note-taking devices and apps. A commonly used note-taking device is a smartpen (Patti & Garland, 2015). Smartpens are electronic pens that create audio recordings or digital images which can be uploaded to a computer. Some smartpens work in conjunction with special dot paper that allows the student to access an audio recording of the portion of a lecture associated with the point at which the note was written. This can be utilized even if the written note contains partial information (Boyle et al., 2015).

In addition to note-taking devices, there are several apps that help students create transcriptions of audio recordings (Boyle et al., 2015). Some apps (e.g., Evernote, https://evernote.com/) utilize a stylus on a tablet screen in addition to having recording capability. Students can add text, images, audio, scans, PDFs, and documents to the notes. Evernote works in conjunction with a computer's text-to-speech feature to create transcriptions of recordings.

Other note-taking apps (e.g., Otter AI, https://otter.ai/) create an audio recording, transcript, and keywords and allow the student to highlight the transcription text. Although digital note-taking devices and software provide benefits to students who struggle with hand-written notes, it is important to balance the use of digital note-taking with the use of hand-written note-taking strategies such as graphic organizers or guided notes (Stacy & Cain, 2015).

Alternative Formats

Students can access alternative formats for textbooks via online sources such as Bookshare (https://www.bookshare.org). These sources provide textbooks as Word documents that can be read by text-to-speech software, as audio recordings on MP3 files, and in EPUB format, a free and open ebook standard used by most ebook readers. Alternative format sources require that a student has a diagnosed disability (e.g., visual impairment, dyslexia) and to have purchased the textbooks before the alternative format can be accessed.

How Can I Make Accommodations and Modifications to Materials?

To implement appropriate adaptations, consider several important principles. The Council for Exceptional Children (CEC; 2005) describes the following principles as "best practices" for implementing accommodations. In Table 13-3, the CEC "best practices" for implementing accommodations are listed with the aligned HLP presented next to each practice. As you read this book always keep in mind you should read the respective chapters on each HLP for more information. It might be that some of those chapters even refer you back to this one.

Accessible Materials

To meet the individual needs of students in the classroom, it may be necessary to incorporate adaptations to make materials accessible. There are many adaptations available, including strategies for accommodations and modifications (McLeskey et al., 2019). Teachers can simplify directions, alter the difficulty level, provide visual supports (such as highlighting relevant information, providing

TABLE 13-3. ALIGNMENT OF "BEST PRACTICES" AND HLPS

"BEST PRACTICES" FOR IMPLEMENTING ACCOMMODATIONS	HLP ALIGNMENT
Accommodations used in assessments should reflect accommodations used in the classroom	HLP 4
Accommodations are aligned to the student's area of need and the student's IEP	HLPs 2, 3, and 12
Accommodations are based upon the student's strengths	HLP 4
Accommodations provide the students an equal opportunity to show what they know	HLP 19
Assessments allow students to use accommodations to demonstrate their knowledge	HLP 4
Accommodations will be evaluated regularly, and only effective ones are continued	HLPs 11 and 15
A multidisciplinary team uses the input of the parent and student to create appropriate accommodations	HLPs 2 and 3
Accommodations are shared with key personnel who work with the student	HLPs 1, 2, and 3
Accommodations are reviewed, revised, and when appropriate, faded over time	HLPs 11 and 15

guided notes, providing and teaching graphic organizers, and teaching mnemonic devices to learn information). These strategies will be described in detail here and allow all students to fully access instructional materials.

Simplify Directions

Directions can be simplified by shortening sentences and substituting familiar words for unfamiliar words. Visual aids can be added to supplement written directions (e.g., using bold text to identify key terms or steps in a process or adding a picture cue). Material on worksheets can be spread over several pages to avoid an overwhelming amount of text, problems, or questions on one page.

Alter the Difficulty Level

Students, in particular those with more significant disabilities, may need the difficulty level of materials altered. Unfortunately, creating multiple worksheets or tests may be time-consuming for the teacher and can stigmatize the student. One alternative is to provide materials for all students that build from easy to difficult concepts. For example, the number of choices on a multiple-choice test may be reduced, providing two choices initially, then adding additional choices as the student becomes more familiar with the content and taking tests. Students can also be provided with a word bank to answer fill-in-the-blank questions. Additionally, students can move at their own pace through online sources such as Khan Academy (https://www.khanacademy.org/), which allows students from preschool to college prep to practice many subjects and accelerate individually. There are also learning apps, such as Math Blaster, which teaches math concepts in a gaming format for PreK through middle school students.

Visual Supports

Many SWD greatly benefit from the use of visual supports throughout classroom instruction. What are visual supports you ask? Visual supports can be defined as communication and teaching aids that provide students with information allowing them to process a message, task, or expectation and providing stimuli to help students focus and complete tasks with more independence (Cohen & Demchak, 2018). Why use visual supports? Rao and Gagie (2006) describe multiple benefits to using visual supports, such as (a) visual supports are a part of everyone's communication system, (b) they can assist in attracting and holding a student's attention, (c) they equip students to focus on the message and reduce anxiety, (d) they can make abstract concepts more concrete, and (e) they can help students express their thoughts. Some examples of visual supports are presented here, including highlighting relevant information, providing guided notes, teaching students to use mnemonic devices, and utilizing a variety of graphic organizers.

Highlight Relevant Material

Highlighting relevant material in the text helps students identify important concepts. Students can be taught strategies, such as making note of text that is bolded, highlighted, or underlined. Teaching students to pay attention to headings, captions, charts, graphs, and pictures is helpful to hone in on the most relevant material. In teacher-created materials, the teacher can make a point of adding highlights to the material to aid students in identifying important concepts. Chang and Ku (2015) found that direct instruction in highlighting or underlying key concepts improved student's note-taking skills.

Guided Notes

Guided notes help students accurately identify key information by filling in blanks on a document prepared by the teacher (Haydon et al., 2011) and help with the idea above—identifying the most relevant information. One of the simplest ways to create guided notes is to make an outline from presentation software (e.g., PowerPoint), replacing key words or phrases with blanks (Konrad et al., 2011). In addition to improving the accuracy of student note-taking and test scores (Haydon et al., 2011), guided notes can improve teacher accountability in staying on schedule with lessons and ensuring the appropriate material is covered in tests (Konrad et al., 2011). A benefit to guided notes, as well as other strategies mentioned in this chapter, is they benefit all students, not just those with disabilities. Many students can struggle to identify key concepts for taking notes; this benefits anyone who needs note-taking support. Figure 13-1 represents guided notes incorporating fill-in-the-blanks, a graphic organizer, and a word bank.

Mnemonic Devices

Another EBP for adapting curricula and materials is making substitutions for text materials. An example of this would be the use of mnemonics. These memory-enhancing strategies provide students with a way to recall unfamiliar information or connect two different concepts (Mastropieri & Scruggs, 1998). An example would be the use of acronyms to remember a list of things, such as the classification taxonomy of living things in science. Mastropieri and Scruggs (1998) suggest recalling the sentence "King Philip's class ordered a family of gentle spaniels" to help prompt a student to recall kingdom, phylum, class, order, family, genus, and species, in order. Additionally, teachers can use mnemonic devices to assist students in remaining focused on doing their work. Shaqwana et al. (2015) describe a mnemonic strategy known as the SOLVE Strategy. It is a mnemonic learning strategy designed to assist students in solving word problems. The students were explicitly taught that SOLVE stood for the following:

The Water Cycle

1. The three states of water are ______________, ______________, and ______________.
2. Liquid water becomes a gas through the process of ______________.
3. When water evaporates from plants, it is called ______________.
4. Water in the gas state is called ______________.
5. When water vapor cools it becomes liquid through the process of ______________ and forms clouds.
6. Water that falls from clouds as rain, snow, or hail is known as ______________.
7. Some water soaks into the ground. This is called ______________.
8. When water does not soak into the ground and flows over the ground, it is called ______________.
9. Water from precipitation or surface runoff helps create large bodies of water called ______________ and ______________.

Fill in the stages of the water cycle:

Word Bank:
Evaporation
Condensation
Precipitation
Transpiration

Figure 13-1. Example of guided notes.

S—Study the problem
O—Organize the facts
L—Line up the problem's steps
V—Verify your plan to solve the problem
E—Evaluate the problem

Graphic Organizers

One scaffolded support (HLP 15) that is beneficial for SWD is the use of a type of visual support—a graphic organizer. "A graphic organizer provides a visual representation of relationships between facts, concepts, and/or ideas" (Boon et al., 2018, pp. 18-19). Providing visual cues can easily be implemented in the general education classroom, which provides services in the Least Restrictive Environment for SWD. Graphic organizers can be paper based or computer based, and this allows for increased accessibility for SWD (Boon et al., 2018). One type of electronic graphic organizer is the computer-based graphic organizer (CBGO). Evmenova et al. (2016) found that CBGOs were very effective for middle schoolers with high incidence disabilities in organizing their thoughts and ideas in writing assignments. Additionally, graphic organizers can be handmade, photocopied, purchased commercially, color coded, or contain graphics.

Graphic organizers are especially helpful for students with a reading or writing disability to assist in taking notes, organize thoughts on paper, and comprehend written texts. See Figure 13-2 for an example of a graphic organizer for summarizing. With this graphic organizer, students summarize a story by writing on the graphic organizer the main character, what the character wanted, the problem, the solution, and the ending. By completing the summarizing activity on a graphic organizer, the student can organize their thoughts and focus on the main parts of the story. The graphic organizer example provided for summarizing is also color coded. Why color code a graphic organizer? Ewoldt and Morgan (2017) describe the potential color-coding graphic organizers have to provide an additional scaffold for SWD. In a study involving elementary students with LD who used color-coded graphic organizers (CCGOs) to assist them in completing a writing task, students showed increased confidence and motivation in their writing and increased understanding of the mechanics of writing (Ewoldt & Morgan, 2017).

What Does HLP 13 Look Like in a K-12 Classroom?

Elementary Example

Mrs. Robin is a third-grade teacher with 20 students in her class. In her class, she has a student, Sara, who has an LD in reading. Sara has difficulty answering comprehension questions and understanding instructions during activities She also has a student, Tucker, who has a visual disability who accesses print using braille. Tucker has very good comprehension skills and a fluent braille reader. She wants Sara and Tucker to fully participate in the classroom activities. The class is currently reading and completing comprehension activities about a book, *The Boy at the Back of the Class,* by Onjali Q. Raúf. She works with her co-teacher (HLP 1) Mr. Craig, a special education teacher, and Mrs. King, Tucker's teacher of students with visual impairments, ahead of time to ensure both students have the accommodations they need to fully participate.

Mrs. Robin has obtained a braille version of the book for Tucker as well as the audio version. She asks Tucker which way he would like to access the book (audio or braille), and he has indicated that he would like to read the braille book with the option to read it as an audio book. Since he has said he would like to access the book through audio and Mrs. Robin has been considering how to accommodate the needs of Sara, who has difficulty reading fluently, she decides to spend 20 minutes each day reading the book aloud to the students while they follow along in their own books.

Mrs. Robin decides to use the visual support of highlighting for the sections of the book she is reading aloud so she can follow along, and Tucker is asked to follow along in his book. Each day, after the book is read aloud to the students, they will be paired together to complete a summary activity about the passage. The students have the option to write their answers, draw pictures, scribe their answers to their partner, complete a graphic organizer, or record their answers orally into a portable audio recorder or classroom computer. These accommodations provided with both Tucker and Sara in mind also assist all the students in the class to be able to access the content by way of UDL.

Secondary Example

Ms. Flores is the special education resource teacher at Arusha Area High School. One of her students, Emma, has dyslexia. Emma's disability in reading also affects her writing and she frequently misspells words in her homework and on tests. Due to her dyslexia, Emma has difficulty taking tests and often answers questions incorrectly because she misunderstands the questions and the

Story Summary *Graphic Organizer* Instructions: After reading the story, summarize the story by thinking about **a character, who wanted something, but there was a problem, so they, and then**? Name: ________________ Date: ________ Name of the story or book: ________________	
THERE WAS A CHARACTER Who is the main character in the story?	
WHO WANTED SOMETHING What did the main character in the story want?	
BUT THERE WAS A PROBLEM What was the problem in the story?	
SO THEY How was the problem solved in the story?	
AND THEN? How did the story end?	

Figure 13-2. Example of graphic organizer: summarizing.

instructions. In developing an IEP for Emma, Ms. Flores realizes she has to take several things into account. While she provides Emma with reading instruction in the resource room, she realizes that Emma struggles with reading in her content area classes and is falling behind. This is not a good place for Emma to try to decode the contents of her textbooks due to the increased cognitive overload. To bypass Emma's disability, Ms. Flores realizes she will need to make use of several accommodations.

First, Ms. Flores provides Emma with assistive technology to make reading in the content areas accessible. Ms. Flores provides Emma with 50% extra time to take tests for her to have time to access the assistive technology. Since the school has licenses for Kurzweil text-to-speech software, Ms. Flores teaches Emma how to use the software and provides her with Microsoft Word documents of her textbooks downloaded from Bookshare. The software reads the texts to Emma to eliminate needing to decode the words. She can highlight particular passages and repeat passages as often as necessary for comprehension. Emma takes her tests in the general education classroom at her desk on a laptop computer with headphones. Additionally, Ms. Flores arranges to have Emma take her tests using Dragon Naturally Speaking speech-to-text software. If Emma has significant dictation, as with an exam with written responses, she is given the option of taking the test in the resource room to avoid giving answers to other test-takers.

Since Emma also has difficulty with spelling, Ms. Flores decides to provide accommodations to help Emma take notes. For note-taking, Ms. Flores helps Emma download Otter AI, which will provide Emma with a transcription of lectures in addition to an audio recording. Key words allow Emma to jump to the portions of the transcription that address those terms. Ms. Flores also helps Emma's content area teachers create guided notes to help Emma and other students write key concepts and stay focused on lectures.

Ms. Flores realizes that Emma could benefit from assistive technology to help her write assignments. To do so, she provides Dragon Naturally Speaking speech-to-text software, which lets Emma dictate her written assignments onto a Word document. As Emma continues to use the software, it adjusts her profile to her speech patterns, including her southern accent.

The strategies Emma learns while making use of her accommodations will allow Emma to keep up with her classmates in content area classes and to demonstrate what she is learning. Emma will be able to continue making use of her accommodations as she moves to post-secondary education.

Summary

In this chapter, we discussed how HLP 13 helps us make adaptations for students with and without disabilities. HLP 13 is defined as,

> Teachers assess individual student needs and adapt curriculum materials and tasks so that students can meet instructional goals. Teachers select materials and tasks based on student needs, use relevant technology, and make modifications by highlighting relevant information, changing task directions, and decreasing amounts of material. Teachers make strategic decisions on content coverage (i.e., essential curriculum elements), the meaningfulness of tasks to meet stated goals, and criteria for student success. (McLeskey et al., 2017, p. 74)

Let us break down the definition of HLP 13 in terms of how, when combined with other HLPs, HLP 13 can be even more powerful in implementation. As you read through the next paragraphs look for the intertwined functionality of the HLPs.

HLP 13 can be most effectively implemented when teachers adapt materials in collaboration with other teachers, related service providers, students, and other key personnel (HLP 1) collaboratively in IEP meetings with input from professionals, family, and the student (HLPs 2 and 3). Adaptations must be based on the student's strengths (HLP 4), include accommodations that are aligned to the student's individual learning goals and IEP (HLP 12), and develop these adaptations in consideration of UDL strategies (HLPs 15, 18, and 19) to assist teachers in meeting the needs of all students. The UDL framework guides the development of teaching strategies to make the curriculum accessible to as many different learners as possible and allows the teacher to proactively prepare the curriculum for as many different students as possible, reducing the need to retroactively provide accommodations.

As described in this chapter, adaptations included accommodations and modifications. Strategies should be systematically and explicitly taught to students (HLPs 8, 16, and 22), include scaffolding (HLP 15) to be implemented effectively, and ensure they are reviewed, revised, and when appropriate, faded over time (HLP 11). Teachers should select materials and tasks based on clearly defined goals that are critical to academic success (HLP 20), and use relevant technology (e.g., providing access to accessible materials and video modeling and prompting) to provide students with the opportunity to show what they know (HLP 19). Additionally, providing students with highlighting key information, using graphic organizers, providing guided notes, and teaching mnemonics increases active student engagement (HLP 18), provides students scaffolded supports (HLP 15), and teaches students cognitive and metacognitive strategies to support learning and independence (HLP 14).

Chapter Review

1. Describe HLP 13 in your own words.
2. Select one strategy highlighted in this chapter and discuss how it can help all students access the curriculum more effectively.
3. Why is it important to understand the differences between accommodations and modification?
4. Make a list of adaptations that could appear on a student's IEP. Categorize by accommodation or modifications.
5. How can teaching with a UDL framework help provide "incidental benefit" to students from the accommodations listed on IEPs that may not be theirs?

References

Banda, D. R., Dogoe, M. S., & Matuszny, R. M. (2011). Review of video prompting studies with persons with developmental Disabilities. *Education and Training in Autism and Developmental Disabilities, 46*, 514-527.

Bone, E. K., & Bouck, E. C. (2017). Accessible text-to-speech options for students who struggle with reading. *Preventing School Failure, 61* (1), 48-55. http://dx.doi.org/10.1080/1045988X.2016.1188366

Boon, R. T., Barbetta, P. M., & Paal, M. (2018). The efficacy of graphic organizers on the writing outcomes of students with learning disabilities: A research synthesis of single-case studies. *Learning Disabilities: A Multidisciplinary Journal, 23*(2), 18-33.

Boyle, J. R., Forchelli, G. A., & Cariss, K. (2015). Note-taking interventions to assist students with disabilities in content area classes. *Preventing School Failure, 59*(3), 186-195. http://doi.org/10.1080/1045988X.2014.903463

Bruno, L. P., Lewis, A. M., Kaldenberg, E. R., Bahr, P. A., & Immerfall, J. (2020). Direct instruction of text-to-speech software for students with intellectual disability. *Education and Training in Autism and Developmental Disabilities, 55*(4), 424-437.

CAST. (2021). *About Universal Design for Learning.* https://www.cast.org/impact/universal-design-for-learning-udl

Chang, W.-C., & Ku, Y.-M. (2015). The effects of note-taking skills instruction on elementary students' reading. *The Journal of Educational Research, 108*(4), 278-291. https://doi.org/10.1080/00220671.2014.886175

Cohen, A., & Demchak, M. (2018). Use of visual supports to increase task independence in students with severe disabilities in inclusive educational settings. *Education & Training in Autism & Developmental Disabilities, 53*(1), 84-99.

Collins, B. C. (2007). *Moderate and severe disabilities: A foundational approach.* Pearson Education Inc.

Collins, B. C. (2012). *Systematic instruction for students with moderate and severe disabilities.* Paul H. Brookes.

Council for Exceptional Children. (2005). Supplement section: Guiding principles for appropriate adaptations and accommodations. *TEACHING Exceptional Children, 38*(1), 53-54.

Disabilities, Opportunities, Internetworking, and Technology. (2021). *What is the difference between accommodation and modification for a student with a disability?* https://www.washington.edu/doit/what-difference-between-accommodation-and-modification-student-disability

Evmenova, A. S., Regan, K., Boykin, A., Good, K., Hughes, M., MacVittie, N., Sacco, D., Ahn, S. Y., & Chirinos, D. (2016). Emphasizing planning for essay writing with a computer-based graphic organizer. *Exceptional Children, 82*(2), 170-191. https://doi.org/10.1177/0014402915591697

Ewoldt, K. B., & Morgan, J. J. (2017). Color-coded graphic organizers for teaching writing to students with learning disabilities. *TEACHING Exceptional Children, 49*(3), 175-184. https://doi.org/10.1177/0040059916681769

Fuchs, L. S., Fuchs, D., & Malone, A. S. (2017). The taxonomy of intervention intensity. *TEACHING Exceptional Children, 50*(1), 35-43. https://doi.org/10.1177/0040059917703962

Haydon, T., Mancil, G. R., Kroeger, S. D., McLeskey, J., & Lin, W. Y. J. (2011). A review of the effectiveness of guided notes for students who struggle learning academic content. *Preventing School Failure, 55*(4), 226-231. https://doi.org/10.1080/1045988X.2010.548415

Hodapp, J. B., & Rachow, C. (2010). Impact of text-to-speech software on access to print: A longitudinal study. In S. Seok, E. L. Meyen, & B. DaCosta (Eds.), *Handbook of research on human cognition and assistive technology: Design, accessibility and transdisciplinary perspectives* (pp. 199-219). Medical Information Science Reference.

Individuals With Disabilities Education Improvement Act, 20 U.S.C. § 1400 (2004).

Konrad, M., Joseph, L. M., & Itoi, M. (2011). Using guided notes to enhance instruction for all students. *Intervention in School and Clinic, 46*(3) 131-140. https://doi.org/10.1177/1053451210378163

Kurth, J. A. (2013). A unit-based approach to adaptations in inclusive classrooms. *TEACHING Exceptional Children, 46*(2), 34-43.

Mastropieri, M. A., & Scruggs, T. E. (1998). Enhancing school success with mnemonic strategies. *Intervention in School & Clinic, 33*(4), 201-208.

McCollum, D., Nation, S., & Gunn, S. (2014). The effects of a speech-to-text software application on written expression for students with various disabilities. *National Forum of Special Education Journal, 25*(1), 1-13.

McLeskey, J., Barringer, M.-D., Billingsley, B., Brownell, M., Jackson, D., Kennedy, M., Lewis, T., Maheady, L., Rodriguez, J., Scheeler, M. C., Winn, J., & Ziegler, D. (2017). *High-leverage practices in special education.* Council for Exceptional Children & CEEDAR Center.

McLeskey, J., Maheady, L., Billingsley, B., Brownell, M. T., & Lewis, T. J. (Eds.). (2019). *High leverage practices for inclusive classrooms.* Routledge.

Novak, K. (2019). UDL: An introduction from pizza parlor to the world. In W. W. Murawski, & K. L. Scott (Eds.), *What really works with Universal Design for Learning* (pp. 1-20). Corwin.

Patti, A. L., & Garland, K. V. (2015). Smartpen applications for meeting the needs of students with learning disabilities in inclusive classrooms. *Journal of Special Education Technology, 30*(4), 238-244. https://doi.org/10.1177/0162643415623025

Rao, S. M., & Gagie, B. (2006). Learning through seeing and doing visual supports for children with autism. *TEACHING Exceptional Children, 38*(6), 26-33.

Raúf, O. Q. (2018). *The Boy at the Back of the Class.* Orion.

Shadiev, R., Hwang, W. Y., Chen, N. S., & Huang, Y. M. (2014). Review of speech-to-text recognition technology for enhancing learning. *Educational Technology & Society, 17*(4), 65-84.

Shaqwana, M., O'Brien, C., Wood, C., & Hitt, S. (2015). Effects of the SOLVE strategy on the mathematical problem-solving skills of secondary students with learning disabilities. *Learning Disabilities Research & Practice, 30*(2), 76-90.

Smith, D. D., Tyler, N. C., & Skow, K. G. (2018). *Introduction to contemporary special education: New horizons* (2nd ed.). Pearson.

Stacy, E. M., & Cain, J. (2015). Note-taking and handouts in the digital age. *American Journal of Pharmaceutical Education, 79*(7), 1-6.

Taylor, J., & Villanueva, M. G. (2014). The power of multimodal representations: Creating and using visual supports for students with high incidence disabilities. *Science and Children, 51*(5), 60-65.

U.S. Department of Education. (2021). *IDEA Sec. 300.39 Special education.* https://sites.ed.gov/idea/regs/b/a/300.39

How Can Students With Disabilities Become Strategic and Independent Learners?

Kyena E. Cornelius, EdD
and Dana L. Wagner, PhD

HLP 14

Teach cognitive and metacognitive strategies to support learning and independence.

INTRODUCTION

Leading students to take ownership of their own learning is challenging, a mixed dilemma. On one hand, we know their history and vulnerability and want to protect them. On the other hand, our job as special educators is to "work ourselves out of a job." From the day a student becomes eligible for special education, we make plans for their transition out of special education. Why does one idea exclude the other? Think about this: If we continue to force their *guaranteed* success, we are enabling dependent learners. If we teach the strategies that lead them to become independent learners, they will be motivated to continue learning and growing. Consider teaching students to use cognitive and metacognitive strategies, the educational equivalent to the Maimonides philosophy: "Give a man a fish, and you feed him for a day. Teach a man to fish, and you feed him for a lifetime."

Owiny, R. L., & Cornelius, K. E. *The Practical Guide to High-Leverage Practices in Special Education: The Purposeful "How" to Enhance Classroom Rigor* (pp. 203-216).

CHAPTER OBJECTIVES

- Describe how teachers get students to monitor their own learning.
- Know how HLP 14 is connected to other HLPs and used alongside evidence-based practices to improve student outcomes.
- Explain ways to explicitly teach cognitive and metacognitive strategies.

KEY TERMS

- **cognitive strategies:** Using the mind (cognition) to solve a problem or complete a task.
- **learning strategies:** An individual student's approach to complete a task.
- **metacognitive strategies:** Strategies used to help students understand how they learn; in other words, strategies designed for students to "think" about their "thinking."
- **Self-Regulated Strategy Development (SRSD):** An evidence-based practice that combines instructional strategies with a means to self-regulate.

Not only do special education teachers teach academic and behavior skills, but they also teach students to persevere through a task as well as to think about and appreciate how they are learning. Every teacher has said, "I want my students to be lifelong learners." That may be true, but do we understand what goes into *lifelong learning*? Effective special educators know they must guide students to this goal. To be more self-directed and independent, proficient learners take ownership of their own learning. They understand how it is connected to other knowledge, understand the demands of a task to effectively demonstrate their learning, and understand how to monitor their acquisition of knowledge. That all sounds great, but how can you actually and practically teach students with disabilities (SWD) *how* to learn?

This task of having students understand how to learn and how to manage their learning seems daunting, because it goes beyond teaching rote facts. It also takes the sole responsibility out of the teachers' hands and puts some significant responsibility on the students. It should not be as scary as it feels; after all, we just said that was our goal, to create efficient and independent learners. This also a goal of Universal Design for Learning (UDL)—for learners to become purposeful, motivated, independent, lifelong learners. The best way to do that is to have students become proficient at (a) selecting the correct strategy for the situation, (b) develop their own learning goals, (c) monitor the progress of that goal, (d) evaluate if the selected strategy is helping them achieve their goal, and (e) alter or change the strategy to adjust to their needs and help them obtain their goal.

In this chapter we will share what High-Leverage Practice (HLP)14—"*Teach cognitive and metacognitive strategies to support learning and independence*" means, and why the team felt this HLP was important enough to be named. We will also point out the related HLPs that you need to implement HLP 14 flawlessly and more successfully. Remember, they are connected and were identified as a group for a reason, to deliver more effective instruction. To that end, we will introduce you to some practical strategies and evidence-based practices (EBPs) to implement with students to increase their learning and independence. Along the way, we will point out the HLPs you will use to facilitate learning and achieve our goal of creating efficient and independent learners.

What Is HLP 14?

HLP 14—"*Teach cognitive and metacognitive strategies to support learning and independence*" seems so easy on the surface. After all, that is teaching—get students to understand the concepts or skills, think about what they are learning, and help them to feel secure that they do understand.

However, when you reflect and think about what you *do* as a teacher to make it actually happen, you might get a little overwhelmed. That is exactly what the HLP writing team, from the Council for Exceptional Children (CEC) and the Collaboration for Effective Educator Development, Accountability, and Reform (CEEDAR) Center, was thinking. They give us a very good definition of the HLP and explain it more by breaking it into steps. First, teachers understand that learning goes beyond just understanding the material taught. To be a proficient learner, students must also use cognitive processes to do several actions at once: (a) solve problems, (b) regulate attention, (c) organize thoughts and materials, and (d) monitor their own thinking. Second, because of this understanding, teachers must purposefully teach cognitive and metacognitive strategies. Those strategies that support memory, attention, and self-regulation of student learning. Third, teachers integrate self-regulation and metacognitive strategies into lessons by modeling their thought process when teaching new skills, and they provide explicit instruction, so that nothing is left to chance, no guessing on the part of the student. Finally, they facilitate the process and know when to step back so that students learn to monitor and evaluate their own performance, analyze their performance in relation to goals they set, and make necessary adjustments to improve their own learning (McLeskey et al., 2017).

How Is HLP 14 Connected to Other HLPs?

When you think about all that goes into metacognition, we are asking students to think, organize, and react. It seems logical then that you use many HLPs when you teach students to take ownership of their own learning. This HLP represents the full range of teaching. The information gathered from assessments (HLPs 4 and 6) and from collaborating with other professions (HLP 1) and students' families (HLP 3) help you plan effective instruction. During the planning, you identify and prioritize goals (HLP 11) and systematically design your instruction to meet those goals (HLP 12). You also consider how you will teach new skills or strategies. Naturally we go to explicit instruction (HLP 16); it is even discussed within the description of HLP 14. Teachers integrate self-regulation and metacognitive strategy instruction "into lessons on academic content through *modeling and explicit instruction*" (McLeskey et al., 2017, p. 25). You also consider how you will provide supports to students and then fade those supports as they learn to take ownership of their own learning (HLP 15), and how you will plan for them to maintain this new skill and generalize it across settings (HLP 21). Of course, during instruction, you want to provide students with many opportunities to engage with their learning (HLP 18) and provide them with positive and constructive feedback (HLPs 8 and 22).

The beauty of metacognitive strategies is that you actually elevate the HLPs and teach students to use them too. As students begin to get more involved with their own learning, they too will set goals (HLP 11), monitor their progress, and adjust strategies (HLP 6). Students will start to think about where else this strategy will be beneficial, both in classes and their community outside of school (HLP 21). As you read on in this chapter, you will read about specific EBPs that were designed to teach cognitive and metacognitive strategies and strategies for content areas that encourage students to be more thoughtful about their learning. Remember some EBPs require you to engage in professional development. Others have easily obtainable resources, either through websites or practitioner journals. We will share both and then provide those resources for you in Table 14-1. In this table, we specifically list the EBP discussed in this chapter, the HLPs used to implement the EBP, and resources where you can find more information.

What Are Cognitive and Metacognitive Strategies?

Before we dive into the strategies, let's take a moment and do a quick refresh from your first-year educational psychology class. Basically, cognition refers to a person's ability to use their mental processes such as memory, problem-solving, attending, and decision-making. Metacognition refers

TABLE 14-1. ALIGNMENT OF HLPS AND RESOURCES FOR EVIDENCE-BASED PRACTICES		
EBP SUPPORT WITH HLP 14	**RELATED HLPS**	**RESOURCES**
Mnemonics	12, 15, 16	https://iris.peabody.vanderbilt.edu/module/ss2/cinit/#content
Self-Regulated Strategy Development	6, 12, 15, 16, 20	https://iris.peabody.vanderbilt.edu/module/sr/ Harris, K. R., Graham, S., Aitken, A. A., Barkel, A., Houston, J., & Ray, A. (2017). Teaching spelling, writing, and reading for writing: Powerful evidence-based practices. *TEACHING Exceptional Children*, 49(4), 262-272. https://doi.org/10.1177/0040059917697250 Shora, N., & Hott, B. (2016). Write on: Improving persuasive writing using the POW+TREE strategy. *Beyond Behavior, 25*(2), 14-20. https://doi.org/10.1177/107429561602500203
Concept maps	15, 19	https://cmap.ihmc.us/
Strategic instruction model learning strategies	4, 5, 11, 15, 16, 18, 21, 22	General information: https://sim.ku.edu/ Professional development opportunities: https://sim.ku.edu/sim-teachers

to these things on a higher level when the person has control over and is keenly aware of their cognition. You have probably heard of this as thinking about thinking. There is overlap of the two, and sometimes the same skill can be both cognition and metacognition. For instance, as a strategic reader, while you are reading this book you are probably asking yourself questions as you read. When those questions help you *increase* your learning, you are using questions as a cognitive strategy, but when you are asking yourself those questions to *monitor* your learning and relating the new information to other knowledge or thinking about how you will use this knowledge, asking where this fits into your teaching practice, then you are using questioning as a metacognitive strategy. Of course, there is a lot more to the two, but defining them is not the purpose of this chapter.

Throughout many chapters in this book, you will read about the great uses of two popular EBPs: mnemonics and graphic organizers. It is logical to expect to see EBPs run across the chapters, because just like the HLPs overlap, their use within the EBPs will too. For the purposes of cognitive and metacognitive strategies, it is important to understand the role mnemonics play in increasing memory. It is well understood that SWD often struggle with memory, which impacts their academic progress (Swanson et al., 2013). Mnemonics, or memory-enhancing devices, have been hugely successful in improving SWD's memory (Mastropieri & Scruggs, 1998). Mnemonics are very flexible and can be useful in many forms. One is the *keyword* mnemonic (Mastropieri et al., 1985), a form of imagery helpful in learning vocabulary. Follow these steps:

1. Select the vocabulary word you need to teach.
2. Choose a keyword that sounds like the word or some part of the target word. It is important that the keyword should be familiar to the students, concrete, and easily pictured.
3. Create a visual that illustrates the definition of the target word.
4. Add the concrete word within the visual of the keyword.

Here is an example: You are preparing to read a story about Charles Lindbergh, *Abducted*, by Diane Webber. Thinking about the word *abduct*, you hear and see a picture of a duck. Duck sounds like *duct*, and so you create a visual of a person with a mask running away from a house holding a bag with a DUCK coming out of it. The stolen duck will help the student see "abduct" in a more concrete way, helping them to learn the new vocabulary. Make sure you give the student repeated practice with any mnemonic.

Probably the most popular mnemonic device is the *letter strategy* mnemonic (Scruggs & Mastropieri, 2000). In this strategy, you use letters from multiple words to create an acronym. This is handy when you need to teach students a sequence to follow or a group of things that belong together. A good example is when teaching students the Great Lakes, you use the acronym HOMES, for Lakes Huron, Ontario, Michigan, Erie, and Superior. When you teach students to use mnemonics, you make this choice strategically as scaffolded support (HLP 15), or perhaps to have students maintain and generalize this knowledge (HLP 21). When you do teach the strategy, it will only be successful if you offer the student repeated practice and many opportunities to engage with the mnemonic (HLP 18).

Another great EBP that is used for both cognitive and metacognitive purposes is graphic organizers (Dexter & Hughes, 2011). Graphic organizers are visual displays of information. They can illustrate relationships between facts and concepts and make these concepts more concrete. They can help students understand various relationships, perhaps a timeline to indicate temporal relationship, or sequencing steps of a process for sequential relationships, or even compare relationships, like the very familiar Venn diagram.

The use of concept maps (Novak & Cañas, 2006) can help students visualize their knowledge growing and becoming more in-depth. Concept maps begin with a central question and the students create a "map" of links and cross links to answer the question. As their knowledge increases, the map gets more full and more connected. This might be used during a unit on the French Revolution in World History. In preparing students for the unit, you want to teach the concept of social class. The student may have initial thoughts and understandings that you want to capture, so you have them write "What is social class and how does it impact politics?" in a circle in the middle of the page, then they start to answer the question and the map grows. You can pull this same concept into current events, and ask how social class impacts American politics? There are some great, free websites that easily store the maps, allowing students to add to them, delete misinformation, and over time create quite an intricate map of the concept and their learning. Have students save them at key points during the unit so they can compare them over time. Using technology (HLP 19) is a great way to engage students (HLP 18) and have them take ownership (metacognition) of their own learning.

How Do I Teach Cognitive and Metacognitive Strategies?

Set Up the Right Classroom Environment

Setting up a classroom environment with expectations, organization, procedures, and routines aligned with your instructional approach is a critical first step toward effective teaching and learning (HLP 7; Archer & Hughes, 2011). In a classroom where strategy instruction is prioritized, teachers expect students to be active participants in their learning from the first step of setting goals and understanding the rationale for those goals through the final step of evaluating their progress and outcomes. Students and teachers are partners throughout the teaching and learning process in an effort for students to take ownership of their learning. Students set goals, make commitments to become independent learners, and come to understand the role of effective and efficient strategies in that process (HLP 11). Teachers understand students' approach to their performance is just as important as the outcome of the task and collect assessment data on students' strategy use and academic skills (HLP 4).

A classroom environment set up for cognitive and metacognitive strategies includes tools for students to self-monitor their progress toward specific goals, such as electronic or paper performance criteria, checklists, and graphs (HLP 6). It includes materials hung in the classroom and in students' electronic or paper folders that support use of strategies—for example, a list of steps with a mnemonic to aid in memorization. Instructional time is devoted to mastering the strategy through systematic and intensive practice in the classroom where it is introduced and support for its use in other settings is provided (HLPs 16 and 20). Teachers include advance and post organizers in their instruction. They emphasize in their feedback to students that success is a result of effort, skills, and a strategic approach to learning and performing (HLP 22).

Understand Four Categories of Metacognition

Metacognition is a critical element of effective strategic instruction (Donker et al., 2014). In strategic learning classroom environments, teachers facilitate students' metacognition across four categories: (a) understanding oneself as a learner, (b) recognizing task demands, (c) knowing specific strategy knowledge, and (d) understanding when to apply a range of strategies across tasks and settings (Lai, 2011). First, you can facilitate students' knowledge about self as a learner through goal setting, self-evaluation, and self-reflection. Helping students recognize their individual strengths, weaknesses, and performance across tasks also is important in building knowledge about self as a learner. Second, you can help students gain knowledge of task demands by teaching them to analyze a complex classroom activity or assignment and break it down into its smallest steps or parts. Third, you can support specific strategy knowledge through collaborative planning in which you identify the most relevant strategies students need to be successful across settings each school year and then systematically and explicitly teach the strategies and ensure students understand their unique purposes. Fourth, you can teach students when to use a range of strategies by creating opportunities for them to practice applying a strategy to a variety of materials and across multiple settings. In the next section, we describe in detail how to effectively teach a specific learning strategy to mastery and support generalization of it across materials and settings.

Use an Effective Instructional Process

The Learning Strategies (LS) curriculum, designed and research validated by experts at Kansas University Center for Research on Learning over the past 4 decades, includes a series of strategies that target a wide range of critical academic and social tasks (Deshler & Lenz, 1989; Deshler & Schumaker, 1993; Hock et al., 2017). Teachers can use the LS curriculum after participating in training by a certified LS professional developer. One distinguishing feature of the LS curriculum is an eight-stage instructional process (Deshler & Lenz, 1989; Deshler & Schumaker, 1993; Hock et al., 2017). The purpose of explaining the eight stages of instruction here is to provide an example of what effective teaching and learning of a specific strategy might look like and to show how several HLPs are implemented in an evidence-based strategic instruction program (Washburn, 2020). The instructional stages include:

1. Pre-test and make commitments
2. Describe the strategy
3. Model the strategy
4. Verbal practice
5. Controlled practice and feedback
6. Advanced practice and feedback
7. Confirm acquisition and make generalization commitments
8. Generalization

In the first stage, pre-test and make commitments, teachers assess students' use of the target strategy to establish a baseline for instruction and ensure students have the prerequisite skills (HLPs 4 and 5). Students make a commitment to learning the strategy while teachers commit to implementing the strategy instruction with integrity (HLP 11). Stage 2, describe the strategy, involves the teacher introducing the strategy by providing a clear, concise, and complete picture of the overt and covert processes and steps, as well as the purpose (HLP 16). The teacher shows cue cards and other materials that support learning the strategy (HLP 15). The next stage, model the strategy, is still heavily teacher-mediated with the teacher demonstrating the cognitive behaviors and overt actions involved in using the strategy (HLP 16). Good think-aloud skills are critical in this stage. Verbal practice, Stage 4, occurs when the instruction begins to shift to a more student-mediated approach (HLP 18). The purpose of this stage is for students to master the key content and steps of the strategy with the assistance of memory devices, such as mnemonics. This stage often involves peer-mediated practice. In Stage 5, controlled practice and feedback, students systematically apply the strategy to controlled materials—materials similar to those used in the model stage and designed to easily fit application of the specific strategy (HLP 15). The responsibility in this stage shifts the strategy use from the teacher model to the student application with the goal of building student confidence and fluency. The student understands the criteria for successful practice, but the specific feedback comes from the teacher, not self-evaluation (HLP 22). Stage 6, advanced practice and feedback, is when the responsibility for strategy use and feedback falls primarily on the student (HLP 15). They practice applying the strategy to materials outside of the LS curriculum, a beginning step in the generalization process (HLP 21). In Stage 7, confirm acquisition and make generalization commitments, the student demonstrates mastery of the strategy content and application, typically through progress monitoring data they have been charting throughout the process, as well as a summative post-test (HLP 21). Just as the student made a commitment to learn the strategy in Stage 1, they commit to using it across tasks and settings in Stage 7. The teacher supports the student in planning for generalization and makes a commitment to provide guidance and feedback in the student's generalized application of the strategy (HLP 22). The final stage, generalization, is when the plan for the student's use of the strategy across tasks and settings is implemented (HLP 21).

How Do I Integrate Self-Regulation?

Self-regulation is a critical component of cognitive and metacognitive strategies. A useful framework for integrating a comprehensive set of self-regulation skills includes the following: (a) goal setting, (b) self-monitoring and self-evaluation, (c) self-talk (also referred to as self-instruction or self-statements), and (d) self-reinforcement (Graham et al., 1992). Goal setting should be specific and attainable. It is a good time to teach students how to task analyze complex skills. There are several potential benefits of goal setting—increasing student engagement, ownership, and self-determination, as well as improving their attention to what is most important. With self-monitoring and self-evaluation, students assess, record, and evaluate their own performance. It is important for teachers to ensure the target academic or social behavior is clearly defined, to explicitly teach the self-monitoring and self-evaluation procedures, and monitor students' practice. Self-monitoring and self-evaluation can be positive for students in that the activities provide immediate feedback and are designed to improve self-awareness and, ultimately, independence. Self-reinforcement occurs after evaluation in which students reinforce their performance. The reinforcement can be related to effort, progress, or an outcome. Self-talk (self-instruction, self-statements) is the process of students coaching themselves through a task, typically following a series of steps (which they might remember with the help of a mnemonic). The value of self-talk is that it can promote independence and student control over their own learning in addition to making efficient use of practice time in a classroom. Graham et al. (1992) defined six different types of self-talk, which provides another framework for planning and implementing quality self-regulation instruction within your classroom. They include

(a) problem definition (defining the nature and demands of a task), (b) focusing attention/planning (attending to a task and making plans for approaching it), (c) strategy related (selecting and using a strategy), (d) coping (dealing with difficulties), (e) self-evaluation (identifying errors and correcting them), and (f) self-reinforcement (rewarding oneself). The last two categories, self-evaluation and self-reinforcement, are also target areas that are more involved than just self-talk, as described earlier.

When Do You "Step Back" and Let Students Monitor and Evaluate Their Own Learning?

An EBP designed to help you teach and students to learn the entire process is Self-Regulated Strategy Development (SRSD). Initially developed and researched as a writing intervention, SRSD has been used successfully as an instructional framework for reading and math as well (Popham et al., 2020). With more than 100 studies conducted, with students from 2nd to 12th grade and multiple disabilities, SRSD improves not only academic performance but student motivation and self-efficacy (Harris et al., 2017).

Like the LS discussed above, SRSD has six phases: (a) develop and activate background knowledge (b) discuss it, (c) model it, (d) memorize it, (e) support it, and (f) provide independent practice (Harris et al., 2013). By implementing these six phases with fidelity you will promote student ownership of their learning and independent use of instructional strategies in 4 to 8 weeks (Harris et al., 2017). One very popular strategy at the elementary level is POW+TREE. Using this mnemonic, students *Pick* an idea, *Organize* notes, *Write* and say more. Then, they select a *Topic* sentence, list the *Reasons*, *Explain* the reasons, and conclude with an *Ending* (Harris et al., 2017). Using this strategy, students will increase their writing output. It reminds them to not only give a reason for their thoughts but to give multiple reasons. Using the image of a tree, students see, just as a tree has multiple branches, a topic has multiple reasons. The mnemonic also reminds students they need to explain their reasons.

Obviously, one strategy will not address all writing needs. Students still will need explicit instruction for grammar, spelling, and other deficits. However, as you continue to use SRSD instruction, you will instill in students a foundation for demonstrating their knowledge through writing. As they develop, you will see the length and depth of students' written product increase, which will give you the confidence to fully release students to work independently. Stepping back will become natural when you see students succeed. By following the SRSD framework, you will see through your own data, and that of the students, that they are succeeding. As students recognize their success, they become motivated learners (Graham et al., 1992).

What Does HLP 14 Look Like in a K-12 Classroom?

Elementary Example

Mrs. Brace, a fourth-grade general education teacher, and Mr. Franklin, a special education teacher, were co-planning for an upcoming writing unit. They began with a pre-assessment writing prompt: "Do you think the school day should be longer or shorter? Explain your answer." As they reviewed the students' narratives, they noticed several students, not just those with disabilities, were giving brief answers and not giving fully developed opinions and reasons, but merely stating an answer to the question. Many narratives began "shorter" or "longer" but not part of a complete sentence. Several students gave one or two sentences related to the topic, but some responses did not even appear on topic. Mr. Franklin suggested they introduce the students to SRSD writing instruction, namely the POW+TREE strategy. Mrs. Brace was very excited to try something new.

***P**ick an Idea*
***O**rganize Your Notes*
***W**rite and Say More*

***T**opic Sentence*
***R**easons*

- *Three or more*
- *Why do I believe this?*
- *Will others believe this?*

***E**xplain Reasons: Say more*
***E**nding: Wrap it up*

Figure 14-1. POW and TREE visual support for student reference. (Adapted from Harris, K. R., Graham, S., Aitken, A. A., Barkel, A., Houston, J., & Ray, A. [2017]. Teaching spelling, writing, and reading for writing: Powerful evidence-based practices. *TEACHING Exceptional Children, 49*[4], 262-272.)

Mr. Franklin began with the first phase of SRSD: Develop and activate background knowledge. The discussion started with students sharing their knowledge and understanding of persuasion. What does it mean, how do you persuade someone to do something, and the discussion continued into examples of when they want to convince their parents to buy them a new toy or take them to a movie. Once the teachers are assured students understand what it means to be persuasive and use persuasion to get something, they move on to Phase 2, discussing the POW+TREE strategy. Mrs. Brace shares how this strategy will help them become better at writing a persuasive essay. She says, "This strategy has an image and phrases to help you learn and remember all of the steps." She introduces the POW+TREE visual (Figure 14-1) that has an explosive POW and a vibrant tree. Mr. Franklin holds up the visual and points as Mrs. Brace explains each letter's purpose. She goes on to explain how this will help them organize their thoughts and explain their reason more clearly.

Mr. Franklin shares the graphic organizer they will use with this strategy (Figure 14-2). He also has a copy of the graphic organizer displayed on the board for him to use during the third phase, modeling. He begins typing as he describes his "thinking." He provides a prompt, "Should the school cafeteria sell candy?" He models his thinking process to develop his opinion and types his thoughts into the Pick an Idea section, "I do not think the school cafeteria should sell candy." He continues with modeling the use of this strategy with the graphic organizer. Once Mr. Franklin has finished the steps of the mnemonic, Mrs. Brace steps in for the fourth phase, memorizing the strategy/mnemonic. She has the students stand up and form a circle around the room. They play a variation of the game "hot potato." She passes a small stuffed animal to the first student asking for the first letter of mnemonic; they pass the animal to their neighbor who tells what the letter stands for in the mnemonic. They do this for a couple of rounds. To check for understanding, the teachers randomly call on students

POW

Pick an Idea

Organize Your Notes

Write and Say More

TREE

Topic Sentence

Reasons (Hint: Include three or more reasons. Why do I believe this? Will my readers believe this?)

1.
2.
3.

Explain Reasons

Ending

Figure 14-2. Sample POW and TREE graphic organizer.

and ask questions about the mnemonic. This stage has a lot of practice and repetition to ensure all students have learned the mnemonic.

Mr. Franklin and Mrs. Brace are both involved in the fifth phase of supporting students. They hang the visuals up around the room for students to use as a support. Students complete several guided-practice opportunities to complete persuasive essays using the graphic organizer. Once they have collected the data and checked that students feel successful, they remove the visual supports and graphic organizers. The students are ready for the independent practice phase. They are given a prompt and instructed to write a persuasive essay.

There are several ways to monitor student progress. Mr. Franklin and Mrs. Brace chose to create a scoring rubric of 10 points. Their scores align with the POW+TREE graphic organizer. Students and teachers both score each section with most sections getting 1 point; the R section has 3 points representing the three reasons. The final point can be on alignment that all the pieces fit together. During the practice phase, teachers conference with students and compare their scoring. They correct any misunderstandings and provide feedback to improve student learning.

Secondary Example

Ms. Ramirez, a general education social studies teacher, and Ms. Vang, a special education teacher, were co-teaching an inclusive ninth-grade geography class. They knew from district and classroom assessments most of the students in their co-taught section had difficulties with reading comprehension, especially given content area texts. Ms. Ramirez and Ms. Vang always taught critical vocabulary terms and background knowledge relevant to an assigned reading before students read a section of the text. They explicitly taught students about content area text structure and demonstrated preview strategies. In their English class, the students learned strategies for decoding multisyllabic words and determining the meaning of unfamiliar words. Despite the focused content area reading instruction, the students still demonstrated poor understanding of the class reading materials. Specifically, Ms. Ramirez and Ms. Vang observed that the students had difficulties accurately summarizing what they read. Common errors included stating or writing exactly what was in the text rather than putting the summary in their own words, providing too many or irrelevant details, and mistaking the overall topic for the main idea.

Ms. Vang recently had participated in Strategic Instruction Model (SIM) LS professional development where she was prepared to teach several reading strategies, including *The Fundamentals of Paraphrasing and Summarizing* (Schumaker et al., 2007). During their co-planning prep, Ms. Vang suggested to Ms. Ramirez that she teach the strategy during their co-taught class. Having some familiarity with SIM and LS, Ms. Ramirez agreed the students could benefit from instruction in this EBP. Because only Ms. Vang in this team had received professional development in *The Fundamentals of Paraphrasing and Summarizing*, they planned for her to take the lead in teaching with Ms. Ramirez in an observe and/or assist role.

They confirmed from state and district assessment data, the prerequisite skill students could accurately read at or above fourth-grade–level text. Further, they knew from their classroom assessments that students understood the critical vocabulary in the assigned readings, in part because of their direct teaching of the critical words. The final prerequisite was that the students could write complete sentences. The teachers confirmed this with post-test data from the *LS Proficiency in Sentence Writing*, which students learned in their English class.

Ms. Ramirez and Ms. Vang gave students the pre-test for *The Fundamentals of Paraphrasing and Summarizing* in which students were asked to find and paraphrase the main idea and details of a content area reading passage. The pre-test scores for all students confirmed the need for teaching the strategy to the whole class. Ms. Ramirez and Ms. Vang shared with each student their pre-test results. They described the purpose of *The Fundamentals of Paraphrasing and Summarizing* is to teach students how to put key information into their own words and strategies for finding the main idea and details in content area texts and emphasized how it can help them to be successful in many classes throughout their school career. Next, the teachers asked students to make a commitment to learn the strategy. Each student wrote a sentence or two demonstrating their commitment and signed their name below the statement(s).

Ms. Ramirez and Ms. Vang prepared to teach the strategy by putting together individual folders containing a progress chart, cue cards, and learning and assignment sheets. They also hung copies of the cue cards on the wall. Ms. Vang planned to lead each lesson by reviewing the detailed plans in the instructor manual. Most lessons included the describe and model strategy phases as well as controlled practice and feedback. This instructional loop repeated until the final lessons, which focused on the post-test and generalization stages.

Ms. Vang described and modeled the strategy components and how to follow the steps within the strategy, such as the TM to D Process, which includes: (a) find the topic, (b) find the main idea, and (c) find the details. She demonstrated in a think-aloud what questions students could ask themselves to follow the process in a systematic way, such as "What information in this paragraph tells me more about the main idea?" She showed how to use sentence stems to answer the self-questions. Ms. Vang modeled problem-solving in her think-alouds by considering several options and choosing the best one after continuously referring to the strategy materials, such as cue cards. In addition to cue cards with strategy steps, Ms. Vang showed and demonstrated how to use other supports like a graphic organizer with headings for each part of the TM to D Process—topic, main idea, and detail. She described and modeled checking her work by thinking aloud with evaluation questions aligned with criteria for mastery. For example, when evaluating a detail sentence she wrote, she asked, "Is this correct? Is this specifically related to the main idea?" and talked through the rationale for it being correct. She then asked about a second and third criteria for performance, "Is this written in my own words? Does it make sense?" and again talked through the evaluation. She made errors and corrected them to demonstrate for students how to self-correct. She provided self-reinforcement statements for effort and accurate work, such as "I'm working hard to apply the strategy, following all of the steps, and accurately summarizing what I'm reading as a result."

The students practiced applying the strategy in a systematic way throughout the lessons. They practiced with materials similar to what Ms. Vang modeled. Ms. Vang scaffolded the practice by prompting students to use supports, such as cue cards and graphic organizers, and reminded them of questions and statements they should be using in their thinking. She asked students to explain their processes and thinking. Ms. Vang provided specific feedback and a score on each student practice piece. Students graphed their performance on their progress chart and determined if they were ready to move on or if they needed more practice.

When the students mastered the strategy with the materials designed for controlled practice within the strategy instruction, they practiced using it to summarize paragraphs in their geography textbook. They used self- and peer-evaluation to determine the effectiveness of their strategy use. In addition, the teachers checked their work. The students took the post-test after showing success with the strategy in the class materials. Ms. Vang and Ms. Ramirez were pleased with the results—all students demonstrated mastery. The students described their progress and outcomes to their peers and set goals for continued application across settings.

Summary

Effective special education teachers strive for student success and independence. The purpose of special education is to provide equal access to education for all students, regardless of their disability. Therefore, the goal of special education is to provide the SWD with strategies that lead to success in the general education curriculum. Teaching cognitive and metacognitive strategies will help students master more skills and grow into independent learners, which will lead to greater success with the general education curriculum.

This chapter highlighted some of the strategies and EBPs that can support SWD to be more strategic learners and thus more successful in the general education curriculum. We discussed how HLP 14—"*Teach cognitive and metacognitive strategies to support learning and independence*" is aligned with multiple HLPs and vital to student self-efficacy and self-regulation. We shared the importance of the right classroom environment, establishing student goals, teaching through explicit instruction, monitoring student progress, providing student supports, and providing corrective feedback. When used together these practices can help you create persistent and self-motivated, independent learners.

Chapter Review

1. How are cognitive and metacognitive strategies related but different?
2. Why should we explicitly teach students the **why** of learning?
3. Describe a cognitive strategy you will use in your classroom and how it is aligned to at least three different HLPs.
4. Explain how you will teach students to monitor their own learning.

References

Archer, A. L., & Hughes, C. A. (2011). *Explicit instruction: Effective and efficient teaching*. Guilford Press.

Deshler, D. D., & Lenz, B. K. (1989). The strategies instructional approach. *International Journal of Disability, Development and Education, 36*(3), 203-224.

Deshler, D. D., & Schumaker, J. B. (1993). Strategy mastery by at-risk students: Not a simple matter. *The Elementary School Journal, 94*(2), 153-167.

Dexter, D. D., & Hughes, C. A. (2011). Graphic organizers and students with learning disabilities: A meta-analysis. *Learning Disability Quarterly, 34*(1), 51-72.

Donker, A. S., De Boer, H., Kostons, D., Van Ewijk, C. D., & van der Werf, M. P. (2014). Effectiveness of learning strategy instruction on academic performance: A meta-analysis. *Educational Research Review, 11*, 1-26.

Graham, S., Harris, K. R., & Reid, R. (1992). Developing self-regulated learners. *Focus on Exceptional Children, 24*, 116.

Harris, K. R., Graham, S., Aitken, A. A., Barkel, A., Houston, J., & Ray, A. (2017). Teaching spelling, writing, and reading for writing: Powerful evidence-based practices. *TEACHING Exceptional Children, 49*(4), 262-272. https://doi.org/10.1177/0040059917697250

Harris, K. R., Graham, S., Friedlander, B., & Laud, L. (2013). Bring powerful writing strategies into your classroom! Why and how. *The Reading Teacher, 66*(7), 538-542. https://doi.org/10.1002/TRTR.1156

Hock, M. F., Bulgren, J. A., & Brasseur-Hock, I. F. (2017). The strategic instruction model: The less addressed aspects of effective instruction for high school students with learning disabilities. *Learning Disabilities Research & Practice, 32*(3), 166-179.

Lai, E. R. (2011). Metacognition: A literature review. *Always learning: Pearson research report, 24*, 1-40.

Mastropieri, M. A., & Scruggs, T. E. (1998). Enhancing school success with mnemonic strategies. *Intervention in School and Clinic, 33*(4), 201-208.

Mastropieri, M. A., Scruggs, T. E., Levin, J. R., Gaffney, J., & McLoone, B. (1985). Mnemonic vocabulary instruction for learning disabled students. *Learning Disability Quarterly, 8*, 57-63.

McLeskey, J., Barringer, M.-D., Billingsley, B., Brownell, M., Jackson, D., Kennedy, M., Lewis, T., Maheady, L., Rodriguez, J., Scheeler, M. C., Winn, J., & Ziegler, D. (2017). *High-leverage practices in special education*. Council for Exceptional Children & CEEDAR Center.

Novak, J. D., & Cañas, A. J. (2006). The origins of the concept mapping tool and the continuing evolution of the tool. *Information Visualization, 5*(3), 175-184. https://doi.org/10.1057/palgrave.ivs.9500126

Popham, M., Adams, S., & Hodge, J. (2020). Self-regulated strategy development to teach mathematics problem solving. *Intervention in School and Clinic, 55*(3), 154-161. https://doi.org/10.1177/1053451219842197

Schumaker, J., Knight, J., & Deshler, D. (2007). *The fundamentals of paraphrasing and summarizing. Instructor manual.* Edge Enterprises.

Scruggs, T. E., & Mastropieri, M. A. (2000). The effectiveness of mnemonic instruction for students with learning and behavior problems: An update and research synthesis. *Journal of Behavioral Education, 10*, 163-173.

Swanson, H. L., Harris, K. R., & Graham, S. (Eds.). (2013). *Handbook of learning disabilities*. Guilford Press.

Washburn, J. (2020). *A crosswalk: High leverage practices in special education and strategic instruction model (SIM) instruction tools and interventions*. https://resources.finalsite.net/images/v1614711219/fdlrsorg/nr6wg50zghluqabjijai/HLPandSIMCrosswalk_SPED_KUCRL12_15_2020.pdf

Does Scaffolding Support or Stifle Students?

Kiersten K. Hensley, PhD
and Kyena E. Cornelius, EdD

HLP 15
Provide scaffolded supports.

INTRODUCTION

Sometimes it is hard to judge the amount of support that is needed, and sometimes we want to support students too much. What is the "just right" level? When can supports help student learning progress and promote independence? When do supports stifle growth and lead to learned helplessness? So many questions to reflect on while planning your instruction. The bottom line is we need to purposefully plan the supports, then monitor the students' use of them, adjust them as needed, and plan to fade them. The beauty is you; if by chance you scale down too early, you can easily boost them up again. Just like training wheels on a bicycle, supports should be designed to be added, adjusted, and removed all at a moment's notice.

Owiny, R. L., & Cornelius, K. E. *The Practical Guide to High-Leverage Practices in Special Education: The Purposeful "How" to Enhance Classroom Rigor* (pp. 217-228).

CHAPTER OBJECTIVES

- Describe the temporary nature and purpose of scaffolded supports.
- Know how HLP 15 is connected to other HLPs and used alongside evidence-based practices to improve student outcomes.
- Explain how scaffolded supports leads to students taking ownership of learning.

KEY TERMS

- **gradual release:** When a teacher designs learning activities that shift responsibility from the teacher to the student over time.
- **scaffolding supports:** Breaking learning up into chunks. When a teacher adds something to the lesson to enhance student learning.
- **zone of proximal development:** The "space" between what a student can do independently and what they can do with support.

Can you imagine being told to do something for the first time and not getting any help? Think about teaching your own children, or any young child, to make a bed. Would you stand in the doorway and say, "make the bed," "just do it," "I know you can do this," "you're a champ, come on, you got this!" Of course not, because that is not teaching; that is cheerleading. Adult support is going to be needed. Even if they have watched you do this before, they are still going to need help. You may start by modeling for them how you pull the sheets up to the top of the bed. Then, you show them how to smooth the sheets and check to see they are hanging evenly on both sides; it continues until you complete the process. You continue to support them by walking and talking through the steps of the chore, breaking it down into bite-size digestible parts. Then, maybe you do it together a few times. Then, gradually you stop doing it, maybe you continue to "coach." Then one day they get it, and are totally independent.

Why would we think teaching content, skills, or behavior is any different? Effective special educators understand that we need to explicitly teach students specific skills, strategies, and content. However, we do not expect them to master independence by just telling them to perform the new skill. Teachers control the environment, or elements of a task they know their student cannot do right now, so the student can focus on the elements they can do. In other words, we provide supports that allow students to perform a task that would normally be beyond their ability level. Gradually, as the student's proficiency increases, we decrease the supports, empowering the student to take on more responsibility. Think beyond the traditional "construction site" analogy you were given when being taught about scaffolding. We think a better analogy would be a bicycle's training wheels or even a batting tee. These are easier to manipulate, and you can take them away and put them back rather easily. You can adjust the training wheel or batting tee by raising or lowering, tightening or loosening, and go back and forth as often as needed. Scaffolded supports in a classroom need to be just as flexible and adjusted regularly. The other reason to relate this High-Leverage Practice (HLP) more to training wheels or batting tees is that in a classroom you sometimes strategically plan out the supports, and at other times you pull one out "on the fly," because you see a need, you are responding to the student in real time.

We cannot stress enough the importance of fading supports as students build proficiency with skills. If we leave the support in place too long, it will become fixed and could lead a student to believe they need it to perform the skill. This promotes learned helplessness. Remember, the intention behind the use of scaffolded supports is to provide students the necessary supports to help them regulate learning as the scaffolding decreases (Hallenbeck, 2002; Sun et al., 2021). In this chapter we will explain the rationale behind selecting HLP 15—"*Provide scaffolded supports*" as a core practice for special education teachers, its relationship to other HLPs, and some evidence-based practices (EBPs) that require you to use this HLP as you implement it. It is imperative that you see scaffolded supports as flexible and temporary and understand how to monitor their use to build student independence.

What Is HLP 15 and How Is It Connected to Other HLPs?

The purpose of identifying a set of core practices was to support the preparation of and development of special education teachers (McLeskey et al., 2019). McLeskey and colleagues (2017) offer a definition of this HLP that outlines a process to implement it. The definition begins with the temporary nature of scaffolded supports; they are there so the student can successfully complete a task they do not yet have the ability to perform independently. These supports are in place for the student to complete the task with a high rate of success. They continue by sharing the five steps or elements of the process. First, effective special education teachers select powerful supports (i.e., visuals, verbal prompts, materials). Second, they calibrate, or adjust, the supports based on the student performance and understanding of the given task. Third, effective special education teachers use scaffolded supports flexibly. Fourth, they use dynamic assessment to evaluate the support's effectiveness. Finally, they gradually remove or fade the support to bolster student independence. Noting again, some scaffolded supports are selected prior to planning a lesson and others are provided responsively during instruction. There are two equally important keys to being successful in using scaffolded supports: Fully understand the task, skill, or content being taught, and know your student well enough to observe changes in their development and proficiency.

As you have read repeatedly throughout this book, no HLP is "performed in isolation." Of course not, that was not the intent of McLeskey and team (2017) or Ball and Forzani (2011) when they identified a set of core practices for general educators. These fundamentals of teaching are meant to be a collective, just as any practice takes on multiple tasks as you become proficient. Let us go back to the baseball tee, mentioned earlier. When you first walk onto a baseball field, you focus just on the ball sitting on the tee. Next, you think about how to hold the bat, temporarily forgetting about the ball. Finally, you have the bat gripped and you form your stance, pull the bat up, take a moment, look at the ball, and swing. You probably missed the ball that was stationary on your first try. However, the point is you went through each element as an isolated practice. Now picture Albert Pujols (an outstanding first baseman for the St. Louis Cardinals) walking up to the plate. Do you imagine he thinks of each of these steps in isolation? It is a collection of actions that have become his muscle memory. As you become more proficient with your teaching practice, you will start to see how naturally multiple HLPs work together within your muscle memory. For instance, as you are planning new instruction you are thinking, "What does my student need to know, and how will I get them there?" (HLP 11). You are identifying and prioritizing goals. Also, you think about the curriculum and where your student is now in relation to the standards, using multiple sources of data and student assessment data (HLPs 4 and 6). You plan how you get them to that goal, systematically designing instruction toward a specific goal (HLP 12). As you plan your instruction you want to use explicit instruction (HLP 16) and provide students with multiple active engagement opportunities (HLP 18), all while giving them positive and constructive feedback (HLPs 8 and 22). Sometimes you see the need to modify or adjust the curriculum or outcome (HLP 13). Of course, you are selecting powerful visuals, verbal prompts, and material supports. You are also wondering if maybe some instructional technology (HLP 19) might be warranted, and if your student might need more intensive instruction (HLP 20).

Scaffolded supports are often included as elements of EBPs. Throughout the next sections we will share some EBPs and research supported strategies that naturally include or ARE scaffolded supports. That should seem logical, since part of the definition shared earlier states that scaffolded supports exist so students can successfully complete a task, they do not yet have the ability to perform

Table 15-1. Alignment of HLPs and Resources for Evidence-Based Practices

EBP SUPPORT WITH HLP 15	RELATED HLPS	RESOURCES
Curriculum-based measurements	4, 6, 20	https://www.interventioncentral.org/ https://dibels.uoregon.edu/ https://iris.peabody.vanderbilt.edu/module/pmm/#content
Mnemonics	12, 15, 16	https://iris.peabody.vanderbilt.edu/module/ss2/cinit/#content
SRSD	14, 16, 20, 22	https://iris.peabody.vanderbilt.edu/module/sr/
Concrete-Representational-Abstract (CRA)	12, 14, 20, 22	https://education.missouri.edu/ebi/interventions/ https://iris.peabody.vanderbilt.edu/module/math/
Graphic organizers	13, 14, 18, 21	https://www.canva.com/graphic-organizers/templates/ https://graphicorganizer.net/
Universal Design for Learning	12, 18, 19	https://www.cast.org/ Murawski, W. W., & Scott, K. L. (Eds.). (2019). *What really works with Universal Design for Learning*. Corwin Press.
Content Enhancement Routines	12, 14, 16, 21, 22	https://kucrl.ku.edu/sim-content-enhancement-routines

independently. This aligns perfectly with why we use EBPs, because these practices have demonstrated, through empirical research, that they have a positive effect on student learning (Leko et al., 2019). Providing scaffolded supports to students while they are learning new skills gives them the confidence to persevere through tasks. They trust the teacher will support them and chunk the learning to their current level of understanding. If we want students to be successful with any learning, we must create the environment that promotes learning and use the practices that demonstrate the most promise. Table 15-1 provides a list of the EBPs discussed in this chapter, the other HLPs used with HLP 15 to implement the EBP, and useful resources for more information about each practice.

What Practices Support Scaffolding?

Several EBPs and instructional frameworks have demonstrated positive effects on student learning. Next, we give a brief overview of some and show their alignment with HLP 5. However, providing an exhaustive list goes beyond the scope of this chapter. As you read on in this chapter, you will see more detail provided and some practice examples of some key practices and frameworks.

Universal Design for Learning

UDL is a framework for the design of curriculum and instruction based on the concept of reducing curricular and instructional barriers, providing choices, and scaffolding learning for all students (Rose, 2000). The UDL framework is organized around three principles of providing options for representation, expression, and engagement. This is meant to be available for all students, and as part of the curriculum and instructional planning process (HLP 12), not as an afterthought to change or provide additional instruction just to struggling learners. When implemented correctly, UDL will provide engagement (HLP 18) and have students more invested in their learning.

Critical Examples

The intentional use of specific types of examples can also be a key EBP in scaffolding student learning. We can see this in use in a few different ways and it can be used across content areas. Worked solutions give learners examples of similar problems that have already been solved along with visual or written prompts (Riccomini & Morano, 2019). Parallel modeling is the use of examples that share some characteristics of the problem the student is being asked to solve, giving some scaffolded support to the student while not simply asking them to do the same problem (Coltman et al., 2002). Another type of critical example is simplified problems. Coltman and colleagues explain that when using simplified problems, students can be supported in gaining experience and independence in applying a concept, but through the use of simplified calculations or content (HLP 11).

Explicit Instruction

Explicit instruction is its own HLP (HLP 16), EBP (Archer & Hughes, 2011), and a framework for designing instruction. Explicitly designed instruction can also be considered a scaffold to support student learning. The five instructional components of explicit instruction really show how the practice leads to scaffolding student learning:

1. Segment complex skills
2. Draw attention to key features through modeling
3. Use systematically faded supports and prompts
4. Provide opportunities for response and feedback
5. Arrange purposeful practice opportunities (Hughes et al., 2017)

Concrete-Representational-Abstract Framework

This framework is an explicit instructional framework (HLP 16) and EBP (Agrawal & Morrin, 2016), where students learn mathematical concepts by developing an understanding of the concept using manipulatives and real-life situations (concrete), moving to pictorial representations and drawings (representational), which then support working through problems using a traditional algorithm (abstract). The CRA framework provides support for students to develop both conceptual and procedural understanding at the same time.

Graphic Organizers and Visuals

Graphic organizers help link to pre-existing knowledge, helping learners make connections and retain information by creating networks of linked ideas or schemas (Dye, 2000). Graphic organizers provide support for understanding vocabulary, organizing concepts and relations, developing ideas, and can be used across content areas. Reilly and Ross (2019) demonstrated that when a predetermined set of graphic organizers (Thinking Maps) is used across a school and teachers use consistent language for supporting students to use the tools, student growth on state-level assessments surpasses the growth of schools in the same district at significant levels. Graphic organizers can also be a support to students as they develop and convey their own ideas for writing and sharing information (Ewoldt & Morgan, 2017). There is also the added flexibility of using graphic organizers that are paper based or technology based (HLP 19).

Content Enhancement Routines

The use of graphic organizers is so powerful that the research team at the University of Kansas also have developed a series of routines that are each paired with a graphic device. Content Enhancement Routines (CERs) have empirical support in promoting student learning (Bulgren et al., 2007). They were designed and studied before the HLPs were identified, but you can see the use of HLPs 13, 14, 15, and 18 in their design. According to Bulgren and colleagues (2007), "CERs emphasize active student engagement, construction of knowledge, use of graphics, note taking, student interaction, and strategic cognitive and metacognitive approaches to learning" (p. 123). It is important to note that CERs require professional development by a trained professional approved by the the University of Kansas Center for Research on Learning. More information can be found at https://sim.ku.edu/sim-content-enhancement-routines.

Mnemonic Strategies

Mnemonic strategies use letters or words in an easily remembered pattern to recall key terms or steps in a process (Mastropieri & Scruggs, 1998). One example of a mnemonic strategy to scaffold student writing is the cues that are part of Self-Regulated Strategy Development (SRSD), such as SCAN to support revisions:

S = Sense: Does it make sense?
C = Connected: Is it connected to my belief?
A = Add: Can you add more?
N = Note errors

Students are prompted to SCAN each sentence and use the prompts to revise their writing (Graham & MacArthur, 1988).

How Do I Select the Right "Powerful" Support?

Effective scaffolding should be within the zone of proximal development (Vygotsky, 1978) which is the gap between what a student can already do independently and what the student needs support to accomplish. Before choosing and implementing a specific support, teachers need to know where that zone of proximal development is for students within a content area. What do students know? Where are the points that students begin to struggle? This can be determined through formal and informal class wide and individual assessments, observations, and conversations.

As the teacher, you also need to match the content and instructional need, having a combination of pre-planned and "on the fly" supports along with explicitly instructing on the use of the supports. If you have taught for a while, you know which supports are good to match with content and can plan for those prior to instruction. For example, there are multiple mnemonic strategies designed specifically for mathematical problem-solving, such as STAR. The acronym stands for **S**earch the problem, **T**ranslate into picture form, **A**nswer the problem, and **R**eview the solution. This may be a scaffolded strategy you teach to all students, and you include it in your planning.

How Do I Use Scaffolded Supports Flexibly?

For "on the fly" supports, you must be responsive to a student need that presents itself but is not necessarily part of your planning. Maybe you have a student struggling to understand a concept through the readings and activities from the lesson, so you need to quickly find alternatives to scaffold their learning. This could be through creating a quick graphic organizer to help the student make connections between new information and what they already know. It could be finding some videos or images to provide a visual. You may need to provide more models or break a task into smaller parts. Even with the most extensive planning, you will need to have additional scaffolding strategies available to pull out at a moment's notice.

You also need to be flexible in the use of supports and see them with multiple purposes and across contents. Perhaps you are teaching the principle of cause and effect in history; the student is struggling to understand so you provide a verbal example, creating a real-life situation involving cause and effect. This "on the fly" support helps start the discussion. You know you will need to do something more with this topic tomorrow, so you adjust a graphic organizer you used to teach story plots with rising and falling action in English. This same graphic organizer can be used to help the student identify the action, what caused it, and the effects. This flexibility can also lead to the student independently using the support in other courses. Teaching the use of a variety of supports and then encouraging the student to use them is part of fading the support.

You can also be flexible in your use of scaffolded supports by understanding some students may struggle with memory issues and after coming back to school after winter or spring break they may have forgotten elements of a skill or task. You may have filed that support away, removed words from a word wall, or taken down some helpful poster outlining steps of a process. It is okay to pull that support back out and use it again for a time until the student has gained their confidence, and then you adjust it a bit or fade it all together.

How Do I Adjust and Fade Scaffolded Supports?

Scaffolded supports are not permanent. They are meant to support in the stages of learning a new skill and then scale back as the student becomes more proficient. You have to continually assess understanding and use of the scaffolded support to know when to start to scale back. This is not about going cold turkey and completely removing scaffolding, but more of a gradual fade. Perhaps you are using the provision of worked examples. In the beginning, you used complete examples that are directly related to the problem the student is working to accomplish. There may be written cues to describe the steps. Once the student can complete the problem with the provided example and written cue, start by removing some of the written cues. The next step may be to remove *all* the written cues. When the student can complete the problem without the written cue, you might provide problems that are similar, but not as closely related. Eventually, you get to the point where you provide one or two examples, and then fade that to the student working independently with no scaffolded examples.

It is also important to remember to prepare your paraprofessionals to provide, adjust, and fade scaffolded supports (Radford et al., 2015). They need to understand and be prepared to instruct students on how to use scaffolds and know when to adjust and fade based on the use of assessment and observation. This will take some training and support for your paraprofessionals, but helping them to be confident in providing scaffolding will go a long way in providing appropriate and effective scaffolded supports for students.

Without fading supports you run the risk of stifling independence. When students become too reliant on a teacher, paraprofessional, or even a support, they may exhibit learned helplessness. Learned helplessness is a phenomenon often discussed with great concern in special education. The

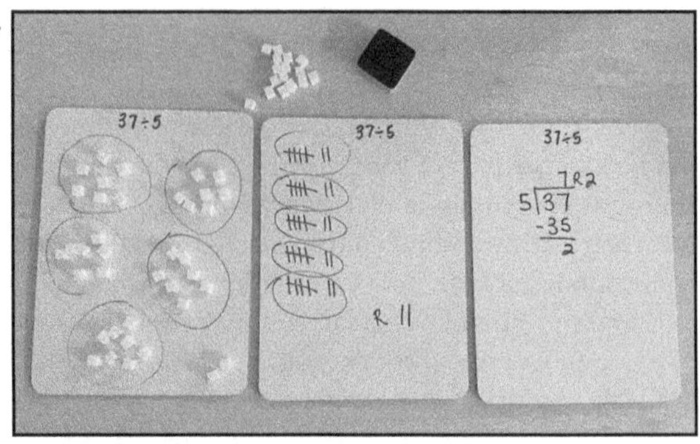

Figure 15-1. Illustration of concrete, representation, abstract.

situation causes students to feel powerless about a situation (e.g., learning, test taking) and just wait for others to support them or even do the task for them (Murawski & Hughes, 2021). Students with learned helplessness generally believe they cannot learn. Students with disabilities are more likely to experience learned helplessness and become overwhelmed with feelings of inability or they believe they fit some stereotype of disability. These emotions tied to their disability can have a negative impact on their own self-perceptions and on their expectations of success. That is why it is important to fade supports in a timely manner. We are not implying there is a clock in play here; what we are saying is monitor students as their ability and confidence grow, then fade the supports.

The student may want to keep using some supports, especially those used as an organizational tool. That is great! The student choosing the support and independently crafting a graphic organizer is different from you handing them the support or even reminding them to use one. In this case, the student has perhaps learned to accommodate their own weaknesses, thought about each support they have been given over time, and independently selected the one for this situation. That is a combination of HLPs 14 and 21. They used metacognition skills related to their organizational abilities, and remembered a strategy they had mastered, and are now using that strategy in another time and place. This is no longer a scaffolded support; it is an independently chosen accommodation. This is a goal achieved.

What Does HLP 15 Look Like in a K-12 Classroom?

Elementary Example

Mrs. Stanford is a special education teacher who co-teaches with Mrs. Doyle in her third-grade classroom. There are a few students who have individualized education program goals in mathematics, but Mrs. Stanford and Mrs. Doyle have purposefully planned mathematics instruction to follow the CRA framework to scaffold student learning. They are beginning by planning for the standard of representing and solving problems involving multiplication and division within 100.

First, they will pre-assess all students, regardless of disability status. When they assess, they will be asking students to show how they solve multiplication and division problems in a concrete manner while using manipulatives. Even though the goal will be for students to use the abstract algorithm to solve problems in the most efficient manner, they will not be assessing for the abstract. Many students can solve problems using the algorithm, but do not understand the concept, so it is important that they are assessed (HLP 6) using manipulatives to check for depth of conceptual understanding.

When instruction begins, Mrs. Stanford and Mrs. Doyle know who has shown that they do not have a conceptual understanding of the topic and will make sure to teach using concrete manipulatives while teaching the algorithm at the same time (Figure 15-1). This helps all students see the relation between the concrete and the abstract algorithm, and all students have access to manipulatives.

As students show proficiency using manipulatives, they fade the concrete and move to using a visual representation, or drawing, while still using the abstract algorithm. If a student struggles with the visual representation, they can easily move back to the concrete. Once they show proficiency using the visual representation alongside the algorithm, then the scaffold is faded, and the student uses just the abstract algorithm. It is key, however, that students have access to manipulatives when they feel they need to check their own understanding and give representation to their thinking.

Secondary Example

Mr. Walker is a special education teacher at Construction Zone Middle School. He co-teaches two science and two math classes with Mr. Foreman. He also has one resource period that supports students with disabilities that have either a co-taught or general education math or science class. He uses that time by preteaching and reteaching concepts from the general education math and science content classes, as well as teaching or supporting students' organizational skills. On Friday, Maya walks into the resource class crying, Mike is fuming, and Hunter just looks dazed. These three students have Mr. Foreman also, but they are not in a co-taught section. They are in a section of honors science. Mr. Foreman had handed them a nine-page very technical science article and told them to write a detailed essay on the flaws of the author's hypothesis and turn it in by Wednesday.

It is time for an "on the fly" scaffolded support. Mr. Walker reassures the students they have the ability, tells them all to take a deep breath, and then asks them to walk him through the assignment. As the students talk, he writes down what they say, stopping them when needed to prompt a different step. The exchange looks like this:

Mr. Walker: "Where do we start?"

Mike: "We need to read the article."

Mr. Walker: "That is a good start, but are there specific questions you want to ask as you read?" as he writes READ ARTICLE on the board.

Maya: "Yes, like what is a stupid hypothesis?"

Hunter: "That is where the scientist says what they think is going to happen; it's their guess."

Mr. Walker: "That is good, Hunter, but it is more than just a guess. What else do you know about a hypothesis?"

Hunter: "It is what they believe will happen based on some other reason. They have some experience, but not enough to know what will happen."

Mr. Walker: "Exactly. Remember our definition: a proposed explanation made on the basis of limited evidence as a starting point for further investigation." Then he writes IDENTIFY HYPOTHESIS.

Mike jumps in: "And then we have to find what is wrong with the hypothesis."

Mr. Walker: "That sounds right to me, Mike. If you are to find the flaws, it means you need to find what is wrong with the hypothesis." While writing FIND THE FLAWS, he verbally prompts them to continue, "Did Mr. Foreman tell you how many flaws you should find?"

Hunter: "Yes, we need at least three with *EVIDENCE*," he says, shaking his head and holding up three fingers, imitating Mr. Foreman.

Mr. Walker corrects Hunter's behavior of mocking Mr. Foreman and then continues to write and probe the students.

The conversation continues until the students have finished their list. Mr. Walker helps them construct a graphic organizer to use while they read (Figure 15-2). This will help them write their essay later. Finally, Mr. Walker helps them determine the timetable for completing the essay and then instructs them to bring their completed graphic organizers and essay drafts to class on Tuesday.

<table>
<tr><td colspan="3">Name of Article:</td></tr>
<tr><td>Hypothesis:</td><td colspan="2">Basis of Hypothesis:</td></tr>
<tr><td>Flaw 1:</td><td>Flaw 2:</td><td>Flaw 3:</td></tr>
<tr><td>Evidence provided in article:</td><td>Evidence provided in article:</td><td>Evidence provided in article:</td></tr>
</table>

Figure 15-2. Graphic organizer constructed in class.

Summary

All students, but especially those with disabilities, need scaffolded supports while learning new skills, content, and behaviors. Effective special education teachers know to explicitly teach them (HLP 16), evaluate their impact (HLP 6), and then fade them (Kennedy et al., 2021). Students need to be supported while learning, but also provided with enough engagement strategies (HLP 18) and practice to learn the skill, until they can demonstrate that over time and across settings (HLP 21). When teachers support student learning and give them enough positive and constructive feedback (HLPs 8 and 22), they will learn.

Effective special education teachers know their students and know the content to understand which supports are powerful, select and implement them, and then monitor their use to adjust the support to benefit students. Teaching students to use supports requires the same techniques as teaching content. You plan for the support, determine how long you anticipate the student will need it, and upfront plan the gradual release of learning over to students to fade the support. You explicitly teach, monitor student learning, and based on that data, at times provide more intensive instruction as needed, and you always plan for long-term learning.

Being flexible is the nature of a special educator's job. So why not be flexible with scaffolded supports? Some work, and some do not; adjust. Some supports can be used in multiple ways; if they work, use them across content and instructional settings. Some supports may work for some students and not others. It is okay; find one that will work, and if you use multiple supports for the same content, that just means you have multiple learners.

Valuable special educators scaffold supports and know when to increase and when to fade their use. They focus on the purpose of scaffolded supports to provide students with the necessary supports to assist in regulating their own learning (Hallenbeck, 2002). Do not enable students when the support is no longer needed; you might stifle their independence. By keeping supports in place too long, students may become dependent on them. Promoting learned helplessness will not make you indispensable to the student; everyone is replaceable. Remember, a special educator's job is to work themselves out of a job. Teach students to be independent. Teach students to think about their learning and how to apply it for themselves.

CHAPTER REVIEW

1. Name one powerful scaffolded support. Describe how you would use, monitor, and fade this support.
2. Which HLPs do you feel could not be used without HLP 15? Give an example to support your answer.
3. What is the difference between supporting students and stifling them?
4. Which EBPs discussed are designed to be scaffolded supports? Why do you believe this to be true?

REFERENCES

Agrawal, J., & Morin, L. L. (2016). Evidence-based practices: Applications of concrete representational abstract framework across math concepts for students with mathematics disabilities. *Learning Disabilities Research & Practice, 31*(1), 34-44. https://doi.org/10.1111/ldrp.12093

Archer, A. L., & Hughes, C. A. (2011). *Explicit instruction: Effective and efficient teaching.* Guilford Press.

Ball, D. L., & Forzani, F. (2011). *Identifying high-leverage practices for teacher education.* In American Educational Research Association Annual Meeting, Philadelphia, Pennsylvania.

Bulgren, J., Deshler, D. D., & Lenz, B. K. (2007). Engaging adolescents with LD in higher order thinking about history concepts using integrated content enhancement routines. *Journal of Learning Disabilities, 40*(2), 121-133.

Coltman, P., Petyaeva, D., & Anghileri, J. (2002). Scaffolding learning through meaningful tasks and adult interaction. *Early Years: An International Journal of Research and Development, 22*(1), 39-49.

Dye, G. A. (2000). Graphic organizers to the rescue! Helping students link—and remember—information. *TEACHING Exceptional Children, 32*(3), 72-76.

Ewoldt, K. B., & Morgan, J. J. (2017). Color-coded graphic organizers for teaching writing to students with learning disabilities. *TEACHING Exceptional Children, 49*(3), 175-184. https://doi.org/10.1177/0040059916681769

Graham, S., & MacArthur, C. (1988). Improving learning disabled students' skills at revising essays produced on a word processor: Self-instructional strategy training. *The Journal of Special Education, 22*(2), 133-152.

Hallenbeck, M. J. (2002). Taking charge: Adolescents with learning disabilities assume responsibility for their own writing. *Learning Disability Quarterly, 25*(4), 227-246.

Hughes, C. A., Morris, J. R., Therrien, W. J., & Benson, S. K. (2017). Explicit instruction: Historical and contemporary contexts. *Learning Disabilities Research & Practice, 32*(3), 140-148.

Kennedy, M. J., Romig, J. E., & Peeples, K. (2021). *HLP 15: Use scaffolded supports.* https://highleveragepractices.org/hlp-15-use-scaffolded-supports

Leko, M. M., Roberts, C., Peyton, D., & Pua, D. (2019). Selecting evidence-based practices: What works for me. *Intervention in School and Clinic, 54*(5), 286-294.

Mastropieri, M. A., & Scruggs, T. E. (1998). Enhancing school success with mnemonic strategies. *Intervention in School and Clinic, 33*(4), 201-208.

McLeskey, J., Barringer, M.-D., Billingsley, B., Brownell, M., Jackson, D., Kennedy, M., Lewis, T., Maheady, L., Rodriguez, J., Scheeler, M. C., Winn, J., & Ziegler, D. (2017). *High-leverage practices in special education.* Council for Exceptional Children & CEEDAR Center.

McLeskey, J., Billingsley, B., Brownell, M. T., Maheady, L., & Lewis, T. J. (2019). What are high-leverage practices for special education teachers and why are they important? *Remedial and Special Education, 40*(6), 331-337. https:/doi.org/10.1177/0741932518773477

Murawski, W. W., & Hughes, C. E. (2021). Special educators in inclusive settings: Take steps for self-advocacy! *TEACHING Exceptional Children, 53*(3), 184-193. https://doi.org/10.1177/0040059920982263

Radford, J., Bosanquet, P., Webster, R., & Blatchford, P. (2015). Scaffolding learning for independence: Clarifying teacher and teaching assistant roles for children with special educational needs. *Learning and Instruction, 36*, 1-10.

Reilly, J. M., & Ross, S. M. (2019). *The effects of thinking maps in raising student achievement: A retrospective study of outcomes from implementing schools. Center for Research and Reform in Education (CRRE).* Johns Hopkins University. https://www.thinkingmaps.com/cdn/JHU-CRRE-Evaluation-of-Thinking-Maps.pdf

Riccomini, P. J., & Morano, S. (2019). Guided practice for complex, multistep procedures in algebra: Scaffolding through worked solutions. *TEACHING Exceptional Children*, *51*(6), 445-454. https://doi.org/10.1177/0040059919848737

Rose, D. (2000). Universal design for learning. *Journal of Special Education Technology*, *15*(3), 45-49.

Sun, L., Ruokamo, H., Siklander, P., Li, B., & Devlin, K. (2021). Primary school students' perceptions of scaffolding in digital game-based learning in mathematics. *Learning, Culture and Social Interaction*, *28*, 100457.

Therrien, W. J., Benson, S. K., Hughes, C. A., & Morris, J. R. (2017). Explicit instruction and next generation science standards aligned classrooms: A fit or a split? *Learning Disabilities Research & Practice*, *32*(3), 149-154.

Vygotsky, L. S. (1978). *Mind in society: The development of higher psychological processes*. Harvard University Press.

Can I Truly Ensure Students Learn?

Ruby L. Owiny, PhD

HLP 16

Use explicit instruction.

INTRODUCTION

Explicit instruction (EI) is an evidence-based practice (EBP) by itself, making it a powerful High-Leverage Practice (HLP) for students to learn efficiently and at high levels. The elements of EI, combined with other EBPs, helps students to learn strategies to enhance their memory while teachers can be confident that their instruction is effective when implementing EI with fidelity. EI connects with multiple other HLPs, allowing teachers to implement multiple HLPs with EI lessons and allowing students access to quality instruction for mastering individualized education program objectives and the general education curriculum. Implementing EI allows students to master key skills, complex concepts, and knowledge while problem-solving and connecting learning to new concepts.

Owiny, R. L., & Cornelius, K. E. *The Practical Guide to High-Leverage Practices in Special Education: The Purposeful "How" to Enhance Classroom Rigor* (pp. 229-242).

CHAPTER OBJECTIVES

- → Define EI.
- → Explain elements of EI.
- → Design a lesson using the principles of EI.

KEY TERMS

- **active engagement:** Students are provided with opportunities to interact with concepts throughout the lesson in a meaningful way and in a variety of activities.
- **Backward design/Understanding by Design (UbD):** A framework for designing instruction with the end goal in mind before developing lessons and teaching them.
- **Cornell note-taking strategy:** A strategy for taking notes during a lecture.
- **guided notes:** An evidence-based practice for students to learn to take effective notes during class lecture.
- **modeling:** Providing a visual and/or verbal example of performing a skill that allows students to first see it in action before doing it.
- **opportunities to respond (OTRs):** The times teachers provide for students to actively participate during instruction to keep them engaged and learning at high rates.
- **scaffolding:** A process of adding or removing supports for students to master concepts.
- **think-aloud:** A form of modeling in which the teacher verbalizes the thought process for completing a task or performing a mental process.

Teachers frequently ask what they can do to ensure their students learn at high levels. While this is the million-dollar question, we have established in this book that there are some practices that we know, through research and through experience, that when used with fidelity, will benefit our students. Explicit instruction (EI) is one such practice. Not only is it a High-Leverage Practice (HLP), but also an evidence-based practice (EBP). Students will benefit and learn at high levels when taught using EI.

There is an abundance of research to support the use of EI for a myriad of academic skills, academically-related skills, grade levels, and disabilities (McLeskey et al., 2017). This research provides evidence for the versatility of EI in meeting a variety of needs across diverse populations. EI is beneficial for its use of multiple effective instruction principles coupled with varied student grouping, promotion of active engagement, and scaffolding of skills through an I Do, We Do, You Do model (McLeskey et al., 2017). Because of this strong research base and the foundation upon which EI is based, teachers can be confident that, when implemented correctly, their students' learning needs will be met.

A compelling feature of EI, along with the other HLPs, goes beyond just students with disabilities (SWD); we know they will benefit, but what is so compelling is that *all* students will benefit. Therefore, whether you are teaching in a self-contained special education classroom, a resource room, or co-teaching in a general education classroom, instruction that follows the EI elements will allow the provision of specially designed instruction for students with individualized education programs (IEPs) while also providing the opportunity for *all* students to achieve at higher levels.

This chapter will briefly describe EI but spend much of the chapter discussing other EBPs that will enhance an EI lesson. While EI itself is an EBP, each phase of instruction comes with its own decisions on how to deliver the instruction and engage students in responding and interacting with the content. Making the lesson engaging for students by motivating them with a purpose is vital. Ensuring you use other HLPs and EBPs will help increase the options you have to engage students and get them involved in their learning.

WHAT IS HLP 16?

HLP 16—"*Use explicit instruction*" is defined as:

> Teachers make content, skills, and concepts explicit by showing and telling students what to do or think while solving problems, enacting strategies, completing tasks, and classifying concepts. Teachers use explicit instruction when students are learning new material and complex concepts and skills. They strategically choose examples and non-examples and language to facilitate student understanding, anticipate common misconceptions, highlight essential content, and remove distracting information. They model and scaffold steps or processes needed to understand content and concepts, apply skills, and complete tasks successfully and independently. (McLeskey et al., 2017, p. 80)

Oftentimes SWD, due to how their disability is specifically impacted by cognitive processing, do not learn implicitly and need EI. This is not to say that students without disabilities will not also need EI. Imagine yourself at a swim meet. You are sitting in the bleachers watching the swimmers move their arms in an arc above the water and their legs come up from the water and make a splash. What you cannot see from the bleachers is what is happening under the water. You would need to be in the water yourself watching from underneath the surface or have a video camera recording what is happening underneath the surface. An SWD might identify what is above the surface, or what is most obvious, but will possibly not be able to identify what is below the surface, or that which is less obvious. They may figure out a simple pattern on their own, but when an exception arises with that pattern, they may not be able to figure out why the exception occurs or when it should occur. This is where EI plays a vital role. It helps to make that which is implicit more explicit to generate greater understanding in a more efficient manner.

Continuing with our swimming example, a student may sometimes be able to observe a swimmer and deduce that where they see an arc above the water, beginning at the swimmer's waist and ending above their head would require another arc, inverted under the water, for the arm to return to the waist and complete the arc above the water repeatedly. However, many times, figuring out that the swimmer is making a full circle to complete a freestyle stroke will require EI to "see" what is below the surface.

Putting this into academic terms, a student may more easily learn the short vowel sound for the letter *a* and identify many words that have the short *a* sound. This same child may not be able to independently identify the sound that *au*, such as in *caught*, and will need EI to learn it and identify other words that have that same sound. Similarly, a student may know that it is polite to say "Hello" when seeing someone, but may not realize the greeting is not spoken every time you encounter that person in the classroom throughout the day, especially among elementary school classmates. One needs only to say "Hello" first thing in the morning when entering the classroom. Some students may need to be taught explicitly when it is appropriate to say "Hello" and when it is not needed.

In sum, the implementation of EI benefits all students across a variety of content areas, skills, and concepts. It can be used in any setting—special education classroom or general education classroom. It helps make instruction intentional and clear for high levels of student learning. EI requires strategic planning with an I Do, We Do, You Do framework.

HOW IS HLP 16 CONNECTED TO OTHER HLPS?

As we explain throughout this book, HLPs are not intended for implementation in isolation, rather they are expected to be implemented in tandem with each other. Some HLPs connect more closely with some than with others. For HLP 16—"*Use explicit instruction*," HLP 7—"*Establish a consistent, organized, and respectful learning environment*" is key to delivering quality instruction. As Chapter 7 established, a quality environment is necessary for any learning to occur. With EI, it is important to establish group norms for this type of lesson to keep pacing of the lesson at an appropriate speed. In their seminal research, Brophy and Good (1986) address pacing of the lesson as the "opportunity to learn" and "content covered." Both components of pacing are important. However, without a well-established classroom environment where students know expectations will be carried through, content coverage and opportunities for learning will be interrupted for the teacher to address inappropriate behavior.

HLPs 8 and 22—"*Provide positive and constructive feedback to guide students' learning and behavior*" align closely to EI as the framework includes "provide immediate affirmative and corrective feedback" as one of the 16 elements (Archer & Hughes, 2011). Immediacy is part of the definition of positive and constructive feedback. Positive feedback ensures a positive learning environment in which students feel safe to take risks in their learning to meet their learning needs. Constructive feedback is an essential part of guided and independent practice (phases of the EI framework), as teachers monitor student practice of a new concept. This feedback helps students to understand where their errors are and how to correct misconceptions they made before those errors become part of their learning, making unlearning more difficult.

EI can be used to teach social skills (HLP 9) and cognitive and metacognitive strategies (HLP 14). Systematically designing instruction toward a specific goal (HLP 12) is a key factor in EI and helps you sequence learning to optimize outcomes. Additionally, providing scaffolded supports (HLP 15) is in the very nature of EI to ensure students master objectives and perform skills with a high rate of accuracy before moving on.

Furthermore, HLP 18—"*Use strategies to promote active student engagement*" is also a key component of EI. Active student engagement typically involves opportunities to respond (OTRs), which is an EBP. Teachers should continually evaluate how often they provide OTRs for their students, with the understanding that the more students engage with content through responding in a variety of ways, increases student achievement and makes learning more efficient (Owiny et al., 2018). Multiple strategies for increasing OTRs are provided in Chapter 18.

Finally, HLP 21—"*Teach students to maintain and generalize new learning across time and settings*" is an element of EI to help ensure students can perform the skill and engage with the content across a variety of relevant settings throughout time. Essentially, once a student learns how to multiply in a classroom using manipulatives, they should eventually be able to use that skill in their community, such as when they are buying favors or treats for a birthday party. If they want their guests to receive multiple favors or have a variety of treats to eat, they might need to use multiplication to determine how many they need. Learning the skill in isolation does not result in lifelong learning, which occurs with maintenance and generalization. This chapter will more fully explain each HLP as it relates to HLP 16.

Why Is Explicit Instruction Important?

Many of us, when given the opportunity, will choose a treatment or strategy that is "tried and true" over a new-fangled approach that is not yet proven. EI is that "tried and true" instructional approach. In their seminal research, on which many special education researchers base their own research, Brophy and Good (1986) address those teacher behaviors that lead to student achievement while Rosenshine and Stevens (1986) identified teaching functions. Similar to HLPs, teaching functions are those instructional behaviors or strategies that teachers employ knowing that their students will achieve at higher levels than if they did not use those behaviors or strategies.

The 16 elements of EI plus the strategies for organizing a classroom for instruction, outlined by Archer and Hughes (2011), are in line with these teaching functions and teaching behaviors. Additionally, Kameenui and Simmons (1990) describe how to design instructional strategies to prevent learning issues or to intervene for students when learning problems occurred. The principles of instruction they address in their book are included in EI. This chapter includes principles based in

Brophy and Good's (1986) work, along with Kameenui and Simmons' (1990) work. Additionally, the work of Archer and Hughes (2011) is the hallmark of this chapter. However, this chapter only skims the surface of their work. Please reference their book for more in-depth information on effective design and delivery of EI.

What Evidence-Based Practices Can Be Used in an Explicit Instruction Lesson?

Modeling is a key part of EI. In the description of this HLP, it states that teachers should "make content, skills, and concepts explicit by showing and telling students what to do or think while solving problems, enacting strategies, completing tasks, and classifying concepts" (McLeskey et al., 2017, p. 80). Modeling allows the teacher to teach a concept or skill by showing *and* telling. In fact, the What Works Clearinghouse (n.d.) lists modeling as one of the EBPs in their infographic, *Evidence-Based Teaching Practices*. Modeling is demonstrating the task or skill you want students to do, even to include self-regulation strategies. Modeling is appropriate for numerous concepts and skills, such as teaching phonics, how to conduct a science experiment, how to balance a chemistry equation, how to write a research project, or even how to think through a process or self-talk to complete a task that may appear too difficult. Modeling is beneficial for students whether learning in a face-to-face setting or in a virtual classroom, synchronous and asynchronous. Video modeling, explained in more detail in Chapter 19 and an EBP, can be an effective method for modeling a concept and posting it to a classroom learning management system whether it is intended for a fully online classroom or as an accommodation for face-to-face instruction.

Traditionally, video modeling was designed for students and their caregivers to review the video to remember (or learn) how to perform the task. However, as discussed previously, it can be effective for all students at all levels. Research supports video modeling as an EBP for students with autism spectrum disorder (ASD; Wong et al., 2015) and in a recent study, students with ASD successfully met learning objectives for computing fractions with a combination of video modeling and manipulatives (Yakubova et al., 2020). Additionally, Satsangi and Hammer (2018) identified positive results in the use of video modeling and the use of EI among students with learning disabilities, also in mathematics.

Modeling benefits all students, whether they have a disability, are learning English as a new language, or are gifted. Mims and colleagues (2012) used a modified system of least prompts procedure in a study with students in middle school with diagnoses of intellectual disability or ASD. In this study, a think aloud was inserted into the second prompt of the system of least prompts during read-aloud sessions focused on comprehension. The think-aloud procedure included re-reading a short passage containing the correct response to the question, stating the correct answer, re-reading the question, and waiting for the student to respond. Students showed an increase in comprehension with this modified process.

Think-alouds are the describing piece of modeling and they are evidence-based (Kamil et al., 2008), which gives teachers confidence that using them can help students learn at higher rates. In fact, think-alouds, as part of the EI modeling phase, are recommended as one of the interventions to use for students struggling with math by the National Center of Education Evaluation and Regional Assistance (Fuchs et al., 2021). They make explicit what is happening in one's brain, like the swimming example mentioned earlier in this chapter. A think-aloud helps students to "see inside one's head" to know what one is thinking (Archer & Hughes, 2011). It allows students to experience the thought process that goes into the implementation of a comprehension strategy or developing a counter-argument in a debate, for example. Think-alouds benefit all students and is a form of representing content, thus is a way of implementing Universal Design for Learning (UDL).

Scaffolding material is vital to student success. Because this is the focus of Chapter 15, we will not go into great depth here, but briefly describe how it applies to EI. EI is delivered using scaffolding. Scaffolding allows students to learn steps or processes in a strategic, near errorless manner with appropriate supports in place. The steps or processes build to help students to understand more in-depth content and concepts, apply skills, and complete tasks successfully and independently. In an EI lesson, students are led through the learning process with more teacher support at the beginning of a lesson to develop the foundation for knowledge and application of concepts and skills with gradual release to the student to perform the skill independently (Archer & Hughes, 2011).

This gradual release of responsibility is often referred to as I Do, We Do, You Do (Mariage et al., 2022). As explained above, EI lessons begin with the teacher briefly explaining the concept or skill and demonstrating its use with examples; this is the I Do or *modeling phase*. Second, examples are provided for the students to work through the process with teacher guidance; this is the We Do or *guided practice phase*. Once students demonstrate understanding of the concept, the You Do phase of the lesson begins, or the *unguided/independent practice*, with the students working independently while the teacher monitors work to correct errors or misconceptions. The teacher can also point out what is being done well and praise students for their work (Mariage et al., 2022). This three-step scaffolded process is effective for allowing students to see and hear the concept and get support while practicing. This helps to build confidence and connect prior knowledge to new knowledge (Archer & Hughes, 2011).

The EBP of strategy instruction can be used during an EI lesson to teach students a method for approaching a task or remembering a concept. Strategies help students to become independent, self-guided learners, which is also a goal of UDL. Once students develop a repertoire of strategies, such as cognitive and metacognitive strategies identified in HLP 14 or behavioral strategies to regulate their behavior independently, students can perform tasks and skills with minimal intervention, which is the ultimate goal of learning—to develop independence in performing a skill or task. There are many strategies from taking deep breaths to control anxiety or following a given number of steps to overcome anger that address social-emotional needs. There are also strategies for checking work, remaining on task, remembering a list of items, and following a process. Strategies can be taught using the EI model of I Do, We Do, You Do for students to develop skills to be successful independent learners (IRIS Center, 2016).

Wiggins and McTighe (2005) describe instructional design as backward design or Understanding by Design (UbD) because teachers often attempt to fit standards and objectives into their pre-chosen activities, rather than starting with the end in mind and asking, "What do students need to know or do and how do I design instruction to get there?" Thus, it feels backward to start with the end goal and then determine the instructional activities to help students master the objective. Many of the foundational principles of backward design and EI overlap. Both require a strong goal or objective and careful sequencing of instructional activities to lead students to proficiency. Additionally, both UbD and EI require strategic planning to carefully choose exactly how the content will be taught with examples and non-examples and precise language to facilitate student understanding, while anticipating common misconceptions, highlighting essential content, and removing distracting information. Both seek to develop deep understanding of concepts and the ability to perform skills proficiently.

In UbD, teachers work through three phases of instructional planning. Wiggins and McTighe (2005) provide prompts for teachers to ask as they prepare instruction. In Stage 1, they consider the national, state, and local standards they must address along with their strengths and passions in alignment with big ideas and enduring questions that lead students to deep understandings. In Stage 2, teachers determine what evidence they will accept from students to demonstrate mastery of the skill or concept while addressing key assessment principles such as validity, reliability, and sufficiency. Also in this stage, teachers should consider the multiple ways students could express their learning to ensure implementation of UDL in their instructional design. Finally, in Stage 3, the fun begins. This is when the instructional activities are planned. Teachers determine the multiple methods of representation of content and how to engage learners in the content. What activities will interest students and effectively teach them the content? This is where EBPs, such as strategy instruction explained previously, should be considered and the ones that will best match the content should be planned.

Contrasting UbD with EI, a similar pattern for lesson design is followed. Teachers must determine the end goal, whether it is an IEP objective, a prerequisite skill, or general education content. From there, the teacher must determine the best way to both assess the skill and teach it in an effective manner. EI emphasizes clear and precise language, organized and focused lessons, and frequent responding, all hallmarks of UbD as well. When developing EI lessons, teachers would do well to also consider the phases of UbD. See Table 16-1 for prompts to consider when designing a UbD-friendly EI lesson. The prompts for UbD instructional considerations are adapted from *The UbD Design Matrix* (Wiggins & McTighe, 2005, p. 34) and chosen for their connection to effective EI lesson design. The prompts for EI lesson considerations are adapted from the components of an EI lesson provided in Archer and Hughes (2011).

How Do I Plan for an Explicit Instruction Lesson?

While this chapter does not explain all 16 elements of EI, a few are described. Using all of the elements, as described in Archer and Hughes (2011), is key to the effective implementation of EI. Remember, Archer and Hughes wrote an entire book explaining EI, so we cannot possibly cover everything in one chapter; however, the goal of this chapter is to give you what you need to get started and then the authors of this book urge you to read Archer and Hughes's book for more in-depth detail.

When considering how to start in your planning for an EI lesson, starting with Phase 1 of UbD Considerations in Table 16-1 will help you get off on the right foot. For your lesson or unit, identify what students need to know. This information can come from IEP goals and objectives or the general curriculum. Additionally, there may be some prerequisite skills needed before a student can begin developing a new skill. This will give you what you need to identify an end point, or the destination, for your instruction. From there, you can create a learning goal or target.

Beninghof (2022) explains the importance of learning targets. They help students to make progress, step-by-step, toward meeting their IEP goals and objectives and mastering the general education curriculum. Breaking down a larger task, such as writing a research paper, into smaller objectives helps students and their teachers to see progress in microbursts, which motivates them to keep moving toward the larger target. For writing a research paper, a lot of steps go into creating the final product. Breaking it down into smaller objectives, such as the student will be able to articulate a main idea, and then moving to the student will be able to add details to describe the main idea, as two of several learning targets, allows short-term progress to be made en route to the longer-term product. Additionally, a learning target provides a way to know when the student has reached the destination for that lesson or unit.

Once you have determined the skill, process, or knowledge on which to focus your lesson or unit and created a learning objective or target, move on to planning the opening of your EI lesson. Consider what prerequisite skills might need to be reviewed and how to explain the learning target to students. Explaining the learning target can include the purpose for learning, also, which is the engagement principle of UDL. This can help motivate students to engage in learning the concept.

Phase 2 of UbD planning is consideration of assessments or, in the terminology of Wiggins and McTighe (2005), acceptable evidence. In other words, how will students prove, or demonstrate, their understanding? To implement the action and expression principle of UDL, multiple means of evidence should be planned across the lesson or unit. In the body of the EI lesson, students should be actively engaged in responding to the content throughout all phases of learning. This is where HLP 16 interfaces with HLP 18. Students should be actively responding in various ways, even during

Table 16-1. Explicit Instruction Lesson Alignment to Understanding by Design

UBD INSTRUCTIONAL CONSIDERATIONS		EI LESSON CONSIDERATIONS	
Phase 1	• What are the key ideas students need to learn? • What do students need to be able to know and do after mastery of this lesson or unit?	Opening	• How can I articulate the goal of the lesson in a student-friendly manner? • Which prerequisite skills must students have to perform this skill or learn new knowledge? • What is the relevance of this knowledge or skill to students' learning or their lives?
Phase 2	• What is acceptable evidence of concept or skill mastery? • How much evidence is sufficient to demonstrate mastery? • What evidence will reliably measure what the student knows and can do?	Body	• How should I explain the new knowledge or skill? • What is the best way to model the concept using a variety of examples and non-examples? • How can students be actively engaged in learning during modeling? • What should be included in guided practice? • What prompts will be used as students practice the new concept to ensure they practice correctly? • How will students practice independently in a meaningful way that allows them to demonstrate mastery of the new concept?
Phase 3	• What learning activities will allow students to best master the goals for this lesson or unit? • What evidence-based practices are most suitable for developing proficiency?	Closing	• What information will be provided in a short review of the concept? • How will the next lesson be previewed to get students excited?

teacher modeling in the I Do phase. Active responding can include speaking, writing, manipulating objects on their desk, moving their bodies a certain way, clicking a mouse, or other ways. Chapter 18 provides ideas for engaging students in active responding.

Finally, teachers should prepare Phase 3, the learning activities. These activities occur throughout the EI lesson. One should ask, "What learning activities will best help students master the lesson goal or learning target?" The answer to this question should include a variety of activities across a variety of modalities to be UDL compliant for the representation module and to engage students most effectively in mastering the learning target. Remember, the activities will be used throughout the lesson so plan enough examples, problems, and other practice opportunities. You will need a couple in your model, a few in the guided practice, enough to ensure students have enough confidence to complete even more of these practice opportunities in the unguided/independent practice phase of the lesson.

For the closing of the EI lesson, consider how to best review the concept addressed in the lesson and preview the next lesson. This allows for implementation of all three principles of UDL, depending on how the review and preview are planned. Students can become intrigued about the next lesson as the engagement principle while actively expressing their learning from the current lesson for action and expression. Finally, the review provides another opportunity for representation of the content while also providing some representation for the next lesson.

Preparing an EI lesson with the principles of UbD along with strategy instruction, scaffolding, and modeling while implementing the 16 elements of effective EI will allow teachers to have confidence that they are meeting the IEP needs of their students while also allowing them to access the general education curriculum to develop proficiency. The beauty of HLP 16 is that EI not only benefits SWD, but it benefits any student by providing systematic, explicit, and direct instruction, which also incorporates HLP 12.

What Does HLP 16 Look Like in a K-12 Classroom?

Elementary Example

Ms. Wolyn teaches special education at Oriole Elementary School. Beylor has an IEP goal in English Language Arts related to writing paragraphs, along with several other students on Ms. Wolyn's caseload. Ms. Wolyn believes in the power of modeling and guided practice. She sees the benefit in monitoring independent practice and providing feedback. She has experienced students being successful in mastering learning targets with an I Do, We Do, You Do model of instruction.

The first step in developing her lesson is to analyze the IEP objective: When given a writing prompt, Beylor will write a paragraph with at least five sentences containing a topic sentence, a minimum of three detail sentences, and a concluding sentence with 80% accuracy in four of five trials as measured by a writing checklist. Ms. Wolyn has data to show that Beylor, along with three other students who have a similar goal, can write a sentence with a noun, verb, and include some adjectives while using appropriate punctuation. They can create a topic sentence from a prompt but struggle to identify details. For example, when asked to write a paragraph about her favorite thing to do, Beylor responded, "I like to swim." When prompted to add details, she stated, "Because it's fun." Ms. Wolyn decides to create a lesson in which students work to develop their details to support the main idea. She decides that acceptable evidence will be either written or verbal responses to prompts, knowing that students do not always have the skills to state their response, let alone write it. Their written response can be in the form of sentences or a drawing with labels for the details to provide multiple opportunities for action and expression in ways that are most meaningful to the student to allow them to show mastery of the lesson target.

Table 16-2. Cue Card with Prompts for Adding Details to a Main Idea

ASK YOURSELF	YOUR IDEA
Who do I like to _______ with?	
What about _______ makes it fun for me?	
When do I like to _______?	
Where do I like to _______?	
How would I describe _______ to my friends without using the words, "fun" or "because I like it"?	
Why is _______ my favorite thing to do?	

Finally, Ms. Wolyn decides which activities to use for teaching the concept, adding details to your main idea. Using the I Do, We Do, You Do phases, she decides to do a think aloud for the I Do phase with the prompt, "What is your favorite thing to do?" She will introduce a laminated cue card with prompts using "WH" questions for adding details to their writing (Table 16-2). Ms. Wolyn thinks aloud, "What is my favorite thing to do? Hmmmm... My favorite thing to do is to go on a hike in the woods. I will write the answer to that question. Next, I need to add some details. The next WH question is 'Who'—Who do I like to hike with? Well, besides my family, I love to hike with my dog, Nova. I will write this sentence, 'I like to hike with my family and my dog, Nova.'" Ms. Wolyn continues until she has modeled adding details to a main idea by using the cue card.

For the We Do phase, Ms. Wolyn decides to show students a picture of a child playing soccer and guides the students to identify reasons soccer might be that child's favorite activity. She decided on soccer because her students have recently finished a unit in physical education, and three of her students are from Mexico where soccer is popular, and two of those students have a parent who plays in a community adult league and the third student plays soccer himself. Beylor's uncle played soccer in Tanzania, and she enjoyed watching his games until her family moved to the United States. Students write their shared ideas on their laminated cue card, as Ms. Wolyn writes it on a projected cue card. When finished, Ms. Wolyn directs students to take a picture with their iPad of their finished cue card to save for future reference.

For the You Do phase, Ms. Wolyn directs students to choose from a variety of prompts to answer in whichever manner they choose. If they choose a verbal response, they must give their response to Ms. Wolyn or the paraeducator, Ms. Linnah. Verbal responses will be recorded for use in later lessons as students work through writing their paragraphs. Beylor chose to draw a picture and label it by answering the questions: Where do I like to swim? Who do I like to swim with? Why do I like to swim (at the beach)? Her response is in Figure 16-1.

Secondary Example

Mr. Olila co-teaches (HLP 1) with Ms. Irena in 10th-grade World History. Emmanuel has a goal to take notes in class. Mr. Olila and Ms. Irena discuss the fact that many students in the class do not have the skills to take quality notes. They decide to teach an explicit lesson on note taking. This lesson will help Emmanuel to meet his IEP goal: When given a note-taking template, Emmanuel will independently take notes with appropriate details during a class lecture/discussion with 80% accuracy in 8 out of 10 trials as measured by a note-taking checklist. The learning target is set, students will take appropriate notes, and the acceptable evidence is established, notes taken either electronically or

Figure 16-1. Beylor's details for the writing prompt.

Name: ____________ Date: ____________ Class Period: ____________

Subject: ____________ Unit: ____________ Topic: ____________

Key Points	**Details**

Summary

Figure 16-2. Cornell note-taking template.

paper/pencil, so Phases 1 and 2 of planning a UbD friendly lesson are done. Mr. Olila and Ms. Irena now need to decide on learning activities to best meet the needs of their students.

Mr. Olila and Ms. Irena decide to teach this lesson over 3 days. Day 1 will consist of the opening and the I Do phase. They decide that for the opening of the lesson, they will explain why note taking is important and give an anecdote of an example of when note taking benefitted a student when studying for a test and a non-example of when poor note taking confused a student when reviewing notes to complete homework. They will use these relevant examples while also using humor to engage students through the UDL principle of engagement. For the I Do phase of the lesson, they will model taking notes with a template using the Cornell note-taking strategy (Figure 16-2), a form of guided notes that is an EBP (Haydon et al., 2011; Konrad, 2009). They will use the co-teaching approach, team teaching, to teach the lesson. Ms. Irena will model note taking using the document camera to project her paper onto the smartboard while Mr. Olila gives the lecture. Mr. Olila will pause periodically for Ms. Irena to do a think aloud to model the notes she has already taken and to decide if she needs to add any details. A copy of the notes will be shared with students in their online classroom, and a physical copy will be provided to any student who wishes to have one. Throughout the lesson, both teachers will ask students questions, do some Turn and Talks, and a Think-Pair-Share to keep students engaged in the lesson while they observe the modeled note taking. They will complete an exit slip in which they will summarize the Cornell note-taking strategy and provide a two-sentence summary of the lesson topic for that day.

Day 2 will consist of the We Do phase of the lesson. Team teaching will continue, this time with Ms. Irena leading the lecture and Mr. Olila leading the note taking. During this guided practice, students will take notes while listening to two mini-lectures. For the first mini-lecture, students will take notes either on their iPads using the electronic template or via written form using a hard copy of the template or creating the template in their history notebook. Mr. Olila will take notes using the document camera again, stopping Ms. Irena periodically to prompt students about details to record and ask them to share with each other what they have already written. Both Mr. Olila and Ms. Irena will walk around the room, monitoring students as they record their notes. At the end of the first mini-lecture, teachers will debrief with students about their notes, allowing them to compare them to the notes Mr. Olila took which are projected. For the second mini-lecture, a similar procedure will be followed, except this time, Mr. Olila will not take notes simultaneously with students. Ms. Irena has chunked the lecture into three parts. Students will be directed to take notes during the lecture and at pre-selected stopping points, Mr. Olila will provide feedback on what he saw as students took notes and have them guide him, with prompting, on what to write on his template. Students will be given an opportunity to edit their notes before going on to the next section of the lecture. This procedure will be repeated for the next two sections of the mini-lecture.

On Day 3, the You Do phase will be taught. Mr. Olila and Ms. Irena will parallel teach this lesson so they can monitor students' note taking in a smaller teacher to student ratio. As Mr. Olila and Ms. Irena teach the same content in the same way, they can easily monitor.

Summary

EI is an effective EBP to help SWD and those without to learn what is below the surface that they cannot see. It makes visible or *explicit* that which is invisible or implicit to the learner. It scaffolds (HLP 15) instruction in a way that helps students grasp concepts in smaller chunks that build on one another.

EI alone is powerful, but when combined with other HLPs, it can really pack a punch! Imagine the power of EI when collaborating with a speech-language pathologist to connect vocabulary goals for a student with a communication disorder to general education content or co-teaching an EI lesson with a general educator as HLP 1 encourages. The expertise that can be shared for the benefit of the student in creating an EI lesson is tremendous! The structure of an EI lesson lends itself to a consistent, organized, and respectful learning environment (HLP 7), and social skills (HLP 9) can be taught using strategy instruction to meet social-emotional learning needs.

An argument could be made for EI benefitting from all the instructional HLPs, although this chapter highlights only some of the connections. To truly be an EI lesson, it must be systematically designed (HLP 12), which can include using the principles of UbD to ensure learning endures and is maintained (HLP 21). Strategies (HLP 14) can, and should be, included in EI for behavior and academic needs. As with any instruction, active student responding (HLP 18) should be planned

Table 16-3. Alignment of HLPs and Resources for Evidence-Based Practices

EBP SUPPORT WITH HLP 16	RELATED HLPS	RESOURCES
Opportunities to respond	18	https://explicitinstruction.org/video-elementary/elementary-video-1/ https://www.interventioncentral.org/academic-interventions/general-academic/group-response-techniques
Think-alouds	12, 14, 15	https://strategiesforspecialinterventions.weebly.com/think-alouds.html
Modeling	12, 14, 15, 20	https://iris.peabody.vanderbilt.edu/module/srs/cresource/q2/p06/ https://explicitinstruction.org/video-elementary/elementary-video-8/
Video modeling	12, 14, 15, 20	https://youtu.be/CdYquPJT4Ak
Scaffolding	15	https://iris.peabody.vanderbilt.edu/module/sca/cresource/q2/p06/
Understanding by Design	12, 20, 21	https://cft.vanderbilt.edu/guides-sub-pages/understanding-by-design/ https://jaymctighe.com/resources/
Guided notes	14, 18	https://www.interventioncentral.org/academic-interventions/study-organization/guided-notes-increasing-student-engagement-during-lecture- https://templatelab.com/cornell-notes/
Strategy instruction	14	https://iris.peabody.vanderbilt.edu/module/jj1/cresource/q3/p07/ https://iris.peabody.vanderbilt.edu/module/ss2/cresource/q1/p04/ https://www.ldonline.org/ld-topics/study-skills/using-mnemonic-instruction-teach-math https://blog.brookespublishing.com/5-mnemonic-strategies-to-help-students-succeed-in-school/

throughout all phases of the lesson. Students and teachers alike will quickly realize the intensive nature of EI lessons, when taught with fidelity, aligning it as an intensive intervention (HLP 20). Finally, an element of EI and HLP 22 is providing positive and constructive feedback throughout the lesson to ensure student understanding and to promote motivation and sustainment of effort. Teachers can be confident that they are helping students to efficiently learn and retain new information with EI. For resources related to HLP 16 and the HLPs that connect with it, refer to Table 16-3.

Chapter Review

1. Describe HLP 16 in your own words.
2. Why is EI important?
3. Explain each phase of an EI lesson.

References

Archer, A. L., & Hughes, C. A. (2011). *Explicit instruction: Effective and efficient teaching*. Guilford Press.

Beninghof, A. M. (2022). *Specially designed instruction: Increasing success for students with disabilities*. Routledge.

Brophy, J., & Good, T. L. (1986). Teacher behavior and student achievement. In M.C. Wittrock (Ed.), *Handbook of research on teaching* (3rd ed., pp. 328-375).

Fuchs, L. S., Newman-Gonchar, R., Schumacher, R., Dougherty, B., Bucka, N., Karp, K. S., Woodward, J., Clarke, B., Jordan, N. C., Gersten, R., Jayanthi, M., Keating, B., & Morgan, S. (2021). *Assisting students struggling with mathematics: Intervention in the elementary grades (WWC 2021006)*. National Center for Education Evaluation and Regional Assistance (NCEE), Institute of Education Sciences, U.S. Department of Education. http://whatworks.ed.gov/

Haydon, T., Mancil, G. R., Kroeger, S. D., McLeskey J., & Wan-Yu J. L. (2011). A review of the effectiveness of guided notes for students who struggle learning academic content. *Preventing School Failure*, 55(4), 226-231.

IRIS Center. (2016). *Youth with disabilities in juvenile corrections (part 1): Improving instruction*. https://iris.peabody.vanderbilt.edu/module/jj1/

Kameenui, E. J., & Simmons, D. C. (1990). *Designing instructional strategies: The prevention of academic learning problems*. Merrill Publishing Company.

Kamil, M. L., Borman, G. D., Dole, J., Kral, C. C., Salinger, T., and Torgesen, J. (2008). *Improving adolescent literacy: Effective classroom and intervention practices: A Practice Guide* (NCEE #2008-4027). National Center for Education Evaluation and Regional Assistance, Institute of Education Sciences, U.S. Department of Education. http://ies.ed.gov/ncee/wwc

Konrad, M., Joseph, L. M., & Eveleigh, E. (2009). A meta-analytic review of guided notes. *Education and Treatment of Children*, 32(3), 421-444.

Mariage, T. V., Winn, J., Tucker, N., & Elliott, R. (2022). Provide scaffolded supports. In J. McLeskey, L. Maheady, B. Billinglsey, M. T. Brownell, & T. J. Lewis (Eds.), *High leverage practices for inclusive classrooms* (2nd ed., pp. 218-234). Routledge. https://doi.org/10.4324/9781003148609-21

Mastropieri, M. A., & Scruggs, T. E. (2014). *The inclusive classroom*. Pearson.

McLeskey, J., Barringer, M.-D., Billingsley, B., Brownell, M., Jackson, D., Kennedy, M., Lewis, T., Maheady, L., Rodriguez, J., Scheeler, M. C., Winn, J., & Ziegler, D. (2017). *High-leverage practices in special education*. Council for Exceptional Children & CEEDAR Center.

Mims, P. J., Hudson, M. E., & Browder, D. M. (2012). Using read-alouds of grade-level biographies and systematic prompting to promote comprehension for students with moderate and severe developmental disabilities. *Focus on Autism and Other Developmental Disabilities*, 27(2), 67-80.

Owiny, R. L., Spriggs, A., Sartini, E. C., & Mills, J. R. (2018). Evaluating response cards as evidence based. *Preventing School Failure: Alternative Education for Children and Youth*, 62(2), 59-72. https://doi.org/10.1080/1045988X.2017.1344953

Regional Educational Laboratory Southeast. (n.d.). *Evidence-based teaching practices*. https://ies.ed.gov/ncee/edlabs/infographics/pdf/REL_SE_Evidence-based_teaching_practices.pdf

Rosenshine, B., & Stevens, R. (1986). Teaching functions. In M.C. Wittrock (Ed.), *Handbook of research on teaching* (3rd ed., pp. 376-391). Macmillan.

Satsangi, R., & Hammer, R. (2018). Video modeling and explicit instruction: A comparison of strategies for teaching mathematics to students with learning disabilities. *Learning Disabilities Research & Practice*, 34(1), 35-46. https://doi.org/10.1111/ldrp.12189

Wiggins, G., & McTighe, J. (2005). *Understanding by design*. ASCD.

Wong, C., Odom, S. L., Hume, K. A., Cox, A. W., Fettig, A., Kucharczyk, S., Brock, M. E., Plavnick, J. B., Fleury, V. P., & Schultz, T. R. (2015). Evidence-based practices for children, youth, and young adults with autism spectrum disorder: A comprehensive review. *Journal of Autism and Developmental Disorders*, 45, 1951-1966.

Yakubova, G., Hughes, E. M., & Chen, B. B. (2020). Teaching students with ASD to solve fraction computations using a video modeling instructional package. *Research in Developmental Disabilities*, 101, 1-11.

How Does Student Grouping Optimize Learning?

Lawrence J. Maheady, PhD
and Kyena E. Cornelius, EdD

HLP 17
Use flexible grouping.

INTRODUCTION

Hopefully, you are not thinking the model classroom is students sitting single file in rows, facing the "front" of the room, and listening to the teacher drone on. This traditional "sit and get" method is not enjoyable for most students; it is especially detrimental to students with or at risk for disabilities. Likewise, you cannot simply tell students to "get into groups" and expect that will yield fantastic results either. There really is an intentional and strategic process for using flexible grouping. This chapter will offer teachers practical strategies to design purposeful student groupings to deliver effective instruction, improve student engagement, and ultimately improve student learning.

Owiny, R. L., & Cornelius, K. E. *The Practical Guide to High-Leverage Practices in Special Education: The Purposeful "How" to Enhance Classroom Rigor* (pp. 243-254).

CHAPTER OBJECTIVES

- Describe multiple ways to design and use flexible grouping to engage students.
- Differentiate between flexible grouping and cooperative learning.
- Describe the rationale for various student arrangement options.
- Know how HLP 17 is connected to other HLPs and when used together with evidence-based practices can improve student achievement.

KEY TERMS

- **collaborative learning:** Students work collectively, toward a common goal with individual targets or objectives. Students are accountable to each other; they recognize and build off their unique differences.
- **cooperative learning:** Students work interdependently, each are assigned specific roles within the group and each have a clear part to play that other group members rely on for project success.
- **flexible same-ability grouping:** Students take part in many different groups based on the purpose of the assignment. A key element to flexible grouping is collecting, analyzing, and responding to student data to change groups as needed.
- **homogeneous grouping:** Students are grouped together based on their similar academic, social, and emotional abilities. This grouping allows teachers to provide more intensive instruction based on a specific goal. Whether for students who struggle and need reteaching of skills, or high achievers who need supplemental instruction.
- **mixed-ability group:** Students with diverse abilities and backgrounds work together, may consist of students of varying ages, academic levels, interests, or abilities. Allows students to learn from the differences in the group while sharing unique abilities and interests.

Placing students in groups for learning purposes has been an empirically supported classroom practice for more than 40 years (Slavin, 1980). However, research also suggests designing and implementing meaningful student groupings remains a challenge for many teachers (Buchs et al., 2017). Using flexible groupings effectively should help teachers address this formidable challenge.

Special education teachers understand the value of flexible groupings, both homogeneous and heterogeneous groups, to differentiate instruction and meet the needs of many diverse learners (Maheady et al., 2019). Flexible grouping can be used to target a specific academic need, build social skills, and/or establish positive peer relationships. To use flexible grouping effectively, teachers must choose tasks with intentional goals that require and foster collaborative work. In addition, they must provide clear directions to enable groups to work independently and hold students accountable for collective and individual learning. Once students have been assigned to groups, effective teachers strategically and intentionally determine which groups to work with, when, and on which specific tasks. When planned correctly, teachers ensure students are grouped purposefully and each member is viewed as *competent* among their peers, interactions are respectful, and that the collective work of the group capitalizes on the strengths of all, while benefiting each student (Kagan, 2021).

This chapter will help you see how High-Leverage Practice (HLP) 17—"*Use flexible grouping*" is implemented alongside other HLPs and provide you with a variety of empirically supported flexible grouping options. Remember, as noted throughout this book, no HLP was designed to be used in isolation. We hope that by learning the basics of flexible grouping, you will see many connections to all HLPs and understand how this practice can benefit all students.

What Is HLP 17 and How Does It Align With Other HLPs?

When the Council for Exceptional Children (CEC) and the Collaboration for Effective Educator Development, Accountability and Reform (CEEDAR) Center teamed up to identify a set of core practices fundamental to effective special educators, the intent was to support the preparation and development of teacher candidates learning their craft (McLeskey et al., 2017). The team began with the work from a team of general educators (Ball & Forzani, 2011), and further delineated the practices as they apply to special education. Some special education HLPs are unique to our field and others extend and/or align with those developed for general educators. A CEEDAR crosswalk for HLPs suggests that HLP 17 might align well with the HLP "*Setting up and managing small group work*" (www.teachingworks.org). The intent was to define what practices "looked like" in effective specialized instruction. This HLP is aligned with and extends the general education HLP "*Setting up and managing small group work.*"

McLeskey and team (2017) provide definitions and descriptions for each of the 22 HLPs for special education. Each description demonstrates HLP overlap within special education and across general and special education. As noted, HLP 17 aligns with the "*Setting up and managing small group work*" HLP for general educators. It also overlaps with the use of other special education HLPs. McLeskey and colleagues (2017) indicated, for example, that effective special educators plan instruction that targets specific learning goals (HLP 12) using same-ability groups (homogeneous) and mixed-ability groups (heterogeneous). They monitor (HLP 6) peer interactions and provide positive and corrective feedback (HLPs 8 and 22) to support student learning. See Table 17-1 for a list of flexible grouping arrangements and the aligned HLPs.

Smaller groups are also used to accommodate individual learning needs (HLPs 13 and 15), deliver intensive instruction (HLP 20), and teach students to work collaboratively (related to HLPs 9 and 16). Effective special educators choose tasks that require collaboration, provide explicit directions (HLP 16) to promote productive and autonomous group interactions, and embed strategies that maximize learning opportunities and equalize participation (HLP 18). They promote active student engagement (HLP 18), use procedures to hold students accountable for collective and individual learning (HLP 7), and monitor and sustain group performance (HLP 21) through proximity and positive feedback (HLPs 8 and 22).

Flexible grouping can take on many arrangements. Figure 17-1 provides a visual representation of possible groupings from one student to larger whole class instruction. The beauty of these arrangements is they do not limit themselves to a particular classroom setting. The Individuals with Disabilities Education Act (IDEA; 2004) advises schools, and therefore teachers, to provide students with disabilities (SWD) instruction in their Least Restrictive Environment (Yell et al., 2020). You, as a special educator, can use your knowledge of students and effective flexible grouping strategies to collaborate with general educators (see HLP 1) to co-plan and co-instruct in the inclusive classroom (Karten & Murawski, 2020). Each grouping arrangement in Figure 17-1 is equally relevant and purposeful in general education classrooms as they are in more restrictive special education settings (e.g., resource rooms). We are not arguing, however, that the use of small groups is the only legitimate way to proceed. There are ample opportunities for well-designed whole group instruction as well as one-on-one teaching arrangements. After all, there are meaningful options in using flexible grouping. This chapter does focus more on supporting you as you implement small groups in your classroom.

Table 17-1. Flexible Grouping Arrangements and Alignment of HLPs and Resources for Evidence-Based Practices

FLEXIBLE GROUPING OPTIONS	WHEN TO USE ARRANGEMENTS	EBP SUPPORT USE	RELATED HLPS	RESOURCES
Whole Class	To introduce new concepts and skills to support student understanding.	Explicit Instruction (EI) Active Engagement Strategies • Choral Responding • Response Cards • Guided Notes	16, 18	https://highleveragepractices.org/hlp-16-use-explicit-instruction https://highleveragepractices.org/hlp-18-use-strategies-promote-active-student-engagement https://www.interventioncentral.org/rti2/guided_notes
Homogeneous (Same Ability) Small Group	To provide focused, intensive instruction for students with similar instructional strengths, needs, and/or interests.	Data-Based Instruction Direct Instruction • Systematic Phonics Instruction • Concrete-Representational-Abstract Framework	6, 7, 16, 18, 20, 22	https://highleveragepractices.org/hlp-20-provide-intensive-instruction
Heterogeneous (Mixed Ability) Small Group	To reinforce or reteach specific skills, typically follows whole class instruction. To promote student collaboration.	Kagan Cooperative Learning Structures Learning Together Jigsaw	7, 9, 18	www.kaganonline.com

(continued)

Table 17-1 (continued). Flexible Grouping Arrangements and Alignment of HLPs and Resources for Evidence-Based Practices

FLEXIBLE GROUPING OPTIONS	WHEN TO USE ARRANGEMENTS	EBP SUPPORT USE	RELATED HLPS	RESOURCES
Partners Dyads/Buddies	To provide student-led experiences that promote academic and social learning.	Class Wide Peer Tutoring (CWPT) Peer-Assisted Learning Strategies (PALS) Collaborative Strategic Reading (CSR)	13, 14, 21, 22	https://www.peertutoringresource.org/ https://iris.peabody.vanderbilt.edu/ebpractice/classwide-peer-tutoring-beginning-reading/ https://iris.peabody.vanderbilt.edu/module/pals26/ https://iris.peabody.vanderbilt.edu/module/csr/
Individual Instruction	To provide focused, intensive instruction for individual students.	Data-Based Instruction Intensive Instruction	6, 20	https://intensiveintervention.org/ https://highleveragepractices.org/hlp-20-provide-intensive-instruction

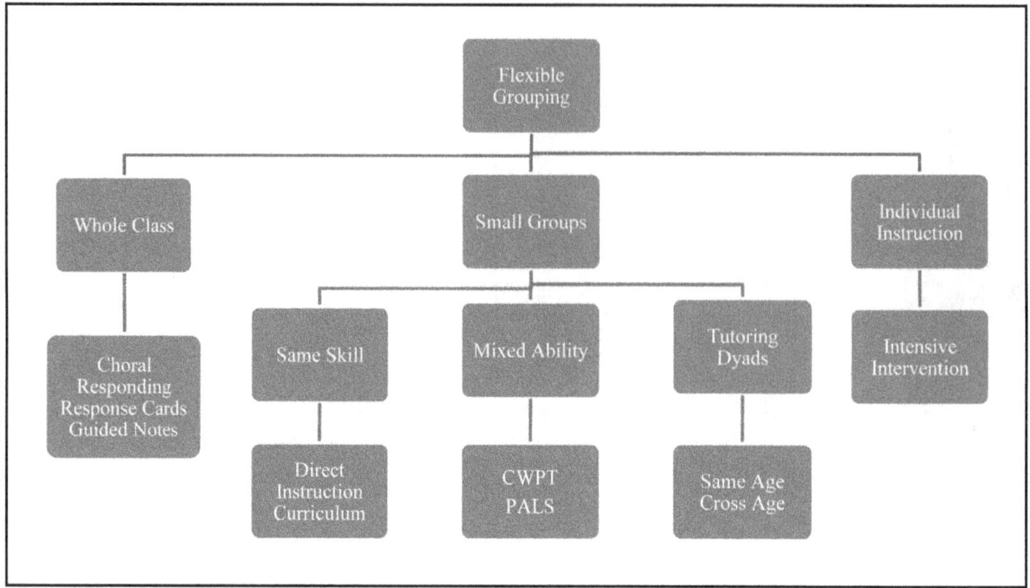

Figure 17-1. Graphic representation of possible teaching arrangements that can be used with flexible grouping.

How Do I Know What Grouping Strategy Is Right for Which Task?

It is easy to think of flexible grouping as synonymous with collaborative learning. Do not be fooled. Collaborative learning fits under the umbrella of flexible grouping. Flexible grouping like the name implies consists of multiple arrangements, used for many purposes and for various durations. Collaborative learning, in contrast, consists of small groupings (e.g., two to six students) and is an evidence-based practice (EBP) for increasing student achievement and motivation, with impressive effect sizes across content areas (e.g., math—Karali & Aydemir, 2018; reading—Slavin, 1980) and age groups (Hattie, 2008; Slavin, 2015). Collaborative learning strategies often include mixed skill groupings; two specific practices with a strong research base are Class Wide Peer Tutoring (CWPT; Maheady et al., 2019) and Peer-Assisted Learning Strategies (PALS; Fuchs et al., 1997), more on these later. Because flexible grouping options range from large whole group instruction, small groups, partners, and one-on-one instruction that change often and for different durations, purpose, and arrangements change often. It is almost impossible to capture *flexible grouping* into a singular, easy to replicate HLP; each arrangement is as unique as the students grouped together (Maheady et al., 2019).

When to Use Whole Class/Whole Group Instruction

Do not be intimidated by whole group instruction. There are times when it is appropriate to expose all students to whole group instruction. It is important to do so, however, using an explicit instruction (HLP 16) framework rather than being the "sage on the stage." Archer and Hughes (2011) noted that students will learn more, and instructional time will be used more wisely when teachers provide (a) clear and explicit models (I Do), (b) several opportunities to respond (HLP 18) using guided practice (We Do), and (c) offer scaffolded supports (HLP 15) until students can engage in independent practice (You Do).

This grouping strategy is best used when teaching new concepts and skills that will benefit all students. During the teacher-led part (I Do), it is critical that teachers first gain student attention and provide clear and concise descriptions and/or demonstrations of the concept or skill. During guided practice (We Do), for example, you can use at least three EBPs (i.e., choral responding, response cards, guided notes) to actively engage most, if not all, students (Blackwell & McLaughlin, 2005). Choral responding is very much like it sounds, all students provide verbal responses *in unison* to teacher signals (Haydon et al., 2013). Successful choral responding is contingent on two conditions: (a) student responses must be short, ideally one to three words, and (b) there can only be one correct answer. This way you can monitor the reply and know where and how to provide praise and corrections.

Response cards are another quick way to engage students in whole group instruction (Owiny et al., 2017). Students use an erasable board or hold up a preprinted picture or color card to respond to teacher prompts. Similar to choral responding, this strategy allows all students to respond simultaneously and lets the teacher scan the room to monitor all student responses and provide necessary feedback. A third engagement strategy for whole group instruction involves the use of guided notes. Guided notes are prepared ahead of class; the teacher makes a handout with cues, sentence starters, and even fills in the blank sections to "guide" students through the lesson/lecture. Students use the handout to follow along with the lecture and write down key facts or concepts being taught (Konrad et al., 2011). Teachers can check completed guided note forms for accuracy of notetaking, and students can use the forms for studying and test purposes.

When to Use Small Homogeneous Grouping

This grouping strategy is used to provide focused, intensive instruction (HLP 20) for students with similar instructional strengths, needs, and/or interests. This could be done in a separate environment such as Tier 2 or 3 instruction in the Response to Intervention (RTI) framework or in the general education classroom when co-teachers engage in different co-teaching approaches such as station teaching or alternative teaching (Karten & Murawski, 2020).

An EBP that works best in small homogeneous grouping is Direct Instruction (DI), same-skill groups (Gersten et al., 1986). Lessons are specifically sequenced and designed to minimize student misunderstanding and maximize learning outcomes (Mason & Otero, 2021). Whether you are engaged in what some refer to as "BIG DI" (Bereiter & Engelmann, 1966), a set of published scripted curricular programs (i.e., Reading Mastery, Connecting Math Concepts), or "little di" (Rosenshine, 1976), a set of teaching behaviors that include (a) structuring concept sequence (HLP 12), (b) using clear and concise instructions (HLP 16), (c) promoting active student responding (HLP 18), (d) providing immediate feedback related to student responses (HLP 12), and (e) minimizing free time (HLP 7), this model is designed for small homogeneous groups of students.

When to Use Small Heterogeneous Grouping

Small heterogeneous groupings are used when you want to distribute student ability, skill, and interest levels across each group. For example, Kagan Cooperative Learning Structures encourage the use of groups that include students who are performing above average, average, and below average. The intent is for students to help one another and learn from each other's differences and unique contributions. Specifically for math needs, Lavasani and Khandan (2011) demonstrated cooperative learning was effective in decreasing math anxiety in students and increased student self-advocacy skills in asking for assistance, both desired outcomes for SWD.

This grouping strategy is effective for the EBP of Collaborative Strategic Reading (CSR; Vaughn & Klingner, 1999), a practice effective in increasing reading comprehension by providing a multicomponent approach. It incorporates before, during, and after reading strategies. Students are placed into groups of up to six students where they each have a pre-assigned role, and rely on each other to complete the given tasks while learning from each other.

When to Use Partner Grouping

Sometimes SWD have difficulty working with more than one peer at a time. In these instances, smaller peer tutoring or partner groupings may be more appropriate. As shown in Figure 17-1, tutoring partners or dyads can include same- or cross-age pairings and tutoring roles can be unidirectional (i.e., one student is always tutor and other is tutee) or reciprocal (i.e., both students serve as tutor and tutees). Student pairings can range from one or two partnerships or include the entire class simultaneously. Juniper Gardens Children's Project CWPT (Greenwood et al., 1997) and PALS, for example, are evidence-based interventions that include weekly competing teams, highly structured tutoring procedures and training, point earning, public posting, contingent rewards, and direct practice of basic academic skills and content and have been used effectively with students with and without disabilities across multiple grade levels and subject areas.

When to Use Individual Instruction

The primary use of individual instruction is to provide focused, intensive instruction (HLP 20) for individual students. Most students who struggle to learn will make progress with research-based interventions when taught in small homogeneous groups targeting their unique needs (Wanzek et al., 2020). However, there are still students who will require even more intensive interventions. Students with more severe learning and behavioral needs often need more intensive instruction. Perhaps the student may need more time, a slower pace, more opportunities to respond with more specific feedback, or even cognitive processing strategies that peers do not. Regardless of need, intensive individual instruction is a data-driven decision you make based on routine progress monitoring (Lembke et al., 2022).

How Can I Be Sure Everyone Is Engaged and Doing Their Assigned Task?

The one thing you cannot do when using flexible grouping is assume that students will work well and stay on task without supervision or feedback. It is critical, therefore, to use proximity cues while students work together. That is, you move around the classroom in a predetermined but unpredictable pattern. Your movements will inhibit off-task behavior to some extent, and your feedback (i.e., positive and corrective) can reinforce students for working well together. You can also assess whether they are doing daily assignments by examining work products. What percentage of assignments were completed accurately and on time? Did everyone pull their weight and participate sufficiently during group work? Some have suggested that having all group members review and initial their work products is another good way to maintain group productivity.

What Does HLP 17 Look Like in a K-12 Classroom?

As noted, flexible grouping can take on many forms. Here, we provide two examples on how CWPT and cooperative learning practices were used to meet the needs of elementary and secondary students enrolled in inclusive classrooms.

Elementary Example

Mr. Rodriguez was a third-grade teacher who expressed concern that three SWD in his inclusion class were not making sufficient progress in math fluency as documented by district-adopted, curriculum-based assessment measures (i.e., aimswebPlus). Mr. Rodriguez received professional development and peer coaching on the use of CWPT as part of his graduate program. He enrolled in two required graduate research courses, completed an illustrative review of the CWPT literature, and designed a single case research study to examine the impact of the intervention on three target students' math fluency (i.e., digits correct per minute).

During baseline lessons, he used his normal teaching routine of providing explicit instruction, followed by guided practice, and 15 minutes of independent seatwork to build math computational fluency. At the end of each class, students completed 3-minute math assessments using AIMSWEB. He then trained the whole class to use CWPT procedures *instead of* working alone during independent work time (i.e., 15 minutes per day, 4 days per week). Using a multiple-baseline design across number facts, he compared target student math fluency during CWPT vs. baseline instruction. There were four major CWPT components:

1. Weekly competing teams.
2. Structured, tutoring procedures.
3. Daily point earning, public posting, and group rewards.
4. Direct practice of math facts.

Students were trained to use CWPT with fidelity in about 30 minutes. Each week, the class was divided randomly (i.e., drawing red or blue paper slips from a covered box) into two teams that remained together for a week. Within teams, students were paired for daily CWPT practice. (Initially, the teacher paired students who he thought would work well together. After they were using tutoring procedures well, he started to pair students more liberally.) Students took turns serving as tutors and tutees for 5 minutes each. Tutors presented math computation problems, tutees solved them orally and in writing, and tutors provided immediate oral feedback (e.g., "that's it" or "try again") and points based on the accuracy of student responses (i.e., 2 points for correct responses, 1 point for "corrected" responses, and 0 points for incorrect answers). To correct inaccurate responses, tutees wrote math facts accurately three times each. If they failed to correct responses, they got 0 points and moved to the next problems.

The goal for students was to earn as many points as they can before a timer went off (i.e., 5 minutes). Tutoring partners then reversed roles and followed the same procedures for another 5 minutes. While the students were working, Mr. Rodriquez circulated and awarded "bonus points" for good tutoring behavior (e.g., awarding appropriate number of points, starting immediately and working throughout sessions, providing positive comments). At the end of each session, students totaled their daily points, including bonus points, and entered them on a publicly displayed tutoring scoreboard. Daily individual points were totaled into cumulative blue and red team scores. The team with the higher total at the end of the week earned "Team of the Week" certificates that were (a) signed by all members and (b) posted prominently in the classroom.

Mr. Rodriquez found that CWPT produced immediate and noticeable increases in all three target students' fluency rates across different sets of math facts. In fact, their fluency rates almost doubled when CWPT was implemented. These data showed that even SWD who were struggling the most improved their math fluency when CWPT was being used. Mr. Rodriquez also noted that most average achieving students improved their fluency rates and the majority rated CWPT procedures and outcomes favorably. These findings extended CWPT positive effects to a new population and outcome measure (i.e., district-adopted progress monitoring measure) and helped Mr. Rodriquez's students meet district-adopted math benchmarks.

Secondary Example

Ms. Chang was an experienced high school science teacher who taught five sections of biology to ninth graders in a culturally diverse, high-poverty school district. Although she had received accolades and awards for her science teaching, she was struggling with one section containing many students with academic challenges. She found it particularly difficult to engage them in content-related discussions and only a few students participated regularly. This was problematic because their lack of active participation was reflected in below-average performance on district-adopted science assessments.

Ms. Chang tried different ways to engage students and improve their science understanding. She used project-based assignments, unstructured small groups, "flipped" the classroom, and offered more choices in class assignments. She infused culturally responsive science topics (e.g., local geography and environmental issues), spoke privately with low-performing students, and offered rewards for improved performance. No strategies worked, few students participated in class discussions, and academic performance remained below average.

Ms. Chang participated in a 2-day summer training program on Kagan Cooperative Learning Structures and agreed to participate in a research study examining the effects of one structure, Numbered Heads Together (NHT), on her students' performance on weekly science assessments (McMillen et al., 2016). She initially taught her class using "typical" teaching practices (i.e., EI, see HLP 16) and assessed their understanding by (a) directing questions to everyone, (b) calling on hand-raising volunteers, and (c) providing positive and corrective feedback (HLP 22). At the end of each week, students independently completed five- or six-item science quizzes administered and scored electronically.

Ms. Chang then used NHT instead of hand raising during science lessons and continued to monitor student performance on weekly quizzes. First, she broke her class into small (three or four members), *mixed-skilled* teams who sat closely with individual whiteboards in hand. Students were numbered one to four and listened while the teacher led science lessons. Ms. Chang directed each content question to the class and said, "put your heads together and come up with the best answers you can." Students wrote individual responses on whiteboards, stood up when completed, shared responses, agreed on best answers, and sat down when finished. The teacher then used a spinner app on her iPad to randomly select numbers (i.e., one to four) to determine team responders. All numbered students stood and responded in unison by showing whiteboard responses. Ms. Chang also checked for individual student understanding and asked other team members for agreements, expansions, and/or possible applications.

Ms. Chang found that almost all students (i.e., mean = 91%) wrote responses on whiteboards and shared them with teammates compared to an average of 12% (i.e., two or three students) who raised their hands to respond. NHT also raised the class's weekly science quiz scores by an average of 16% (57% vs. 73%) over baseline instruction, or the equivalent of two letter grades. Quiz scores were always higher using NHT, students rated the cooperative learning structure favorably, and Ms. Chang felt that it was an effective, efficient, and fun way to engage more students during group lessons.

Summary

Hopefully, you are starting to see the value of using flexible grouping in your classroom, while at the same time understanding the complexity and need for purposeful planning of different grouping strategies. As you reflect on various ways you can use this HLP, do not forget the importance of how it fits with other HLPs to implement some valuable EBPs.

Flexible grouping provides a variety of ways to provide instruction to SWD, both in general and special education settings. You should use flexible grouping to target specific learning goals (HLP 12), provide intensive instruction (HLP 20), and accommodate individual learning needs (HLP 13), while scaffolding skills (HLP 15) to improve student learning. Regardless of the grouping arrangements used, teachers must monitor pupil progress (HLP 6), provide constructive feedback (HLPs 8 and 22), and adjust instruction as necessary (also part of HLP 6). Using flexible grouping also increases active student engagement (HLP 18) and holds students accountable for collective and individual learning, helping to maintain a respectful learning environment (HLP 7).

You should identify and use specific EBPs for delivering instruction in various grouping strategies. For instance, DI is well suited for same-skill small groups. Dyad tutoring partners work well with same age and cross age groups to deliver instruction. The EBPs of CWPT, PALS, and NHT are specific EBPs that can be used with dyads as well as multiple partner small groups.

Flexible grouping strategies, like all HLPs, are not content specific. You can design same-skill small groups for reading instruction using DI with systematic phonics instruction or concrete-to-representational-to-abstract sequence of instruction (CRA) in math. Smaller groups work well for CSR, where a group of up to six students are assigned specific roles, rely on, and help teach each other reading comprehension skills. Collaborative learning is also valuable in decreasing math anxiety and increasing student self-advocacy skills.

In closing, we cannot emphasize enough, flexible grouping is not a single practice or set of practices that can be easily replicated. Students are intentionally grouped for a specific purpose and taught the role they are to play in the group, from the expectations of the classroom to the role of tutor and tutee in dyads, to the various roles of a collaborative learning group. Effective teachers create procedures to hold students accountable for both group and individual learning. They also monitor groups and learning to provide feedback and adjust learning as needed to promote achievement.

Chapter Review

1. How are flexible groupings and collaborative learning related, yet different?
2. Why is it important to be strategic about the grouping strategy selected? Name one strategy described in the chapter and how you would place students in the group.
3. Name three EBPs discussed in this chapter and the grouping strategy most effective for implementation.
4. What other HLPs are used in conjunction with flexible grouping? Provide your own description of how they are connected.
5. Why is it important to use multiple grouping strategies?

References

Archer, A. L., & Hughes, C. A. (2011). *Explicit instruction: Effective and efficient teaching.* Guilford Press.

Ball, D. L., & Forzani, F. M. (2011). Building a common core for learning to teach: And connecting professional learning to practice. *American Educator*, *35*(2), 17-21.

Bereiter, C., & Engelmann, S. (1966). Observations on the use of direct instruction with young disadvantaged children. *Journal of School Psychology*, *4*(3), 55-62.

Blackwell, A. J., & McLaughlin, T. F. (2005). Using guided Notes, choral responding, and response cards to increase student performance. *International Journal of Special Education*, *20*(2), 1-5.

Buchs, C., Filippou, D., Pulfrey, C., & Volpé, Y. (2017). Challenges for cooperative learning implementation: Reports from elementary school teachers. *Journal of Education for Teaching*, *43*(3), 296-306.

Colón, G., Zgliczynski, T., & Maheady, L. (2022). Using flexible grouping. In J. McLeskey, L. Maheady, B. Billingsley, M. T. Brownell, & T. J. Lewis (Eds.), *High leverage practices for inclusive classrooms* (2nd ed., pp. 265-281). Routledge. https://doi.org/10.4324/9781003148609-23

Fuchs, D., Fuchs, L. S., Mathes, P. G., & Simmons, D. C. (1997). Peer-assisted learning strategies: Making classrooms more responsive to diversity. *American Educational Research Journal, 34*(1), 174-206.

Gersten, R., Woodward, J., & Darch, C. (1986). Direct instruction: A research-based approach to curriculum design and teaching. *Exceptional Children, 53*(1), 17-31.

Greenwood, C. R., & Maheady, L. (1997). Measurable change in student performance: Forgotten standard in teacher preparation? *Teacher Education and Special Education, 20*(3), 265-275.

Hattie, J. (2008). *Visible learning: A synthesis of over 800 meta-analyses relating to achievement.* Routledge.

Haydon, T., Marsicano, R., & Scott, T. M. (2013). A comparison of choral and individual responding: A review of the literature. *Preventing School Failure: Alternative Education for Children and Youth, 57*(4), 181-188.

Individuals With Disabilities Education Act, 20 U.S.C. § 1400 (2004).

Kagan, S. (2021). The structural approach and Kagan structures. In N. Davidson (Ed.), *Pioneering perspective in cooperative learning: Theory, research, and classroom practice for diverse approaches to CL* (pp. 77-127). Routledge.

Karali, Y., & Aydemir, H. (2018). The effect of cooperative learning on the academic achievement and attitude of students in mathematics class. *Educational Research and Reviews, 13*(21), 712-722.

Karten, T. J., & Murawski, W. W. (2020). *Co-teaching do's, don'ts, and do betters.* Association for Supervision & Curriculum Development.

Khan, A., & Akhtar, M. (2017). Investigating the effectiveness of cooperative learning method on teaching of English grammar. *Bulletin of Education and Research, 39*(1), 1-16.

Konrad, M., Joseph, L. M., & Itoi, M. (2011). Using guided notes to enhance instruction for all students. *Intervention in School and Clinic, 46*(3), 131-140.

Lavasani, M. G., & Khandan, F. (2011). The effect of cooperative learning on math anxiety and help seeking behavior. *Procedia Social and Behavioral Sciences, 15*, 271-276.

Lembke, E. S., Smith, A., & Newman-Thomas, C. (2022). Using student assessment data, analyzing instructional practices, and making necessary adjustments that improve student outcomes. In J. McLeskey, L. Maheady, L., B. Billingsley, M. T. Brownell, & T. J. Lewis (Eds). *High leverage practices for inclusive classrooms* (2nd ed., pp. 85-101). Routledge. https://doi.org/10.4324/9781003148609-10

Maheady, L., Zgliczynski, T., & Colon, G. (2019). *Using flexible grouping.* In J. McLeskey, L. Maheady, B. Billingsley, M. Brownell, & T. Lewis (Eds.), High leverage practices for inclusive educational settings (pp. 327-333). Routledge.

Mason, L., & Otero, M. (2021). Just how effective is direct instruction? *Perspectives on Behavior Science, 44*(2), 225-244. https://doi.org/10.1007/s40614-021-00295

McLeskey, J., Barringer, M.-D., Billingsley, B., Brownell, M., Jackson, D., Kennedy, M., Lewis, T., Maheady, L., Rodriguez, J., Scheeler, M. C., Winn, J., & Ziegler, D. (2017). *High-leverage practices in special education.* Council for Exceptional Children & CEEDAR Center.

McMillen, C., Mallette, B., Smith, C., Rey, J., Jabot, J., & Maheady, L. (2016). Effects of Numbered Heads Together on the science quiz performance of 9th grade students. *Journal of Evidence-Based Practices for Schools, 15*(1), 65-89.

Owiny, R. L., Spriggs, A. D., Sartini, E. C., & Mills, J. R. (2017). Evaluating response cards as evidence based. *Preventing School Failure: Alternative Education for Children & Youth.* https://doi.org/10.1080/1045988X.2017.1344953

Peltier, C., & Vannest, K. J. (2018). Using the concrete representational abstract (CRA) instructional framework for mathematics with students with emotional and behavioral disorders. *Preventing School Failure: Alternative Education for Children and Youth, 62*(2), 73-82.

Rosenshine, B. (1976). Recent research on teaching behaviors and student achievement. *Journal of Teacher Education, 27*(1), 61-64.

Slavin, R. E. (1980). Cooperative learning. *Review of Educational Research, 50*(2), 315-342.

Slavin, R. E. (2015). Cooperative learning in elementary schools. *Education 3-13, 43*(1), 5-14.

TeachingWorks Resource Library. (2022). *Curriculum resources.* https://library.teachingworks.org/curriculum-resources/high-leverage-practices/

Vaughn, S., & Klingner, J. K. (1999). Teaching reading comprehension through collaborative strategic reading. *Intervention in School and Clinic, 34*(5), 284-292.

Wanzek, J., Al Otaiba, S., & McMaster, K. L. (2020). *Intensive reading interventions for the elementary grades.* Guilford Press.

Yell, M. L., Katsiyannis, A., Ennis, R. P., Losinski, M., & Bateman, D. (2020). Making legally sound placement decisions. *TEACHING Exceptional Children, 52*(5), 291-303. https://doi.org/10.1177/004005992090

How Do I Keep Students Involved in Learning?

Ruby L. Owiny, PhD

HLP 18

Use strategies to promote active student engagement.

INTRODUCTION

High-Leverage Practice (HLP) 18 promotes active student engagement through the use of a variety of strategies. Active student engagement is directly related to academic and behavioral achievement for students with and without disabilities. Teachers should consider which strategies best help students to stay focused on instruction and engaged to ensure higher levels of achievement. A consideration should be given to ensuring high levels of student engagement through a variety of strategies. This chapter not only explains HLP 18 and the rationale behind it but also identifies evidence-based strategies and explains those strategies for readers to implement in their teaching practice.

Owiny, R. L., & Cornelius, K. E. *The Practical Guide to High-Leverage Practices in Special Education: The Purposeful "How" to Enhance Classroom Rigor* (pp. 255-270).

CHAPTER OBJECTIVES

- Define active student engagement.
- Describe how to implement active student engagement in teaching practice.
- Explain specific evidence-based practices to implement active student engagement in teaching practice.

KEY TERMS

- **active student responding:** A method of measuring active student engagement.
- **choral responding:** Students responding all together, at the same time.
- **opportunities to respond (OTRs):** Each time a student is provided an occasion to respond to a stimulus.
- **peer-assisted learning:** A specific research-based, class-wide, peer-mediated program in which students are paired together with one being a stronger student; students take turns being the teacher and the learner.
- **peer tutoring:** Students are paired with one being the tutor and one being the tutee.
- **response cards:** High- or low-tech for which students use to respond to prompts by writing on, holding up or pointing to a card or whiteboard, or clicking an electronic response.
- **self-regulation:** One's ability to manage one's emotions and responses.
- **student engagement:** The opportunities teachers provide for students to respond to instruction.
- **Think-Pair-Share:** A responding technique in which students respond to a prompt independently, share with a peer, and combine with other groups to explain thoughts and ideas.
- **visual prompts:** A drawing, chart, picture, clipart, or photograph to represent a task or an activity.

Teachers often lament that their students are not paying attention in class. As is human nature, we can quickly move the lamenting to complaining and make it the students' fault. But, what if we change the narrative? What if we address the *problem* as a teacher issue rather than a student one? What if we identified ways to keep our students engaged? Made our teaching more interesting to students? Any educator will agree that active student engagement equates to higher levels of achievement. However, we frequently fall into a rut of doing the same old thing, the same old way, and expecting different results. Hey, wait a minute—that is the definition of insanity! We do not know about you, but there are certainly times we get bored and it might just be because we are not changing things up. We seem stuck doing the same things we did when we started our teaching careers. It might just be time to try something new.

This chapter is all about student engagement, and not just any student engagement, but active student engagement. Unlike passive learners, engaged learners are excited about learning. When you use strategies that keep students actively participating in their learning you will both reap many benefits.

What Is Active Student Engagement?

Active student engagement is a key factor in both students' on-task behavior and academic achievement. It makes sense that teachers want students to be on-task; they will learn more, right? Maybe, but simply being on-task is not enough. After all, students can appear to be on-task but, in reality, are daydreaming. Students must be actively learning to maximize their achievement and reduce off-task behaviors (Heward, 2022). Maintaining attention to task is easier for students when they are actively involved in opportunities to respond (OTRs), an evidence-based practice (EBP) for increasing student achievement (MacSuga-Gage & Simonsen, 2015). In fact, the practices described in this chapter have a research base to do both: maximize learning **and** increase on-task behavior. After all, the goal is for students to become active engaged learners rather than passive ones.

Active student engagement involves opportunities for students to respond to instruction, such as written or verbal responses, for sure, but in fact, student responding can occur in multiple ways. Active student engagement also includes four other components: (a) connecting instruction to students' lives, (b) peer-assisted learning (e.g., cooperative learning or peer tutoring), (c) student self-regulation, and (d) technology use (McLeskey et al., 2017). This chapter provides you with practices you can use in your teaching to increase active student engagement in your classroom.

What Is HLP 18?

High-Leverage Practice (HLP) 18—"*Use strategies to promote active student engagement*" is defined as:

> Teachers use a variety of instructional strategies that result in active student responding. Active student engagement is critical to academic success. Teachers must initially build positive student-teacher relationships to foster engagement and motivate reluctant learners. They promote engagement by connecting learning to students' lives (e.g., knowing students' academic and cultural backgrounds) and using a variety of teacher-led (e.g., choral responding and response cards), peer-assisted (e.g., cooperative learning and peer tutoring), student-regulated (e.g., self-management), and technology-supported strategies shown empirically to increase student engagement. They monitor student engagement and provide positive and constructive feedback to sustain performance. (McLeskey et al., 2017, p. 24)

That may seem overwhelming, but we are going to break it down for you into its important components. Before we do that, we will talk about why active student engagement is so important. As mentioned above, OTR increases student engagement and is a way of keeping students actively participating in the instructional process, which only helps them in the long run. There are many ways to provide OTR using low- or high-tech activities. For example, Kahoot is quite popular. Teachers can create quizzes for students to access as a group or individually. Students receive immediate feedback and can race to see who is able to respond the quickest. The teacher also gets immediate feedback. They can see results of each item instantly to know how accurately students are responding. A low-tech activity could involve two colored index cards, red and green. The teacher can ask yes/no or true/false questions and the students could raise the corresponding color (e.g., green for true or yes and red for false or no). As you can imagine, the more students are actively participating in their own learning, the more they will learn and have fun while doing, making engagement that much better.

Why Is Active Student Engagement Important?

In addition to increasing students' on-task behavior, reducing inappropriate behaviors, and increasing their achievement, students are certainly more likely to enjoy learning when they are actively involved rather than passively listening. Thus, students being actively engaged makes your job a bit easier.

Classroom engagement can also keep students engaged in school. Students who are apathetic toward learning often become disillusioned about their future and drop out of school (Ecker-Lyster & Niileksela, 2016). Students with disabilities (SWD) are at great risk of dropping out of high school, a much greater risk than their non-disabled peers, leading to poor post-secondary outcomes (Morningstar et al., 2017). In fact, students with high incidence disabilities, such as learning disabilities or ADHD, are more likely to experience challenges in classroom and school participation, which set the stage for poor academic and behavioral performance (Walker & Barry, 2018) and increasing the likelihood they will become disengaged and drop out.

Increasing student engagement not only benefits students, but provides opportunities for formative assessment and the ability to provide on-the-spot feedback (HLPs 8 and 22). This allows for immediate information on how well students are learning the lesson concepts (Heward, 2022), make in-the-moment adjustments, and use the informal data you are collecting through student responses to make informed decisions about future (as in tomorrow!) lessons. *How do you need to adjust? Are there some students who need a deeper dive or who need some remediation? Are students ready to move on to a new concept?* These and many other questions can be answered through active student responding. This information helps you perform HLP 6—"*Use student assessment data, analyze instructional practices, and make necessary adjustments that improve student outcomes.*" See Chapter 6 for more information on that. This is another example of how the HLPs go together and are implemented simultaneously; they really do have an intertwined functionality. However, the purpose of this chapter is to provide ways you can increase active student responding. As you read, we encourage you to consider further ways you can connect HLP 6 with HLP 18.

We can agree that student motivation and achievement are important. Now focus on how relationships can influence student engagement, and why relationship building is important when planning for *active* student engagement. When considering the five ways to provide for active student responding included in the definition of this HLP, understanding why these are included in this HLP is important. First, consider why it is important to connect learning through relevant content. Relevant content allows students to feel as though they belong and are valued in the classroom and school (affective engagement; McLeskey et al., 2017). Accordingly, students are more likely to value their learning and take ownership of their education when they can see themselves reflected in the curriculum and understand why the lesson or unit is relevant to their lives. Making content relevant requires cultural responsiveness (incorporating the assets and strengths of students' culture) to not only plan instruction but also use a variety of techniques that allow students to be comfortable in responding to instruction, such as role-playing or storytelling (IRIS Center, 2012). Furthermore, understanding students' academic and cultural backgrounds allows you to build positive, personal relationships (McLeskey et al., 2017). It is natural to see then, that by increasing students' interest and building positive relationships, teachers will increase the likelihood that students will be motivated to learn and demonstrate "stick-to-it-iveness" when learning gets challenging.

Student self-regulation is known to be the greatest predictor of academic success (Blair, 2002) and can be developed through three components: consistent and predictable environments (HLP 7), positive social relationships with peers and teachers (HLP 9), and strategies that emphasize focus and memory (Sanchez, 2017). Given that the first two components of self-regulation are addressed in other chapters, including Chapter 14, which addresses strategies to promote learning and independence, this chapter will provide you with some ideas for strategies that will help enhance students' focus and memory. We believe you will agree that when students are focused and remember content, they are more capable of being actively engaged in the lesson.

Technology-supported strategies can include assistive technology or even instructional technology. Is there not an HLP on that? There absolutely is! See Chapter 19 for information on technology. This chapter will incorporate technology as a means of implementing active engagement strategies. Technology can often motivate students to respond when more traditional ways fail. Technology can not only enhance what you are doing in your classroom but also provide you with options for e-learning. High-tech and low-tech activities can help enhance engagement through provision of novel activities.

How Much Active Responding Is Enough?

There are multiple ways to consider the frequency of active student engagement. Active student responding is the most direct method of measuring active engagement. This involves simply counting the times a student makes a specific response to instruction and calculating a rate per minute or simply reporting the number of responses in a given time period (Heward, 2022). There are other ways to measure active engagement in relation to active student responding, including OTR, time on task, instructional time, allocated time, and available time. For our purposes, OTR will be a focus in the practices we discuss in this chapter for increasing active student responding. An OTR is simply any time a teacher requests a response from a student (Owiny et al., 2017). The teacher can provide a prompt with varied response types from students: written, verbal, or even gestures (Simonsen et al., 2010). The more OTR provided, the more students have the opportunity to engage with the content and develop proficiency while also maximizing success for students with skill deficits (Adamson & Lewis, 2017). While research provides many excellent reasons to increase OTR, many teachers still do not use it to its recommended levels as per the Council for Exceptional Children (CEC; 1987) of four to six OTRs per minute (Stichter et al., 2009). This chapter will give you some ideas on strategies you can use to increase your use of OTR in varied ways to keep students engaged and their experiences fresh and exciting.

What Strategies Can I Use to Increase Active Engagement?

We will break this section into four parts to provide you with ideas for each component of active student engagement. We focus on practical and evidence-based practices for connecting learning to students' lives.

Student Interests and Strengths

We will start with an obvious way to connect—students' interests. Are you annoyed at your students who are always pulling out their Pokémon cards at inopportune times? Is there a way you could incorporate their love of Pokémon into a lesson? Maybe you could allow your students to write a how-to piece on how to trade cards providing the tips and tricks of the trade or graph how many of each type of card students have in the class. The key here is to hone in on what students like and use that to your advantage, because when you do, it actually benefits your students, too. They will be more likely to focus on a lesson when it includes something they enjoy.

Another way to approach connections to content and students' lives is through a strengths-based approach. Armstrong (2012) describes this approach through the lens of neurodiversity, the notion that allows us to think about brain diversity in the same way we think about biodiversity. There are many, many types of plants. We would not diagnose a rose as being deformed or having a disability because it does not look like a sunflower. We understand there are different types of flowers. They look and smell different and certain types grow better in particular areas. Why not take that approach to our students? Instead of seeing our students through the lens of their disability or their deficits, why not look at them through the lens of their strengths (Armstrong, 2012)? For example, instead of bemoaning a student who is "always on the move," why not channel that energy into the classroom and incorporate movement into your lessons or provide hands-on learning for students to demonstrate their learning in a manner meaningful to them? For SWD, we can create a paradigm shift. What characteristics of their disability are a strength? Do they hyper-focus? How can we leverage that? How can we see what we call a disability and see it as a form of diversity with characteristics to celebrate and exploit for the student's benefit? A strengths-based approach is certainly in line with this HLP.

Both student interests and strengths-based instruction lend themselves to culturally responsive teaching (Rodriguez & Hardin, 2017). We need to think about two more elements—students' academic and cultural backgrounds. For SWD, it is vital that we not only consider their needs related to their disability but we can leverage their cultural and linguistic backgrounds to benefit them. How can I do that, you might ask? Start with getting to know your students and their families through face-to-face conversations or via the phone, email, text, or even videoconferencing. Provide students with a survey (paper or electronic, such as Google Forms or Survey Monkey) to complete with their families to inquire about their family values, how they view community, adult authority, and gender roles—three important aspects of culture teachers should consider (Gay, 2018). Invite parents to meet you at a fast-food restaurant or a coffee shop to get to know them. This might be less intimidating than meeting you at school. Incorporate materials related to your students' backgrounds throughout the school year (e.g., not just during Black History Month or Hispanic Heritage Month). Learn about special events or activities your students are involved in. Ask them about those events and activities to learn about them. Attend those events when invited, as you are able (Rodriguez & Hardin, 2017). This gives you a direct line into your students' lives and builds trust and respect with them and their families. Incorporate those events and activities into your instruction. It might be as simple as creating a word problem related to baseball and using your student's name who is on a baseball team, or it could be modeling how to conduct research by leading students through researching the significance of a bar/bat mitzvah or fasting during Ramadan. Incorporating your students' interests, cultures, and religions into your instruction helps students to feel seen, heard, and loved, while also allowing them to learn about their peers who might have different interests, be from different cultures, or have a different religion from them.

Varying Student Responses

There are a myriad of strategies available to you to motivate all students to respond simultaneously to your instruction at any grade level or for any content area. Nagro et al. (2016) describe whole group responding by using *hand signals*. For example, raising a hand with one finger up means a student has a new idea to share while two fingers means they want to add a thought to the point currently being discussed. Comprehension checks or self-reflection can easily be incorporated into instruction using hand signals. For comprehension checks, students can respond to, "How well do I understand?" by putting up one finger for "I have no idea" and four fingers for "I've got it!" (Nagro et al., 2016). For self-reflection, students could respond to the question, "I did my best work" or "I was kind and respectful to my peers and teachers" by raising one finger for "I didn't do very well" and five fingers for "I rocked it!"

Choral responding is another method for seamlessly incorporating whole group response into a lesson. Students respond orally, in unison, to questions asked by the teacher. It is important to remember the three criteria for choral responding as described by Heward (2022): (a) each question can only have one correct answer; (b) the question must be able to be answered with just a couple of words; and (c) questions can be presented at a brisk pace (and should be). "In unison" is key to pacing and student learning and will take practice. It is also important to remind students that you are going for errorless learning and to only respond if they absolutely know the correct answer. You will become quite adept at "reading the classroom" and knowing whether everyone responded or not, so do not worry about that. It just takes practice. Oftentimes a signal such as a snap, clap, or hand drop is used to alert students when to respond. For example, the teacher may ask, "Which type of triangle has three angles less than 90 degrees each?" Pause for wait time and then finger snap. All students respond, "Acute triangle." If all students do not respond together or you hear some incorrect responses, you can incorporate a correction procedure (part of explicit instruction; HLP 16). The correction procedure includes three steps. First, repeat the question. Second, state the correct answer. Third, state all students should respond together and provide the question with wait time and a signal again. Repeat until all students reply correctly and together. When you first begin to use

Table 18-1. Correction Procedure

STEPS	EXAMPLE
1. State correct answer.	Teacher: "The capital of Illinois is Springfield."
2. Repeat the question.	Teacher: "What is the capital of Illinois?"
3. State the correct answer.	Teacher: "The capital of Illinois is Springfield."
4. State the question again.	Teacher: "What is the capital of Illinois?"
5. Give attention signal for all students to respond together.	{Signal: Clap} Students: Springfield.
6. Repeat Steps 1 to 5 until all students respond correctly and together.	

choral responding, it will take some time for students to learn the procedures, but once they learn it, reminders to respond together will decrease drastically. See Table 18-1 for a full sequence of each step in the procedure.

Another strategy is *response cards*. Response cards are an EBP (Owiny et al., 2017) and are easy to implement. There are low-tech and high-tech options. When using response cards, students hold up, point to, or click an electronic response. Response cards can be pre-made cards made from file folders, index cards, construction paper, etc. For dichotomous responses, two colors of construction paper can be glued together, cut into smaller cards, if desired, and laminated. Each student can have the card and can respond to yes/no, true/false, or choose one option questions. For example, if you would like chicken nuggets for lunch, hold up the blue side of your card. If you would like pizza for lunch, hold up the purple side of your card. Is the formula for calculating the area of a square = width x height? Hold up yellow for yes and pink for no. Another example: Mexico is part of North America. Green stands for true and red stands for false. You could also create blank response cards with laminated construction paper, card stock, or manila folders. This creates a personal wipe-off board for each student in an inexpensive manner. More durable whiteboards, already made, can be purchased from various department stores or teacher supply stores. You can also go to a home improvement store and ask for white laminated bathroom board to be cut into whichever size you would like (e.g., 8 ½ x 11 inches). The options for response cards truly are endless. Nagro et al. (2016) describe putting sets of response cards on metal rings for students to keep them in one place. Weather-related items, such as sunny, rainy, and cloudy, can be created for younger children to use during calendar time. Number cards can be used for answers to math problems. Vocabulary cards can be used to practice definitions, synonyms, antonyms, parts of speech, and the list could continue. Truly, the sky is the limit.

Response cards can also be high-tech, such as with the use of a clicker system. In addition to synchronous responding, asynchronous responding can occur using Kahoot, Nearpod, or EdPuzzle. These are nice response options for use with stations, independent work, or even e-learning. Students are engaged and expected to respond to their learning via the assigned platform.

Think-Pair-Share is an option that allows students to formulate a response before sharing with anyone. It is a well-researched strategy, simple to use, and incorporates cooperative learning (Prater, 2018). For students who need processing time, this can be a great lifeline. You can pose a question to students, which can be either a short response or a longer response, including higher-order thinking. Students first formulate their response by simply thinking of their idea, writing it down, highlighting it in a text, etc. Once adequate wait time is provided, students are directed to share their idea first with a partner and then with the whole group. Students can receive immediate feedback from their peers, too, which adds to the power of this strategy (Himmele & Himmele, 2017). Not only is HLP 18 being incorporated into instruction but also HLP 22.

Peer-assisted learning allows students to learn from one another. This can be in cooperative groups or peer tutoring. Research on cooperative learning shows strong support for the development of, and increase in, students' abilities to think at higher levels while increasing academic achievement especially in reading and mathematics (Slavin, 2013). These data support higher-level thinking skill increases across intellect, race, ethnicity, or disability (Slavin, 1995). There are multiple benefits for students, but especially for students who struggle with social skills. Cooperative groups can help them develop and hone their interpersonal skills, while being held accountable to their part in the group and generating knowledge from within themselves and the group (Kilbane & Milman, 2014). For high school students, developing social skills plus honing critical thinking skills through cooperative groups involved in project-based learning will set them up for real-world job opportunities (Mandel, 2003). Today's job force needs individuals who can problem solve, think critically, and collaborate with others (Geisinger, 2016). Cooperative learning allows students to actively respond to content being learned and helps develop lifelong skills important to their long-term success.

Peer tutoring is another option for increasing active student responding. In peer tutoring, student pairs become the tutors and tutees. Generally, a higher-achieving student will teach or review material with a lower-achieving student (Hott et al., 2012). Like other strategies, peer tutoring can benefit students at all ages and in all content areas. Careful teaching of expectations and procedures are important for success, however. A benefit of peer tutoring for SWD, in particular, is that they get multiple OTR and can receive immediate feedback in this one-to-one setting. Peer tutoring has a strong research-base supporting its benefit, including in online settings (Vasquez & Slocum, 2012).

There are several ways peer tutoring can be implemented in a classroom. Classwide peer tutoring, partner tutoring, cross-age tutoring, and reciprocal tutoring are some commonly used ways (Hott et al., 2012). As you probably guessed, classwide peer tutoring involves partnering the entire class for structured learning sessions, while partner tutoring involves a student the teacher has targeted specifically for peer tutoring, rather than the whole class.

Peer-assisted learning (PAL) is another way to engage students in active learning. PAL can be implemented with partners or in small groups in any content area (Walkup-Amos, 2020) and any level from elementary to secondary (Hott et al., 2012). PAL can provide one-on-one assistance for a student who is struggling with learning a concept by pairing that student with a student who has developed proficiency in that same concept. This is another way the HLPs tie together. Flexible grouping, HLP 17, can be accomplished through PAL in partner work or cooperative learning groups. PAL is well documented as a strategy to increase achievement as they engage students in active learning (Prater, 2018). Not only does PAL benefit academic achievement, but it can improve social interactions between students when social skills are explicitly taught (HLP 9; Walkup-Amos, 2020).

The Question Exploration Routine is one of the many Content Enhancement Routines developed at the University of Kansas. The Question Exploration Routine helps students explore ideas and main questions of a lesson or unit and engage with the material at a more personal level (Bulgren et al., 2009). You can use this EBP to promote student engagement with individuals, peers, and groups. Studies have shown these practices improve classroom test scores for students at the secondary level (Bulgren et al., 2011; Schumaker et al., 2020). You will introduce the unit by introducing and discussing the critical question of the unit. This one step helps students engage in those objectives we typically share but that students do not necessarily pay attention. Then students discuss the key vocabulary and explain or define it with student-friendly language. When students actively discuss and use vocabulary, their learning becomes more authentic than just looking up the terms in the glossary of the text. Just as the name implies, students explore other questions that will help support their learning. Using a graphic organizer, students can partner or work in collaborative groups to generate questions. As you proceed with the lesson or even a whole unit, have students refer to the tool to answer the questions. The final question on the organizer is the home run of learning; students relating what they just learned to their own personal experience. It is important to note, the study strategies developed by the University of Kansas Center for Research and Learning, like most EBPs, require training; a link to the center can be found in Table 18-2, along with many resources to support the practices discussed in this chapter.

Self-Regulation

Difficulty with self-regulation is a common challenge among SWD, across disability categories (Korinek & deFur, 2016). As mentioned previously, Chapter 14 addresses self-regulation through cognitive and metacognitive strategies for student learning and independence (HLP 14). This section will address strategies that enhance students' focus and memory, key components of self-regulation, and of active engagement.

The prefrontal cortex, which controls the limbic system, is the area of the brain that controls self-regulation and can be developed using strategies to improve focus and memory (Sanchez, 2017). Ullman and Pullman (2015) discovered that improved declarative memory (i.e., fact-based or event-based information) improved other brain functions, which can increase the probability of greater success throughout life. So how does a teacher help their students improve focus and memory? We will look at some ways below.

Do not be afraid of repetition. Foundational information that is essential to future learning should be solid in a student's repertoire. Identify ways to make repetition fun. Play games with your whole class or in small groups. To practice math facts or comparisons, students can play "Hot Hand." In partners, one student shuffles a deck of cards (with Kings, Queens, Jacks, and Jokers removed) and deals half the deck to themself and their partner. Each partner turns over two cards and either adds, subtracts, or multiplies the two numbers. Highest sum, difference, or product wins and that student keeps the cards. For comparisons, students turn over just one card and whomever has the greatest number or the smallest number, depending on whether you are playing a round of "greater than" or "less than," wins that round. Once all cards are gone, the player with the most cards wins. This makes learning fun, allows for frequent responding, and provides the repetition students need to solidify foundational knowledge in their memories.

Finally, to aid in both memory, focus, and independence, provide visual prompts with checklists, schedules, and steps to completing multi-step processes, such as long division or handwashing (Carr et al., 2014; Carter et al., 2011). The National Autism Center (2009) identified visual schedules to be an EBP for those with autism spectrum disorder, as did Knight, Sartini, and Spriggs (2014) who added that visual schedules coupled with systematic instruction (HLP 12) meets criteria for EBP. The beauty of visual schedules is they can benefit anyone who needs support with memory, focus, and independence. Visual activity schedules can be as simple as the daily schedule posted on the whiteboard or as a permanent sign in the classroom. It can have just words or symbols or pictures to pair with the words. Visual activity schedules can also be for separate subject areas as an agenda for the class period (e.g., bell ringer, opening activity, instructional presentation, guided practice, independent practice). It could be in the form of an individual-sized schedule for just one student or larger for the whole class. The options are truly endless! A benefit of visual activity schedules is that they are effective in allowing individuals with intellectual disabilities to complete tasks with little to no assistance, leading to greater independence (van Dijk & Gage, 2019). To help you get started, Figure 18-1 provides an example of a visual activity schedule for the class periods in a school day.

Checklists are also a good option for assisting with memory, focus, and independence and, like visual schedules, benefit any student who needs support in these areas. Checklists can help students remain engaged while independently completing tasks. These checklists (also called *task analysis*) can be provided for daily living skills such as handwashing, baking cookies, or getting ready for bed.

Table 18-2. Alignment of HLPs and Resources for Evidence-Based Practices

EBP SUPPORT WITH HLP 18	RELATED HLPS	RESOURCES
Peer-assisted learning	17	https://www.youtube.com/watch?v=J9NN7g7W-pU https://iris.peabody.vanderbilt.edu/module/palsk1/ https://iris.peabody.vanderbilt.edu/module/pals26/ https://iris.peabody.vanderbilt.edu/module/palshs/
Repetition	7, 14	http://www.ascd.org/publications/educational-leadership/oct12/vol70/num02/100-Repetitions.aspx Datchuk, S. M., & Hier, B. O. (2019). Fluency practice: Techniques for building automaticity in foundational knowledge and skills. *TEACHING Exceptional Children, 51*(6), 424-435. https://doi.org/10.1177/0040059919847213
Checklists/ task analysis	7, 14, 15	https://afirm.fpg.unc.edu/task-analysis http://aacintervention.com/home/180009852/180009852/tips/2010/12dec2010/Editing%20Using%20CUPS.pdf
Choral responding	16	https://www.tandfonline.com/doi/abs/10.1080/1045988X.2012.682184 http://www.rcsthinkfromthemiddle.com/choral-response.html
Response cards	13, 15	https://www.ncbi.nlm.nih.gov/pmc/articles/PMC2790933 https://www.youtube.com/watch?v=3tggOkAKY1Y https://www.youtube.com/watch?v=94jKw9ZNWIA
Think-Pair-Share	17, 22	https://www.kent.edu/ctl/think-pair-share http://www.theteachertoolkit.com/index.php/tool/think-pair-share
Peer tutoring	17, 22	https://ies.ed.gov/ncee/wwc/InterventionReport/81 https://www.tandfonline.com/doi/abs/10.1080/10573569.2017.1302372?journalCode=urwl20
Visual prompts	15	https://www.yourtherapysource.com/blog1/2020/11/03/what-is-a-visual-prompt/ https://lessonpix.com/

(continued)

Table 18-2 (continued). Alignment of HLPs and Resources for Evidence-Based Practices

Opportunities to respond	15, 16	https://ebi.missouri.edu/?p=1337 https://louisville.edu/education/abri/primarylevel/otr/behavior https://www.education.uw.edu/ibestt/wp-content/uploads/2018/02/Opportunities-to-Respond.pdf
Active student responding	15, 16	https://www.totalparticipationtechniques.com/total-participation-techniques-m9gyf https://www.sciencedirect.com/science/article/abs/pii/S0883035516301082 https://highleveragepractices.org/hlp-18-use-strategies-promote-active-student-engagement
Question Exploration Routine	14, 15	https://sim.ku.edu/sim-content-enhancement-routines https://eric.ed.gov/?id=ED469289

They can be for academic processes such as how to write an essay, how to complete a story problem, or how to balance a checkbook. A commonly used strategy in writing is to edit work using the acronym CUPS (capitalization, usage, punctuation, spelling). A checklist using an adapted version of CUPS is found in Figure 18-2. Colorful font or visual cues can further enhance the power of the checklist for students. Checklists, like visual activity schedules, can be posted for all to see, such as handwashing steps often posted in restrooms, or can be individually sized for a student to put in a notebook or on a binder ring to carry with them and use as necessary. In fact, Uberti et al. (2004) went a step further in not only providing individual copies of a checklist to students but provided a checklist based on error analysis (for addition problems with and without regrouping). The data showed that these individualized checklists benefited students with learning disabilities and those who were English-language learners.

Supporting focus, memory, and independence are key to student success and active engagement in the classroom and broader school experience. When students can focus on tasks, remember the key concepts necessary for completing the tasks, and complete those tasks independently, they are more likely to meet expectations for college, career, and independent living upon graduation. They are empowered to complete tasks on their own, which can lead to greater self-efficacy and goal setting.

The strategies addressed in this chapter are but a sampling of those you can use to increase student engagement in your classroom. It is important to not only use these strategies, along with others that your students enjoy, but also to continuously provide positive and constructive feedback to sustain performance (HLP 22). Feedback will allow your students to get evaluative information on how they are performing as they gain confidence in the skills and processes they are learning.

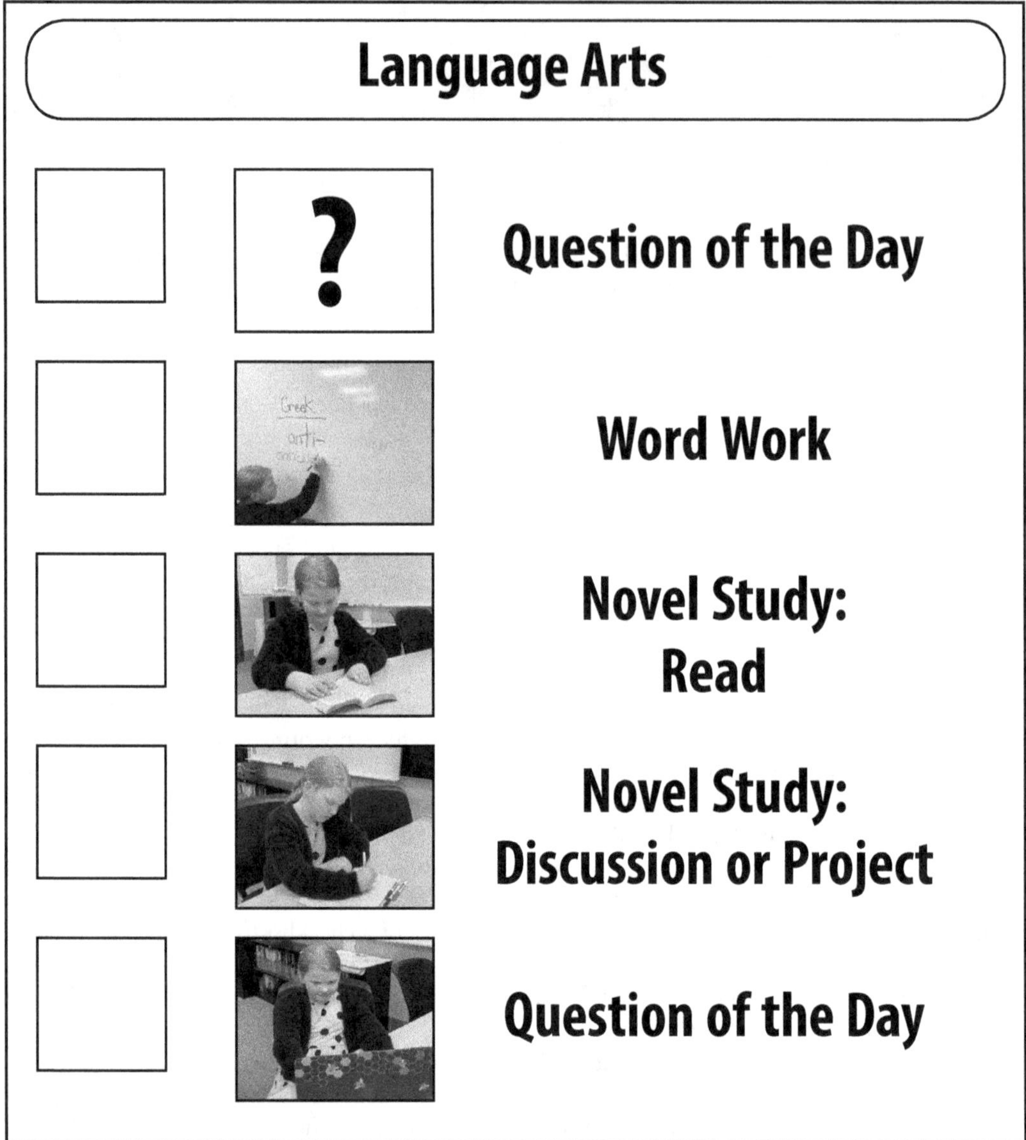

Figure 18-1. English Language Arts mini-schedule.

What Does HLP 18 Look Like in a K-12 Classroom?

Elementary Example

Mrs. Walerczak has a small group of eight third-grade students for instruction on their reading goals. Their individualized education program contain goals for vocabulary, fluency, and comprehension. In addition to systematic instruction (HLP 12), Mrs. Walerczak uses visual cues and choral responding to introduce vocabulary words for today's lesson. She first holds up a card with the word, a student-friendly definition, and a picture cue, then says the word while pointing to it, snaps her fingers, and students respond by repeating the word. She follows the same steps for the student-friendly definitions, tracing her finger under the words as she and the students read them. To practice fluency, Mrs. Walerczak displays a poem, which she reads first to the students. Next, she directs students to

Checking Grammar, Spelling, & Mechanics
Directions: Read over your writing and check for the following:
______ Do I have a **capital letter** at the beginning of every sentence?
______ Do I have a **capital letter** for every proper noun?
______ Do I have **noun and verb agreement**? Hint: Squiggly lines under your words in Google Docs or Microsoft Word can indicate a potential grammar mistake.
______ Do I have proper **punctuation** at the end of every sentence?
______ Have I checked for **spelling**? Hint: Squiggly lines under your words in Google Docs or Microsoft Word often indicate a misspelling.

Figure 18-2. Checklist for editing a writing task.

read it with her, then they read it together without her in an I Do, We Do, You Do instructional sequence. This allows students to have two OTR by chorally reading the poem. Finally, Mrs. Walerczak asks comprehension questions about the poem using a Think-Pair-Share format. First, she asks the question, gives wait time for students to come up with an answer in their head, and then directs students to turn and talk to their elbow partner (this is a pre-established procedure). Once they share their ideas, they decide on one answer together to share with the class, if called on. The five comprehension questions continue in that manner until all have been answered.

Secondary Example

Mr. Brace uses this same HLP to engage his high school students. Mr. Brace and his co-teacher are getting ready to introduce a new unit in U.S. History, so they prepare the students for the content by explicitly teaching vocabulary needed for students to understand and master the concepts. They will use whiteboards, Think-Pair-Share, and a question exploration guide graphic organizer from the Question Exploration Routine (Figure 18-3; Bulgren et al., 2009) to engage students with the material. First, they introduce the unit and talk about the broad concept. During this phase of the lesson, they provide many OTR for students to activate prior learning. Then they explicitly teach the vocabulary giving students multiple opportunities to say and write the new words on whiteboards. Once the students begin to demonstrate understanding, the teachers move on to engaging students with Think-Pair-Share of combining student-friendly definitions and using the vocabulary. Next, students work with a partner and collaborative teams to complete the question exploration guide. Mr. Brace gets them started by modeling his expectation and presents the critical question for the unit. Then students work with a partner to complete the key term section with explanations or student-friendly definitions. They get into collaborative teams, share out their definitions and explanations once finished with partner work. The next step is to have teams generate supporting questions the students hope to have answered as they navigate the unit. Finally, student teams share out to the class what questions they generated.

Summary

As we have mentioned throughout this chapter, implementing HLP 18—"*Use strategies to promote active student engagement*," there are several other HLPs that can be used in combination. Table 18-2 shows those HLPs that we have addressed alongside HLP 18 in this chapter. Many of the HLPs are used hand-in-hand with one another and very few are as powerful alone as they are together. Combined, we can increase student achievement through student engagement with quality

Unit Question Exploration	
Name:	Date:
Class:	Unit Title:
Lesson Title:	Critical Question:
1. What are the vocabulary and definitions for this unit?	
Vocabulary	*Definition*
2. What are some questions you have about this unit?	
Question	*Answer*
3. What is the main idea to be addressed in this unit?	
4. Apply the main idea. Make connections to your experiences and your knowledge about the world.	

Figure 18-3. Question Exploration Routine. (Adapted from Bulgren, J. A., Marquis, J. G., Lenz, B. K., Schumaker, J. B., & Deshler, D. D. (2009). Effectiveness of question exploration to enhance students' written expression of content knowledge and comprehension. *Reading & Writing Quarterly, 25,* 271-289.)

classroom management (HLP 7) and systematically designing instruction to meet learning goals (HLP 12). Implementing assistive and instructional technologies (HLP 19) allows students to access learning and experience it in different ways by being active participants. Providing feedback improves instructional outcomes (HLP 8) and using both positive and corrective feedback (HLP 22) increases students' correct academic and behavioral responses. Additionally, the use of explicit instruction (HLP 16) provides opportunities for students to actively engage in learning in an errorless manner while using cognitive and metacognitive strategies (HLP 14). When we systematically provide opportunities for students to practice skills over time, we increase maintenance of these skills. By extending practice in varied environments across content areas, when appropriate, we increase the opportunities for students to generalize their learning, which allows them to transfer that learning into other appropriate situations (HLP 21).

In sum, providing many OTR through active student responding in your lessons will increase student engagement leading to increased achievement. Table 18-2 also provides resources for you to learn more about the strategies included in this chapter and the HLPs used to implement the strategies. We encourage you to explore those resources and to seek out your own. Also, it would be wise to collect data on your teaching by recording how many OTR you provide in your lessons and set a goal to continually increase that number to work toward the goal of four to six per minute as set by the Council for Exceptional Children (1987) and Stichter et al. (2009). Collecting the data and reflecting on how you can improve is also a way to implement HLP 6 to ensure your practice encourages active student responding.

Chapter Review

1. Describe HLP 18 in your own words.
2. Why is active student engagement important?
3. How does knowing students' interests help to increase their engagement in class?
4. In what ways does HLP 18 connect with other HLPs?
5. Choose a strategy you learned in this chapter and identify how you could implement it in a lesson.

References

Adamson, R. M., & Lewis, T. J. (2017). A comparison of three opportunity-to-respond strategies on the academic engaged time among high school students who present challenging behavior. *Behavioral Disorders, 42*(2), 41-51. https://doi.org/10.1177/0198742916688644

Armstrong, T. (2012). *Neurodiversity in the classroom: Strength-based strategies to help students with special needs succeed in school and life*. ASCD.

Blair, C. (2002). School readiness: Integrating cognition and emotion in a neurobiological conceptualization of children's functioning at school entry. *American Psychologist, 57*(2), 111-127.

Bulgren, J. A., Marquis, J. G., Lenz, B. K., Deshler, D. D., & Schumaker, J. B. (2011). The effectiveness of a question-exploration routine for enhancing the content learning of secondary students. *Journal of Educational Psychology, 103*(3), 578. https://doi.org/10.1037/a0023930

Bulgren, J. A., Marquis, J. G., Lenz, B. K., Schumaker, J. B., & Deshler, D. D. (2009). Effectiveness of question exploration to enhance students' written expression of content knowledge and comprehension. *Reading & Writing Quarterly, 25*, 271-289.

Carr, M. E., Moodre, D. W., & Anderson, A. (2014). Self-management interventions with autism: A meta-analysis of single-subject research. *Exceptional Children, 81*, 28-44.

Carter, E. W., Lane, K., L., Crnobori, M., Bruhn, A. L., & Oakes, W. P. (2011). Self-determination interventions for students with and at risk for emotional and behavioral disorders: Mapping the knowledge base. *Behavioral Disorders, 36*, 100-116.

Council for Exceptional Children. (1987). *Academy for effective instruction: Working with mildly handicapped students*. Author.

Ecker-Lyster, M., & Niileksela, C. (2016). Keeping students on track to graduate: A synthesis of school dropout trends, prevention, and intervention initiatives. *Journal of At-Risk Issues, 19*(2), 24-31.

Gay, G. (2018). *Culturally responsive teaching: Theory, research, and practice* (3rd ed.). Teachers College Press.

Geisinger, K. F. (2016). 21st century skills: What are they and how do we assess them? *Applied Measurement in Education, 29*(4), 245-249. https://doi.org/10.1080/08957347.2016.1209207

Heward, W. L. (2022). Use strategies to promote active student engagement. In J. McLeskey, L. Maheady, B. Billingsley, M. T. Brownell, & T. J. Lewis (Eds.), *High leverage practices for inclusive classrooms* (2nd ed., pp. 282-294). Routledge. https://doi.org?10.4324/9781003148609-24

Himmele, P., & Himmele, W. (2017). *Total participation techniques: Making every student an active learner*. ASCD.

Hott, B. L., Walker, J. D., & Shani, J. (2012). *Peer tutoring. Council for Learning Disabilities info sheet*. https://council-for-learning-disabilities.org/peer-tutoring-flexible-peer-mediated-strategy-that-involves-students-serving-as-academic-tutors

IRIS Center. (2012). *Classroom diversity: An introduction to student differences*. https://iris.peabody.vanderbilt.edu/module/div/

Kilbane, C. R., & Milman, N. B. (2014). *Teaching models: Designing instruction for 21st century learners*. Pearson.

Knight, V., Sartini, E., & Spriggs, A. D. (2014). Evaluating visual activity schedules as evidence-based practice for individuals with autism spectrum disorder. *Journal of Autism and Developmental Disorders, 45*, 157-178.

Korinek, L., & deFur, S. H. (2016). Supporting student self-regulation to access the general education curriculum. *TEACHING Exceptional Children, 48*(5), 232-242. https://doi.org/10.1177/0040059915626134.

MacSuga-Gage, A. S., & Simonsen, B. (2015). Examining the effects of teacher-directed opportunities to respond on student outcomes: A systematic review of the literature. *Education and Treatment of Children, 38*(2), 211-240.

Mandel, S. (2003). *Cooperative work groups: Preparing students for the real world*. Corwin.

McLeskey, J., Barringer, M.-D., Billingsley, B., Brownell, M., Jackson, D., Kennedy, M., Lewis, T., Maheady, L., Rodriquez, J., Scheeler, M. C., Winn, J., & Ziegler, D. (2017). *High-leverage practices in special education.* Council for Exceptional Children & CEEDAR Center.

Morningstar, M. E., Lombardi, A., Fowler, C. H., & Test, D. W. (2017). College and career readiness framework for secondary students with disabilities. *Career Development and Transition for Exceptional Individuals, 40*, 79-91. https://doi.org/10.1177/2165143415589926

Nagro, S. A., Hooks, S. D., Fraser, D. W., & Cornelius, K. E. (2016). Whole-group response strategies to promote student engagement in inclusive classrooms. *TEACHING Exceptional Children, 48*, 243-249. http://doi.org/10.1177/0040059916640749

National Autism Center. (2009). *The National Autism Center's national standards report.* National Autism Center.

Owiny, R. L., Spriggs, A. D., Sartini, E. C., & Mills, J. R. (2017). *Evaluating response cards as evidence based.* Preventing School Failure: Alternative Education for Children & Youth. https://doi.org/10.1080/1045988X.2017.1344953

Prater, M. A. (2018). *Teaching students with high-incidence disabilities: Strategies for diverse classrooms.* SAGE.

Rodriquez, J., & Hardin, S. E. (2017). Culturally responsive teaching to support all learners. In W. W. Murawski & K. L. Scott (Eds.), *What really works with exceptional learners* (pp. 117-132). Corwin.

Sanchez, H. (2017). Thanks for the memories: Brain-based learning at its best. In W. W. Murawski & K. L. Scott (Eds.), *What really works with exceptional learners* (pp. 117-132). Corwin.

Schumaker, J. B., Fisher, J. B., Walsh, L. D., & Lancaster, P. E. (2020). Effects of multimedia versus live professional development on teachers' and students' performance related to the question exploration routine. *Learning Disabilities Research & Practice*, 35(4), 180-200. https://doi.org/10.1111/ldrp.12232

Simonsen, B., Myers, D., & DeLuca, C. (2010). Teaching teachers to use prompts, opportunities to respond, and specific praise. *Teacher Education and Special Education, 33*(4), 300–318. https://doi.org/10.1177/0888406409359905

Slavin, R. E. (1995). *Cooperative learning: Theory, research, and practice* (2nd ed.). Prentice Hall.

Slavin, R. E. (2013). Effective programmes in reading and mathematics: Lessons from the best lessons encyclopedia. *School Effectiveness and School Improvement, 24*(4), 383-391. https://doi.org/10.1080/09243453.2013.797913

Stichter, J. P., Lewis, T. J., Whittaker, T. A., Richter, M., Johnson, N. W., & Trussell, R. P. (2009). Assessing teacher use of opportunities to respond and effective classroom management strategies: Comparisons among high- and low-risk elementary schools. *Journal of Positive Behavior Interventions, 11*, 68-81.

Uberti, H. Z., Mastropieri, M. A., & Scruggs, T. E. (2004). Check it off: Individualizing a math algorithm for students with disabilities via self-monitoring checklists. *Intervention in School & Clinic, 39*(5), 269-275.

Ullman, M. T., & Pullman, M. Y. (2015). Adapt and overcome: Can a single brain system compensate for autism, dyslexia, and OCD? *Scientific American Mind, 51*, 24-25.

van Dijk, W., & Gage, N. A. (2019). The effectiveness of visual activity schedules for individuals with intellectual disabilities: A meta-analysis. *Journal of Intellectual & Developmental Disability, 44*(4), 384-395.

Vasquez, E., & Slocum, T. A. (2012). Evaluation of synchronous online tutoring for students at risk of reading failure. *Exceptional Children, 78*, 221-235.

Walker, J. D., & Barry, C. (2018). Assessing and supporting social skill needs for students with high-incidence disabilities. *TEACHING Exceptional Children, 51*(1), 18-30. https://doi.org//10.1177/0040059918790219

Walkup-Amos, T. (2020). Creating inclusive music classrooms through peer-assisted learning strategies. *TEACHING Exceptional Children*, 52(3), 138-146. https://doi.org/10.1177/0040059919891185

How Do I Consider Assistive and Instructional Technologies in My Instruction?

Alice L. Rhodes, PhD
and Ruby L. Owiny, PhD

HLP 19
Use assistive and instructional technologies.

INTRODUCTION

High-Leverage Practice (HLP) 19 is a necessary consideration for meeting the needs of students with disabilities (SWD). Some students benefit from instructional technology to acquire new skills and to develop fluency with those skills. Other students need assistive technology to navigate through their school and community, engage in meaningful conversations with peers, and demonstrate their learning. This chapter defines instructional and assistive technology, describes procedures for considering assistive and instructional technology, and describes how to implement instructional and assistive technology in the classroom. All of this is explained using a Universal Design for Learning framework to allow all students to fully participate in school and the community while providing for the unique needs of SWD in a manner that maintains their dignity, reduces stigma, and allows them access to the learning environment.

Owiny, R. L., & Cornelius, K. E. *The Practical Guide to High-Leverage Practices in Special Education: The Purposeful "How" to Enhance Classroom Rigor* (pp. 271-284).

CHAPTER OBJECTIVES

- Define the terms assistive technology and instructional technology.
- Describe the procedures for considering assistive and instructional technologies for students within the Universal Design for Learning framework.
- Explain the importance of augmentative and alternative communication for students to access the general education curriculum.
- Understand the importance of assistive and instructional technology to all students' success within the Universal Design for Learning framework.
- Implement the use of assistive technology and instructional technology in the classroom.

KEY TERMS

- **assistive technology device:** Any item, piece of equipment, or product utilized for increasing, maintaining, and improving the functional capabilities of students with disabilities.
- **assistive technology services:** Any service that assists a student with a disability select, acquire, and use an assistive technology device. It includes such services as evaluation, purchasing, selecting, coordinating, and training or technical assistance for the students, parents, and professionals.
- **augmentative and alternative communication (AAC):** Includes all forms of communication (other than oral speech) used to express thoughts, needs, wants, and ideas, such as communication boards, sign language or speech-generating devices used by individuals unable to communicate readily through oral speech.
- **content-specific instructional technologies:** Any technology (e.g., application, website, or software) that helps students learn content-specific material.
- **general instructional technologies:** Any technology (e.g., application, website, or software) that assists a teacher in providing instruction and support to students with the purpose of meeting specific needs in any content area.
- **Student, Environment, Task, and Tools (SETT) framework:** Assists practitioners in making decisions about assistive technology for students with disabilities considered in the framework.

Technology is a part of our daily lives which became especially apparent during the COVID-19 pandemic when schools and universities were required to provide some type of remote instruction to students. As the world became even more reliant on technology, many experienced what individuals with disabilities experience daily. Technology often supports their learning, daily living, social interactions, and independence. Considering the need for assistive technology (AT) and instructional technology (IT) to support students with disabilities (SWD) has been part of the law since the reauthorization of Individuals with Disabilities Education Act in 1997. Since then, individualized education program (IEP) teams have been required to consider what, if any, AT or IT might be needed for a student to access the general education curriculum successfully.

In fact, this is the premise of Universal Design for Learning (UDL)—to remove barriers to learning so **all** students can access the general curriculum in a meaningful, engaging manner. The implementation of assistive and instructional technologies can help remove barriers for SWD, and even for those without diagnosed disabilities, by providing access in ways not otherwise possible. UDL is based on the notion that all students should be able to access the instruction, but inflexibility in developing goals, methods, materials, and assessments often produces roadblocks to learning rather than accessibility (Novak, 2019). Often students can feel singled out if they are the only one using a particular support, such as a pencil gripper or calculator. But, what if pencil grippers and calculators were available to whomever wanted to use them? This is an example of AT and UDL being considered simultaneously and meets the needs of more students at one time while addressing more diversity, making universal decisions rather than individual ones (Delisio & Bukaty, 2019).

As you will learn in this chapter, AT and IT include various digital technologies. Research into the use of digital technologies in inclusive classrooms shows a positive connection to student engagement and learning. In fact, as Dazzeo and Rao (2020) describe the increase in technology use in schools and recognize the impact of technology and instructional strategies for providing scaffolding for students with a variety of needs, thus removing barriers to their learning. Utilizing sound instructional strategies *and* technology increases student achievement. Digital technology aligns well with the UDL framework to benefit students in the following ways: (a) technology expands the ways materials can be presented to students that include supports and multiple representations built in, (b) creates engagement and interest, (c) allows for multiple means for expressing what they know, (d) presents ways to collaborate, and (e) presents ways to provide incremental supports to meet learning needs (Dazzeo & Rao, 2020). As McLeskey et al. (2017) note, SWD benefit from the consideration of AT and IT that could support them in meeting their IEP goals and accessing the general education curriculum. Identifying appropriate AT and IT removes barriers to accessing instruction, allowing students to fully participate in the general education curriculum and demonstrate what they know in meaningful ways.

This chapter addresses High-Leverage Practice (HLP) 19: *Use Assistive and Instructional Technologies* by explaining what it is, the difference between AT and IT, how decisions should be made, and the evidence-based practices (EBPs) for assessing and implementing AT and IT to meet individual student needs. As a result of this chapter, you will add ideas to your toolbox to effectively use both AT and IT to support your students with IEPs, but truly, all students will benefit.

It is important for special educators to remember that an IEP team is in place for good reason—for collaboration and team decision-making (HLPs 1 and 3). The idea of determining if a student needs AT and subsequently deciding which AT will benefit the student is daunting, not to mention the considerations of IT! Special educators do not need to take on this responsibility alone; the IEP team assists in this by having someone on the team that is an expert in AT and IT. Not to mention, states and school districts have whole offices designated to AT and are more than willing to consult with teachers to help identify the most appropriate IT and AT device or service for a student to access the general education curriculum effectively to best support learning.

What Is HLP 19?

HLP 19—"*Use assistive and instructional technologies*" is defined as:

> Teachers select and implement assistive and instructional technologies to support the needs of SWD. They choose and use augmentative and alternative communication devices and assistive and instructional technology products to promote student learning and independence. They evaluate new technology options given student needs; make informed instructional decisions grounded in evidence, professional wisdom, and students' IEP goals; and advocate for administrative support in technology implementation. Teachers use the universal design for learning (UDL) framework to select, plan, implement and evaluate essential student outcomes. (McLeskey et al., 2017, p. 87)

We will address these three components of HLP 19: IT, AT, and augmentative and alternative communication (AAC).

AAC is also part of AT. AAC includes items and services specifically for a particular student to communicate. These devices enable students to initiate conversation, respond to others, and maintain conversations. AAC can be low-, medium-, or high-tech. For example, the Picture Exchange Communication System (PECS) uses pictures on cards, making it low-tech (www.pecsusa.com).

These are often put into a binder for easy access. The Go Talk 20+ (https://www.attainmentcompany.com/gotalk-20) is a medium-tech device that supports communication, while the Tobii Dynavox i-110 (https://us.tobiidynavox.com/pages/i-110-2) is a high-tech speech-generating device to support communication. High-tech AAC are devices that allow for the storage and retrieval of messages.

Without these devices, students essentially do not have a voice or way to communicate with others. It is important that teachers understand that last sentence. It bears repeating—without AAC, a student is left without a way to communicate. In other words, the student has no way of communicating their needs, wants, and desires. Imagine being so thirsty, your throat and mouth are dry, and you desperately need water, but you must rely on someone else to get that. Now imagine you have no way of letting anyone know you need the water. This can be horrifying. Now imagine this is your daily existence. Students who require AAC for communication need to have access to it whenever communication could take place. This means at home, school, in the community, on the playground, anywhere a student needs to communicate. It is irresponsible for teachers to take away these devices, as frequently happens, as a punishment or for other reasons. It takes away the student's voice. Alternatively, schools sometimes do not allow the device to go home, leaving the student without a way to communicate on the bus or at home, unless provisions are made for the student to have multiple devices. It is important to remember that the devices must always be in working order (charged, fresh batteries, etc.) for the student to successfully communicate wherever they may be. IEP teams should consider what training is needed for school personnel, parents, and possibly the student to maintain proper working devices.

Why Are Assistive and Instructional Technologies Important to Consider?

As one might imagine, the use of IT and AT in the classroom is vital for the academic, behavioral, and social success of students. It is also a consideration for implementing UDL to remove barriers and provide access to the general education curriculum for all students. The action and expression principle includes optimizing tools and AT (Checkpoint 4.2; CAST, 2018). The premise of Checkpoint 4.2 is the notion that all learners, at some point in their educational career, need assistance navigating through their educational environment, whether that is the physical environment or the curriculum. We can all think of a class or a particular skill that was unusually difficult for us. You likely would have appreciated your teacher removing barriers by providing multiple methods for you to learn the material and demonstrate your learning. We know we would have appreciated that, especially when learning to multiply fractions. Imagine the possibilities for IT to help a student overcome a struggle with learning a particular concept. Software applications such as IXL or iReady provide individualized practice with concepts aligned with national and state standards. When struggling with multiplying fractions, then, both of these applications tailor practice items to incrementally assist the student in developing an understanding of the concept and honing prerequisite skills to be successful.

Not only does technology give students a voice who otherwise may be voiceless, as in the case of AAC, technology also makes learning accessible to students when it may not otherwise be; again, think UDL. IT is a way to meet student needs while preparing instruction using the principles of UDL by making learning more meaningful, engaging, and accessible. With the world wide web, teachers can take students on field trips to places they cannot go physically. For a teacher in Oregon to take their students to see Plimoth Patuxet in Massachusetts is nearly impossible. Yet, this same teacher can go to the web and take their students on a virtual field trip through Scholastic (https://youtu.be/p5qi3Meqy24). Experiencing a place via a video can be more engaging than simply reading about it in a textbook. However, the beauty of thinking the UDL way is both can be provided for students. They can experience a virtual field trip *and* read the book, or be given the choice of how they want to access that part of their learning. Here is another example of IT: An elementary teacher may want her students to practice reasoning skills, but needs a way for students to do so independently, so they send them to their iPads to use the application, ST Math. In a secondary classroom, a social studies teacher may want their students to engage in an online Scavenger Hunt (e.g., Webquest) and send students to various websites to gather information to answer an essential question. These are all IT that all students can access. Some students with certain disabilities, such as visual impairment or motor impairment, may need some accommodations, but generally, they can access these resources. Therefore, IT, both general and content-specific, enhances instruction and makes learning fun and engaging for all students.

What role, then, does AT play in the classroom? AT levels the playing field. It makes an otherwise inaccessible activity or task accessible. It is very important, when making decisions about AT, that one understands AT is on a continuum of complexity. On one end of the continuum are low-tech devices—items that are readily available, inexpensive, and do not have batteries or require electricity to work—but as technology progresses through the continuum, it becomes more complex (Koch, 2017). For example, a student with working memory challenges may need to use highlighters (low-tech) to color code material to find information easily and be able to remember it. A student with poor fine motor skills may need a pencil gripper or a "fat" pencil (low-tech) to help grasp the writing utensil, or the student may need binder clips (low-tech) on pages to grip them for turning. A student with a visual impairment or visual processing disorder may need text enlarged using a desktop electronic magnifier (medium-tech) in order to read material clearly. A student might need to use text-to-speech software (high-tech) to access a textbook chapter or need to use an electric wheelchair (high-tech) to navigate their environment. These low-, medium-, and high-tech examples make learning accessible to the student.

How Can Instructional Technologies Be Embedded in Instruction?

IT is meant to be used, not only for SWD but for all students (Israel & Willams, 2022). Special educators should consider IT as a means of enhancing instruction for all of their students. When working with a general educator (HLP 1), special educators should remember that IT is intended to support all students and be willing to share ideas for how the general educator might incorporate such technologies into instruction to support not only the students with IEPs in the general education classroom but all other learners as well. IT includes general technologies that can be used across all content areas, such as word processing or voice-to-text software and applications and content-specific technologies that are specific only to one particular content area. Content-specific technology could include calculators for mathematics, dissection apps for science, or content-specific websites, such as the Smithsonian Museums (si.edu), for social studies, science, or the arts.

It is no surprise that technology can enhance instruction. Teachers learned during the COVID-19 pandemic that IT can be used to deliver instruction as well. As Collins (2012) points out, technology can assist teachers to provide systematic instruction (HLP 12) with new content, drill and practice for discrete skills, or practicing skill performance, such as in chained tasks. An EBP, Self-Regulated Strategy Development (SRSD; see HLP 14), is an oft-used strategy for struggling writers due to its effectiveness (Rowland et al., 2020). While traditionally, the SRSD strategy is used for physically writing or typing pieces, IT can be effective for students as they use the SRSD in written expression (Rowland et al., 2020). For more information about SRSD and other cognitive and metacognitive strategies, see Chapter 14. Three technologies suggested are voice-to-text software, word prediction software, and digital graphic organizers. These ITs benefit SWD who have difficulty putting words from their head onto paper, organizing their ideas into a cohesive writing piece, and spelling. Teachers know that it is not only SWD that experience these struggles, therefore, IT can serve universal accommodations, in other words, a means of implementing UDL, benefitting all students, not only those with disabilities.

Video modeling (VM) and video self-modeling (VSM) are EBPs that can be used to teach almost any academic, social, motor, or functional life skill across disabilities and age ranges. VM is also a part of HLP 13 when used as a means to adapt materials (e.g., instruction) for specific learning goals. VM can also be provided through a variety of devices—tablets, laptops, or even smartphones; anywhere a video can be played, VM can be displayed! VM is a beneficial intervention across both a range of ages and content areas, such as math, reading, social studies, and even social behaviors (Boon et al., 2020; Cihak et al., 2012). In addition, VM can enhance the achievement of students across a range of disabilities, including autism spectrum disorder; in academic, functional, and vocational skills (Kellems & Morningstar, 2012); visual impairments (Chang et al., 2020); and learning disabilities (LD; Boon et al., 2020). The best news, and the reason this intervention is included in this chapter, is that VM is proven to be an EBP (Cox & AFIRM team, 2018).

Many have watched a YouTube video to learn how to do something—everything from changing a tire, cooking a particular recipe, or how to knit, draw, tie a tie, etc. Those videos can be considered VM. While it sounds extremely simple, it does take some planning and intentionality to create a high-quality VM session. Cox and the team at AFIRM (2018) describe how to create a video model. A link to the information brief is included in Table 19-1. Once the video is created, students can watch the video as many times as they need to learn the skill or task or simply for review. Remember that students will need adult supervision, the materials to perform the task, and frequent reinforcement as they acquire the new skill or task.

VSM is very similar to VM, except in the case of VSM, the student serves as the model for themselves. This, too, is an EBP and is widely used across ages, disabilities, content areas, and skills or tasks (Diorio et al., 2019; Reyes et al., 2021; Sadler, 2019). VSM has even been successful with students in a general education classroom to transition more quickly with fewer issues when doing so (McNiff et al., 2019). Keep in mind that it might take several sessions to get through a full task if the task is chained, meaning the task has multiple steps such as hand washing or solving three-digit multiplication with regrouping. As the student is acquiring the skill or task, they will need prompting (HLPs 15 and 22) through each step and may perform some steps incorrectly. Thankfully, there is editing software to make this step easier.

An emerging practice is content acquisition podcasts (CAPs), which are designed using instructional design principles and EBPs. They are short, multimedia vignettes that provide instruction. CAPs adhere to specific design principles, such as strong images, clear and precise narration, and sometimes on-screen text (Teacher Education Division, n.d.). They follow the design principles from Mayer's Cognitive Theory of Multimedia Learning (CTML; Mayer, 2008). These design principles help to "reduce cognitive load" and increase learning through "high quality instruction using multimedia" (Teacher Education Division, n.d.). Originally intended for teacher professional development and supported with multiple studies as being effective for training pre-service teachers (Green et al., 2020; Kennedy et al., 2014; Kennedy et al., 2018; McNamara et al., 2020), this model has been adapted to create CAP-S with the S for students. The beauty of CAP-S is it inherently embeds UDL into the videos, removing barriers and making learning accessible and engaging to all students. In fact, Kennedy et al. (2014) identified that CAP-S benefitted students with LD and those without any identified disability in vocabulary acquisition using design principles from UDL and CTML, along with EBPs for teaching vocabulary. In addition, Kennedy et al. (2014) provide step-by-step production directions for creating CAP-S.

The benefit of creating CAP-S is that most teachers have relatively easy access to the materials needed for creating their own CAP-S. Content, a computer (laptop or desktop), slide creation applications or software (e.g., PowerPoint, Pages, or Google Slides), and video production software, such as Apple's iMovie for Mac computers or Microsoft Windows' MovieMaker for PCs, are all relatively easily available for teachers. To further understand how to create CAP-S, a link to a completed CAP-S is listed in Table 19-1. Keep in mind that CAP-S provides a way for UDL implementation through the use of IT. It is a way to keep students engaged with relevant content in a method that is relevant to them. It is also a way to represent the content in a clear manner as an alternative method to traditional instruction.

Table 19-1. Alignment of HLPs and Resources for Evidence-Based Practices

EBP SUPPORT WITH HLP 19	RELATED HLPS	RESOURCES
Augmentative and alternative communication	1, 3, 4, 9, 12, 15, 16, 18	https://www.asha.org/public/speech/disorders/aac/ https://youtu.be/zmsdLzQW5G0
Differentiated instruction	4, 6, 13, 17, 22	https://intensiveintervention.org https://www.understood.org/en/articles/differentiated-instruction-what-you-need-to-know
Universal Design for Learning	4, 13, 14, 15, 16, 17, 18, 20, 21, 22	https://udl-irn.org/about/ https://www.novakeducation.com/blog/what-is-udl-infographic
Video modeling	9, 13, 15	Video Modeling https://youtu.be/Q_-Z6zzMQ50 Video Self-Modeling https://youtu.be/rKKh-a-2OJM https://youtu.be/GS9IFwuM_G8 https://files.eric.ed.gov/fulltext/ED605910.pdf
Assistive technology-accessibility software and materials	12, 13, 15	https://www.isetcec.org/ https://iris.peabody.vanderbilt.edu/module/at/#content
CAP-S	12, 13, 14, 15, 16	Creating CAP-S https://vimeo.com/24179998 Example of CAP-S https://vimeo.com/24169318 https://vimeo.com/24168886

What Is Assistive Technology?

The Individuals with Disabilities Education Improvement Act (IDEIA, 2004) defines an AT device as any item, piece of equipment, or product system, whether acquired commercially off the shelf, modified, or customized, that is used to increase, maintain, or improve functional capabilities of a child with a disability. AT devices and services are considered necessary in helping to bridge the gap between a student's strengths, limitations, and current skills and the expectations of educational and community contexts (Douglas et al., 2012).

Unlike IT, AT may or may not be available for everyone. AT, by design, is intended specifically to meet the individual needs of students with specific needs. By definition, AT "includes any item, equipment, or product system, whether commercially acquired off the shelf, modified, or customized that is used to increase, maintain, or improve the functional capabilities of a child with a disability" (Hashey et al., 2020). Some AT is simply not appropriate for just any student but rather meets a specific need for a targeted student. The beauty of some AT being accessible to all students is the ease in which the SWD can be included in the general education program with minimal disruption or unwanted attention.

AT devices are commonly divided into categories of low-tech, medium-tech, and high-tech. Low-tech AT includes items that can be easily obtained, inexpensive, usually do not require batteries or electricity (e.g., raised line paper, pencil grips), and that can be made available to all students. Medium-tech AT includes items that usually require batteries and are digital (e.g., talking calculators, digital recorders). High-tech AT includes items that have sophisticated features, meet specific needs of the user, and include rechargeable batteries (e.g., iPads, voice-activated software). AT helps students in all areas of disability.

Research into the positive impact of AT for individuals with disabilities has been conducted over the last decade in a variety of areas, from teaching reading comprehension skills (Stoner et al., 2011) and phonics (Ahlgrim-Delzell et al., 2016) to teaching communication skills (van der Meer et al., 2011) utilizing AT devices such as Apple iPads, iPods, and iPhones, computers, specialized software, and other devices. To consider AT for students, teachers must evaluate the usefulness of new technology that is available for classroom use based upon student needs. They must make informed instructional decisions that use professional wisdom, are grounded in research, consider the student's IEP goals, and advocate for support from administration in the implementation of technology (McLeskey et al., 2017).

The SETT Framework

SETT is an acronym that stands for student, environment, tasks, and tools. It was developed to help collaborative teams create student-centered, environmentally sound, and task-focused tool systems (Jones et al., 2021). It includes considering: (a) the needs of the student, (b) the environment in which the AT will be utilized, (c) the task the student will be required to complete, and finally (d) the AT tools that would be best for the student when considering the student, environment, and the tasks. See Table 19-2 for some questions to ask to evaluate which AT might be beneficial for an SWD.

Quality Indicators of Assistive Technology

The primary purpose of Quality Indicators of Assistive Technology (QIAT) is "to guide thoughtful development, provision, and evaluation of AT services for students with disabilities" (QIAT Leadership Team, 2015, p. 4). The authors provide eight areas for implementation considerations. Each of the eight areas contains five to seven indicators that further clarify characteristics for implementation. The QIAT aligns well with the HLPs; after all, the HLPs are the *purposeful how* needed to implement EBP as the QIAT provides a purposeful guide to the implementation of AT (QIAT Leadership Team, 2015). These eight QIAT areas align with the HLP as noted in Table 19-3.

Accessibility Software and Materials and Assistive Technology

AT enables SWD to engage in learning activities they may otherwise not have been able to. For example, in English Language Arts, AT devices help students to respond in a variety of ways. For example, presentation software (e.g., PowerPoint, Keynote) can be used to teach sight words (Yaw et al., 2011) with students able to use text-to-voice software to hear the word read to them and can then read it back after hearing it. Text-to-voice or voice-to-text systems, such as what is available in Google applications or through other software companies, allow students to have material read to them by highlighting text and clicking play or by hitting a record button and speaking into a device's microphone while the application types the words being spoken. A writing assignment may be challenging for a student with dysgraphia to complete with a pencil and paper, but scribing while the software types it may enable the student to successfully complete the writing task. Additionally, most software currently available allows students to use spell check or grammar checkers to correct spelling and

Table 19-2. Considerations Using the Student, Environment, Asks, and Tools Framework

WHAT WILL BEST SUIT THE STUDENT?	
Considerations:	*Ask:*
Student	1. What does the student need to be able to do independently and cannot yet do? 2. What are the specific needs that contribute to this concern? 3. What are the student's interests? 4. What are the student's current abilities related to these concerns?
Environment	1. Where will the student use the AT? 2. How many students are in the environment? 3. What are the attitudes or expectations of the individuals in that environment? 4. What challenges for access might exist?
Task	1. What activities require AT to complete? 2. What AT will support the student in achieving educational goals? 3. What are the specific demands for each environment in which the student participates? 4. What are the functional demands on the student?
Tools	1. What AT will help the student accomplish goals? 2. How feasible is training and consistent use of the AT for the student to use independently? 3. What training is needed by stakeholders and the student? 4. Will the student be better able to meet goals with this device?

grammar errors. These options provide opportunities for ease in implementing UDL for all students. For example, there are plenty of applications that can be purchased for practicing academic skills and some have corrective and positive feedback already built in, such as providing auditory positive feedback for correct answers or corrective feedback when students make an error (Seok et al., 2015).

Augmentative and Alternative Communication

One type of AT is AAC, defined as including all forms of communication used to express thoughts, needs, wants, and ideas when the student is unable to respond verbally, due to the disability. It is vital that students who have complex communication needs have access to the AAC that best meets their needs. Like with AT, AAC is also described in terms of low-, medium-, and high-tech. However, AAC is divided into the additional categories of aided and unaided. Unaided AAC includes sign language or gesturing that can be performed without supplementary devices. Aided AAC requires individuals to use external tools such as low-tech picture cards, high tech computer software, and tablets with AAC apps that may include speech generation (Ganz et al., 2019).

Table 19-3. Quality Indicators of Assistive Technology Alignment With High-Leverage Practices

QIAT IMPLEMENTATION AREA	HLPS
1. Consideration of AT devices and services	1, 2, 3, 4, 11
2. Assessment of AT needs	4
3. Documentation of AT in a student's IEP	1, 2, 13
4. Implementation of AT	8/22, 13, 15, 16, 18
5. Evaluation of the Effectiveness of the AT	11
6. AT transition	11
7. Administrative support	1, 2
8. AT training and professional development	1, 2

The Picture Exchange Communication System (PECS) is a form of AAC wherein students use pictures as a way to communicate, request, and express ideas. There are three goals of PECS: teach students to initiate conversations, approach a communication partner, and utilize the pictures to communicate a clear message. There are six phases that begin with learning to exchange single picture cards for objects up to students learning to answer questions and make comments (Cihak et al., 2012). PECS can increase students' independent initiations and requests (Cihak et al., 2012). Using VM to teach students a new skill (i.e., acquisition of PECS) allows students to acquire the skills quicker than without the use of VM, and teachers can be confident in their interventions as both are evidence-based (Cihak et al., 2012).

Students can use their high- or low-tech AAC devices to respond during instruction such as selecting answers on an iPad, with an appropriately chosen app, to signify their response (Ahlgrim-Delzell et al., 2016; Hudson et al., 2015). The use of AAC allows participants to communicate and demonstrate their learning in a meaningful way, chosen to match the user's abilities and needs.

What Does HLP 19 Look Like in a K-12 Classroom?

Elementary Example

Mr. France is a third-grade teacher with 22 students. Some of his students are Ramón, with an LD in reading; Paul and Emma who love video games; and Amanda who has cerebral palsy, which impacts her fine motor skills and verbal communication. When Mr. France begins to plan his next science unit, he knows that designing it using the principles of UDL will help all students access the curriculum in meaningful ways. He decides to enlist students Paul and Emma to help him create a video game using Tynker, a coding app for kids that his class has been learning to use. Paul and Emma work together well and have mastered multiple levels of Tynker coding. He gives them the key terms and concepts for the unit and asks the digital literacy coach (HLP 1) to work with them to create this game. Mr. France knows that Ramón prefers to use audiobooks to reduce the cognitive load reading independently requires, so he puts in a request to the school librarian for the books to be used in the unit and gets those downloaded on the school iPads for Ramón, as well as for any student who would prefer to listen to the text rather than read it. Mr. France knows it will be difficult for Amanda to maneuver through the video game due to her underdeveloped fine motor skills, so he makes sure they have an adaptive Bluetooth-enabled switch to connect to the iPad so Amanda has a larger surface by which to navigate through the video game independently. Finally, he knows that questioning techniques will be used in both large and small groups, so he works with the speech-language pathologist to make sure responses necessary for answering questions specific to the science concepts are programmed into Amanda's voice output communication aid so she will be able to initiate and respond to questions. Of course, Amanda will have access to previously learned core vocabulary and phrases for responding and initiating that are already programmed into her device, so she can respond in a wide variety of ways. Mr. France worked with the special educator, Ms. Britton, to ensure that key terms were identified and written in kid-friendly definitions. Ms. Britton developed a vocabulary sheet with a picture cue for each word, the word, and the kid-friendly definition. This was sent out to all students as a Google Doc (with text-to-speech capability) on their iPads and also printed out to put in their science notebooks, allowing them two ways to access the documents. Mr. France and Ms. Britton wrote an introductory letter for all parents but with Amanda's parents in mind, particularly, so they would be aware of the new buttons on her communication device and be able to practice terms with her. With this pre-planning complete, Mr. France is in pretty good shape with all the materials ready and preparations made for all his students to participate meaningfully in this upcoming unit. The collaboration between Mr. France and Ms. Britton also provided the appropriate information for Ramón and Amanda to practice content-area vocabulary, an IEP goal for them both. This allows both Mr. France and Ms. Britton to gather appropriate data for IEP goal monitoring. The monitoring is naturally embedded into classroom activities, quizzes, and projects so it does not feel like any extra work on either teacher's part.

Secondary Example

Mrs. King is a ninth-grade social studies teacher who is beginning a unit on economics. She has 22 students in her sixth-period social studies class. In her class, she has three students with specific needs related to disability. Payton has attention-deficit/hyperactivity disorder, inattentive type (ADHD), and an LD in math. Henry is a student with a physical disability who uses a speech-generated AAC device to communicate and a power wheelchair for mobility. Jay is gifted and talented in leadership. As part of the unit, Mrs. King would like to plan for the sixth-period class to sell donuts in the afternoon to teachers and staff in the building. She knows that this will require students to move around the building and in the classroom, handle money and keep detailed accounts, and reflect daily on what was learned.

In consultation with the gifted and talented teacher, she has decided to appoint Jay as the coordinator of the deliveries. Jay is a natural leader, but procrastinates on his work sometimes, so this will motivate him since others will depend on him daily. She wants Henry and Payton to fully participate in the activities, too, so she works with her co-teacher (HLP 1), Mrs. Nellie, a special education teacher. Together, they decide to divide students into groups of four to six who will each take part in the donut deliveries every week in rotation for 3 weeks. She has Henry and Payton in separate peer groups with general education students who will be good peer models. Jay will be coordinating groups and activities along with the teachers and other students.

After Mrs. Nellie and Mrs. King collaborated and spent a few days assessing (HLP 4) the most appropriate vocabulary to program and teach Henry to use on his AAC device, they taught the peers (HLPs 1, 8, and 15) how to assist Henry in communicating with the teachers and staff when selling the donuts. For Payton, Mrs. Nellie suggested that she have access to her tablet to reference the calculator and have reminders set for her of tasks needing to be completed during deliveries. As they consulted about using the classroom iPads, it was decided that each group would have access to two tablets when completing deliveries as this would benefit all students to have reminders of tasks they needed to complete, a calculator for confirming change needed, and a spreadsheet app for keeping the accounts.

Summary

In this chapter, we discussed how HLP 19 helps teachers to consider AT and IT in their instruction. When combined with other HLPs (Collaboration, Assessment, Social/Emotional/Behavioral, and Instruction), HLP 19 can be even more powerful in implementation. Table 19-1 illustrates how EBPs and HLPs work together and provides the reader with resources for further understanding of how to implement each EBP. Collaboration is essential when determining what IT, AT, or AAC is necessary for meeting the needs of students. Collaboration with speech-language pathologists, general educators, and technology experts helps special educators to fully understand a student's needs and the range of technologies available (HLP 1). With collaboration, there is also support in making decisions to choose technology that will best meet the needs of students and allow them full participation in the school and the community. Collaboration with a student's family (HLP 3) helps educators to learn the goals the family has for their child and what technology has been used in the past, what worked, and what did not.

Collaboration could not occur without assessment from multiple sources (HLP 4). Determining the student's abilities, desires, and needs through various assessments allows for wise decision-making. Ongoing assessment allows for determining if the appropriate technology is being used or if a change should be made (HLP 6). AT, including AAC, provides a student with a voice when they may not otherwise have one, allows for mobility throughout the school and community, and facilitates social interaction (HLP 9). It will be no surprise that IT and AT certainly impact instruction as this HLP is part of the Instruction HLPs. Curriculum can be adapted for specific needs (HLP 13), and allow for the acquisition of strategy use (HLP 14). Teaching the use of AT can involve explicit instruction (HLP 16), while IT could help to provide intensive instruction that students need for making progress (HLP 20). Several IT applications provide positive and constructive feedback to help students to develop skills in a self-paced manner (HLP 22). HLP 19 illustrates again, as with the other HLPs, that the HLPs are best implemented in concert with others for the most benefit to students.

Chapter Review

1. Describe HLP 19 in your own words.
2. Describe the difference between an assistive technology "device" and assistive technology "services" according to IDEIA, 2004.
3. Make a list, with examples, of how instructional technologies can be embedded in instruction.
4. Define the term "assistive technology" or "AT."

References

Ahlgrim-Delzell, L., Browder, D. M., Wood, L., Stanger, C., Preston, A. I., & Kemp-Inman, A. (2016). Systematic instruction of phonics skills using an iPad for students with developmental disabilities who are AAC users. *The Journal of Special Education*, *50*(2), 86-97. https://doi.org/10.1177/0022466915622140

Boon, R. T., Urton, K., Grünke, M., & Ko, E. H. (2020). Video modeling interventions for students with learning disabilities: A systematic review. *Learning Disabilities: A Contemporary Journal*, *18*(1), 49-69.

CAST. (2018). *Universal design for learning guidelines version 2.2*. http://udlguidelines.cast.org

Chang, C. J., Lo, C. O., & Chuang, S. C. (2020). Applying video modeling to promote the handwriting accuracy of students with low vision using mobile technology. *Journal of Visual Impairment & Blindness*, *114*(5), 406-420.

Cihak, D. F., Smith, C. C., Cornett, A., & Coleman, M. B. (2012). The use of video modeling with the picture exchange communication system to increase independent communication initiations in preschoolers with autism and developmental delays. *Focus on Autism and Other Developmental Disabilities*, *27*(1), 3-11. https://doi.org/10.1177/1088357611428426

Collins, B. C. (2012). *Systematic instruction for students with moderate and severe disabilities*. Paul H. Brookes Publishing.

Cox, A., & AFIRM Team. (2018). *Video modeling*. National Professional Development Center on Autism Spectrum Disorders, FPG Child Development Center, University of North Carolina. http://afirm.fpg.unc.edu/video-modeling

Dazzeo, R., & Rao, K. (2020). Digital Frayer model supporting vocabulary acquisition with technology and UDL. *TEACHING Exceptional Children*, *53*(1), 34-42. https://doi.org/10.1177/0040059920911951

Delisio, L. A., & Bukaty, C. A. (2019). UDL and assistive technology: Utilizing technology beyond mere accessibility. In W. W. Murawski & K. L. Scott (Eds.), *What really works with universal design for learning* (pp. 157-171). Corwin.

Diorio, R., Bray, M., Sanetti, L., & Kehle, T. (2019). Using video self-modeling to increase compliance to classroom requests in students with autism spectrum disorder. *International Journal of School & Educational Psychology*, *7*(1), 145-157.

Douglas, K. H., Wojcik, B. W., & Tompson, J. R. (2012). Is there an app for that? *Journal of Special Education Technology*, *27*(2), 59-70.

Ganz, J., Hong, E. R., Leuthold, E., & Yllades, V. (2019). Naturalistic augmentative and alternative communication instruction for practitioners and individuals with autism. *Intervention in School and Clinic*, *55*(1), 58-64. https://doi.org/10.1177/1053451219833012

Green, K. B., Stuckey, A., Towson, J. A., Robbins, S. H., & Bucholz, J. L. (2020). Special education preservice teacher knowledge of mathematics methods: The effects of content acquisition podcasts (CAPS). *Journal of Special Education Technology*, *35*(3), 145-154.

Hashey, A. I., Kaczorowski, T. L., & Di Cesare, D. M. (2020). *High-leverage practices (HLPs) in special education: Instruction guide #6*. Council for Exceptional Children.

Hudson, M. E., Zambone, A., & Brickhouse, J. (2015). Teaching early numeracy skills using single switch voice-output devices to students with severe multiple disabilities. *Journal of Developmental and Physical Disabilities*, *28*(1), 153-175. https://doi.org/10.1007/s10882-015-9451-3

Individuals With Disabilities Education Improvement Act, 20 U.S.C. § 1400 (2004).

Israel, M., & Williams, J. (2022). Use assistive and instructional technologies. In J. McLeskey, L. Maheady, B. Billingsley, M. T. Brownell, & T. J. Lewis (Eds.), *High leverage practices for inclusive classrooms* (2nd ed., pp. 295-312). Routledge. https://doi.org/10.4324/9781003148609-26

Jones, B. A., Peterson-Ahmad, M., Fields, M., & Williams, N. (2021). Training preservice teachers to match assistive technology to student needs. Journal of Special Education Technology, *36*(4), 271-283 https://doi.org/10.1177/0162643420918337

Kellems, R. O., & Morningstar, M. E. (2012). Using video modeling delivered through ipods to teach vocational tasks to young adults with autism spectrum disorders. *Career Development and Transition for Exceptional Individuals*, *35*(3), 155-167.

Kennedy, M. J., Kellems, R. O., Thomas, C. N., & Newton, J. R. (2014). Using content acquisition podcasts to deliver core content to preservice teacher candidates. *Intervention in School and Clinic*, *50*(3), 163-168. https://doi.org/10.1177/1053451214542046

Kennedy, M. J., Rodgers, W. J., Romig, J. E., Mathews, H. M., & Peeples, K. N. (2018). Introducing the content acquisition podcast professional development process: Supporting vocabulary instruction for inclusive middle school science teachers. *Teacher Education and Special Education*, *41*(2), 140-157. https://doi.org/10.1177/0888406417745655

Koch, K. (2017). Stay in the box! Embedded assistive technology improves access for students with disabilities. *Education Sciences*, *7*(4), 82.

Mayer, R. E. (2008). *Multimedia learning* (2nd ed.). Cambridge University Press.

McLeskey, J., Barringer, M.-D., Billingsley, B., Brownell, M., Jackson, D., Kennedy, M., Lewis, T., Maheady, L., Rodriguez, J., Scheeler, M. C., Winn, J., & Ziegler, D. (2017). *High-leverage practices in special education*. Council for Exceptional Children & CEEDAR Center.

McNamara, S. W. T., Wilson, K. R., & Petersen, A. (2020). Content acquisition podcasts' impact on pre-service teachers' understanding of language and disability. *British Journal of Educational Technology*, *51*(6), 2513-2528.

McNiff, M. T., Maag, J. W., & Peterson, R. L. (2019). Group video self-modeling to improve the classroom transition speeds for elementary students. *Journal of Positive Behavior Interventions*, *21*(2), 117-127.

Novak, K. (2019). UDL: An introduction from pizza parlor to the world. In W. W. Murawski & K. L. Scott (Eds.), *What really works with universal design for learning* (pp. 1-18). Corwin.

QIAT Leadership Team. (2015). *Quality indicators for assistive technology: A comprehensive guide to assistive technology services*. CAST Professional Publishing.

Reyes, E. N., Wood, C. L., Walker, V. L., Voggt, A. P., & Vestal, A. R. (2021). Effects of video self-modeling and system of least prompts on completion of transitional routines for a student with extensive support needs in inclusive settings. *Journal of Positive Behavior Interventions*, 1-11. https://doi.org/10.1177/1098300721990291

Rowland, A., Smith, S. J., & Lowrey, K. A. (2020). Connecting evidence-based writing strategies with readily available technology solutions. *TEACHING Exceptional Children*, *53*(3), 253-255. https://doi.org/10.1177/0040059920954778

Sadler, K. M. (2019). Video self-modeling and functional behavior assessment to modify behaviors in students with autism spectrum disorder and intellectual disabilities. *Education and Training in Autism and Developmental Disabilities*, *54*(4), 406-419.

Seok, S., DaCosta, B., & Min Yu, B. (2015). Spelling practice intervention: A comparison of tablet PC and picture cards as spelling practice methods for students with developmental disabilities. *Education and Training in Autism and Developmental Disabilities*, *50*(1), 84-94.

Stoner, J. B., Beck, A. R., Dennis, M., & Parette, H. (2011). The use of instructional technology in direct vocabulary instruction. *Journal of Special Education Technology*, *26*(3), 35-46.

Teacher Education Division. (n.d.). *Content acquisition podcasts.* https://tedcec.org/sites/default/files/2020-12/Content_Acquisition_Podcasts.pdf

van der Meer, L., Kagohara, D., Achmadi, D., Green, V. A., Herrington, C., Sigafoos, J., O'Reilly, M. F., Lancioni, G. E., Lang, R., & Rispoli M. (2011). Teaching functional use of an iPod-based speech-generating device to individuals with developmental disabilities. *Journal of Special Education Technology*, *26*, 1-11.

Yaw, J. S., Skinner, C. H., Parkhurst, J., Taylor, C. M., Booher, J., & Chambers, K. (2011). Extending research on a computer-based sight-word reading intervention to a student with autism. *Journal of Behavioral Education*, *20*(1), 44-54. https://doi-org.go.asbury.edu/10.1007/s10864-010-9118-1

When Is Instruction Intensive Enough?

Ruby L. Owiny, PhD

HLP 20

Provide intensive instruction.

INTRODUCTION

The highest level of intensive instruction is implemented in Tier 3 of any tiered system of support. Response to Intervention (RTI), Positive Behavioral Interventions and Supports (PBIS), and Multi-Tiered System of Supports (MTSS) all rely on evidence-based core curriculum in which all students receive high-quality instruction at Tier 1. Statistically, about 20% of students will need more intense instruction than what Tier 1 offers universally. Tier 2 provides greater intensity for instruction and meets the needs of about 15% of students placed there. However, approximately 5% need the highest level of intensive instruction. This chapter focuses on Tier 3 interventions and explains how teachers can make sound decisions to identify validated interventions. This chapter also addresses the cognitive process necessary for success in school and life. Some students need academic or behavioral interventions along with cognitive strategies or sometimes only need cognitive strategies to be successful.

Owiny, R. L., & Cornelius, K. E. *The Practical Guide to High-Leverage Practices in Special Education: The Purposeful "How" to Enhance Classroom Rigor* (pp. 285-301).

CHAPTER OBJECTIVES

- Define intensive instruction.
- Determine how to make instructional decisions to provide intensive instruction to students with disabilities.
- Identify evidence-based practices that support implementation of intensive instruction.

KEY TERMS

- **cognitive flexibility:** Ability to shift seamlessly between ideas, thoughts, people, or activities.
- **cognitive load:** How much information working memory can hold at one time.
- **executive functioning:** Cognitive functions that aid students in organizing, regulating, initiating, or monitoring learning; includes cognitive flexibility, inhibitory control, and working memory.
- **inhibitory control:** The ability to focus on appropriate stimuli over a period of time without becoming distracted by other stimuli around them.
- **Multi-Tiered System of Supports (MTSS):** Holistic approach to support academic, behavior, physical, mental, and social needs.
- **Positive Behavioral Interventions and Supports (PBIS):** Tiered approach to primarily supporting behavior needs.
- **Response to Intervention (RTI):** Tiered approach to primarily supporting academic needs in the English Language Arts and mathematics; alternative approach to diagnosing specific learning disabilities.
- **working memory:** Information held in the brain for a short period of time for the purpose of completing a task.

Intensive instruction is a key component of Multi-Tiered System of Supports (MTSS), Response to Intervention (RTI), and Positive Behavioral Interventions and Supports (PBIS) in Tier 3 instruction (Harn et al., 2015). Special educators frequently deliver the instruction at Tier 3 and must be well trained in how to identify validated practices, learn how to implement those practices with fidelity, determine the level of intensity a student needs, determine how to best group students, and how to address cognitive processing and executive functioning needs as part of the services provided. This chapter examines these features of a well-planned, thorough intensive intervention at Tier 3.

It is important to note that RTI is a multi-tiered approach, focused on academic achievement with the goal to ensure high-quality Tier 1 instruction for all students, fill in learning gaps, and support students in Tier 2 with more intensive instruction and supports with Tier 3 providing the most intensive supports. This approach is also intended to serve as an alternative to the "wait to fail" model and the discrepancy model of identification of students with learning disabilities. When students do not make adequate progress in Tiers 1 and 2, needing intensive supports from Tier 3, students are then frequently, but not necessarily, identified with a learning disability and placed, with parent permission, into special education.

On the other hand, PBIS is also a multi-tiered approach, focused on behavioral support. Each tier functions similarly to those of RTI with Tier 3 being a place to potentially identify a student with an emotional or behavioral disorder and subsequent placement in special education. A key distinction in PBIS is an emphasis on community support and collaboration between students, their families, and their schools. Interventions are designed to address the function of a student's behavior to individualize a plan to support the student well.

Whereas RTI focuses mainly on academic support and PBIS primarily focuses on behavioral support, MTSS is more comprehensive and focuses support on academic needs, and behavioral needs, along with supporting the whole student, which includes physical, mental, and social supports as well.

The frameworks within MTSS, RTI, and PBIS are designed to include evidence-based interventions at all tiers with progress monitoring occurring to ensure appropriate progress toward academic (MTSS and RTI) and behavioral (MTSS and PBIS) standards, while MTSS also includes supports for other aspects of a student's well-being. Each framework includes universal screening to determine student progress across the school population and identify those students who might need Tier 2 supports. Continuous progress monitoring and assessment are also keys to each framework, as is providing more supports as students need more intensive interventions in Tiers 2 and 3 while still receiving core instruction at Tier 1.

For the purpose of this chapter, the focus is on Tier 3 interventions with evidence-based practices (EBPs) that can generally be used regardless of the framework a particular school has implemented. A student may need intensive support at Tier 3 for reading or math instruction. Another student may benefit from intensive support at Tier 3 for behavioral needs, while another student may need mental health interventions at Tier 3 to support their overall well-being and coping. Regardless of the area of need, this chapter speaks to Tier 3 in general.

What Is HLP 20?

High-Leverage Practice (HLP) 20—"*Provide intensive instruction*" is defined by McLeskey et al. (2017) as:

> Teachers match the intensity of instruction to the intensity of the student's learning and behavioral challenges. Intensive instruction involves working with students with similar needs on a small number of high priority, clearly defined skills or concepts critical to academic success. Teachers group students based on common learning needs; clearly define learning goals; and use systematic, explicit, and well-paced instruction. They frequently monitor students' progress and adjust their instruction accordingly. Within intensive instruction, students have many opportunities to respond and receive immediate, corrective feedback with teachers and peers to practice what they are learning. (p. 89)

When considering intensive instruction, we must use the tiered pyramid model as an illustration. The three-tiered systems commonly implemented in schools, PBIS, MTSS, and RTI, are tiered systems. Each tier involves more intensive instruction as one "moves up the tiers." Tier 1 instruction is designed for all students to receive high-quality, research-based instruction in academics (RTI), behavior (PBIS), or both (MTSS) that is proactive and preventive. When a student is not making appropriate progress (approximately 20% of students do not), they may receive more focused instruction at Tier 2 with the expectation that knowledge gaps can be quickly remediated, and Tier 2 intervention will no longer be needed. As one might imagine, that is not always the case for every student. About 5% of students will need Tier 3 instruction due to their more intense needs. HLP 20 addresses the intensive instruction necessary at Tier 3 for students to be most successful. The familiar pyramid is provided for you in Figure 20-1.

HLP 20 involves the need for teachers to match the intensity of instruction to the intensity of the learning or behavioral needs and grouping students with similar needs to provide instruction on the most important skills that are clearly defined and important for building a strong academic or behavioral foundation. Systematic, explicit, well-paced instruction that involves frequent progress monitoring and data-driven decision-making is key to HLP 20, and to the success of students in Tier 3. When delivering intensive instruction, teachers ensure that students have many opportunities to respond and provide immediate, corrective feedback to students as they practice skills. Peers also are provided with opportunities to provide feedback to one another.

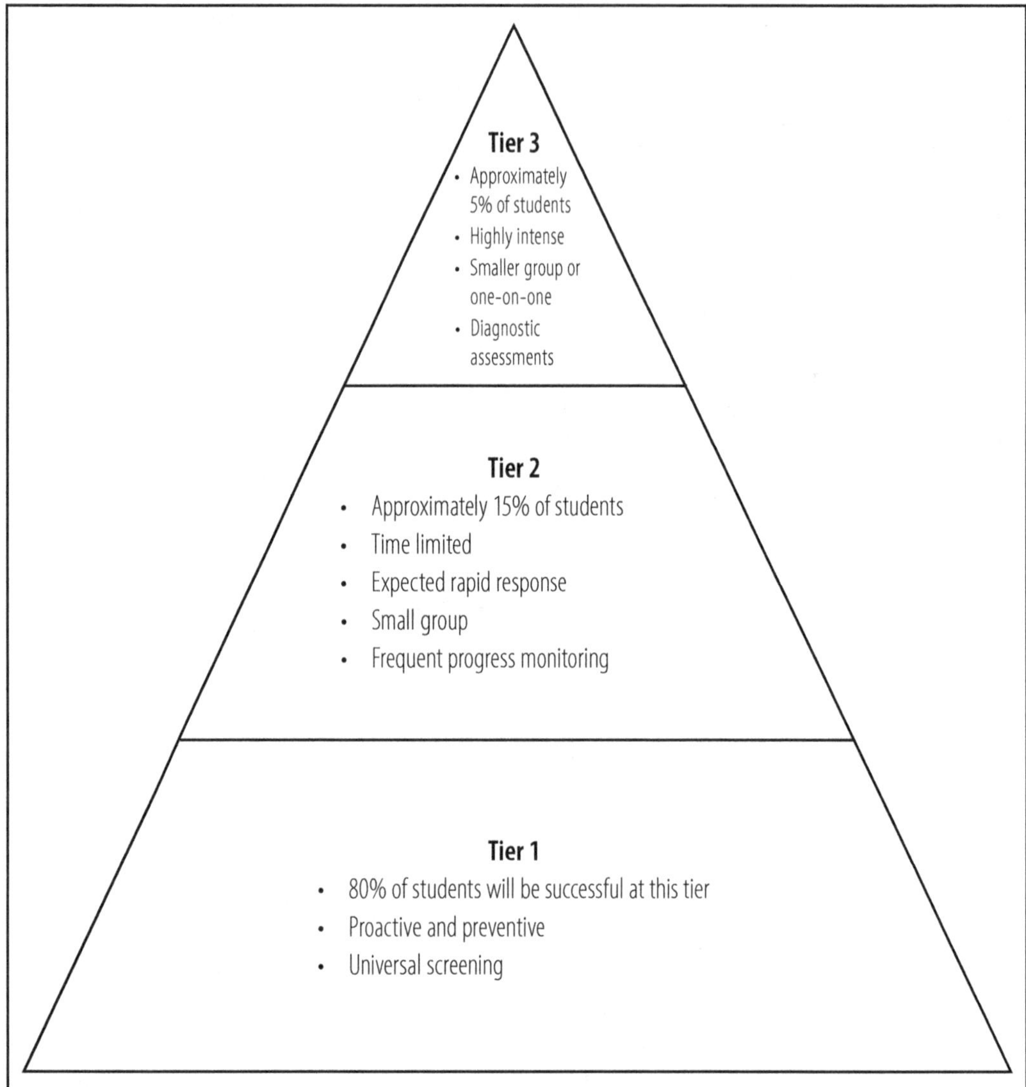

Figure 20-1. Tiered systems of support: RTI, PBIS, or MTSS. (Adapted from Harn, B., Basaraba, D., Chard, D., & Fritz, R. [2015]. The impact of schoolwide prevention efforts: Lessons learned from implementing independent academic and behavior support systems. *Learning Disabilities: A Contemporary Journal, 13*[1], 3-20.)

It is important, as a special educator, to understand how to deliver intensive instruction as this is highly likely to be the type of instruction that your students with disabilities (SWD) will need, at least for part of their school day. This chapter will help you to know what considerations should be taken and how to prepare for intensive instruction.

How Is HLP 20 Connected to Other HLPs?

It is no surprise, at this point, if you have read any of the other chapters in this book, that HLP 20 works in tandem with other HLPs; they all share intertwined functionality. If you have read Chapters 1 through 19 or glanced ahead to Chapters 21 or 22, you may even have some thoughts on where the connections lie. Shall we see if your ideas are in line with the HLPs listed below?

As you might imagine, collaboration is involved in providing intensive instruction. Educators cannot afford to live on their own proverbial islands, they need the expertise of each other to best meet the needs of students. The varying types and levels of expertise in a school are akin to an orchestra. An orchestra would not sound as it should if, one day, the violins suddenly decided to carry the melody on their own and the flutes walked off the stage. All instruments, playing together with their correct parts, creates a beautiful symphony. The same is true for educators. Collaborating with colleagues and parents (HLPs 1 and 3) is vital for student success. To make sound instructional decisions for students, assessment data must be gathered from a range of sources (HLP 4). These data together help to form a robust picture of the student's strengths and weaknesses to inform how instruction should be designed to allow the student to achieve at higher levels.

Frequent progress monitoring is a vital part of intensive instruction to have appropriate data to make informed instructional decisions to adjust instruction as necessary to meet student needs (HLP 6). Teaching social skills (HLP 9) can require intensive instruction and is part of the PBIS and MTSS framework related to pro-social behavior. In HLP 10, a behavior support plan (BSP) can require intensive behavioral instruction to support the student. In fact, it should be expected that teaching a replacement behavior involves intensive instruction to help the student become proficient in changing an aberrant behavior to a positive, pro-social one.

In the description of intensive instruction, it is stated "use systematic, explicit, and well-paced instruction" (McLeskey et al., 2017, p. 89). Thus, HLPs 12, 15, and 16 are practices that should be included in the delivery of intensive instruction. Clearly defined learning goals relate to HLP 11 while HLPs 18 and 22 provide opportunities to respond and immediate, corrective feedback, respectively. These practices are major components of intensive instruction. Cognitive strategies are also important when providing intensive instruction. These involve both cognitive and metacognitive strategies (HLP 14). Finally, it is important for students to generalize or transfer their learning to demonstrate a deep understanding, indicating learning will endure across settings and time (HLP 21). Students need on-going corrective and positive feedback to become fluent in performing a skill and for that transference to occur. With positive feedback, students are more willing to take risks and try out skills in new places. For information on what these HLPs are, and EBPs recommended to implement them, please refer to the appropriate chapter for more information. This chapter is focused on the "how to" of intensive instruction in terms of matching intensity to needs, determining how to identify a validated supplemental intervention, and the cognitive processing strategies necessary to embed in intensive instruction to ensure higher levels of student achievement.

How Do I Match the Intensity of Instruction to the Intensity of a Student's Needs?

When a student is not achieving appropriately with only Tier 1 supports, they should be provided with more intensive instruction at Tier 2 with highly effective instruction. There is a percentage of students who, statistically, will need more intensive Tier 3 supports, due to a disability or other reasons. Therefore, as special educators, it is vital to understand how to determine intensification for instruction at Tier 3, the level you are most likely tasked with teaching.

If a student is receiving appropriate instruction in an evidence-based curriculum and that curriculum is being taught with fidelity, the teacher must analyze progress monitoring data to determine next steps (Fuchs et al., 2014). It is important to monitor progress on a frequent and regular basis to ensure that the student is making adequate progress. In the event the student is not making adequate progress at Tier 2 and moves to Tier 3 or is in Tier 3 but needs even more intensive support, decisions must be made for how to intensify instruction.

There are two main categories for intensifying instruction: organizational or instructional (Wanzek et al., 2020). Organizational decisions include a student spending more time receiving the intervention, receiving instruction in a smaller group, or both. When analyzing assessment data, ask questions such as, "How intense is this need?" If progress is incredibly slow, as in a graph of the data show a nearly flat slope, then the need is quite intense. This leads to further questions that require an answer, "Does the student need more time during the school day or week in intervention?" and "Does the student need a smaller group or one-on-one instruction to make greater progress?" If the answer is yes to one or both of these questions, teachers must decide how much more time and which size of group will likely best suit the student's needs.

For making instructional delivery intensifications, Wanzek et al. (2020) explain six methods: (a) more explicit instruction; (b) more systematic instruction; (c) increasing opportunities for responding, practice, and review; (d) providing more specific and corrective feedback; (e) providing instruction in cognitive processing strategies; and (f) including direct instruction for transfer of skills. For the first four of these methods, this book has full chapters brimming with EBPs for implementing those methods/HLPs. In subsequent sections of this chapter, cognitive processing strategies and teaching for maintenance and generalization (or transfer) of skills will be more fully described.

For the purposes of this section of the chapter, let us discuss how to make these decisions. It will likely come as no surprise that making decisions based on data is critical for determining how best to intensify instruction. An EBP, commonly implemented for HLP 20, is data–based individualization (DBI). For full implementation of DBI, see Walker and Kearns (2022) for a description. For our purposes, we are honing in on analysis of data for decision-making. Using the DBI process, this chapter assumes a high-quality, research-based program, implemented with fidelity and appropriate progress monitoring, is established and data are collected from multiple sources. From there, decisions are determined through examination of the assessment data. The team should analyze the data together with the purpose of hypothesizing why the student is not making expected progress (Walker & Kearns, 2022). Once the hypothesis is determined, adaptations to the intervention can be decided. See Figure 20-2 for a sample flowchart for hypothesizing and decision-making that includes Wanzek et al.'s (2020) recommended organizational and instructional considerations.

How Do I Work With My Team to Determine a Validated Supplemental Intervention?

An essential component of all tiers in any tiered system of supports, whether it is PBIS, RTI, or MTSS, is the implementation of validated supplemental interventions with fidelity. Therefore, choosing a validated intervention and receiving adequate training is the foundation of a strong tiered system of supports. One may ask how to determine which interventions are validated and which are not, and which are validated to support the specific population of students they are working with. This section of the chapter will provide guidance for selection of validated interventions to meet the needs of individual students.

There are several resources one can search for evidence-based interventions, which are summarized in Table 20-1. These resources are fantastic when the specific intervention one is searching for is actually included on that particular bank of interventions. However, how does one validate interventions that are not included in those resources? Keep reading. A framework follows.

Leko et al. (2019) provide helpful insight into how to evaluate an intervention to determine if it is an EBP. There are three levels of evidence for evaluating interventions with EBP being the top, ultimate level with a high level of rigorous research supporting the effectiveness of the intervention. The other two levels, research-based and emerging practice, have fewer research studies supporting positive outcomes for SWD as is the case for research-based interventions, while emerging practice is based in theory, practitioner expertise, or "good ideas" with little to no research to back up the effectiveness of the intervention. Interventions used at Tier 3 for intensive instruction must be based on the highest level of evidence. Students with the most involved needs and greatest learning gaps can ill afford to be taught with interventions that "just sound good." They deserve to be taught using EBP.

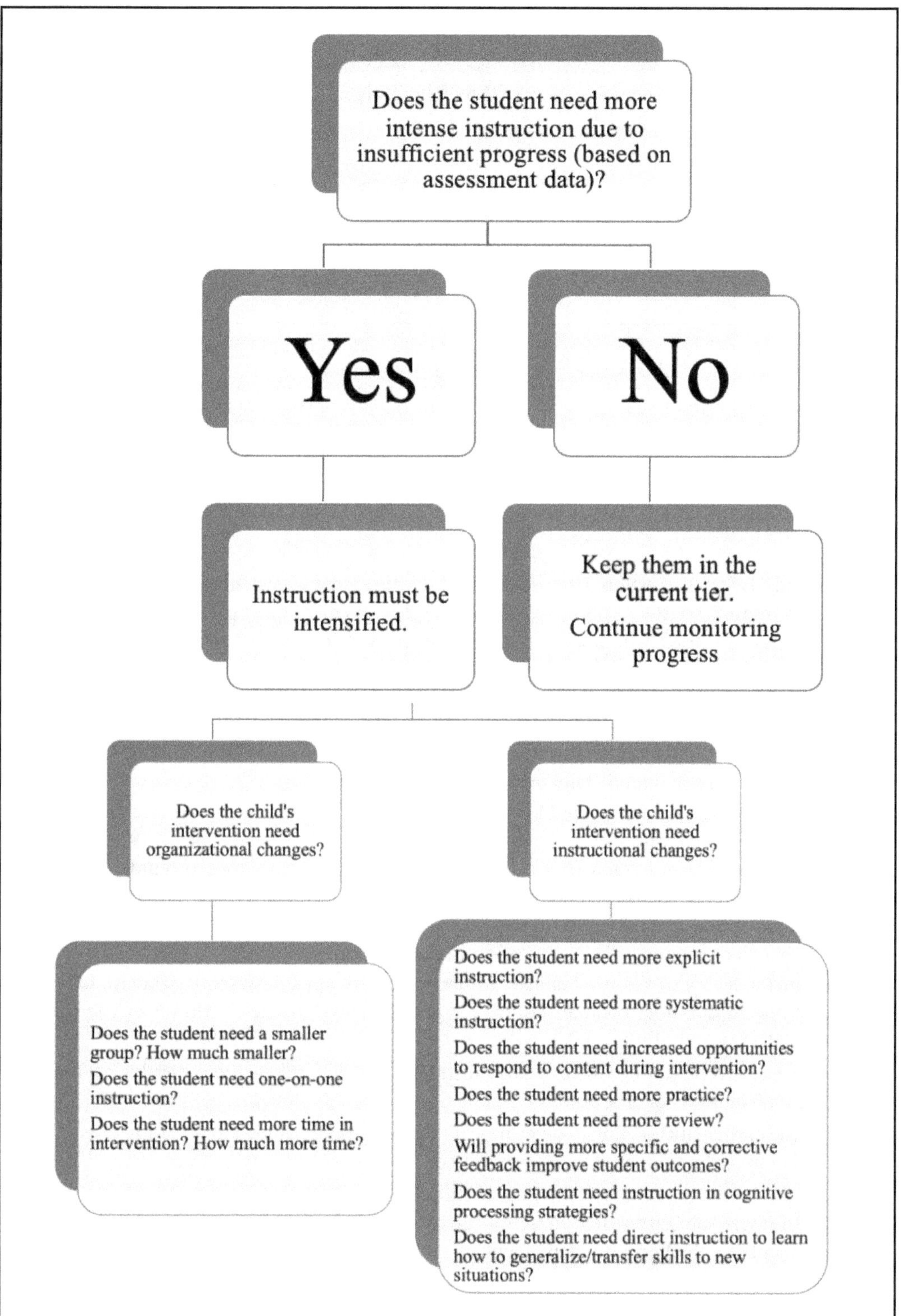

Figure 20-2. Making sound decisions to intensify instruction.

TABLE 20-1. RESOURCES FOR EVIDENCE-BASED INTERVENTIONS

SOURCE	WEBSITE	DESCRIPTION
What Works Clearinghouse	https://ies.ed.gov/ncee/WWC	Provide reviews of research to determine which studies meet rigorous standards and provide summaries of the findings for practitioner use in determining evidence-based interventions.
National Center on Intensive Intervention	https://intensiveintervention.org/	Provide resources for stakeholders to ensure quality implementation of intensive intervention using DBI.
Center on PBIS	https://www.pbis.org/pbis/what-is-pbis	Provide resources for implementation of the PBIS framework in schools.
RTI Action Network	http://www.rtinetwork.org/	Provide resources for stakeholders to implement RTI on a large-scale.
IRIS Center	https://iris.peabody.vanderbilt.edu/	Provide a variety of resources for meeting the instructional and behavioral needs of students.

This leads us to the question: How does one determine what is evidence based? First, search for intervention from one of the resources listed in Table 20-1, as mentioned prior. If the intervention is not listed in one of those resources, it is possible the intervention has not gone through analysis yet or the studies included in the analysis did not provide adequate evidence at the time the analysis was conducted. It is possible new data have been published but a new analysis has not been updated. At this point, school personnel have a decision to make, forgo the intervention for another one or follow these steps to identify if the research validates the practice. This is a more time-intensive process for school personnel but could reap dividends.

Below are the steps recommended for conducting an analysis of available research to determine if the intervention is likely an EBP. These steps are synthesized from Leko et al. (2019), the National Center on Intensive Intervention (n.d.) document on clarifying questions to guide intervention changes, and VanDerHeyden's (n.d.) recommendations. For ease in analyzing data identified in the research articles found, you may want to use Table 20-2 as an organizational tool for taking notes to reference when determining if the intervention is, indeed, evidence based.

1. Conduct a search in Google Scholar, a library database, or a university database for the intervention in question. Include settings for peer-reviewed articles, within 5 to 10 years, and included a research study.
2. Download several recent articles whose abstracts show the independent variable for the study is the intervention being reviewed.
3. Scan the participants section to determine if the population included in the study resembles the population of the student(s) being considered.
4. Scan the results to identify if the intervention impacted student achievement in a significant way. In single-subject research design, a functional relationship between the intervention (independent variable) and the dependent variable (the data collected) should be identified. In group research studies, statistics should show a strong effect size (e.g., the closer to 1.0 the more impact of the intervention on the dependent variable).
5. Read through the discussion. Does the impact of the intervention as it relates to training needed, the process to implement, and the impact on student achievement make this a viable intervention for you, as the implementer, and your student/s? If others, such as paraeducators, could also be implementers, consider the complexity of the intervention and the feasibility of transference of implementation to other school personnel (Leko et al., 2019).

Table 20-2. Template to Analyze a Research Article

Intervention: ______________________				
Guiding Question: Is this intervention effective for ______________________?				
Academic Research Literature: Use the grid below to document the literature identified. This will help summarize the literature to help determine if this intervention is evidence-based.				
Article	**Participants**	**Results**	**Benefits/Concerns**	**Feasibility**
Title Authors	What was the population included in the study? Disabilities? Race/ethnicity? Grade level? Gender? Socioeconomic status?	Statistical results, quantitative themes/ shifts, social validity/ significance	What benefits were identified? What concerns for implementation might you have?	Is the benefit worth the cost? Is it possible to implement with fidelity? Can appropriate personnel be trained? Could this intervention benefit the student/s in question? How much time is needed?

6. Research the cost. Is the cost viable? In other words, can your school or district afford to purchase the curriculum necessary to implement the intervention and afford training for implementation fidelity?
7. How much time per day/week is necessary for the implementation of this intervention? Is this feasible given the potential "return on investment"? In other words, does the time involved lead to a high probability of accelerated student growth? Is the time necessary able to be provided in the student's school day? Are there personnel available to provide the intervention for the time required?

What Are the Cognitive Processing Strategies I Need to Embed in My Intensive Instruction?

Students may experience intensive intervention needs based on cognitive processing deficits that hinder academic achievement. Therefore, cognitive strategy instruction is important (Bryant et al., 2021). Peterson et al. (2019) state addressing cognitive processing as a further method for intensifying instruction. These processes can be related to executive functioning needs (e.g., working memory, inhibitory control, or cognitive flexibility) or in other cognitive processes such as goal setting or self-monitoring. Additionally, self-talk can be taught to help students choose and apply strategies they already know and to maintain attention to task. Keep in mind, also, that students may need supports to reduce cognitive load (e.g., graphic organizers, cue cards, mnemonic devices) to fully perform the tasks needed for academic success. This section describes each of these needs through the lens of EBPs and with the caveat that cognitive processing strategies should not be taught in isolation, but rather in conjunction with academic instruction as well (Bryant et al., 2021; Wanzek et al., 2020). For more information about cognitive strategies, read Chapter 14.

Executive functioning skills guide the processing that occurs when a student organizes, regulates, initiates, or monitors learning (Walker & Russell, 2019). Another way of stating it is "a group of processes that allows individuals to self-regulate the ways in which they interact with their environment" (Strosnider & Sharpe, 2019). These skills, controlled by the brain, serve a function similar to a GPS. Imagine a road trip without having any idea how to navigate to your destination except knowing how to get out of your neighborhood. You would make many wrong turns, stops and starts, and end in frustration and possibly not make it to your destination at all or arrive considerably late and disheveled. The GPS organizes your trip, gives you step-by-step directions, a visual map, and can even pause to give you a pitstop for gasoline or a lunch break. Executive functioning performs a similar purpose for learning and daily living. When all skills are fully developed, a student can retain information, manage multiple pieces of information to synthesize into new ideas, and hold that information in storage (working memory). They can also focus on appropriate stimuli over a period of time without becoming distracted by other stimuli around them (inhibitory control), and they can shift between thoughts, ideas, concepts, people, or activities with ease (cognitive flexibility; Owiny et al., 2023). Imagine a student who is disorganized in their thinking, cannot retain information provided to them just minutes ago, or they are unable to shift their thought processes to another task easily. This is like your road trip. No GPS, little to no direction, and loads of frustration. Many SWD have comorbid executive functioning deficits as well, which can significantly impact reading and mathematics, two primary areas targeted by tiered systems of support (e.g., RTI or MTSS; Bryant et al., 2021; Owiny et al., 2023; Wanzek et al., 2020). There are multiple models for describing and grouping executive functioning skills; for the purposes of this chapter, they are grouped into working memory, inhibitory control, and cognitive flexibility as Walker and Russell (2019) and Owiny et al. (2023) categorize them.

Working Memory

Working memory includes auditory memory and visual-spatial memory to efficiently hold and use relevant information to complete a task (Strosnider & Sharpe, 2019). Digital or hard copy calendars can be one way to support working memory. Train students to use a calendar to record due dates, exams, quizzes, readings, extracurricular activities, etc., to refer to it for planning their evening or their week and to remember what is coming up to help plan for accomplishing the task. Mnemonics, as discussed in Chapters 13, 14, 15, and 21, are also EBPs that support working memory (Strosnider & Sharpe, 2019). Some further strategies to support working memory are presented in Table 20-3 for a starting point or for new ideas to support this area of executive functioning skills. Additionally, it is important to consider how to reduce cognitive load. Teachers can help reduce the cognitive load for a student by providing a strategy to help the student temporarily hold the information from an external source (Owiny et al., 2023). Consider a trip to the supermarket to purchase ingredients to make meals from a prepared meal plan. One typically creates a list of the items needed to go to the supermarket and bring home the necessary ingredients. How often might one forget an item on the list if the list is left at home or the device the list is created on loses power while in the supermarket? Creating the list serves as a strategy and becomes an external source to hold the information long enough to do the shopping. Once shopping is over, the list no longer needs to be remembered. Parts of it may go back in storage, such as remembering a 15-lb bag of flour was purchased, and others will be forgotten, such as the bag of chocolates purchased to hide in one's desk.

Table 20-3. Strategies to Support Executive Functioning Skills

EXECUTIVE FUNCTIONING SKILL	STRATEGY	DESCRIPTION
Working Memory	Provide examples	Helps solidify learning and allows a student to see what the end goal looks like
	Mnemonics	Images, rhymes, or acrostics to help remember vocabulary, lists, etc.
	Graphic organizers	Helps students to organize their learning and remember steps to a process or key components to a concept
	Highlighting	Helps students to visually clue in on the most important information and ignore extraneous information
Inhibitory Control	Goal-setting	Helps students to remain focused on a goal to completion
	Cue cards	Lists steps or processes for using a strategy or completing a task; helps students to stay on-task to task completion
	Short breaks	Brief breaks in learning, such as a restroom break, getting a drink, or talking with a friend helps to reduce cognitive load, give a break, and help the student to refocus to continue with the task at hand
	Movement	Quick exercise or activity to break up long periods of sitting
Cognitive Flexibility	Self-talk	Students can use questions to reflect on what they need to do, what they are learning, how they are feeling, etc. and use a strategy, such as deep breathing, making a list, etc. to help them get or stay on track
	Self-advocacy	Students communicate with teachers, in an appropriate manner, what is working for them, what they need help with, what is frustrating them, etc.
	Note-taking template	Helps students to shift from listening to writing notes
	Checklists	Break down a process or task into individual steps

Inhibitory Control

Diamond (2013) states that inhibitory control or inhibition is, "controlling one's attention, behavior, thoughts, and/or emotions to override a strong internal predisposition or external lure." In other words, inhibitory control allows a student to ignore stimuli that would otherwise distract them from the task at hand. The stimuli can come from within the student, such as a thought of, "This is too hard. Let me ask to go to the bathroom." Stimuli can come from without, such as a class of students running outside to the playground and the student can observe the chaos from their desk by the window. Learning to control those impulses to remain focused and on-task is important for long-term academic achievement. A strategy to develop inhibitory control can include self-monitoring. Self-monitoring can help students to focus on such tasks as reading the full directions before completing a task and ensuring they have all the materials needed to complete that task. Self-monitoring is important for comprehension to help students focus on a short passage, check their understanding, and quickly review what they have read before moving on (Walker & Russell, 2019). Self-monitoring can also help with controlling one's behavioral impulses. Students can be taught to monitor their behavior with a quick check-in, such as are my hands, feet, and materials in my own space and are my eyes on my own work. A checklist can help students monitor their work or behavior as well. For example, a common acronym for writing mechanics is CUPS for Capitalization, Usage, Punctuation, and Spelling. A checklist could be laminated and stuck in the pocket of each student's writing notebook. When finished with a writing piece, they can pull that out, along with a marker and an old, clean sock (to use as an eraser for a clean card, ready for the next use) and quickly check their work. Alternatively, a student could have a cue card for monitoring their on-task behavior, such as what might be used in a PBIS framework for Tier 1 or 2. The card could say, "During this class period, I (1) followed directions, (2) completed assigned tasks, and (3) completed my assigned work." The student could record a response by circling a smiley face, straight face, or sad face for yes, mostly, or no, respectively. See Table 20-3 for more suggestions to support inhibitory control.

Cognitive Flexibility

Cognitive flexibility involves a student's ability to seamlessly shift between different demands, ideas, or even tasks. It is evident in a difficulty to multi-task, such as listening and taking notes, difficulty leaving a task unfinished to move on to another task, or to change direction while completing a task such as in reading comprehension. Table 20-3 provides further ideas for supporting cognitive flexibility beyond the example below.

Shifting from a recall question, such as "Who was the main character?" to a higher-level synthesis question, such as "Analyze the role of Benvolio and Tybalt in the plot of *Romeo and Juliet*" requires cognitive flexibility. Making this shift can be difficult for students. Modeling the thought process of how to make these cognitive shifts makes an implicit process more explicit. For example, a teacher could conduct a think-aloud about what they think about while completing a comprehension task. A sample script could be something like this:

> I have a question to answer about the main character in the closing argument in the trial of Tom Robinson that I've just read from *To Kill a Mockingbird*. In this passage, Atticus Finch is giving the closing speech, therefore I know that he is the main character. Now, I need to analyze how his morality is evidenced in his speech. This takes a mental shift in thinking, not a recall level, but a synthesis level. I need to look at both the broader message and the minute details. Atticus calls out Mayella Ewell, the accuser, in his closing argument by saying,
>
> > I say guilt, gentlemen, because it was guilt that motivated her. She has committed no crime, she has merely broken a rigid and time-honoured {sic} code of our society, a code so severe that whoever breaks it is hounded from our midst as unfit to live with. She is the victim of cruel poverty and ignorance, but I cannot pity her: she is white. She knew full well the enormity of her offense, but because her desires were stronger than the code she was breaking, she persisted in breaking it. She persisted, and her subsequent reaction is something that all of us have known at one time or another. She did something every child has done—she tried to put the evidence of her offense away from her. But in this case she was no child hiding stolen contraband: she struck out at her victim—of necessity she must put him away from her—he must be removed from her presence, from this world. She must destroy the evidence of her offence {sic}. (Lee, 1960, p. 231)
>
> From this passage, I can use evidence from the text. Mayella broke a cultural norm, not a law. As we read on through the passage, Atticus does not want her to be punished, but to acknowledge what she did wrong to prove Tim Robinson's innocence. Not only would this help his client, Tim, but it would help the community heal from the lie she told, leading to intense pain in the community.

This think-aloud serves as just one example for supporting cognitive flexibility. Playing games that require shifting, such as crossword puzzles, logic games, or even riddles and brain teasers, help students to develop more flexible thinking. Table 20-3 provides more examples to implement in the classroom.

What Does HLP 20 Look Like in a K-12 Classroom?

Elementary Example

Mary and James are teacher candidates assigned to Gator Elementary School for their field experience. They have been partnered with Ms. Kamm the school intervention specialist as their mentor teacher. The candidates have discussed the RTI framework in many of their courses and are currently enrolled in an elementary literacy methods class. They are excited to have a chance to implement what they are learning in their preparation program. The candidates had an initial meeting and school tour last week, but today they are "on the clock."

Teachers at Gator Elementary School administer curriculum-based measurements (CBMs) to assess reading and math skills three times a year. Ms. Kamm has the results from the universal screening and comes into the classroom with the results from the first-grade students' reading assessment. She shares the student scores with Mary and James and asks them to identify students that could be viewed as "struggling" learners. The candidates compare the scores with the assessment benchmark norms and highlight the students who score below the 40th percentile as being at "some risk" and students who scored below the 20th percentile as "at risk." Ms. Kamm is pleased at their knowledge and the process they used to identify the students. She then shares a list of students that teachers have already said they wanted to "watch" more closely; she asks the candidates to compare the lists. There are a few "outliers"; a couple of students scored high, yet their teacher had them noted with concerns. Ms. Kamm said she would address those unique students, but she wanted the candidates to focus on where the highest needs were and could they see common patterns. James noticed right away that three students scored only a 1 or 2 on the letter naming assessment. Mary said she was more concerned with students who scored low on the phonemic segmentation assessment. Ms. Kamm, pleased with the students' comments and dialogue, asked them to identify students they would recommend for Tier 2 intervention support, and could they by these assessments group the students into small homogeneous groups (HLP 17) and use the assessment data (HLP 6) to suggest an intervention. James very quickly said, "Before we group students based on this assessment, should we also look at the intervention curriculum for a placement test and the observation notes from the teachers?" Mary added, "We can't just place students in groups based on these scores, we need multiple pieces of information (HLP 4) just like James said." Ms. Kamm praised the candidates for their thoroughness. They continued to pour over the results and discuss next steps. Ms. Kamm shared the two interventions they should use as a starting point. The candidates made a list of the students who would need a placement test for which intervention and connected with the general education teachers to schedule time with the students.

Once the candidates had all the information, they grouped students and started planning their intervention lessons. They worked with Ms. Kamm and the general education teachers to schedule times for the students with the greatest need, those classified as "at risk," to receive pull-out interventions. They also planned with the general education teachers to deliver interventions to the students with "some risk" in the general education classroom during the reading instruction. Mary and James planned together but then alternated where each of them delivered the interventions. In their lesson planning, they noted the multiple practice opportunities (HLP 18) students would have and would build in extra just in case they were needed, noting specific feedback (HLP 22) prompts they might offer students. They also planned their lessons using systematically designed instruction (HLP 12), and each lesson was planned using an explicit instruction (HLP 16) template. They also determined that after every fifth intervention day they would administer the CBMs again to monitor progress and record the students' response to the intervention.

Each week they met together and discussed how the lesson delivery went. They analyzed student data and discussed the results with Ms. Kamm. Ms. Kamm would also observe their lesson delivery and provide them feedback on their performance. The candidates would use their graphs of student data and their notes from the lesson plans to make changes to instruction as needed. Sometimes that meant more practice opportunities, sometimes it meant changing student groupings, or sometimes even the pacing of the lessons. After a few lessons with these changes, they would determine if the student responded to the intensity and if not was it time to change the intervention. As the students made progress, the candidates grew more confident in their abilities.

Secondary Example

Mrs. Wingate is new to Dakota High School; she is nervous about adjusting her instruction without the CBM progress monitoring data she used at the elementary school. She teaches both in a co-taught classroom and a resource room. As she reads through the English standards and examines the grade-level curriculum, she asks her co-teacher, Ms. Appleton, how she monitors students. Ms. Appleton is unsure about the question, "I just use the district benchmark assessment at the end of each quarter." She admits she does not have an ongoing practice but feels she must be doing "okay" because most of her students are passing the benchmark assessments. Mrs. Wingate decides to look at the district pacing guide and see how the benchmarks are aligned with the curriculum.

She does see the alignment, but these are only quarterly summative assessments. She will need something different to gauge the changes she may need to make if she needs to intensify her instruction. She sits down with the curriculum standards and the district essential standards. She knows she will be teaching vocabulary and reading comprehension to meet student individualized education program goals. She creates her own CBMs (HLP 6) for these skills using the guidelines from a text (Reed et al., 2012) used in her preparation program. She uses novels from the grade-level curriculum to help construct the CBMs and makes sure to embed a question on the assessment about various strategies the students use to answer the questions (HLPs 14 and 21).

Every time she administers a CBM, she records the score and compares it to the previous score. She tracks the progress and uses information from the assessment to adjust her instruction. Sometimes this means she reteaches a strategy for students to monitor their own learning, or she introduces a new strategy specific to the students' errors. She will often collaborate with colleagues about ways to intensify her instruction. This helps her with pacing and adding more practice. However, when she needs more strategies, and even a new intervention, she uses the resources like those in Table 20-1.

Summary

As this chapter explained, it takes a team of stakeholders to make wise decisions for how to best intensify instruction for students (HLP 3). Often, while the general educator provides instruction at Tier 1, the special educator provides more intensive instruction at Tier 3. This requires collaboration (HLP 1) in and of itself, let alone the team making decisions on how best to provide intervention for students. To make those wise decisions on how to intensify instruction, stakeholders need data from multiple sources to analyze to determine next steps (HLPs 4 and 6).

When intensification of instruction for behavioral needs is present, it is important to remember HLP 9, teach social skills, and HLP 10, conduct functional behavioral assessments and develop behavior support plans. Students with behavioral needs must participate in intensive instruction to develop the social skills they need to successfully navigate school and community social situations. Additionally, the Instructional HLPs provide a method for intensifying instruction, not only for academic skills, but also for behavioral skills. These HLPs (11, 12, 14, 16, 18, and 22) provide students with the focused instruction they need to meet their goals because their teachers know how to prioritize those goals (HLP 11), they know how to systematically and explicitly design instruction to help students reach their goals (HLPs 12 and 16), and instruction in metacognitive and cognitive strategies (HLP 14) help students develop the executive functioning skills and metacognition necessary for academic and behavioral success. Finally, by offering multiple opportunities for students to respond to their learning (HLP 18), they can acquire skills more quickly to meet their goals. With positive and corrective feedback (HLP 22), students can learn how to perform the skills with proficiency and develop competency in generalizing, or transferring, their knowledge to novel settings or across time.

Combining these HLPs to design more intensive instruction through organizational or instructional methods helps ensure students learn at higher levels. Knowing how to identify and implement interventions that are validated provides teachers with confidence that the practices and curriculum they are using, when implemented with fidelity, will give students what they need to be successful in meeting learning outcomes. Finally, combining academic and behavioral interventions with cognitive strategy instruction helps students to develop the internal processing skills necessary to organize their learning, efficiently use material stored in working memory, and maintain attention to task through to completion. The principles included in HLP 20 set students up for higher levels of achievement when implemented with high levels of fidelity. Additionally, Table 20-4 provides suggested resources for the EBPs mentioned in this chapter while showing the connection of the EBPs that help to implement HLP 20 with other HLPs. This connection of EBPs to other HLPs serves as a reminder of the interconnected functionality of the HLPs, which when used in tandem, provide the most benefit to students.

Chapter Review

1. Describe HLP 20 in your own words.
2. Explain how to intensify support for a student with intensive academic or behavioral needs at Tier 3.
3. Describe how you could identify a validated intervention. Practice by using Table 20-2 to analyze a research article.
4. List the three areas of executive functioning.
5. Choose one example of support for each of the three areas of executive functioning. How does each example support that particular area of executive functioning? How could you implement that strategy in your classroom?

Table 20-4. Alignment of HLPs and Resources for Evidence-Based Practices

EBP SUPPORT WITH HLP 20	RELATED HLPS	RESOURCES
Explicit instruction	9, 10, 11, 16	https://intensiveintervention.org/resource/What-Every-Educator-Needs-to-Know-About-Explicit-Instruction https://highleveragepractices.org/hlp-16-use-explicit-instruction
Systematic instruction	9, 10, 11, 12	https://highleveragepractices.org/hlp-12-systematically-design-instruction-toward-specific-learning-goal https://youtu.be/YDRsmxPA-J8
Opportunities for responding, practice, and review	9, 10, 11, 18	https://highleveragepractices.org/hlp-18-use-strategies-promote-active-student-engagement https://files.eric.ed.gov/fulltext/ED591076.pdf
Specific and corrective feedback	9, 10, 11, 22	https://ctb.ku.edu/en/table-of-contents/advocacy/encouragement-education/corrective-feedback/main https://intensiveintervention.org/explicit-instruction-supporting-practices-feedback-pace
Cognitive processing strategies	9, 10, 11, 14	https://iris.peabody.vanderbilt.edu/module/dbi1/cresource/q2/p06/ https://cft.vanderbilt.edu/guides-sub-pages/metacognition/
Direct instruction	9, 10, 11, 15	https://www.nifdi.org/15/index.php?option=com_content&view=article&id=52&Itemid=27 https://youtu.be/KmxHsC3DvAo
Data-based instruction	1, 3, 4, 6, 9, 10, 11, 20	https://otus.com/guides/data-driven-instruction/ https://iris.peabody.vanderbilt.edu/module/dbi2/cresource/q2/p08/

References

Bryant, D. P., Bryant, B. R., & Shin, M. (2021). Mathematics interventions. In D. P. Bryant (Ed.), *Intensifying mathematics interventions for struggling students.* Guilford Press.

Diamond, A. (2013). Executive functions. *Annual Review of Psychology, 64,* 135-168.

Fuchs, D., Fuchs, L. S., & Vaughn S. (2014). What is intensive instruction and why is it important? *TEACHING Exceptional Children, 46*(4), 13-18.

Harn, B., Basaraba, D., Chard, D., & Fritz, R. (2015). The impact of schoolwide prevention efforts: Lessons learned from implementing independent academic and behavior support systems. *Learning Disabilities: A Contemporary Journal, 13*(1), 3-20.

Lee, H. (1960). *To kill a mockingbird.* Grand Central Publishing.

Leko, M. M., Roberts, C., Peyton, D., & Pua, D. (2019). Selecting evidence-based practices: What works for me. *Intervention in School and Clinic, 54*(5), 286-294. https://doi.org/10.1177/10534512188191

McLeskey, J., Barringer, M.-D., Billingsley, B., Brownell, M., Jackson, D., Kennedy, M., Lewis, T., Maheady, L., Rodriquez, J., Scheeler, M. C., Winn, J., & Ziegler, D. (2017). *High-leverage practices in special education.* Council for Exceptional Children & CEEDAR Center.

National Center on Intensive Intervention. (n.d.). *Clarifying questions to create a hypothesis to guide intervention changes: Question bank.* https://intensiveintervention.org/sites/default/files/Clarifying_Questions_Hypothesis_508.pdf

Owiny, R. L., Walker, J. D., Boothe, K. A., & Lohmann, M. J. (2023). Creating expert learners in remote classrooms: Strategies & technology to support executive functioning skills. In P. Griswold, M. Urgolo-Huckvale, & K. McNeal (Eds.), *Engaging students with disabilities in remote learning environments.* IGI Global.

Peterson, A., Danielson, L., & Fuchs, D. (2019). Introduction to intensive intervention. In R. Z. Edmonds, A. G. Gandhi, & Danielson, L. (Eds.), *Essentials of intensive intervention.* Guilford Press.

Reed, D. K., Wexler, J., & Vaughn, S. (2012). *RTI for reading at the secondary level.* Guilford Press.

Strosnider, R., & Sharpe, V. S. (2019). *The executive function guidebook: Strategies to help all students achieve success.* Corwin.

VanDerHeyden, A. (n.d.). *Examples of effective RtI use and decision making: Part 1 overview.* RTI Action Network. http://www.rtinetwork.org/essential/assessment/data-based/examples-of-effective-rti-use-and-decision-making-part-1-overview

Walker, J. D., & Russell, V. (2019). UDL and executive functioning: Unlock the capacity for learning. In W. W. Murawski & Scott, K. L. (Eds.), *What really works with Universal Design for Learning.* Corwin Press.

Walker, M. A., & Kearns, D. (2022). Provide intensive intervention using data-based individualization. In J. McLeskey, L. Maheady, B. Billingsley, M. T. Brownell, T. J. Lewis (Eds.), *High leverage practices for inclusive classrooms.* (2nd ed.). Routledge.

Wanzek, J., Al Otaiba, S., & McMaster, K. L. (2020). *Intensive reading interventions for the elementary grades.* Guilford Press.

What Do I Need to Include so Students Maintain Their Learning, Not Only for Tomorrow, but Next Week, Next Year, and Forever?

Jennifer A. Sears, PhD
and Kyena E. Cornelius, EdD

HLP 21

Teach students to maintain and generalize new learning across time and settings.

INTRODUCTION

"When will I use this again in my life": the statement teachers of all ages hear repeatedly in their classrooms. How do we make what we are doing in our classrooms relevant across settings? As teachers, we inherently know exactly how students will use the information in the future. We know fractions relate to cooking, learning about text features will help in college, but the fact remains we need to teach students with disabilities explicitly how they can maintain and generalize these skills to other settings. In this chapter you will learn how to make teaching relevant, so students are able to not only maintain skills they have learned in your classrooms but to generalize these skills across settings.

Owiny, R. L., & Cornelius, K. E. *The Practical Guide to High-Leverage Practices in Special Education: The Purposeful "How" to Enhance Classroom Rigor* (pp. 303-313).

CHAPTER OBJECTIVES

- Identify multiple ways to maintain and generalize new learning across time and settings.
- Know how HLP 21 is connected to other HLPs and used alongside evidence-based practices to improve student outcomes.
- Explain the importance of explicitly teaching for maintenance and generalization to ensure student achievement.

KEY TERMS

- **generalizability:** Retaining a skill across setting, time, and people. Generalization happens when the learned skill occurs across these three dimensions without reteaching.
- **maintenance:** Retaining a skill over time.
- **mastery:** A level of understanding beyond proficiency, at least 95% accuracy toward achieving a goal.
- **proficiency:** A deep level of understanding, but perhaps with some room for improvement; a level of 75% to 90% accuracy toward achieving a goal.
- **self-directed:** Strategies students use to monitor and regulate their own behavior and learning.

If the purpose of school is to have students acquire knowledge in specific subject areas, then it is essential students are able to take what they have learned in school and maintain that knowledge and use it across different settings. How many times have we heard a student say "I don't know why I have to learn this, I will never use this in real life." As educators, our role is not only to teach our students specific skills but to also help them to maintain these skills and generalize them to "real life" situations. In order to do this, teachers must develop ways to help students to do this naturally, and one day, independently.

For students with disabilities (SWD), it is essential to develop skills students can utilize in order to maintain and generalize what they have learned across settings. However, this essential skill is one that is particularly challenging for SWD, especially for those identified with autism spectrum disorders and intellectual disabilities (McLeskey et al., 2017). Skill development for students follows the process of acquisition, fluency, maintenance, and then generalization. Maintenance is described as the ability to continue to utilize a skill after initial instruction has occurred. An example of this could be learning multiplication facts. After a student is taught how to multiply, and has become fluent in calculating multipliers, they are able to then maintain skills and use it outside of direct instruction. In order to show generalization, however, the student must be able to apply this skill to outside of the teaching environment. Keeping with the multiplication example, to generalize multiplication, a student is able to use this skill while shopping to know the cost of multiple items at the same price. Pretend the student is completing a worksheet in math class but no direct instruction is taking place, and they complete all of the problems accurately. They can do this time and time again in the classroom where they learned to multiply, even when months have passed since the instruction ended; this is maintenance. But, now say they are out with three friends and they want to each get a slice of pizza, at $3.00 per slice. They know for four slices of pizza they will need $12.00. This is generalization.

Some specific generalization strategies include sequential modification, training to generalize, natural maintaining contingencies, training with sufficient exemplars, training loosely, using indiscriminable contingencies, and program control stimuli (Markelz et al., 2022). Through the use of these individual strategies, students are able to generalize information across settings. For example, in the practice of training with sufficient exemplars, the teacher may reinforce a student raising their hand to ask a question instead of interrupting instruction. The teacher will then speak to other adults in the school (general education teacher, therapist, etc.) about the strategy and how the student is reinforced. In turn, when the student raises their hand in a different setting, they are reinforced in the same way. This will help the student in generalizing this specific strategy across settings.

The purpose of this chapter is for practitioners to understand how High-Leverage Practice (HLP) 21 relates to the other HLPs, understand evidence-based practices (EBPs) that will assist in students' maintenance and generalization of content and skills, and to offer resources to help practitioners implement HLP 21. By the end of this chapter, you will understand more about ways to intertwine several HLPs to implement the EBPs needed for student success. Without multiple HLPs in play at the same time, teachers cannot become effective practitioners. We hope by learning more about maintenance and generalization, you will start to see all the interconnected fibers that make HLPs a vibrant fabric of teaching and understand how these practices are vital to all student learning.

What Is HLP 21?

Beyond identifying HLP 21 as "*Teach students to maintain and generalize new learning across time and setting*," the team of researchers from the Council for Exceptional Children (CEC) and the Collaboration for Effective Educator Development, Accountability and Reform (CEEDAR) Center, gave a definition to help teachers understand the three major elements of the HLP. First, effective teachers are to use *specific techniques*, meaning a set of techniques with empirical research to justify their use, to teach students to exhibit their newly acquired knowledge and skills across time and setting. Second, teachers promote maintenance of skills by strategically using schedules of reinforcement, giving students numerous reviews and reteaching missing components of the skill or content; they also teach skills reinforced in the student's community, where they function beyond the classroom. Third, teachers do not naturally assume learning happens; they systematically design instruction and experiences and build in numerous examples requiring students to apply their learning over time and in other settings. When this is planned and implemented with consistency, students learn to use their new skills and demonstrate their new knowledge in places and situations other than the classroom where the skill or knowledge was taught, and they maintain these skills without ongoing instruction (McLeskey et al., 2017).

Purpose and Importance in Classroom Practice

Students must learn how to take what they are learning in one classroom and bring it into different settings. This could be bringing strategies learned that are behavioral into the home setting or academic into the work setting. Often, what is done in a classroom is done in isolation, and the four walls of the classroom are a sanctuary not to be disturbed. This way of thinking is what leads ineffective teachers to assume learning just naturally occurs. However, SWD are often in multiple settings throughout their school day. They may work with general education teachers, special education teachers, therapists, and paraprofessionals, along with other adults and students in the school. If we, as teachers, teach our students to take what they have learned in one setting and generalize it across other settings, the students are better able to make the connection outside of school as well. For example, if a student learns a strategy in their reading instruction to find essential information in text, the student can then take the strategy into a math class and find the essential information in a word problem. In turn, because students now possess this skill, they can take the same strategy into their social studies class and find essential information about a historical figure or into science class and find the essential steps in a lab activity. The student has demonstrated not only have they maintained this skill, but they have also generalized it across settings.

How Is HLP 21 Connected to Other HLPs?

When the HLPs were initially introduced by the CEC, they were intended to be practices that reflect the essence of effective practices in special education (McLeskey et al., 2017). These essential practices were meant to transcend content areas and be used in every classroom. Further, the practices were designed as a comprehensive list of practices used together, not to be considered in isolation as one practice implemented with students to teach something. Just as with many activities in life where you perform multiple actions at once, consider a sport: you grip a piece of equipment, watch at the ball, consider the other players, be aware of the playing field, etc. Each HLP depends on the others to be considered complete. HLP 21—"*Teach students to maintain and generalize new learning across time and settings*" is no exception. In fact, HLP 21 depends on many other HLPs to be implemented well.

In order for students to maintain and generalize their learning across settings, those who are in these other settings need to be part of the planning, teaching, and follow-through process of this, meaning the special educator must collaborate with other professionals to increase student success (HLP 1) as well as families (HLP 3). Educators, professionals, and families must all be on the same page and communicate effectively. For instance, if a student is working on a self-regulation skill of raising their hand in class, and this is being monitored by a special educator, the general educator whose class the student pushes into must know this is a targeted skill. Additionally, if there is a behavior plan the student is currently using to monitor this progress, the general educator, elective teachers, and others must know this is something the student is learning in order to celebrate the successes or to correct the incorrect components of the skill the student is currently learning.

As students learn new skills and knowledge, they need positive and constructive feedback to guide their learning and behavior (HLPs 8 and 22). Using the example from above, it is essential to be providing positive and constructive feedback to students while they are working on the maintenance and generalization phases of learning. Students must have frequent and specific feedback as they move forward in their learning.

Several of the HLPs in the domain of instruction are essential to success with HLP 21. These include HLP 11—"*Identify and prioritize long- and short-term goals,*" HLP 12—"*Systematically design instruction toward a specific learning goal,*" HLP 15—"*Provide scaffolded supports,*" HLP 16—"*Use explicit instruction,*" and HLP 20—"*Provide intensive instruction.*" In order to get students to own their learning and demonstrate it over time and in multiple settings, you must determine what skills or knowledge need to be taught and how you are going to break it up into learnable segments. You must systematically design instruction to see how those learnable segments build on each other, without having scaffolded supports in place, or fading support over time; students will not feel safe attempting new learning. This is another reason the best lesson plans include the template of explicit instruction: a model of the skill by the teacher, guided practice where the teacher and students perform the skill together, and unguided practice where the student performs the skill without the teacher. Of course, we can also agree SWD need intensive instruction designed with the specific learning needs and current performance levels in mind. Teachers are encouraged to use each of these HLPs, along with HLP 6, using student data to analyze and adapt instruction to improve student learning. Each of these chapters provide even more ways these HLPs are a vibrantly woven fabric. By designing instruction toward a goal you want your student to maintain, scaffolding the instruction (while using explicit instruction during intensive instruction), providing feedback, and collecting data on skill acquisition, students may be in a better place to maintain and generalize their learning across settings. See Table 21-1 for a list of these and other HLPs connected to HLP 11, along with several EBPs to promote maintenance and generalization.

Table 21-1. Alignment of HLPs and Resources for Evidence-Based Practices

EBP SUPPORT WITH HLP 21	RELATED HLPS	RESOURCES
Mnemonics	12, 15, 16	https://iris.peabody.vanderbilt.edu/module/ss2/cinit/#content
Self-Regulation • SRSD • Self-determination	14, 15, 16, 20	https://iris.peabody.vanderbilt.edu/module/sr/
Secondary Transition Planning	3, 4, 11, 14, 16	https://iris.peabody.vanderbilt.edu/module/tran/
Comprehension Strategies • Text Features • CSR	14, 15, 16, 20	https://iris.peabody.vanderbilt.edu/module/csr/ Capin, P., & Vaughn, S. (2017). Improving reading and social studies learning for secondary students with reading disabilities. *TEACHING Exceptional Children*, 49(4), 249-261.
Concrete-Representational-Abstract	14, 15, 16, 20	https://iris.peabody.vanderbilt.edu/module/math/#content
Plan for Generalization	6, 11, 12, 13, 14, 15, 16, 20	Burt, J. L., & Whitney, T. (2018). From resource room to the real world: Facilitating generalization of intervention outcomes. *TEACHING Exceptional Children, 50*(6), 364-372.

What Specific Techniques Should I Use to Systematically Plan for Maintenance and Generalization?

Maintaining and generalizing learning across settings allows students to take what they have learned in isolation in a classroom or therapist's office and take those same strategies into the "real world." These strategies range from behavior and social-emotional strategies to strategies learned in an academic classroom. For instance, think about the specific course work and the EBPs you learned as a student in your teacher preparation program, you were first taught them in a methods course, then when your professor felt you had a good understanding of the practices, you used them under supervision with students. After graduation, you started teaching in your own classroom, and now you implement these practices naturally. This is an example of maintaining and generalizing the information you learned. Some of the EBPs you learned are perfect to partner with HLP 21.

For instance, in your math methods course you probably learned about Concrete-Representational-Abstract (CRA; Mercer & Miller, 1992). The first thing you do as a classroom teacher is gather manipulatives so you can guarantee students learned the math concepts you wanted to teach. Then you plan the lessons using the manipulatives and scaffold the student learning until the students maintain and generalize their knowledge and can complete the calculations using the numbers in a traditional algorithm.

Another common teaching strategy is the use of mnemonics (Putnam, 2015). Mnemonics are memory devices. Believe it or not, we can trace mnemonics back to the ancient Greeks (Yates, 1966). Remember when you learned the colors of the rainbow: ROY G BIV means red, orange, yellow, green, blue, indigo, and violet. How about when you learned the order of operations: PEMDAS stands for parentheses, exponents, multiplication, division, addition, and subtraction? These are acronyms to help you learn and maintain something. There are also imagery mnemonics where you create a picture in your mind to help you remember; in Spanish the word for tiger is *tigre*, so you could picture a tiger that has turned *gray*. We also use rhymes and jingles. Remember this one: *i* before *e*, except after *c*, and when sounding like *a*, as in neighbor and weigh? Mnemonics are powerful for helping students to maintain and generalize information.

One EBP that uses mnemonics is Self-Regulated Strategy Development (SRSD; Harris et al., 2006). This specific strategy is used primarily in writing where students learn, use, and adopt strategies used by successful writers, for instance, POW-TREE (refer back to Chapter 14 for a full explanation of this strategy). The strategy itself is a multi-step process including:

- **P**—Pick an idea
- **O**—Organize my notes
- **W**—Write and say more
- **T**—Topic sentence
- **R**—Reasons
- **E**—Explanation
- **E**—Ending

For reading comprehension, a strategy frequently used is teaching students to rely on text features (Butler et al., 2021; Fischer et al., 2008). Begin teaching this strategy by explaining different text features such as examining the title, headings, key vocabulary, why some text or vocabulary is bold or in italics, and the purpose of headings. Next, teach students to use these features to understand and make meaning of the text they are about to read. Teachers subsequently build in opportunities for them to use these skills across content areas. When you tell students why they are doing these things, and show them their successes, they will start to use the strategy independently in other settings and for life (this "why" of learning is also related to the engagement principle in Universal Design for Learning).

Another EBP related to this HLP, as discussed earlier, is CRA for mathematics instruction (refer back to Chapter 15 for more on this strategy). Through this practice, students start with a concrete representation of the concept, often manipulatives such as fraction circles, dice, unifix cubes, etc. are used. Next the teacher takes the same concept and has students draw a representation of the concept. Finally, the student uses the algorithm and symbols to represent the mathematical concept. Throughout the process, review and reteaching are used to ensure the student continues to understand the concept. You can help students generalize this learning across settings, and in the community, by explicitly teaching (HLP 16) the use of math in cooking and shopping.

How Do Teachers Strategically Promote Maintenance of Skills?

While utilizing strategies with students is essential, these strategies cannot just be done in isolation, for students to truly maintain the strategies across settings, teachers must systematically promote the maintenance of these skills. This can be done in a number of ways throughout the school day.

One way teachers do this is by using schedules of reinforcement. The teacher starts with using continuous reinforcement where a behavior is immediately followed by reinforcement through the use of Class Dojo; for example, or any number of reward systems. Each time a student raises their hand they are given a "check" or "point" for doing this correctly. Gradually, the teacher begins to remove the reinforcer. However, when the teacher begins to see the behavior dwindling, reteaching and reviewing of the skill may need to be implemented.

This can similarly be done in the content areas as well. In math, students learn the concept of fractions. The teacher may use the EBP of the CRA strategy to teach the concept to the students where they begin with fraction circle manipulatives, move to drawing pictures, and eventually are able to add, subtract, multiply, and divide fractions. However, the question remains, "When will I use this?" Teachers can bring cooking into the instruction. Students must rework recipes and use the concepts previously learned in math class to compute measurements to complete a recipe. The teacher has now generalized the skill of fractions across settings and into the community, and the students show maintenance of the strategy. The same can be done with decimals where students begin shopping for items and using money.

Similarly in reading, the Collaborative Strategic Reading (CSR; Capin & Vaughn, 2017) strategy is used. In this strategy, the concepts of prior knowledge, vocabulary development, questioning techniques, and opportunities to practice are used to improve reading skills. By teaching this strategy in English Language Arts, the teacher can utilize the same skill in social studies or science. This strategy also explicitly teaches students the roles and responsibilities of collaborative work groups. Students are assigned a role, given cue cards with prompts to help facilitate discussions, and given time to practice before working with peers on a task. Within the groups, students "chunk" material, are given many opportunities to quickly state the main idea (e.g., "give the gist"), and when someone is incorrect a peer reviews and reteaches the material in student-friendly language. This strategy is not only valuable for reading in the English Language Arts classroom but throughout the student's academic career. How often are SWD placed in collaborative groups without instruction on what they are to do? Teachers think they are doing something good for the students, and building peer engagement, but without knowing what to do in a group, the student will feel lost and overwhelmed. We encourage you to explicitly teach students these roles, not only for CSR groups, but for every content class in which they participate. For more on purposeful grouping strategies, please see Chapter 17.

How Can Teachers Plan for Natural Experiences to Build Generalization?

The ability to use a skill across time, setting, and with multiple people is the goal of all learning, for students with and without disabilities. Think about this, would we ever want a typically developing student to learn mathematical concepts of addition and subtraction, and then never expect them to balance their personal finances? The same holds true for SWD. We just need to be more systematic and strategic about planning our instruction. Burt and Whitney (2018) provide special educators five easy steps, and convenient to the purpose of this book, all are aligned to HLPs. Step 1, define the range of settings where you would like to see the skill (HLPs 11 and 12). Think about all the classrooms and environments you want the student to use the skill. Step 2, determine the relevant stimulus activities, setting circumstances, and response examples (HLPs 13 and 15). List the activities, when and where they would be present, and consider the correct way for the student to use the skill. What supports will be needed for transferring this skill across settings? Step 3, think about where "overgeneralization" could occur. Just as you plan for examples and non-examples in explicit instruction (HLP 16), you should discuss settings where this skill may not be warranted and how the student will self-regulate (HLP 14). Step 4, plan and sequence teaching examples (HLPs 11, 12, and 15). What are all the possible scenarios where the student will use the skills, develop opportunities for them to practice, sometimes repeatedly? Step 5, deliver instruction with progress monitoring (HLPs 6, 16, and 20). Outline the lesson and make sure to share the relevance of the skill in other settings and build in opportunities to practice as much as needed; of course you progress monitor their learning!

What Does HLP 21 Look Like in a K-12 Classroom?

Elementary Example

Ms. Moreno is a fourth-grade special education teacher who co-teaches with Ms. Wright, a fourth-grade general education teacher. Ms. Moreno primarily teaches students with math needs, both in a resource classroom and with Ms. Wright. The teachers collaboratively plan lessons and determine ways they can continue practice from the resource room into the general education classroom (HLP 1). Recently, the school opened a school store where Patrick and Adeline have started working. While Ms. Moreno or her paraprofessional, Ms. Reece, is there with the students, both students are struggling with calculating how many points students need in order to purchase different items (HLP 11).

To begin, the teachers used explicit instruction of multiplication (HLP 16). Together, the teachers break down the steps of multiplication starting with repeated addition (HLP 15). They bring in Cheerios and M&Ms to create equal groups of numbers to allow students practice with repeated addition. The students use dice to create their own math problems and in small groups practice the skill.

Next, the teachers begin to discuss the concept of multiplication. Students continue to practice with both the manipulatives the teachers used the day prior, and when ready, begin to draw pictures of the math problems as they create the examples. Ms. Moreno takes a small group of students who have the manipulatives in front of them while drawing the representation. At the same time, Ms. Wright has moved onto just drawing the pictures without the manipulative representation.

The teachers begin to bring in the concept of using numbers for multiplication, each day, adding to the concept. They use a video of "School House Rock" to introduce the next skip counting number. The students pair up with other students who are working on the same number (e.g., 2s, 3s, 4s) and do number walks through the school, quizzing each other on the multiplication facts. When the student indicates they are "ready," they take a quiz on the specific multiplication facts, reviewing the previous facts they had memorized. Frequently, the principal and instructional coach join the students on their multiplication walks to quiz students and work together with them. As they learn different fact families, the student gets a star on the classroom chart.

For Patrick and Adeline, the concept is continued into the school store. As students come to the store to shop for items using the points they acquire through a school-wide positive behavior support system, Patrick and Adeline begin to use their multiplication skills. One day as they were preparing to open the store, Ms. Reece asked the students, "If a pencil is 2 points and Kameron wants 3 pencils, how many points will they need?" Through this, Patrick and Adeline begin to generalize the concept of multiplication across different settings.

Secondary Example

Mr. Murphy is a high school special education teacher. He teaches students in both a resource and general education co-taught classrooms. He spends a lot of time and effort on preparing students to be self-advocates. How can students become independent if teachers are always "covering" for them? He thinks about two students in particular. Kya is a quiet student and extremely shy and reports she is intimidated by some of her general education teachers. Juan, on the other hand, is very impulsive and usually speaks before he can put his thoughts together. Both of these students need to learn to articulate their needs, and they need to understand their accommodations and why they are needed. Kya wants to go on to a 4-year university and become a preschool teacher; she plans on attending the local community college in a couple of years before transferring to the state university. Juan loves everything automotive and wants to go to a technical school to pursue a career in auto body repair. Both of these students are able to achieve these goals, but first they will need to learn to self-advocate.

Mr. Murphy decides to explicitly teach the students about their accommodations and why they were selected. He has them review and discuss their individualized education program (IEP) accommodations list. Kya and Juan both have accommodations for assistance with organization and extended time (time and a half) for written assignments. Mr. Murphy recognizes the students will need to help to master, maintain, and generalize an organizational strategy. Both Kya and Juan have had teachers and paraprofessionals do this activity for so long, they have taken on some "learned helplessness" in this regard. However, to build their self-advocacy skills, Mr. Murphy decides to focus on the accommodation of extended time. Mr. Murphy knows they will need to self-advocate for the extended time accommodation in their post-secondary education. Both students will finish high school next year; he has 2 years to build this skill.

Once the students graduate, they will transition out of special education but still qualify for accommodations in their post-secondary institution of learning under Section 504 of the Rehabilitation Act. This Civil Rights law still protects students from discrimination when they get to college and allows for reasonable accommodation. However, the process of requesting and receiving accommodations in college is not the same as in high school. One of the major differences is they will not have a "case manager" assigned to monitor the accommodations and their progress. They will have to self-advocate for themselves. Kya has been identified with dyslexia, and Juan with attention-deficit/hyperactivity disorder. Since both are recognized as disabilities, they will be eligible for reasonable accommodations, but they will need documentation of the disability.

Colleges also have different requirements for documentation of the disability. Mr. Murphy adds a note to have Kya and Juan research the disability service offices of the institutions they want to attend as one of the first steps in learning to self-advocate for their accommodations. He follows the guidance of Burt and Whitney (2018) to ensure generalization. First, to establish a range of generalization settings, Mr. Murphy identifies a long-term goal (HLP 11) for students to generalize the skill.

- Goal: Students will explain their disability to all content area teachers and ask for the accommodation of extended time provided in their IEP.

He establishes short-term goals (STG) to help break this skill down and build success across settings. These also coincide with the second, third, and fourth steps: make relevant stimulus activities, setting circumstances, and response examples; plan for overgeneralization; and select and sequence teaching examples.

- STG 1: Given weekly in-class practice, students will create and read a script to explain their disability to the teacher and peers.
- STG 2: Following content course assignments, students will document, in a journal, how they use "extended time" for various assignments to help explain the personal value of this accommodation.
- STG 3: Without a script or prompts, students will explain their disability and needed accommodations to their guidance counselor.
- STG 4: Without scripts or prompts, students will explain the accommodation of extended time to content area teachers to access the accommodation.

Mr. Murphy collaborates with Mrs. Bruner, the guidance counselor (HLP 1), so they both understand the goals and determine a way to monitor students' progress (HLP 6) and the fifth step of the Burt and Whitney model. He teaches the students what "extended time" means and why they each have this accommodation. Finally, he sequences the instruction and activities to ensure student success.

Summary

The ability to maintain and generalize skills across time and settings is a key component of learning. This is the same at all stages of life for just about every skill we want to teach students. Fortunately, in special education, we have some great EBPs that naturally set us up for this HLP. The problem is, as we often hear, "there aren't enough hours in the day," and "we have an implementation issue" or a research-to-practice gap (Greenwood & Abbot, 2001). So, do we run out of instructional time, or do we fail to implement the EBP as it was designed? It is probably a little bit of both, not to mention all of those well-intentioned professionals that also enabled learned helplessness. A famous quote misattributed to a former United States poet laureate would apply to this situation, "Do the best you can until you know better. Then when you know better, do better."

Remember, plan for maintenance and generalization. Use specific techniques proven to be effective. Make sure you implement schedules of reinforcement, build in lots of opportunities for review, then progress monitor to target missing skills, and reteach. Repeat the review and opportunities for practice as needed, and expect they will be needed. Do not assume generalization just happens. Systematically build in experiences for students to demonstrate and use their new skills in other settings. Work with your colleagues to have them prompt students and support their transition of knowledge across settings and with different people. This will be the most effective way to achieve your goal of creating independence among your students. We cannot expect them to rely on us or other professionals for the rest of their lives on things that are within their ability to learn and do. Hopefully, after reading this chapter, you now have some great ideas to build your knowledge so you can say, you now "know better," and with time and practice you will **do better**.

Chapter Review

1. Describe the difference between maintenance and generalization.
2. How would you determine a student has reached maintenance?
3. Provide an example of how you would teach for generalization across (a) time, (b) setting, and (c) people.
4. Determine an important skill you want to teach to generalization. Plan out the instruction. Be sure to include relevance and the natural environment. For bonus points, list all HLPs you will use to implement your instruction.

References

Burt, J. L., & Whitney, T. (2018). From resource room to the real world: Facilitating generalization of intervention outcomes. *TEACHING Exceptional Children*, *50*(6), 364-372. https://doi.org/10.1177/0040059918777246

Butler, W. S., Hord, C., & Watts-Taffe, S. (2021). Increasing secondary students' comprehension through explicit attention to narrative text structure. *TEACHING Exceptional Children*, *54*(6), 394-403. https://doi.org/10.1177/00400599211025548

Capin, P., & Vaughn, S. (2017). Improving reading and social studies learning for secondary students with reading disabilities. *TEACHING Exceptional Children*, *49*(4), 249-261.

Fisher, D., Frey, N., & Lapp, D. (2008). Shared readings: Modeling comprehension, vocabulary, text structures, and text features for older readers. *The Reading Teacher*, *61*(7), 548-556.

Greenwood, C. R., & Abbott, M. (2001). The research to practice gap in special education. *Teacher Education and Special Education*, *24*(4), 276-289.

Harris, K. R., Graham, S., & Mason, L. H. (2006). Improving the writing, knowledge, and motivation of struggling young writers: Effects of self-regulated strategy development with and without peer support. *American Educational Research Journal*, *43*(2), 295-340.

Levin, J. R. (1993). Mnemonic strategies and classroom learning: A twenty-year report card. *The Elementary School Journal*, *94*(2), 235-244.

Markelz, A. M., Scheeler, M. C., & Lee, D. L. (2022). Teach students to maintain and generalize new learning across time and settings. In McLeskey, J., Maheady, L., Billingsley, B., Brownell, M. T., & Lewis, T. J. (Eds.), *High leverage practices for inclusive classrooms,* (2nd ed., pp. 330-342). Routledge. http://doi.org/10:4324/9781003148609-24

McLeskey, J., Barringer, M.-D., Billingsley, B., Brownell, M., Jackson, D., Kennedy, M., Lewis, T., Maheady, L., Rodriguez, J., Scheeler, M. C., Winn, J., & Ziegler, D. (2017). *High-leverage practices in special education.* Council for Exceptional Children & CEEDAR Center.

Mercer, C. D., & Miller, S. P. (1992). Teaching students with learning problems in math to acquire, understand, and apply basic math facts. *Remedial and Special Education, 13*(3), 19-35.

Putnam, A. L. (2015). Mnemonics in education: Current research and applications. *Translational Issues in Psychological Science, 1*(2), 130.

Yates, F. (1966). *The art of memory.* The University of Chicago Press.

What Feedback Should We Give Students to Guide Learning?

Kyena E. Cornelius, EdD

HLP 22

Provide positive and constructive feedback to guide students' learning and behavior.

INTRODUCTION

Feedback is one of the most discussed practices in education. Of all the actions a teacher can do, effective feedback has more impact on the students than anything. The word choice and usage of feedback phrases can lift a student and elevate their learning. It can also be devastating. Think about the adage we tell children: "Sticks and stones may hurt my bones, but words will never harm me." If only that were true. Effective teachers and especially those working with students with disabilities know to provide clear and specific feedback that is goal directed. Feedback is powerful, so powerful and important it is named as a High-Leverage Practice twice.

Owiny, R. L., & Cornelius, K. E. *The Practical Guide to High-Leverage Practices in Special Education: The Purposeful "How" to Enhance Classroom Rigor* (pp. 315-326).

CHAPTER OBJECTIVES

- Describe the elements a feedback statement needs to be positive and constructive.
- Explain why the elements of feedback are necessary to improve student outcomes.
- Know how HLP 22 is connected to other HLPs and can be used to guide student learning.
- Break down a feedback statement and adjust it to be positive and constructive.

KEY TERMS

- **contingent:** Occurring or if certain circumstances occur.
- **corrective:** Designed to counteract the undesirable.
- **immediate:** Occurring instantly or close in time.
- **positive:** Consisting of or characterized by the presence of features rather than their absence.
- **specific:** Clearly defined examples or identified with detail.

Effective special education teachers provide positive and constructive feedback to guide student learning and behavior to achieve desired outcomes more accurately and to be time efficient. Feedback is so important and emphasized so often that the research team that identified the core practices for special education named it twice! That was no accident! You have already read about the practice of providing feedback in Chapter 8 in the section for Social/Emotional/Behavioral High-Leverage Practices (HLPs). So, why should you read this chapter? Because feedback is that important. You do not have to take my word for it—the seminal article entitled *The Power of Feedback* (Hattie & Timperley, 2007) has been cited in more than 16,100 publications, and that is just at the time this chapter is being written. It is quite possible that number will have surpassed 18,000 by the time you are reading this. To make my point, if you were to look at the reference list for this chapter and that of Chapter 8, you will find most of those articles and book chapters also cite Hattie and Timperley. They state the purpose of feedback is to reduce "the discrepancies between current understanding/performance and a desired goal" (p. 86). Effective feedback answers three questions: (a) where am I going, (b) how am I going, and (c) where to next?

It is also important to understand that the feedback we give students to change their behavior and improve their learning has subtle nuances between tasks, skills, and most importantly, the students themselves. The elements are consistent though. Cornelius and Nagro (2014) defined performance feedback as a "critique of observed behavior that is immediate, specific, positive, and corrective when needed, designed to move the recipient toward a desired performance" (p. 135). And to reiterate the point made earlier, yes, they cited Hattie and Timperley (2007) also. In this chapter, we will look more into each of these elements—(a) clear and specific, (b) focused on the task, (c) immediate, (d) positive, and (e) corrective—to help you provide feedback that will guide your students' learning.

What Is HLP 22 and How Is It Connected to Other HLPs?

As you have read throughout the book, and with any literature on the HLPs in special education, the research team started with the HLPs identified by Ball and Forzani (2011). Guess what? Feedback is there too, *Providing Feedback to Students*. They describe this practice as: "Effective feedback helps focus students' attention on specific qualities of their work; it highlights areas needing improvement and delineates ways to improve" (https://www.teachingworks.org/high-leverage-practices/). For special educators, the research team describes the practice and gives teachers exact steps to follow. They begin with the purpose, "The purpose of feedback is to guide student learning and behavior and increase student motivation, engagement, and independence, leading to improved student learning and behavior" (McLeskey et al., 2017, p. 25). They go on to inform special educators to deliver feedback strategically that is specific to a goal, emphasizing that feedback is most powerful when (a) the student is aware of the goal; (b) it informs the student about areas that need improving; and (c) provides specific information to help them improve. Do you see the three questions again? Just in case you missed them; aware of the goal, *where am I going*; informs the areas that need improving, *how am I going*; and provides help to improve, *where to next*. The Council for Exceptional Children (CEC) and the Collaboration for Effective Educator Development, Accountability, and Reform (CEEDAR) Center team go on to encourage special educators not to be limited in the feedback they offer, but to be creative and remember that feedback can be verbal, nonverbal, or written. However, they urge teachers to not be flexible on elements of timeliness, contingent or dependent on the task, genuine, meaningful, age appropriate, and at a rate that matches the progression of the task. For example, a student will need more feedback as they are learning a skill, then less as they become more proficient, and even less as they have mastered the skill. Feedback should be ongoing until students have fully reached the goal.

All HLPs work in concert with each other. That is the nature of teaching. The HLPs are core practices that can be enacted simultaneously, and as you become more proficient with your teaching practice it will be almost like a skilled musician not thinking about their finger position, body posture, or even "reading the notes." It becomes natural to just feel and see the music. Look at how the description above flows naturally into HLP 15, provide scaffolded supports, you naturally fade the support of feedback as the student achieves the task goal. It is also easy to see HLP 21, because we want every student to maintain and generalize the tasks we teach. However, by now we are confident you see others. As you teach students your classroom routines and establish a consistent, organized, and respectful learning environment (HLP 7) they will need feedback. When you teach social skills (HLP 9), students will need feedback. These are covered more completely and directly in Chapter 8 as they too, fall in the domain of Social/Emotional/Behavioral HLPs. In this chapter, we will focus more on using feedback as you systematically design instruction (HLP 12). It is important to plan for feedback as you plan for lessons. Effective special educators anticipate common errors and misunderstandings, and plan for their correction and clarification. When you teach students to think and organize their learning, and to self-monitor their learning to become more independent (HLP 14), you need to provide them detailed feedback about their current understanding that will lead them to better maximize their learning. As already mentioned, feedback is one way we scaffold learning (HLP 15) for students. When looking at the explicit way we teach students, we model (I Do), we provide guided support (We Do), and when students are ready, we provide opportunities that are unguided (You Do; HLP 16). Students will require ongoing feedback at different rates of intensity, at the different phases of the instruction. When you strategically group students in different flexible arrangements (HLP 17) they will need both feedback that they are performing the task of their group role correctly, and performance feedback regarding the desired instructional task of the group. Whenever you purposefully use strategies to engage students (HLP 18) you are providing them an opportunity to respond to the learning task, naturally they will need feedback on their progress toward mastering the learning task. As students learn to use their assistive technology (HLP 19) they will need feedback until they are independent. The more intensive the instruction (HLP 20), the more feedback the student will need. As students work to maintain and generalize their learning (HLP 21), they will need feedback. As you can see, basically every HLP in which you directly interact with students, you provide feedback. Couple this idea with the theme of this book—HLPs are how you implement evidence-based practices (EBPs); consequently, every time you instruct students, you need to provide feedback! See Table 22-1 for a list of HLPs related to HLP 22, and some of the EBPs discussed in this chapter.

Table 22-1. Alignment of HLPs and Resources for Evidence-Based Practices

EBP SUPPORT WITH HLP 22	RELATED HLPS	RESOURCES
Concrete-Representational-Abstract	11, 12, 13, 15, 16, 18, 20, 21	https://iris.peabody.vanderbilt.edu/module/math/
Direct Instruction	12, 13, 15, 16, 17, 18, 20, 21	https://www.nifdi.org/15/index.php?option=com_content&view=article&id=52&Itemid=27 https://www.learninga-z.com/site/resources/breakroom-blog/direct-instruction?source=google&medium=cpc&campaign_id=16440209676&creative=&keyword=&matchtype=&network=x&device=c&gclid=Cj0KCQjwyt-ZBhCNARIsAKH1177aRHZ4OgALDg3dzhvjgrv3iDdmWJmUeW04rQ9plK9_nl_R4_YEvBEaAv8xEALw_wcB
Explicit Instruction	12, 13, 15, 16, 17, 18, 20, 21	Archer, A. L., & Hughes, C. A. (2011). *Explicit instruction: Effective and efficient teaching.* Guilford Press. https://highleveragepractices.org/hlp-16-use-explicit-instruction https://explicitinstruction.org/
Help-Seeking Strategy	15, 16, 18, 19, 21	https://www.edutopia.org/article/teaching-students-how-ask-help
Peer Tutoring	16, 18, 21	http://acentral.education/accommodations/peer-tutoring
Self-Monitoring Strategy	15, 16, 18, 19, 21	https://iris.peabody.vanderbilt.edu/module/sr/#content

How Do I Scaffold Feedback for Student Learning?

The feedback we provide to students needs to be directed at their current *level* of learning. Hattie and Timperley (2007) share four levels of learning: task level, process level, self-regulation level, and self level. For the purposes of this chapter, we will follow the lead of O'Brien and colleagues (2022) and focus on the first three. These scaffolded levels help deliver more targeted and specific feedback. At the task level, students are just learning the new skill; they are understanding the task and just beginning to "do" the task. Students need to receive immediate feedback to let them know if they are performing the task correctly. For instance, as students are learning that proper nouns all begin with an uppercase letter, a teacher gives students a list of six nouns: Mars, planet, London, city, John, man. As she is circulating, she sees a student who has written all six words with initial uppercase letters. She provides this feedback, "Monique, you began all the words with uppercase letters. Some of the words are proper nouns, but some are common nouns. Can you tell me the rule for proper nouns again?" Monique says, "All proper nouns begin with an uppercase letter." "That is right, proper nouns do begin with an uppercase letter. Can you tell me our definition of 'proper noun'?" Monique replies, "A special noun that *names* a particular person, place, or thing." "Very good, Monique, you are exactly right, a proper noun names a particular person, place, or thing. Mars is a particular place; it is the planet next to Earth. However, is 'planet' a particular place? I will tell you, there are three proper nouns and three common nouns. You need to go back and look at these words again and determine which are common and which ones are proper. Do they name a particular person, place, or thing?" Did you notice the teacher did not just correct Monique, she provided the feedback to help Monique continue to learn the task, and then left her with a goal.

The next level of feedback is when students are learning a process to accomplish a task, the process level feedback. Use this level when you want students to focus on a strategy to complete a task. Students already have some level of understanding of the task and the process to use but need to continue with a strategy or find a different one to complete the task. This is the feedback that goes beyond learning the task but deepens student understanding of learning. Process level feedback not only focuses on the strategy but also using information to search for cues to have students accurately accomplish and improve their final product. Specific feedback may include asking students about the strategies they used to check for errors or search for more information.

Mrs. Gray is working with a group of students who are using multiple texts to analyze how two authors writing about the same topic share different evidence or different interpretations of facts. Nancy is a student with writing organization goals, who needs to elaborate with supporting details to enhance the essay. Martin is proficient at using one text to find details and evidence but needs to learn to use two texts equally to compare the authors' ideas. As Mrs. Gray observes the two working, she observes that both students are falling into their comfort zones: Nancy is rushing and not adding details, and Martin only has one text open. She leans over and tells Nancy, "This opening paragraph is amazing! You have a very strong topic sentence; I like how you pointed out that famous authors don't always agree! You have also provided three examples to organize the next three paragraphs of the essay. However, your next paragraphs don't have much explanation or detail from the texts. Let's think about what we need to do next. What strategy did you use while reading through the two different readings?" She then turns to Martin and says, "Martin, you have really dissected the first reading! The insights you have drawn from the author's use of figurative language is spot on! You are absolutely right, when someone is 'burning with the desire to learn,' they are very interested in the topic and want to learn more. But what did you notice about the second author's use of more fact-based, expository text? How can you dig into that reading to understand more about his word choice? What other assignment does this remind you of? How can you use what you did there, to help find more in the second reading?" Mrs. Gray then turns to the students and employs HLP 17—"*Use flexible grouping*" to draw on each student's strengths so they can help each other and collaborate to use multiple strategies to strengthen their essays. She gives each of them a follow-up goal for their essay and a goal for working together to support each other to complete the task.

The final level of feedback is related to self-regulation. This higher level provides students with support to help them think about their thinking, their feelings, and the actions needed to complete an academic goal. Teachers use this feedback to help students self-manage their own progress. Students are encouraged to think about and reflect on their own thinking (metacognition; HLP 14) to self-assess and self-monitor. Feedback at this level is used when you are confident students have mastered the task, and you want to maintain and generalize (HLP 21) their learning. Mr. Curtis is helping students proofread and check their work before submitting it. Colin is working on the write up for a science lab while Caroline is going over a history assignment she completed and looking through her text and class notes to check her answers. Mr. Curtis speaks to the students: "Colin, now that you have completed the lab report, read through it again and check your responses. As you do, be sure to think about how you came up with your responses, ask yourself 'How confident am I that I responded fully to every prompt?', and consider 'why' you know you are ready to submit." Colin uses a self-monitoring strategy and refers to the checklist he created to check his responses (Zimmerman, 2002). Mr. Curtis turns to Caroline and says, "I like that you used all the resources you were given for this assignment. Look at your answers, how do they compare to the examples your history teacher, Ms. Finch, provided in the example? What else do you need to think about in completing this assignment?" Caroline looks through her notes, and sees she has some information missing. She turns to a peer and asks for their notes from class and asks to talk through Ms. Finch's example. This help-seeking strategy is one that builds on her existing knowledge and seeks to discuss with a peer for deeper understanding increasing her engagement with the content (Karabenick & Knapp, 1991; Linnenbrink & Pintrich, 2003).

What Types of Feedback Would Increase Student Motivation, Engagement, and Independence?

Remember, "feedback can be helpful or harmful depending on how it is conveyed" (Archer & Hughes, 2011, p. 175). It can also be helpful or harmful depending on the student characteristics (O'Brien et al., 2022). Individualized feedback happens when teachers know their students and their backgrounds and experiences. Based on a student's cultural background, they may prefer different types of feedback. Cultural studies researchers refer to collective or individualistic cultures. Generally, many people from Asia and South America are considered collective and prefer group directed feedback, while people from northwest Europe, Canada, and the United States are considered individualistic and prefer personalized feedback (deVries et al., 2022). As you work with students, get to know them and their backgrounds and personal preferences to deliver the most impactful feedback. When feedback is used effectively it moves the student closer to the desired performance; therefore, it should be *clear* and *specific*; focused on the product, not the student; *immediate*; stated in a *positive* manner; and *corrective* as needed (Cornelius & Nagro, 2014).

Clear and Specific Feedback

Effective feedback cannot leave anything open to interpretation. It must be clear and specific, whether responding to a correct or incorrect answer. When responding to a correct answer while a student is at the task level of scaffolded feedback, you run the risk of empty praise. Just saying "nice job" is empty as the student may not know what was nice about their effort. Instead, be very clear and specific, "You are correct, the M in Mars should be an uppercase letter, because it is a proper noun. Good thinking, Monique." Similarly, when the student is incorrect, do not tell them they are wrong or give them correct answers. Provide them with clear and specific feedback that helps them revise their own answers. "I see you have an uppercase P for planet. Monique, can you tell me the rule for proper nouns? That is correct, a proper noun is a noun that names a specific person, place, or thing. Is planet a proper noun?" In this case, the teacher helps Monique to understand the task and provide effective meaningful feedback.

Focused on the Product, Not the Student

Effective feedback is directed toward the student's work or performance of a task, not the student themself. Think about the teacher's performance feedback in our example of process level feedback. "Martin, you have really dissected the first reading! The insights you have drawn from the author's use of figurative language is spot on! You are absolutely right, when someone is 'burning with the desire to learn,' they are very interested in the topic and want to learn more." Highlighting the correct use of figurative language has an academic focus and will move the student along in their learning. Whereas, if Mrs. Gray merely told the student, "Yes, that is awesome! You are brilliant," it would not improve their learning and might even cause the student to stop trying to learn more; this message communicates they have *arrived* at mastery and can stop learning.

Immediate

The closer in proximity the feedback is to the trial/attempt of the task, the more impact it will have, especially for struggling learners (Decker & Buggey, 2014). When feedback is provided to students as they are performing the new task, it gives them the opportunity to engage with the task with more opportunities for a correct response. Remember practice does not make perfect, practice makes permanent. Give students the opportunity to revise their learning before they practice multiple times independently. Think back to Monique learning the use of uppercase letters for proper nouns. What if the teacher had not stopped Monique, given her clear and specific feedback and the opportunity to revise and engage again, but instead given this assignment for homework, and then released Monique to practice alone? When Monique came in the next day, the feedback would not have been as effective, **and** the teacher would have to take time to "unteach" the bad learning.

Positive in Nature

Hopefully, by now, you understand this does not mean you say nice, empty praise statements. Praise and positive are not synonyms. Some feedback is praise, but not all positive feedback is praise. Positive feedback highlights a process or task by pointing out what is present, not focusing on what you do not observe. Effective feedback should be delivered in a positive manner and used to encourage students to extend their knowledge (Scheeler et al., 2004). The goal here is to highlight what the student has done, acknowledge their work, and extend it or correct it. Looking back at Mr. Curtis's feedback to Colin, he said, "Now that you have completed the lab report, read through it again and check your responses. As you do, be sure to think about how you came up with your responses, ask yourself 'How confident am I that I responded fully to every prompt?', and consider 'why' you know you are ready to submit." He acknowledges the work Colin has done, recognizes the student feels he has completed it, but wants to emphasize and extend Colin's use of the self-monitoring strategy. He did not take anything away from the student or even withhold feedback, he simply provided steps forward. He provided positive feedback.

Corrective When Needed

When feedback is directed to student misunderstandings, you can anticipate errors and correct them as they happen before they become habits. One of the hallmarks of the EBP of Direct Instruction is the immediacy of error correction procedures and the follow-up practice opportunities provided to students (Stockard et al., 2018). As a student is learning to read, they will make errors, whether it is skipping a word or misreading a letter sound. When this happens, it is best to stop the student, correct their error, and provide them another practice opportunity, and then another opportunity a few minutes later, which is called *delayed practice*. For example, a student may read the word "bad" for "bag". The teacher would stop the student and say, "This word is bag. What word?" asking the student to repeat and then reread the word "*bag.*" Later, after the student had read another line or two, the teacher would go back, point to the word "bag," and say, "What is this word?" This type of feedback is more direct and offered at the task-level. This is much more effective than allowing the student to read "bad" for several attempts and then correcting them after the lesson. However, corrective feedback is not only useful at the task level but also effective at the process and self-regulated levels and needs to be just as intentional.

How Does Feedback Answer the Three Questions of Effective Feedback?

Remember effective feedback is purposeful. It intentionally has the student focus on their performance and leads them to reflect on their performance and engage with three questions: (a) What is my goal? (b) What is my current understanding of the task or skill? and (c) How do I get to the next level? In these questions the student is the "my/I." Hattie and Timperley (2007) refer to this as directional feedback. It "fills a gap" between students' current understanding and what they need to understand.

Where Am I Going?

Feedback that answers this question is focused on the learning goal. Look back at the feedback offered earlier in the chapter. Monique needs to learn that proper nouns begin with uppercase letters. Martin has a goal to analyze two different texts for the same purpose. Colin's goal is to self-monitor his work before he turns it in. Their teachers each intentionally stated or had the student restate the goal and ensured they each understood the goal.

How Am I Doing?

Feedback that answers this question is focused on the student's current understanding. Monique's current understanding, or application of the rule, is to use an uppercase letter for all the nouns. Martin is doing well with figurative language and analyzing a single text. Colin understands completing the lab report meant he needed to answer questions, which he did, but maybe not completely. Their teachers pointed out their current level of understanding and even reinforced this understanding was acceptable, but not the goal.

Where to Next?

Feedback that answers this question gives the student their next steps. What do they need to do now to advance their learning to a higher level? Monique needs to correct the common nouns with uppercase letters. Martin needs to read and use that second text. Colin needs to use the self-monitoring strategy and the checklist he created to check his responses to ensure they are fully answered, and he knows why the lab report is complete.

What Are Some Creative Ways to Provide Feedback?

This is when it becomes time to get out of your own head. Today's students are very technology driven. Why not use that for a creative way to provide feedback? Picture this: You are co-teaching. You and your teaching partner taught students how to transition from a parallel teaching approach to a station teaching approach. It required them to move desks and get materials from another part of the room. You modeled what students should do, you practiced with them, and then you asked them to perform the task as quickly as possible. They did a great job, but there was a little too much unnecessary talking. You want to provide them with feedback before they practice again, so you and your co-teacher create a TikTok video providing the students with performance feedback. You remind them of the goals, acknowledge the time in which they completed the task, their success in getting into the right place, and their ability to get all the materials needed. You set an expectation of the time you want them to achieve today and the noise level you expect. It would be fun, creative, and rewarding for the students.

The research team specifically mentions nonverbal feedback in the definition of HLP 22. Remember though, a simple thumbs up does not provide enough specificity or really any information needed for effective feedback. However, when you see a student stalled, and thinking about their next steps, you can point to the supports around the room. Perhaps the student is learning to use a self-regulation strategy, and you have posted the questions they need to ask themselves when they are initially "finish" with an assignment. Point to the support poster you have hanging up to remind them of their next step. You have reminded them of the goal, told them where they are (ready to ask themself the reflective questions), and helped them establish the next step—use the questions to check their answers and see if they need to add more to their responses.

Another creative way to provide feedback on assignments that have been submitted, especially if it is a draft of an essay or lab report, is to take a screenshot of the student's work and record your feedback in a video or voice over to remind them of the goal, commend them on what they have done correctly, correct what needs to be corrected, and provide them with the next step. Send the student the video or voice recording and let them hear you as they work on their next steps. If they get stuck, they can just replay the recording and not have to wait on you for help.

How Can I Ensure My Feedback Is Effective and Ongoing?

Feedback must use the elements discussed. If you are new to teaching, or just want to make sure you are delivering the most impactful feedback possible, make yourself a note. Write some feedback statements in your plan book. Think about when students are learning a new writing technique or are even new to group work, we give them sentence starters. Why not give yourself some? Write down a few prompts and stems right in your lesson plan, where you will see them for easy reference. Think about the objective of the lesson. Is it a new skill? Then, the students will need task-level feedback. Is the lesson focused on a process? The students will need process level feedback. Similarly, if the lesson involves the students using a cognitive or metacognitive process, the students will need self-regulation level feedback. Write a quick note next to the objective in your lesson plan that says, task, process, or self-regulation. In the body of the lesson, as you write out your guided practice opportunities, write out what you anticipate the student will do. Can you anticipate the error? If so, how can you correct it and move students to the next level?

What Does HLP 22 Look Like in a K-12 Classroom?

Elementary Example

Ms. Greely is a special education teacher working with students in the first and second grades. She does not have a published curriculum but develops her lessons using the EBP of concrete, representational, and abstract (CRA; Agrawal & Morin, 2016). This framework allows her to teach students concepts using manipulatives (concrete). Once they achieve a predetermined level of mastery, the teacher begins to use drawings and pictorial representations (representational). These scaffolded levels of support (HLP 15) promote student understanding of the concepts before completing math problems using traditional algorithms (abstract).

In today's lesson, Ms. Greely is teaching students the "adding on" concept. She knows her students are becoming proficient with the concept that addition is the combining of numbers/objects. However, all the students, when given a problem, will count each individual manipulative. For example, when given a problem of 3 + 6, students will count out three manipulatives and then count out six, arrange them on their placemat, and count each of the items starting with 1. Ms. Greeley would like students to know they can become more efficient if they start with a value of a set and then begin counting the individual manipulatives of the second group. As she gets started, she models a couple of examples while sharing her thought process in a *think-aloud*. She provides several opportunities for the students to perform the task with her in a guided practice. As they complete each practice opportunity, she provides them with positive and constructive feedback. "Miguel, you are correct, you can start at 4 and continue counting as you add on." "Kevin, remember you do not need to start with 1, that is incorrect. How many chips are in this box?...Yes, there are four, so if there are four chips what number should you say first to start adding on?" She continues to provide the feedback each student needs at the task level.

Secondary Example

Ms. Gail is a special education teacher working with Mr. Edwards, a ninth-grade English teacher. They have planned a unit in which students will synthesize multiple texts to write a persuasive essay. In their planning, the teachers develop the learning objectives for the unit. Given three pieces of text, a primary source, a textbook section, and a magazine article, students will synthesize the three to create a persuasive essay with at least three supporting details. They create a "guidelines checklist" for students to reference and use to self-monitor their learning (HLP 14). Ms. Gail creates a prewriting template for students who struggle with planning and organizing written tasks (HLPs 13 and 15). Mr. Edwards has planned to model a complete essay and post it in the online class forum for students to reference as they work. After the initial model and some guided practice activities (HLP 16), the students are given their three sources, the guidelines checklist, and the prewriting template, if needed. The teachers monitor students as they begin to highlight information in the written sources and take notes. Mr. Edwards sees Jim has written his "big idea" down on his prewriting template and highlighted a sentence, copied it onto the template, and then he starts to read the next article. Mr. Edwards says, "Jim, I see you have already identified the overarching theme of the three sources. How did you arrive at that as your theme?" Jim points to the titles of each of the sources. "See, all of the articles have something about *power* in the title, and as I read the articles, they each mentioned how some person got their way." Mr. Edwards commends Jim for his observation, but then challenges him to follow the guideline checklist, "That is an excellent observation, and you are right, each of the people did get what they wanted, and seeing a common word in the title is a good prediction strategy. But what do you remember about 'predictions'? Is the first prediction always correct?" Jim shakes his head and rolls his eyes at the thought of redoing what he started. Mr. Edwards tells him, "I am not saying this is wrong, but I don't think you have enough information to state the theme right now. I want you to be sure you are following the guidelines of the assignment. Continue to read all the articles, *completely*, and use your checklist to make sure you have all the information before you determine the 'big idea.'" Jim admitted he had only read the titles, just skimmed the first paragraph of the readings, and made an assumption.

After the students complete their first drafts, the teachers decide to provide them with written feedback and then conference with them to monitor their progress and provide positive and constructive feedback to guide student learning. Both teachers took half of the class essays and read through the drafts. They marked up the documents with track changes and reflective questions. They each made a short video to send to the student about their work (HLP 19). In the video, the teachers also modeled next steps of the assignment using the guidelines checklist. The day of the conferences, the teachers shared the written feedback with the students and answered any questions the students had at the time. When students went back to working on the assignment, the teacher sent the video in that student's classroom inbox with directions to watch the video if they got stuck and needed a little push to keep working. As students continued to work, you could hear the teachers saying, "How does your essay compare to Mr. Edwards' model?", "What should you do next?", or "How do you know, how can you check?"

Summary

Feedback needs to happen every day in your classroom. An effective special education teacher plans for strategic delivery of performance feedback. They know their students in a way that lets them anticipate errors, correct those errors, and provide more opportunities for the student to practice. They know the student's preferred style of feedback and never provide harmful feedback. Effective special education teachers consider a student's background and provide feedback that honors the student and their culture. They avoid empty praise and understand some praise can halt additional learning.

Feedback is scaffolded depending on the lesson and activities students are performing. It can be task level, providing feedback on new skill acquisition. Feedback can be process level when students are learning strategies to complete a task. It can also be given at the self-regulation level when you are trying to guide students to take ownership of their own performance. Effective feedback answers three questions: (a) where am I going, (b) how am I going, and (c) where to next? When teachers provide constructive feedback, it is clear and specific, it is focused on the task or student work, and not the students themselves. Teachers understand that feedback must be delivered as close to the occurrence of the behavior or learning task as possible; the more immediate the feedback, the more effective it will be. Feedback is always positive in nature; teachers should focus on what is present and not what they did not observe. Feedback must also be corrective, not in a way that shames a student, but matter of factly, without judgment. Students need to understand mistakes are part of learning, and that when you correct them, it is to help them grow and achieve more. Effective feedback extends learning and is necessary for student success.

Chapter Review

1. What are the four elements of effective feedback?
2. Think about the scaffolded levels of feedback. Create two feedback sentence starters for each level to write in a plan book.
3. Describe how effective feedback moves students forward.
4. Why is empty praise harmful feedback?

References

Agrawal, J., & Morin, L. L. (2016). Evidence-based practices: Applications of concrete representational abstract framework across math concepts for students with mathematics disabilities. *Learning Disabilities Research & Practice, 31*(1), 34-44. https://doi.org/10.1111/ldrp.12093

Archer, A. L., & Hughes, C. A. (2011). *Explicit instruction: Effective and efficient teaching.* Guilford Press.

Ball, D. L., & Forzani, F. M. (2011). Building a common core for learning to teach: And connecting professional learning to practice. *American Educator, 35*(2), 17-21.

Chan, P. E., Konrad, M., Gonzalez, V., Peters, M. T., & Ressa, V. A. (2014). The critical role of feedback in formative instructional practices. *Intervention in School and Clinic, 50*(2), 96-104. https://doi.org/10.1177/1053451214536044

Cornelius, K. E., & Nagro, S. A. (2014). Evaluating the evidence base of performance feedback in preservice special education teacher training. *Teacher Education and Special Education, 37*(2), 133-146. https://doi.org/10.1177/0888406414521837

Decker, M. M., & Buggey, T. (2014). Using video self-and peer modeling to facilitate reading fluency in children with learning disabilities. *Journal of Learning Disabilities, 47*(2), 167-177. https://doi.org/10.1177/0022219412450618

de Vries, J., Feskens, R., Keuning, J., & van der Kleij, F. (2022). Comparability of feedback in PISA 2015 across culturally diverse countries. *Education Sciences, 12*(2), 145. https://doi.org/10.3390/ educsci12020145

Hattie, J., & Timperley, H. (2007). The power of feedback. *Review of Educational Research, 77*(1), 81-112.

Karabenick, S. A., & Knapp, J. R. (1991). Relationship of academic help seeking to the use of learning strategies and other instrumental achievement behavior in college students. *Journal of Educational Psychology, 83*(2), 221. https://doi.org/10.1037/0022-0663.83.2.221

Koenka, A. C., & Anderman, E. M. (2019). Personalized feedback as a strategy for improving motivation and performance among middle school students. *Middle School Journal, 50*(5), 15-22. https://doi.org/10.1080/00940771.2019.1674768

Linnenbrink, E. A., & Pintrich, P. R. (2003). The role of self-efficacy beliefs in student engagement and learning in the classroom. *Reading & Writing Quarterly, 19*(2), 119-137. https://doi.org/10.1080/10573560308223

McLeskey, J., Barringer, M.-D., Billingsley, B., Brownell, M., Jackson, D., Kennedy, M., Lewis, T., Maheady, L., Rodriguez, J., Scheeler, M. C., Winn, J., & Ziegler, D. (2017). *High-leverage practices in special education.* Council for Exceptional Children & CEEDAR Center.

O'Brien, K. M., Cumming, M. M., Binkert, G. D., & Ore, D. R. (2022). Providing positive and corrective feedback. In McLeskey, J., Maheady, L., Billingsley, B., Brownell, M. T., & Lewis, T. J. (Eds.), *High leverage practices for inclusive classrooms* (2nd ed., pp. 343-356). Routledge. https://doi.org/10:4324/9781003148609-28

Scheeler, M. C., Ruhl, K. L., & McAfee, J. K. (2004). Providing performance feedback to teachers: A review. *Teacher Education and Special Education, 27*, 396-407. https://doi.org/10.1177/088840640402700407

Stockard, J., Wood, T. W., Coughlin, C., & Rasplica Khoury, C. (2018). The effectiveness of direct instruction curricula: A meta-analysis of a half century of research. *Review of Educational Research, 88*(4), 479-507. https://doi.org/10.3102/003465431775191

TeachingWorks Resource Library. (2022). *Curriculum resources.* https://library.teachingworks.org/curriculum-resources/high-leverage-practices/

Zimmerman, B. J. (2002). Becoming a self-regulated learner: An overview. *Theory Into Practice, 41*(2), 64-70. https://doi.org/0.1207/s15430421tip41

Conclusion

Ruby L. Owiny, PhD
and Kyena E. Cornelius, EdD

The High-Leverage Practices (HLPs) function together to provide special educators, and even general educators, with a description of the effective practices that will improve student achievement when implemented with fidelity and on a regular basis (McLeskey et al., 2017). The challenge for teachers is to understand how to implement each HLP effectively. This book provided guidance on how to implement the HLPs through provision of specific evidence-based practices which will lead to enhanced classroom rigor and increased student success.

The intertwined functionality of the HLPs is key to understanding their implementation—they cannot and should not be used in isolation. For this reason, each chapter intentionally highlights the function of their connectivity. They are not a checklist, rather they work together to create the rigor necessary for teachers to design and implement instruction effectively and for students to achieve at higher levels. This is true of all students regardless of an identified disability, level of need, or where specially designed instruction is delivered. Special educators can also be confident that when implementing the HLPs in their practice, they are also demonstrating proficiency in the Council for Exceptional Children (CEC) standards, as well. Berlinghoff and McLaughlin (2022) discuss this alignment with the updated CEC Practice-Based Standards. This alignment further highlights the importance of the HLPs in teaching practice. To see the alignment between the standards and the HLPs, see the tables that follow.

Throughout this book, you have learned the how-to in terms of implementing the evidence-based practices (EBPs) through the HLPs and now understand the multiple facets of the intertwined functionality between and among the HLPs, EBPs, CEC standards, and culturally responsive teaching to effectively meet the needs of students with disabilities through specially designed instruction in any setting deemed the most appropriate for the student. A bonus to this is when the Least Restrictive Environment is determined to be the general education classroom is that students without individualized education programs benefit as well.

Owiny, R. L., & Cornelius, K. E. *The Practical Guide to High-Leverage Practices in Special Education: The Purposeful "How" to Enhance Classroom Rigor* (pp. 327-341).

Take what you have learned from this book and go make an even greater impact on the achievement and well-being of students with disabilities and their non-disabled peers! Thank you for picking up this book as another step in your journey to being a more effective teacher. Go forth and implement those HLPs!

References

Berlinghoff, D., & McLaughlin, V. L. (Eds.). (2022). *Practice-based standards for the preparation of special educators.* Council for Exceptional Children.

McLeskey, J., Barringer, M.-D., Billingsley, B., Brownell, M., Jackson, D., Kennedy, M., Lewis, T., Maheady, L., Rodriquez, J., Scheeler, M. C., Winn, J., & Ziegler, D. (2017). *High-leverage practices in special education.* Council for Exceptional Children & CEEDAR Center.

Crosswalk: HLPs to CEC Standard Components

HLP	CEC STANDARD COMPONENT
HLP 1: Collaborate with professionals to increase student success.	7.2 Candidates collaborate, communicate, and coordinate with families, paraprofessionals, and other professionals within the educational setting to assess, plan, and implement effective programs and services that promote progress toward measurable outcomes for individuals with and without exceptionalities and their families. 7.3 Candidates collaborate, communicate, and coordinate with professionals and agencies within the community to identify and access services, resources, and supports to meet the identified needs of individuals with exceptionalities and their families. 7.4 Candidates understand their role of working with paraprofessionals to implement efficiently and effectively necessary components of the IEP.
HLP 2: Organize and facilitate effective meetings with professionals and families.	7.1 Candidates utilize communication, group facilitation, and problem-solving strategies in a culturally responsive manner to lead effective meetings and share expertise and knowledge to build team capacity and jointly address students' instructional and behavior needs.
HLP 3: Collaborate with families to support student learning and secure needed services.	1.2 Candidates advocate for improved outcomes for individuals with exceptionalities and their families while addressing the unique needs of those with diverse social, cultural, and linguistic backgrounds. 7.2 Candidates collaborate, communicate, and coordinate with families, paraprofessionals, and other professionals within the educational setting to assess, plan, and implement effective programs and services that promote progress toward measurable outcomes for individuals with and without exceptionalities and their families.

(continued)

Crosswalk: HLPs to CEC Standard Components

HLP	CEC STANDARD COMPONENT
HLP 4: Use multiple sources of information to develop a comprehensive understanding of a student's strengths and needs.	2.1 Candidates apply understanding of human growth and development to create developmentally appropriate and meaningful learning experiences that address individualized strengths and needs of students with exceptionalities. 4.1 Candidates collaboratively develop, select, administer, analyze, and interpret multiple measures of student learning, behavior, and the classroom environment to evaluate and support classroom and school-based systems of intervention for students with and without exceptionalities. 4.2 Candidates develop, select, administer, and interpret multiple, formal and informal, culturally and linguistically appropriate measures and procedures that are valid and reliable, to contribute to eligibility determination for special education services. 4.3 Candidates assess, collaboratively analyze, interpret, and communicate students' progress toward measurable outcomes using technology as appropriate, to inform both short- and long-term planning, and make ongoing adjustments to instruction. 6.3 Candidates systematically use data from a variety of sources to identify the purpose or function served by problem behavior to plan, implement, and evaluate behavioral interventions and social skills programs, including generalization to other environments.
HLP 5: Interpret and communicate assessment information with stakeholders to collaboratively design and implement educational programs.	4.1 Candidates collaboratively develop, select, administer, analyze, and interpret multiple measures of student learning, behavior, and the classroom environment to evaluate and support classroom and school-based systems of intervention for students with and without exceptionalities. 4.3 Candidates assess, collaboratively analyze, interpret, and communicate students' progress toward measurable outcomes using technology as appropriate, to inform both short- and long-term planning, and make ongoing adjustments to instruction.
HLP 6: Use student assessment data, analyze instructional practices, and make necessary adjustments that improve student outcomes.	4.3 Candidates assess, collaboratively analyze, interpret, and communicate students' progress toward measurable outcomes using technology as appropriate, to inform both short- and long-term planning, and make ongoing adjustments to instruction. 5.1 Candidates use findings from multiple assessments, including student self-assessment, that are responsive to cultural and linguistic diversity and specialized as needed, to identify what students know and are able to do. They then interpret the assessment data to appropriately plan and guide instruction to meet rigorous academic and non-academic content and goals for each individual.

(continued)

Crosswalk: HLPs to CEC Standard Components

HLP	CEC STANDARD COMPONENT
HLP 7: Establish a consistent, organized, and respectful learning environment.	6.1 Candidates use effective routines and procedures to create safe, caring, respectful, and productive learning environments for individuals with exceptionalities. 6.2 Candidates use a range of preventive and responsive practices documented as effective to support individuals' social, emotional, and educational well-being.
HLP 8: Provide positive and constructive feedback to guide students' learning and behavior.	5.2 Candidates use effective strategies to promote active student engagement, increase student motivation, increase opportunities to respond, and enhance self-regulation of student learning. 6.2 Candidates use a range of preventive and responsive practices documented as effective to support individuals' social, emotional, and educational well-being.
HLP 9: Teach social behaviors.	5.2 Candidates use effective strategies to promote active student engagement, increase student motivation, increase opportunities to respond, and enhance self-regulation of student learning. 6.2 Candidates use a range of preventive and responsive practices documented as effective to support individuals' social, emotional, and educational well-being. 6.3 Candidates systematically use data from a variety of sources to identify the purpose or function served by problem behavior to plan, implement, and evaluate behavioral interventions and social skills programs, including generalization to other environments.
HLP 10: Conduct functional behavioral assessments to develop individual student behavior support plans.	6.3 Candidates systematically use data from a variety of sources to identify the purpose or function served by problem behavior to plan, implement, and evaluate behavioral interventions and social skills programs, including generalization to other environments.
HLP 11: Identify and prioritize long- and short-term learning goals.	2.2 Candidates use their knowledge and understanding of diverse factors that influence development and learning, including differences related to families, languages, cultures, and communities, and individual differences, including exceptionalities, to plan and implement learning experiences and environments. 3.1 Candidates apply their understanding of academic subject matter content of the general curriculum to inform their programmatic and instructional decisions for individuals with exceptionalities. 5.1 Candidates use findings from multiple assessments, including student self-assessment, that are responsive to cultural and linguistic diversity and specialized as needed, to identify what students know and are able to do. They then interpret the assessment data to appropriately plan and guide instruction to meet rigorous academic and non-academic content and goals for each individual.

(continued)

CROSSWALK: HLPs TO CEC STANDARD COMPONENTS

HLP	CEC STANDARD COMPONENT
HLP 12: Systematically design instruction toward a specific learning goal.	2.2 Candidates use their knowledge and understanding of diverse factors that influence development and learning, including differences related to families, languages, cultures, and communities, and individual differences, including exceptionalities, to plan and implement learning experiences and environments. 3.2 Candidates augment the general education curriculum to address skills and strategies that students with disabilities need to access the core curriculum and function successfully within a variety of contexts as well as the continuum of placement options to assure specially designed instruction is developed and implemented to achieve mastery of curricular standards and individualized goals and objectives. 5.3 Candidates use explicit, systematic instruction to teach content, strategies, and skills to make clear what a learner needs to do or think about while learning.
HLP 13: Adapt curriculum tasks and materials for specific learning goals.	3.1 Candidates apply their understanding of academic subject matter content of the general curriculum to inform their programmatic and instructional decisions for individuals with exceptionalities. 3.2 Candidates augment the general education curriculum to address skills and strategies that students with disabilities need to access the core curriculum and function successfully within a variety of contexts as well as the continuum of placement options to assure specially designed instruction is developed and implemented to achieve mastery of curricular standards and individualized goals and objectives. 5.6 Candidates plan and deliver specialized, individualized instruction that is used to meet the learning needs of each individual.
HLP 14: Teach cognitive and metacognitive strategies to support learning and independence.	3.2 Candidates augment the general education curriculum to address skills and strategies that students with disabilities need to access the core curriculum and function successfully within a variety of contexts as well as the continuum of placement options to assure specially designed instruction is developed and implemented to achieve mastery of curricular standards and individualized goals and objectives. 5.3 Candidates use explicit, systematic instruction to teach content, strategies, and skills to make clear what a learner needs to do or think about while learning. 5.6 Candidates plan and deliver specialized, individualized instruction that is used to meet the learning needs of each individual.

(continued)

CROSSWALK: HLPs TO CEC STANDARD COMPONENTS

HLP	CEC STANDARD COMPONENT
HLP 15: Provide scaffolded supports.	3.2 Candidates augment the general education curriculum to address skills and strategies that students with disabilities need to access the core curriculum and function successfully within a variety of contexts as well as the continuum of placement options to assure specially designed instruction is developed and implemented to achieve mastery of curricular standards and individualized goals and objectives.
	5.6 Candidates plan and deliver specialized, individualized instruction that is used to meet the learning needs of each individual.
	6.3 Candidates systematically use data from a variety of sources to identify the purpose or function served by problem behavior to plan, implement, and evaluate behavioral interventions and social skills programs, including generalization to other environments.
HLP 16: Use explicit instruction.	5.3 Candidates use explicit, systematic instruction to teach content, strategies, and skills to make clear what a learner needs to do or think about while learning.
	6.3 Candidates systematically use data from a variety of sources to identify the purpose or function served by problem behavior to plan, implement, and evaluate behavioral interventions and social skills programs, including generalization to other environments.
HLP 17: Use flexible grouping.	5.4 Candidates use flexible grouping to support the use of instruction that is adapted to meet the needs of each individual and group.
	5.5 Candidates organize and manage focused, intensive small group instruction to meet the learning needs of each individual.
HLP 18: Use strategies to promote active student engagement.	5.2 Candidates use effective strategies to promote active student engagement, increase student motivation, increase opportunities to respond, and enhance self-regulation of student learning.
HLP 19: Use assistive and instructional technologies.	4.3 Candidates assess, collaboratively analyze, interpret, and communicate students' progress toward measurable outcomes using technology as appropriate, to inform both short- and long-term planning, and make ongoing adjustments to instruction.
	5.1 Candidates use findings from multiple assessments, including student self-assessment, that are responsive to cultural and linguistic diversity and specialized as needed, to identify what students know and are able to do. They then interpret the assessment data to appropriately plan and guide instruction to meet rigorous academic and non-academic content and goals for each individual.
	5.2 Candidates use effective strategies to promote active student engagement, increase student motivation, increase opportunities to respond, and enhance self-regulation of student learning.
	5.6 Candidates plan and deliver specialized, individualized instruction that is used to meet the learning needs of each individual.

(continued)

Crosswalk: HLPs to CEC Standard Components

HLP	CEC STANDARD COMPONENT
HLP 20: Provide intensive instruction.	5.5 Candidates organize and manage focused, intensive small group instruction to meet the learning needs of each individual. 5.6 Candidates plan and deliver specialized, individualized instruction that is used to meet the learning needs of each individual.
HLP 21: Teach students to maintain and generalize new learning across time and settings.	3.2 Candidates augment the general education curriculum to address skills and strategies that students with disabilities need to access the core curriculum and function successfully within a variety of contexts as well as the continuum of placement options to assure specially designed instruction is developed and implemented to achieve mastery of curricular standards and individualized goals and objectives. 6.3 Candidates systematically use data from a variety of sources to identify the purpose or function served by problem behavior to plan, implement, and evaluate behavioral interventions and social skills programs, including generalization to other environments.
HLP 22: Provide positive and constructive feedback to guide students' learning and behavior.	5.2 Candidates use effective strategies to promote active student engagement, increase student motivation, increase opportunities to respond, and enhance self-regulation of student learning. 6.2 Candidates use a range of preventive and responsive practices documented as effective to support individuals' social, emotional, and educational well-being.
Note: This table is reproduced with permission. Berlinghoff, D., & McLaughlin, V. L. (Eds.). (2022). *Practice-based standards for the preparation of special educators*. Council for Exceptional Children.	

Crosswalk: CEC Standard Components to HLPs

STANDARD 1: ENGAGING IN PROFESSIONAL LEARNING AND PRACTICE WITHIN ETHICAL GUIDELINES	
Candidates practice within ethical and legal guidelines; advocate for improved outcomes for individuals with exceptionalities and their families while considering their social, cultural, and linguistic diversity; and engage in ongoing self-reflection to design and implement professional learning activities.	
CEC STANDARD COMPONENT	**HLP**
1.1 Candidates practice within ethical guidelines and legal policies and procedures.	
1.1 Candidates advocate for improved outcomes for individuals with exceptionalities and their families while addressing the unique needs of those with diverse social, cultural, and linguistic backgrounds.	HLP 3: Collaborate with families to support student learning and secure needed services.
1.1 Candidates design and implement professional learning activities based on ongoing analysis of student learning; self-reflection; professional standards, research and contemporary practices.	
STANDARD 2: UNDERSTANDING AND ADDRESSING EACH INDIVIDUAL'S DEVELOPMENTAL AND LEARNING NEEDS	
Candidates use their understanding of human growth and development; the multiple influences on development, individual differences, diversity, including exceptionalities, and families and communities to plan and implement inclusive learning environments and experiences that provide individuals with exceptionalities high quality learning experiences reflective of each individual's strengths and needs.	
CEC STANDARD COMPONENT	**HLP**
2.1 Candidates apply understanding of human growth and development to create developmentally appropriate and meaningful learning experiences that address individualized strengths and needs of students with exceptionalities.	HLP 4: Use multiple sources of information to develop a comprehensive understanding of a student's strengths and needs.
2.2 Candidates use their knowledge and understanding of diverse factors that influence development and learning, including differences related to families, languages, cultures, and communities, and individual differences, including exceptionalities, to plan and implement learning experiences and environments.	HLP 11: Identify and prioritize long- and short-term learning goals. HLP 12: Systematically design instruction toward a specific learning goal.

(continued)

Crosswalk: CEC Standard Components to HLPs

STANDARD 3: DEMONSTRATING SUBJECT MATTER CONTENT AND SPECIALIZED CURRICULAR KNOWLEDGE	
Candidates apply their understanding of the academic subject matter content of the general curriculum and specialized curricula to inform their programmatic and instructional decisions for learners with exceptionalities.	
CEC STANDARD COMPONENT	**HLP**
3.1 Candidates apply their understanding of academic subject matter content of the general curriculum to inform their programmatic and instructional decisions for individuals with exceptionalities.	HLP 11: Identify and prioritize long- and short-term learning goals. HLP 13: Adapt curriculum tasks and materials for specific learning goals.
3.1 Candidates augment the general education curriculum to address skills and strategies that students with disabilities need to access the core curriculum and function successfully within a variety of contexts as well as the continuum of placement options to assure specially designed instruction is developed and implemented to achieve mastery of curricular standards and individualized goals and objectives.	HLP 12: Systematically design instruction toward a specific learning goal. HLP 13: Adapt curriculum tasks and materials for specific learning goals. HLP 14: Teach cognitive and metacognitive strategies to support learning and independence. HLP 15: Provide scaffolded supports. HLP 21: Teach students to maintain and generalize new learning across time and settings.

(continued)

Crosswalk: CEC Standard Components to HLPs

STANDARD 4: USING ASSESSMENT TO UNDERSTAND THE LEARNER AND THE LEARNING ENVIRONMENT FOR DATA-BASED DECISION-MAKING	
Candidates assess students' learning, behavior, and the classroom environment in order to evaluate and support classroom and school-based problem-solving systems of intervention and instruction. Candidates evaluate students to determine their strengths and needs, contribute to students' eligibility determination, communicate students' progress, inform short and long-term instructional planning, and make ongoing adjustments to instruction using technology as appropriate.	
CEC STANDARD COMPONENT	**HLP**
4.1 Candidates collaboratively develop, select, administer, analyze, and interpret multiple measures of student learning, behavior, and the classroom environment to evaluate and support classroom and school-based systems of intervention for students with and without exceptionalities.	HLP 4: Use multiple sources of information to develop a comprehensive understanding of a student's strengths and needs. HLP 5: Interpret and communicate assessment information with stakeholders to collaboratively design and implement educational programs.
4.1 Candidates develop, select, administer, and interpret multiple, formal and informal, culturally and linguistically appropriate measures and procedures that are valid and reliable, to contribute to eligibility determination for special education services.	HLP 4: Use multiple sources of information to develop a comprehensive understanding of a student's strengths and needs.
4.1 Candidates assess, collaboratively analyze, interpret, and communicate students' progress toward measurable outcomes using technology as appropriate, to inform both short- and long-term planning, and make ongoing adjustments to instruction.	HLP 4: Use multiple sources of information to develop a comprehensive understanding of a student's strengths and needs. HLP 5: Interpret and communicate assessment information with stakeholders to collaboratively design and implement educational programs. HLP 6: Use student assessment data, analyze instructional practices, and make necessary adjustments that improve student outcomes. HLP 19: Use assistive and instructional technologies.

(continued)

Crosswalk: CEC Standard Components to HLPs

STANDARD 5: USING EFFECTIVE INSTRUCTION TO SUPPORT LEARNING	
Candidates use knowledge of individuals' development, learning needs and assessment data to inform decisions about effective instruction. Candidates use explicit instructional strategies and employ strategies to promote active engagement and increased motivation to individualize instruction to support each individual. Candidates use whole group instruction, flexible grouping, small group instruction, and individual instruction. Candidates teach individuals to use meta-/cognitive strategies to support and self-regulate learning.	
CEC STANDARD COMPONENT	**HLP**
5.1 Candidates use findings from multiple assessments, including student self-assessment, that are responsive to cultural and linguistic diversity and specialized as needed, to identify what students know and are able to do. They then interpret the assessment data to appropriately plan and guide instruction to meet rigorous academic and non-academic content and goals for each individual.	HLP 6: Use student assessment data, analyze instructional practices, and make necessary adjustments that improve student outcomes. HLP 11: Identify and prioritize long- and short-term learning goals. HLP 19: Use assistive and instructional technologies.
5.1 Candidates use effective strategies to promote active student engagement, increase student motivation, increase opportunities to respond, and enhance self-regulation of student learning.	HLP 8: Provide positive and constructive feedback to guide students' learning and behavior. HLP 9: Teach social behaviors. HLP 18: Use strategies to promote active student engagement. HLP 19: Use assistive and instructional technologies. HLP 22: Provide positive and constructive feedback to guide students' learning and behavior.

(continued)

Crosswalk: CEC Standard Components to HLPs

STANDARD 5: USING EFFECTIVE INSTRUCTION TO SUPPORT LEARNING	
Candidates use knowledge of individuals' development, learning needs and assessment data to inform decisions about effective instruction. Candidates use explicit instructional strategies and employ strategies to promote active engagement and increased motivation to individualize instruction to support each individual. Candidates use whole group instruction, flexible grouping, small group instruction, and individual instruction. Candidates teach individuals to use meta-/cognitive strategies to support and self-regulate learning.	
CEC STANDARD COMPONENT	**HLP**
5.1 Candidates use explicit, systematic instruction to teach content, strategies, and skills to make clear what a learner needs to do or think about while learning.	HLP 12: Systematically design instruction toward a specific learning goal. HLP 14: Teach cognitive and metacognitive strategies to support learning and independence. HLP 16: Use explicit instruction.
5.1 Candidates use flexible grouping to support the use of instruction that is adapted to meet the needs of each individual and group.	HLP 17: Use flexible grouping.
5.1 Candidates organize and manage focused, intensive small group instruction to meet the learning needs of each individual.	HLP 17: Use flexible grouping. HLP 20: Provide intensive instruction.
5.1 Candidates plan and deliver specialized, individualized instruction that is used to meet the learning needs of each individual.	HLP 13: Adapt curriculum tasks and materials for specific learning goals. HLP 14: Teach cognitive and metacognitive strategies to support learning and independence. HLP 15: Provide scaffolded supports. HLP 19: Use assistive and instructional technologies. HLP 20: Provide intensive instruction.

(continued)

Crosswalk: CEC Standard Components to HLPs

STANDARD 6: SUPPORTING SOCIAL, EMOTIONAL, AND BEHAVIORAL GROWTH

Candidates create and contribute to safe, respectful, and productive learning environments for individuals with exceptionalities through the use of effective routines and procedures and use a range of preventive and responsive practices to support social, emotional and educational wellbeing. They follow ethical and legal guidelines and work collaboratively with families and other professionals to conduct behavioral assessments for intervention and program development.

CEC STANDARD COMPONENT	HLP
6.1 Candidates use effective routines and procedures to create safe, caring, respectful, and productive learning environments for individuals with exceptionalities.	HLP 7: Establish a consistent, organized, and respectful learning environment.
6.2 Candidates use a range of preventive and responsive practices documented as effective to support individuals' social, emotional, and educational well-being.	HLP 7: Establish a consistent, organized, and respectful learning environment. HLP 8: Provide positive and constructive feedback to guide students' learning and behavior. HLP 9: Teach social behaviors. HLP 22: Provide positive and constructive feedback to guide students' learning and behavior.
6.3 Candidates systematically use data from a variety of sources to identify the purpose or function served by problem behavior to plan, implement, and evaluate behavioral interventions and social skills programs, including generalization to other environments.	HLP 4: Use multiple sources of information to develop a comprehensive understanding of a student's strengths and needs. HLP 9: Teach social behaviors. HLP 10: Conduct functional behavioral assessments to develop individual student behavior support plans. HLP 15: Provide scaffolded supports. HLP 16: Use explicit instruction. HLP 21: Teach students to maintain and generalize new learning across time and settings.

(continued)

Crosswalk: CEC Standard Components to HLPs

STANDARD 7: COLLABORATING WITH TEAM MEMBERS	
Candidates apply team processes and communication strategies to collaborate in a culturally responsive manner with families, paraprofessionals, and other professionals within the school, other educational settings, and the community to plan programs and access services for individuals with exceptionalities and their families.	
CEC STANDARD COMPONENT	**HLP**
7.1 Candidates utilize communication, group facilitation, and problem-solving strategies in a culturally responsive manner to lead effective meetings and share expertise and knowledge to build team capacity and jointly address students' instructional and behavior needs.	HLP 2: Organize and facilitate effective meetings with professionals and families.
7.2 Candidates collaborate, communicate, and coordinate with families, paraprofessionals, and other professionals within the educational setting to assess, plan, and implement effective programs and services that promote progress toward measurable outcomes for individuals with and without exceptionalities and their families.	HLP 1: Collaborate with professionals to increase student success. HLP 3: Collaborate with families to support student learning and secure needed services.
7.3 Candidates collaborate, communicate, and coordinate with professionals and agencies within the community to identify and access services, resources, and supports to meet the identified needs of individuals with exceptionalities and their families.	HLP 1: Collaborate with professionals to increase student success.
7.4 Candidates understand their role of working with paraprofessionals to implement efficiently and effectively necessary components of the IEP.	HLP 1: Collaborate with professionals to increase student success.
Note: This table is reproduced with permission. Berlinghoff, D., & McLaughlin, V. L. (Eds.). (2022). *Practice-based standards for the preparation of special educators*. Council for Exceptional Children.	

Financial Disclosures

Dr. Kelly Acosta reported no financial or proprietary interest in the materials presented herein.

Dr. Amber Benedict reported no financial or proprietary interest in the materials presented herein.

Dr. Kathleen A. Boothe reported no financial or proprietary interest in the materials presented herein.

Dr. Kyena E. Cornelius reported no financial or proprietary interest in the materials presented herein.

Dr. Shantel M. Farnan reported no financial or proprietary interest in the materials presented herein.

Amy I. Gaines reported no financial or proprietary interest in the materials presented herein.

Dr. Kiersten K. Hensley reported no financial or proprietary interest in the materials presented herein.

Dr. Kimberly M. Johnson reported no financial or proprietary interest in the materials presented herein.

Dr. Michael J. Kennedy reported no financial or proprietary interest in the materials presented herein.

Dr. Marla J. Lohmann reported no financial or proprietary interest in the materials presented herein.

Dr. Lawrence J. Maheady reported no financial or proprietary interest in the materials presented herein.

Dr. Wendy W. Murawski reported no financial or proprietary interest in the materials presented herein.

Dr. Ruby L. Owiny reported no financial or proprietary interest in the materials presented herein.

Jodie Ray reported no financial or proprietary interest in the materials presented herein.

Dr. Alice L. Rhodes reported no financial or proprietary interest in the materials presented herein.

Dr. Sarah M. Salinas reported no financial or proprietary interest in the materials presented herein.

Dr. Jennifer A. Sears reported no financial or proprietary interest in the materials presented herein.

Dr. Victoria Slocum reported no financial or proprietary interest in the materials presented herein.

Dr. Dana L. Wagner reported no financial or proprietary interest in the materials presented herein.

Dr. Jennifer D. Walker reported no financial or proprietary interest in the materials presented herein.

Index

Printed in the USA
CPSIA information can be obtained
at www.ICGtesting.com
LVHW081716300524
781726LV00005B/450

9 781630 918842